THE MACMILLAN HANDBOOK FOR RETIREMENT

JOHN KEMP
and
BILL TADD

MACMILLAN REFERENCE BOOKS

Copyright © Macmillan London 1987

All rights reserved. No reproduction, copy or transmission of
this publication may be reproduced, copied or transmitted save
with written permission or in accordance with the provision of
the Copyright Act 1956 (as amended). Any person who does any
unauthorised act in relation to this publication may be liable
to criminal prosecution and civil claims for damages

First published 1987 by
THE MACMILLAN PRESS LTD
London and Basingstoke

Associated companies in Auckland, Delhi, Dublin, Gabarone,
Hamburg, Hong Kong, Johannesburg, Kuala Lumpur, Lagos,
Manzini, Melbourne, Mexico City, Nairobi, New York, Singapore,
Tokyo

British Library Cataloguing in Publication Data

The Macmillan handbook for retirement.
  1987–
  1. Retirement——Great Britain——Handbooks
  manuals etc.
  646.7'9'0941   HQ1064.G7

ISBN 0–333–44895–2
Typeset by Wyvern Typesetting Ltd, Bristol

Printed by Richard Clay PLC, Bungay, Suffolk

Contents

PREFACE
PREPARING FOR RETIREMENT 1
   The challenge of retirement 2
   The retirement seminar 11
FINANCE 23
   State pensions and other social security benefits 25
   Occupational pensions 61
   Managing your money 95
   Instant access and deposit accounts 121
   Investments 143
   Taxation 179
   Insurance 193
   Your will be done 217
HEALTH AND WELL-BEING 225
   Physical health and your state of mind 228
   Special problems of men and women 244
   Using the health services 257
   Older relatives – support and care 264
YOUR HOME 277
   Moving to your retirement home 277
   Retiring abroad 315
   Improving your home 325
   Cashing in on your home 335
WORK AND LEISURE 345
   Work after retirement 347
   Holidays 379
   Leisure 397
   Back to School 398
   Hobbies 406

Preface

This book represents well over 50 years' combined experience in the field of retirement planning by John Kemp and Bill Tadd, and their two principal collaborators Dr Beric Wright and Hilary Jones. (Dr H. Beric Wright MB, FRCS, MFOM is a Governor of the foundation for Age Research. He was, until his retirement, Chairman of the BUPA Medical Centre in London and was a founder member and former chairman and president of the Pre-Retirement Association (PRA). Hilary Jones is a freelance journalist and is a former editor for women's Interests on *Choice*. She is also a course organiser for PRA holiday courses.) It is a tribute to all those people they have met over the years willing to share their experiences of retirement – both the triumphs and the pitfalls.

It is designed to be dipped into a chapter or a page at a time as the mood takes you, and will provide the answers to most of the questions you are likely to ask about your retirement, from money to moving house, from health to hobbies. You will find advice on the whole gamut of opportunities and challenges that face any man or woman, single or married, as they approach the great day.

The authors take the view that it is possible to make substantial and worthwhile investments in your retirement well in advance of the actual date (though it is also never too late).

There are obvious investments to be made in your financial future but you can invest equally well in your health by taking sensible steps now. You can also invest in your sense of satisfaction and achievement by planning for the hobbies or work which will occupy you in retirement; in your home either by moving house or adapting your present one; and in your relationships simply by thinking ahead and talking about retirement to your loved ones.

Every effort has been made to supply comprehensive information and to provide you with names and addresses of people and organisations from whom you can find out more for yourselves. We hope that those organisations who believe they have something to contribute to retirement but who have been omitted from this issue will write to us for possible inclusion in the future.

The authors would like to express their thanks to the many people who have contributed to this book in various ways, in particular to Victor Sawle for his invaluable advice and guidance on the financial sections; to Alexander Wilson for his help on the social security system; and to Ron Spill of Legal & General for his contributions to the chapter on occupational pensions.

Retirement has been described as 'The Great Escape' – the ultimate opportunity for fulfilment. But it is your choice what you make of it. We merely hope this volume will help you towards the proud boast of many of those retired people who have been able to say: 'These are the happiest days of my life.'

Preparing for retirement

THE CHALLENGE OF RETIREMENT	2
Perspective on work	2
Making the most of retirement	7
Recipe for success?	10
THE RETIREMENT SEMINAR	11
Courses for individuals	11
Courses for companies	13
USEFUL ADDRESSES	14

THE CHALLENGE OF RETIREMENT

The prospect of retirement affects people in different ways. Emotions can range from ecstatic joy to debilitating terror, and neither reaction is likely to be justified. The transition from full-time work into full-time leisure is seldom so easy that there are no problems at all. Neither is it often as bad as some of us fear it will be. Whatever *you* feel about retirement, whatever illusions you hold about this new stage of your life, one thing is certain – you will be better off if you do a little bit of planning.

That is what this book is all about. You can think of it, if you like, as if it were a holiday brochure. It will offer you all sorts of alternative routes and all manner of interesting diversions, at various prices, all aimed at getting you to your destination – which is a stimulating and enjoyable retirement.

Not that retirement is a holiday – one long afternoon lying in a hammock in the sunshine. The important thing about holidays is that they usually come to an end after a fortnight, after which we go back to our jobs refreshed and invigorated looking forward to showing off our suntans and our photographs to friends and colleagues. The trouble with retirement is that after a fortnight nothing changes. There is no office to go to and, if you are not careful, you might just find yourself waking up and wondering: 'What on earth am I going to do with myself today?'

Perhaps it would be better if you treated this book like a manual for a new career. Because that is exactly what retirement is. The main difference between this job and your old one being that you are now the boss; you must make your own decisions about how to use your time and your skills. If we can help you to make this 'career' the most successful one you have ever undertaken then our efforts will have been worthwhile.

Perspective on work

Retirement is a major change in our lives and can bring problems if we are not prepared. First we need to set our working lives into perspective and think hard about what work has meant for us.

HOW LONG TO GO?

There's no need to start counting the days once you reach retirement age. Your number is unlikely to come up for many years yet.

Most people will recall the biblical lifespan as three score years and ten and surprisingly enough the official lifespan statistics bear this out even today. According to the Government Actuary's Department the expectation of life for a male child in 1986 was 71.07 years (compared with only 48 in 1901) whereas for a woman it was 77.01 (compared with 51.6 in 1901).

But, the very fact that you have already reached close to retirement age means that your expectancy of life is well beyond these estimates. This is because the national statistics take account of the manifest maladies and accidents that can befall us from the day we are born, through the infections of infancy, the accidents of early maturity and the risk of coronary heart and other fell diseases in middle age. The fact that you have survived all these means you are one of the lucky ones who has beaten the average.

Expectation of life from specific ages.

At age (years)	Males	Females
50	24.27	29.33
60	16.39	20.84
65	13.04	16.98
70	10.13	13.40
75	7.72	10.21
80	5.79	7.49

So a man retiring at 65 can expect to live into his 79th year, on average, before his death, whereas a woman at 65 can expect to live, on average, until she is in her 82nd year.

What we will miss about work

After a lifetime of work it is only natural that there are certain aspects we will miss. The most common are:
- a sense of purpose
- social contact
- routine and discipline
- income
- status

Let's take a brief look at each of them in turn.

A sense of purpose Work gives our lives a direction, a sense of purpose and responsibility. The fact that we have a job to do means that we have targets to achieve, budgets to keep to and colleagues to work with. For many people their jobs are the main driving force in their lives. The prospect of losing that job and that sense of doing something worthwhile can be at the root of much fear and anxiety about retirement.

No matter how humble the responsibility, whether it is the responsibility carried by the managing director to keep the company in profit or the responsibility of the maintenance staff who clean up after everyone has gone and make sure that the boilers are on to warm the offices the following day, it gives something that anyone unlucky enough to have been made redundant or unemployed will miss, the sense of being needed.

I recall a personnel officer who attended a week-long retirement planning course with which I was involved. There were about 400 people in the room at the time I was asking delegates what their feelings were as they approached retirement. She called me over and as she began to tell us how resentful she was that she would not be allowed to continue with the job she loved so much, she broke down and sobbed.

Although no-one else in the room proved to be quite so emotional I have no doubt she reflected the feelings of others present in her sense of impending loss. She also articulated the growing feeling of ordinary people who would prefer a more flexible approach to retirement, allowing each person to choose the date of their retirement within, say, a five- or ten-year age band. After all, not everyone wants to work for as long as possible. Plenty of others would welcome the chance to go early even with a reduced pension.

Perhaps the fact that this woman was a single person made the prospect of retirement seem even more of a void, but many a married workaholic with few hobbies and outside interests would have wept with her.

Happily, by the end of the week during which she had the opportunity to talk to many other people in the same boat, her attitude was much more positive and happy. Perhaps you feel like her as you begin this book. If so I hope you will have cause to change your mind by the end. You may even wonder why you wasted so many years clinging to the jobs treadmill.

Social contact Whether you regard yourself as a gregarious, social person or not, there is no escaping the company of other people when you get to work. Team work is often the essence of successful companies and on the shop floor, in committee meetings, the board room or the trades union meeting, we are constantly talking to other people, expressing our views, listening to others and contributing to decision-making.

In many cases our colleagues become our friends. They are interested in us, in our children and grandchildren, they will share our concerns when we, or our loved ones, are ill; they will follow our fortunes in our working lives and we, of course, will be just as interested in them.

Unhappily, far too many people on the approach to retirement have few friends other than their colleagues. While such friendships can last after retirement, it is not so easy to keep in touch outside the context of work.

Routine and discipline Whatever your occupation, having a job does impose disciplines which, in a sense, offer a template for our daily lives.

Every working day most of us get up at a set time. We leave the house at the same time to catch the bus or train that gets us to our place of work. In the evening we return, as often as not, at much the same time each day. Perhaps we have an evening meal with our spouse or families. Maybe we have evening meetings to go to. Then in the summer there is the garden to be tended, the lawn to be cut.

The weekends are fixed by our working lives as well. After all, if there was no work, Saturday and Sunday would be much like any other day of the week. I recall one retired man complaining that the thing he missed most about retirement was his weekends. 'Somehow by the end of the week I felt I had *earned* my weekend of rest,' he said. 'It's not the same now I am retired. Any day of the week can be my weekend.'

Income This is often the main worry of people approaching retirement and it is true that most of us can expect to suffer a reduction in our income when we retire. Though it is hard to generalise, net incomes from pensions and lump sum payments associated with pensions usually amount to something like a half to two thirds of their net incomes while in work. We also miss the prospect of *real* rises in income that can come from promotion or rises above the inflation rate.

However, as we shall demonstrate later in this book, most people will find themselves able to maintain much the same standard of living in retirement as they enjoyed while in full time work, and often finances work out better than we anticipate.

Status We tend to know other people as much by the jobs they do as by their names or the street they live in, and this creates a sense of identity and status. We get used to being introduced socially as 'the manager of Barclays Bank in the High Street' or 'my friend Jack. He's a plumber in business on his own account' (or even by what our husbands or wives do for a living – 'Have you met Freda? Her husband's an architect').

This is not, of course, entirely lost in retirement, people are still pigeonholed by what they *used* to do, but many do miss the status of their former role.

What we will *not* miss

We all know the pressures of keeping down a job in the modern world and though work is obviously important it is not necessarily always a pleasure. There are some aspects which we can cheerfully do without, such as

- travel
- timekeeping
- stress

Travel

Unless you are lucky enough to live over the shop or, at any rate, reasonably close to your place of work, modern travel can be hell. Those who, like me, have spent many years of their lives travelling into London by train, may well be spending up to three hours every day simply getting to and from the office. An hour of that may be spent on a train or tube and the rest driving to and from your local station, and walking to and from your office to the London terminal. Even though you do get used to it, you experience enough icy trains, points failures and traffic jams to be more than pleased when retirement offers a happy release.

Perhaps your job compels you to drive long distances on congested roads or in all weathers. Who on earth would miss all that?

Timekeeping

The tyranny of the clock is one of the things we take for granted in normal working life. 'Time is money', as people like to say and most companies these days are extremely conscious of the hourly costs of their workers. So timekeeping is as much a part of our lives during our working years as eating and breathing.

Most people's employment contracts require them to be in a certain place at a certain time and to remain there until the end of the working day. It is one of the things you accept about having a job. Indeed many senior staff will know that it does not stop there. Often they will have work to take home in the evenings and at weekends, and they are expected to do it to underline their commitment. As often as not they do it willingly, of course, even competitively – demonstrating to colleagues that they can work harder than anyone else – but it is wearing and tiring nevertheless.

Most people, once they have come to terms with retirement, talk of the freedom that retirement has offered them: freedom from having to comply with other people's time schedules; and freedom to work out fresh ones to suit themselves.

Stress
A doctor who rose to the top of his particular tree confessed after retirement that for the first time in years he was able to wake up in the morning feeling genuinely refreshed. 'I used to wake up tired', he said, 'and I suppose I must have gone through the week getting steadily worse. The bonus of retirement for me is that I no longer feel tired.'

What undoubtedly added to his problem was the fact of being under stress. It's surprising how stressful modern living and modern working is. It does not matter what level of job you have, it is always present. You take it home with you, it is still with you at weekends, sometimes it affects your sleep and certainly it affects your family. You will find more about this in the *Health* section (p. 225) but all the points we have mentioned so far help to increase the pressures on us; testing our ability to cope. Unhappily, the pressures can sometimes prove too much and mental illness and breakdowns can result.

Making the most of retirement

Once you have weighed up what work has meant to your life, you will be in a good position to see which aspects will need to be replaced once you are retired in order to maintain a sense of purpose and fulfillment in your life. Many people have mixed feelings as they approach retirement and indeed there are a number of pluses and minuses. Some of your own hopes and fears may well be found in the table below.

Pluses	Minuses
• Freedom	• Reduced income
• Togetherness	• Togetherness
• Opportunity	• Lost social contacts
• Challenge	• Loneliness

Freedom
We have the freedom to:
- do what we want when we want to
- take another job or not as we please
- associate with the people we like, rather than the people we were thrown together with at work
- choose to live where we like
- go on holiday when we like (and when it is cheapest)

Planning your retirement can be a bit daunting at first. After all, in the past you have managed to fit your leisure activities into the space of weekends and the evenings. Now you have all the time there is.

Suppose you live close to your workplace and your working day encompasses no more than eight hours a day, five days a week. If you have an annual holiday entitlement of five weeks, you work 1880 hours a year. If you are one of those unfortunates who travel into London to work and spend three hours a day travelling, then your working life amounts to 2585 hours each year. That's the equivalent of 323 eight hour shifts or 108 whole days and nights to call your own. Now deciding how to use these extra hours is a real challenge.

Opportunity

If you hear a person saying to you: 'I don't know how I ever found time to go to work', you can be sure you have found someone who has taken advantage of the opportunities. There is the opportunity to spend more time with your family, to travel, to spend more time in the garden or working on the house, to take up new hobbies and sporting pastimes, to read more books, watch more television, and a thousand and one other things that life has to offer if only you have the time and the inclination to take advantage of them.

Let me offer one word of advice – make an effort to plan carefully. I have asked thousands of people over the years what they plan to do with their spare time once they have retired and one of the most common replies is something like this: 'Oh, I shall have plenty to do. I want to get the house painted; there are some DIY repairs I want to do on some of the windows; the garden has been dreadfully neglected for years and my wife has been badgering me to build some shelves in the utility room.'

That's fine so far as it goes but it does not constitute a full 'career structure' for retirement. In six months time you probably will have painted the house, built the shelves, tidied up the garden *and* fixed the windows. Then what do you do? Of course plenty of other things demanding your time and skills *might* turn up. But they might not, and you may have benefited by tackling these things in a different way. Perhaps it would be better to spread the workload on the house over a longer period so that you could take up a new hobby or a new sport. After all what's the rush? At least that way you won't wake up one morning with the sinking feeling that you have no reason to get up.

There is nothing sinful or slothful about having nothing to do on a particular day. But somehow even days off are better when planned, even if it is no more of a plan than to say 'It's a nice sunny day today I think I'll sit in the garden instead of working.' At least you retain control and make the decision rather than having it forced on you.

One retired man I know thinks the secret of a successful retirement is always to have something in your diary. 'You can't enjoy leisure to the full unless you have a full diary,' he argues.

Togetherness
Many couples look forward to being able to see more of each other in retirement. A word of warning, however – the reality of more togetherness can be more disharmony. Many wives will tell you that often their husbands seem to think that retirement is for the man alone and does not include his spouse. 'I can't tell you the disloyal thoughts that go through my mind as I continue with the household chores, as I have throughout our married life, while he sits with his feet up reading the morning paper,' one wife told me.

At the very least it might be beneficial for all of us to sit down with our partners long before retirement comes and discuss what you hope is in it for each other. I know it's difficult to be entirely honest in this situation but you could do worse than to write down a list of the pros and cons of retirement as you see them and compare notes.

These remarks don't apply to those of you who live alone, but today many people of both sexes choose to live together for companionship and shared expenses to name but two reasons. And there is no doubt that single people who share homes need to consider the implications for the other partner very carefully. I have been surprised at the number of times I have heard one of two women who share a home express sentiments about retirement which are exactly similar to those voiced by married couples.

DO IT YOUR WAY

Here is a Golden Rule for retirement. Only *you* can decide how retirement is going to work for you. Never mind what other people tell you to do. Never mind what suggestions you read in this book. Do it your way.

There is no secret formula for a successful retirement. There are as many successful formulas as there are people. I know one man who took early retirement and found contentment by abandoning all the old habits imposed by the clock. He abandoned any formal daily schedule, including mealtimes. He ate when he was hungry and went to sleep when he was tired.

In practice this meant that he got up late most mornings, had a cat nap most afternoons and went to bed about three in the morning. Happily it was a way of life that suited his wife as well!

Recipe for success?

People approaching retirement are often interested to ask those who have retired if they can offer a 'recipe' for a successful retirement – rather like a couple of newly-weds asking a couple celebrating their golden wedding for their recipe for marital harmony! The most famous of these recipes was dished up more than 20 years ago by Professor Alastair Heron, one of the founders of the retirement planning movement. His recipe seems to have stood the test of time, though the order of importance of the various ingredients might be arguable.

Professor Heron came up with six essential ingredients for a successful retirement, each one of which he believed to be important if retirement as a whole was to be fulfilling. They were:
- An adequate philosophy of life
- An adequate income
- Good health
- Congenial companions
- Purposeful occupation
- A congenial home

There has been much debate over the years as to the order of importance they should assume, but very little indeed to suggest that they are in any way out of date 20 years on.

Before retirement the order seems quite obvious. Many put 'adequate income' at the top of their sheet of paper, while others put 'good health'. The relationship between the two seems to be that people choose the one they appear to have least of at the time! The other items fall in various places in the list.

After retirement the order changes. Then you find at the top of the list something rather more intangible like 'an adequate philosophy of life' or 'purposeful occupation'. Health always remains fairly close to the top. Whereas money, as often as not, has fallen either to the bottom or near the bottom of the pile. As I said earlier, you may well find that your finances will turn out better than you had hoped.

We have already touched on most of the subjects in Professor Heron's list, except for choosing a suitable home for retirement. You will find more about this later in the book, but probably for the first time in your life your choice of a home can be made on the basis of where you would most *like* to live rather than where you *must* live in order to get to your place of work.

One final thing before you start to delve into the other pages of this book. Never underestimate the capacity of retirement to take you by surprise. It never ceases to amaze me how many colleagues who have been professionally involved in retirement planning over the years have retired themselves and later told me: 'I never realised it would be like that.' One friend claimed it had been almost like a bereavement and most of all he missed his secretary to organise the little things he now had to do for himself, such as post his letters and organise his diary.

Once you get used to the idea you will not want to turn back the clock. Indeed as one retired journalist once told me: 'I spent years reporting the affairs of the rich, the famous and the powerful. It seemed to be the most important thing in life at the time. I had no hobbies and absolutely no other interests outside my job. I viewed retirement like a death sentence. Yet within six months I had almost forgotten the old life, it all seemed so trivial and unimportant. You suddenly realise that life has so much more fulfilment and pleasure to offer. You wouldn't drag me back to Fleet Street for double the salary.'

THE RETIREMENT SEMINAR

Many people find it helpful to talk to others about their retirement plans. A good way of doing this is to attend a retirement planning seminar. There are various types available, many of them organised through the **Pre-Retirement Association**. This section will tell you where to find one and what you can expect from attending a seminar. The first part of this is aimed at individuals and the second part at personnel or pensions staff charged with responsibility for running company seminars.

Courses for individuals

The most common type of seminar is for groups of about 25 to 30 people who spend a day or two listening to a group of experts, asking questions and discussing the issues between themselves.

The Pre-Retirement Association is one of the country's largest providers of courses both to individuals and to industry. The Association is an educational charity which, although it receives some Government funding, exists largely on the income it receives from members, publications and its seminar services.

It runs courses both through its own seminar division known as the *Retirement Preparation Service* and also through the 41 local retirement planning associations who are affiliated to the PRA. A full list of these is given at the end of this chapter. These are usually the most inexpensive form of retirement provision available and are often available to both individuals and local companies. This is where you should start your search for a course.

If there is no local PRA group or they do not have suitable courses it is worth contacting your local adult education department to see if they run evening classes. An increasing number of education authorities do offer retirement planning courses, though they are usually evening classes run over a period of weeks rather than one- or two-day events. Failing that it is worth trying your local branch of the **Workers' Educational Association** (you will find their address either from your local library or the Citizens' Advice Bureau) to see if they run a course.

If you are not able to find a local course (and unhappily this is highly likely for many people) then you may have to choose a residential course or stay overnight at a hotel that is local to another course.

PRA courses
There are three main courses offered:
- A one-day seminar at **Sion College** on London's Embankment close to Blackfriars Underground Station (Circle and District Lines).
- A three-day residential course at **Stanford Hall**, the Co-operative Union's training centre near Market Harborough in Leicestershire.
- A week-long residential course run by the PRA at **Pontins South Devon Holiday Centre** at Paignton, South Devon.

Sion College This is an attractive theological library overlooking the River Thames in Central London which provides a lovely setting for a seminar. A chairman and half a dozen expert speakers spend the day covering the 'essentials' of retirement planning, including mental approach, financial management, social security matters, health, hobbies and accommodation. Lunch is provided together with a copy of the PRA seminar booklet *Your Retirement*. The whole day costs £60 plus £40 for an accompanying spouse. There are about eight courses a year and you can obtain more details and book through the *Retirement Preparation Service* at PRA head office.

Stanford Hall The three-day event at Stanford Hall begins on Friday evening and continues until lunch on Sunday. They are held twice a year in April and October and cost about £100 a head plus VAT. The content of the course is very similar to the one-day event except that there is much more time available to involve delegates in discussion sessions and to answer questions.

A great bonus of the Stanford Hall seminar is the venue itself which is a magnificent former stately home set in huge grounds which includes a lovely lake and many majestic sweet chestnut trees. Booking is through PRA head office.

Pontins Holiday Centre The retirement planning holiday week at Pontins is widely regarded as the best value seminar available. There are two courses a year – in May and September – and the cost is about £116 plus

VAT. This includes accommodation, three meals a day, the various seminar talks and demonstrations, volumes of literature and the free use of Pontins entertainment facilities.

The event is usually attended by up to 500 people at a time and is a mixture of independent and company sponsored delegates who devote the week to planning their futures. It offers a unique mix of people both retired and yet to retire and because of the length of the course develops a particular atmosphere which brings delegates back year after year.

The days are divided into relatively formal lecture sessions attended by all the delegates in the morning when expert speakers cover the main ground of retirement planning and smaller informal afternoon and evening groups which cover a much wider range of subjects than can be tackled in a shorter seminar.

A particular feature of the Pontins courses is the range of hobby activities which newcomers are invited to try out for the first time in the hope that they will find new interests to develop in future. These include ballroom dancing (there is a live band every evening), bridge, painting and drawing, golf, flower arranging, DIY, decorating, gardening, photography and so on. Booking forms are available from PRA head office from mid-January each year. Don't be put off by the venue, the chalets are adequate rather than comfortable, but you will encounter none of the 'Hi-de-hi' atmosphere.

Further information
The **Retirement Preparation Service** is the only organisation which provides a range of seminars available to private individuals as well as company bookings. In practice they are often attended by a mixture of individual and company delegates.

SAGA Holidays also runs week-long courses at Dundee University for groups of up to 40 people. The basic price is £153 for the week which runs from Wednesday to Wednesday.

Local education authorities often produce retirement planning courses. For example **Morley College** runs two courses each term for $2\frac{1}{2}$ hour sessions over ten weeks. They charge £14.50 for ILEA residents and £20.50 for non-residents.

Courses for companies

The table on p. 20 shows the major providers of seminars for company delegates. Although most have standard one- or two-day seminars there is often a good deal of flexibility to meet individual needs. Prices quoted are exclusive of VAT. Many course providers charge extra to meet the expenses of speakers and it is worth checking this point. Seminar costs are allowable as a deductible expense against Corporation Tax.

In general most course providers offer seminars either exclusively for a single company or on a mixed-company basis. This is specially useful to smaller companies for whom a full in-house seminar would be very expensive. Except where stated the fees do not include the cost of accommodation or meals. Unless individual rates are specified the fees are normally for groups of the size stated.

USEFUL ADDRESSES

Morley College
61 Westminster Bridge Road
London SE1 7HT
☎ 01-928 8501

Pre-Retirement Association (PRA)
19 Undine Street
Tooting
London SW17 8PP
☎ 01-767 3225

SAGA Holidays
Enbrook House
Sandgate Hill
Folkestone
Kent CT20 3SG
☎ 0303 47000

PRA affiliated organisations

Age Concern Caithness
P. Yeomans (Secretary)
Westburn
Murkle
Thurso KW14 8SR
☎ 0847 65208

Bedfordshire Pre-Retirement Council
T. Beighton (Hon Secretary)
c/o Retirement Education Centre
6 Rothsay Gardens
Bedford MK40 3QB
☎ 0234 60304/01-387 9729

Berkshire Pre-Retirement Association
A. V. Vickerage (Chairman)
c/o Nabisco Recreation Club
121 Kings Road
Berkshire RG1 3DE
☎ 0734 55440
Office Hours: 10 a.m.–12 Noon Tues & Thurs

Bristol & District Retirement Council
G. W. Sledge (Hon Secretary)
Westbury Adult Centre
Eastfield Road
Westbury-on-Trym
Bristol
Avon BS9 4AE
☎ 0272 620346

Charnwood & District Retirement Council
W. Gibb (Retirement Co-ordinator)
John Storer House
Wards End
Loughborough
Leicestershire LE11 3HA
☎ 0509 30131

Coventry Pre-Retirement Committee
G. E. Lilley (Secretary)
28 Corporation Street
Coventry
West Midlands CV1 1PR
☎ 0203 20381

PREPARING FOR RETIREMENT 15

Croydon Retirement Association
Mrs L. V. Baker (Secretary)
Coombe Cliff Education Centre
Coombe Road
Croydon
Surrey CR0 5SP
☎ 01-680 2018
Course Info ☎ 01-657 6514

Voluntary Action Cumbria
G. Fiddler
Birbeck House
Duke Street
Penrith CA11 7NA
☎ 0768 68086

Dacorum Pre-Retirement Association
Mrs D. Ostan (Hon Secretary)
1 Highridge Road
Apsley
Hemel Hempstead
Hertfordshire HP3 0AG

Essex Pre-Retirement & Retirement Association
D. J. Pasterfield (Hon Secretary)
Welfare & Benefits (1/277)
Ford Motor Co Ltd
Brentwood
Essex CM13 3BW
☎ 0277 253000

GLAP (Greater London Association for Pre-Retirement)
Mrs B. Spiers (Director)
St Margaret Pattens Church
Eastcheap
London EC3M 1HS
☎ 01-623 6630

Guildford Retirement Association
D. Dodd (Hon Secretary)
'Khaya Lami'
Castle Road
Horsell
Woking
Surrey GU21 4EU
☎ 04862 65536

Gwent Pre-Retirement Council
W. T. Brownbill (Secretary)
17 The Walk
New Inn
Pontypool
Gwent NP4 5PU
☎ 049 55 3699

Kent Retirement Association
D. Peroni (Hon Secretary)
33 Lansdown Road
Sittingbourne
Kent ME10 3AY
☎ 0795 70839

Lancashire Pre-Retirement Association
Mrs K. Rothwell
78 Arundel Road
Lytham St Annes
Lancashire FY8 1BN
☎ 0253 735051

Leicester Council for Voluntary Service
E. Dunsdon (Retirement Planning Officer)
32 De Montfort Street
Leicester LE1 7GD
☎ 0533 555600

Merseyside Pre-Retirement Association
A. E. Cockerill (Secretary)
Mount Vernon Green
Hall Lane
Liverpool L7 8TF
☎ 051-709 0990

Norfolk Education for Retirement Association
H. McCloughan (Chairman)
Norwich City College
Ipswich Road
Norwich NR2 2LJ

North Devon Third Age Group
F. P. Drew (Secretary)
Dartington North Devon Trust
Bridge Chambers
Barnstaple
Devon EX31 1HB

North East Pre-Retirement Association
Mrs P. A. Ward (Secretary)
Northern Council for Further Education
5 Grosvenor Villas
Grosvenor Road
Newcastle upon Tyne NE2 2RU

North Hampshire Pre-Retirement and Retirement Association
J. A. M. Laidlaw (Secretary)
1 White Cottages
Plastow Green
nr Headley
Berkshire RG15 8LN
☏ 063523 286

Nottingham & District Pre-Retirement Council
S. H. S. Dove (Chief Executive Officer)
144A High Road
Beeston
Nottingham NG9 2LN
☏ 0602 223824

PRAGMA (Pre-Retirement Association of Greater Manchester)
H. C. West (Secretary)
The St Thomas Centre
Ardwick Green North
Manchester M12 6FZ
☏ 061-273 7451

PREP (Pre-Retirement Education Programmes – Sheffield)
Mrs B. E. Cooper (Course Director)
Milne House
5–11 Bailey Street
Sheffield S1 4EH
☏ 0742 739990

PREP (Pre-Retirement Educational Provision – Hereford)
M. Morgan (Chairman)
Westfield House
Walford
Ross-on-Wye
Herefordshire HR9 5RH
☏ 0989 2424

PRIDE (Pre-Retirement in Devon)
G. Guest (Director)
59 High Street
Totnes TO9 5PB
☏ 0803 865887

Retirement Association of Northern Ireland
Mrs M. Leroux (Chairman)
25a University Road
Belfast BT7 1JG
☏ 02322 21324

St Helens and Knowsley Retirement Association
Dr C. K. Lysons (Secretary)
'Lathom'
Scotchbarn Lane
Whiston
Merseyside L35 7JB
☏ 051-426 5513

The Scottish Retirement Council
S. Graham Hoey (Director)
212 Bath Street
Glasgow G2 4HW
☏ 041-332 9427/8

Dundee & District Retirement Council (In association with the Scottish Retirement Council)
J. Howie (Hon Organiser)
20 Paterson Street
Dundee
☏ 0382 814661/78619

PREPARING FOR RETIREMENT 17

Lothian Retirement Committee (In association with the Scottish Retirement Council)
Mrs H. Kirkland (Secretary)
Community Education Department
Lothian Regional Council
40 Torphichen Street
Edinburgh EH3 8JB
☎ 031-225 5569

Shropshire Pre-Retirement Advisory Group
B. Morris (Secretary)
Shrewsbury College of Arts & Technology
London Road
Shrewsbury
Shropshire SY2 6PR
☎ 0743 51544

South Glamorgan Pre-Retirement Council
H. Joinson (Secretary)
140 King George V Drive
Heath Park
Cardiff
South Glamorgan CF4 4EL
☎ 0222 754515

Southampton Pre-Retirement Committee
J. Melmoth (Secretary)
17 Luccombe Place
Shirley
Southampton
Hampshire SO1 2RL
☎ 0703 773292

Staffordshire Retirement Council
G. F. Gilmore (Chairman)
11A Stafford Street
Stafford
Staffordshire ST16 2BP
☎ 0785 211122

Sunderland Pre-Retirement Council
R. F. Falconer (Chairman)
Action-in-Retirement Centre
Bishopwearmouth Parish Church
High Street West
Sunderland
Tyne & Wear SE1 3ET
☎ 0783 654066

Surrey Retirement Association
B. W. Buttle
Department of Educational Studies
University of Surrey
Guildford GU2 5XH
☎ 0483 571281

Walsall Pre-Retirement Council
K. Seeney (Secretary)
2 Wells Drive
Hillcroft Park
Stafford ST17 0PL

Retirement Council for the North of Warwickshire
S. Reece (Retirement Co-ordinator)
50 Station Street
Atherstone
Warwickshire CV9 1BU
☎ 08277 67099

West Glamorgan Pre-Retirement Council
H. Lloyd (Secretary)
495 Hendrefoilan Road
Killay
Swansea
West Glamorgan SA2 7NU
☎ 0792 207934

Wolverhampton Pre-Retirement Council
S. D. Copland (Secretary)
106 Woodthorne Road South
Tettenhall
Wolverhampton
West Midlands WV6 8XL

Companies offering pre-retirement courses

Allied Dunbar
Allied Dunbar Centre
Swindon SN1 1EL
☎ 0793 28291

Career Plan
Chichester House
Chichester Rents
(Off Chancery Lane)
London WC2A 1EG
☎ 01-242 5775

CEPEC (Centre for Professional Employment Counselling) Ltd
67 Jermyn Street
London SW1Y 6NY
☎ 01-930 0322/2005

DPS Consultants
Dodd's Lane
27 Preston Street
Faversham
Kent ME13 8PE
☎ 0795 531472

Executive Stand-By
310 Chester Road
Hartford
Northwich CW8 2AB
☎ 0606 883849

Future Perfect
17–19 Stratford Place
London W1N 9AF
☎ 01-499 8030

Godwins
Briarcliff House
Kingsmead
Farnborough
Hants GU14 7TE
☎ 0252 544484

Legal & General
Grosvenor House
125 High Street
Croydon
Surrey CR9 3UA
☎ 01-681 5177

Mercer Fraser
4 Southampton Place
London WC1A 2DD
☎ 01-405 4343

Mid-Career Development Centre
77 Morland Road
Croydon CR0 6EA
☎ 01-654 0808

Millstream Conferences
Mill House
South Harting
Petersfield
Hampshire GU31 5JF
☎ 073085 711/331

Noble Lowndes Personal and Financial Services
PO Box 431
53 Eastcheap
London EC3P 3HL
☎ 01-283 2000

Prudential Assurance Pension Fund Services
142 Holborn Bars
London EC1N 2NH
☎ 01-405 9222

Retirement Planning Services Ltd
Manor House
Church Street
Leatherhead
Surrey KT22 8DH
☎ 0372 377811

Retirement Preparation Services
c/o Pre-Retirement Association
19 Undine Street
Tooting
London SW17 8PP
☎ 01-767 3225

Director of the PRA's Holiday Courses is
W. D. Tadd
78 Capel Road
East Barnet
Herts EN4 8JF
☎ 01-449 4506

Ringley Financial Counselling
Ringley House
London Road
Reigate
Surrey RH2 9QH
☎ 07372 22647/45485

Scrimgeour Retirement Services
PO Box 21
20 Copthall Avenue
London EC2R 7JS
☎ 01-600 7595

Sedgwick Personal Financial Management
Bevington House
24/26 Minories
London E1 8DX
☎ 01-377 3456

Standard Life
PO Box 62
3 George Street
Edinburgh EH2 2XZ
☎ 031-225 2552

Providers of pre-retirement courses to company delegates.

Company	Duration	Numbers preferred	Cost	Contact and special notes
Allied Dunbar	1–2 days	20	by negotiation	*Contact* Bhari Jack
Career Plan	1 day upwards	25	by negotiation	*Contact* Sir Timothy Hoare Bt. Like delegates to have held similar positions of responsibility.
CEPEC (Centre for Professional Employment Counselling) Ltd	2–3 days	limited	£695 per couple	*Contact* Genny Watson. Seminars at Sundridge Park Management Centre, Bromley, Kent. Also offers individual service at £800 for couples unwilling to attend seminars.
DPS Consultants	2–3 days	10–18	£425–£450 per couple	*Contact* D. Peter Smith. Uses prestigious Leeds Castle for senior management courses.
Executive Stand-By	1–3 days	20–30	£600–£800	*Contact* J. R. Anglebeck. Has been running courses since 1974.
Future Perfect	Weekends	12 couples	By negotiation	*Contact* John Ottensooser
Godwins	2 days	25	By negotiation	*Contact* Ken Melbourne
Legal & General	1–2 days	About 20	About £600	*Contact* Keith Hughes. One of the first insurance companies to offer retirement planning seminars. Uses independent financial speakers.
Mercer Fraser	1–2 days	30	£1000–£1500	*Contact* Glyn White. Works in association with the **Pre-Retirement Association's Retirement Preparation Service**.
Mid-Career Development Centre	2 days	10	£200 each	*Contact* Kieran Duignan. Seminars run under title of 'Over 50–Finding New Ground.'

Millstream Conferences	3 days	8 couples	Individual: £575 Couples: £985	*Contact* Peter Tuke. Up market venues and course aimed at small groups of senior executives. Meals and accommodation included in fee.
Noble Lowndes Personal and Financial Services	1 day	20–25	£250–£300 for groups. Individuals: £70 (or £95 incl. spouse)	*Contact* Ian Wilson. Generally aimed at staff with salaries of £15,000 a year or more.
Prudential Assurance Pension Fund Services	1 and 2 days	25–30	£115 per person. Companies by negotiation	*Contact* Roy Elms. Price includes lunch.
Retirement Planning Services Ltd	1–3 days	8–20	from £350	*Contact* Tony Wheeler. Offshoot of Hinton Hill the investment advisory group.
Retirement Preparation Service Pre-Retirement Association	1–2 days Weekends Full weeks	25–30 50 450–500	£600–£1000 for company groups. Weekends: £90 per head. Full weeks: £116 per head	*Contact* Bill Bruce. PRA were first in the field and have widest range of courses available. Many of speakers on all seminars were trained by them.
Ringley Financial Counselling	1–2 days	26	£200 per person	*Contact* A. J. Gillett. Also produces range of audio-visual presentations on related subjects.
Scrimgeour Retirement Services	Mostly 2 days	12–24	By negotiation	*Contact* Arnold Kentridge
Sedgwick Personal Financial Management	½ day upwards	30	From £200	*Contact* D. Sargeant
Standard Life	1 day Occasional weekends	24	£550 for company groups. £55 for individuals (£95 couples)	*Contact* D. M. Calder. Lunch included in fee.

This man is too busy to think for himself

All too often, retirement is the last thing today's busy executive has the time – or desire – to think about. Its implications are little short of alarming. It is conveniently pushed to the back of the mind.

Where it stays, on permanent hold.

As a result, the transition can be very sudden. Loss of self-esteem is common. Personal relationships can suffer. And the drop in income can often lead to difficult financial juggling.

You, more than anyone, are aware of this. But, after all, your responsibilities *do* actively cease when an employee leaves the company. So how can you help before then?

The art of pre-retirement education is to talk through the possible problems that may arise and help individuals to discover their own solutions. By careful counselling and gentle persuasion you can be of immeasurable service.

It's an area in which we can help, too. We've produced a retirement pack, including our specially commissioned video which deals sympathetically with preparing for this time of life. It also includes the 200 page Allied Dunbar Retirement Planning Guide and a special brochure on in-house retirement planning that's been prepared in conjunction with the Pre-Retirement Association.

The whole package costs just £50. It could be a major responsibility of yours to cut out the coupon.

Send it to: Bhari Jack, Retirement Planning Consultant, Allied Dunbar Assurance plc, Allied Dunbar Centre, Swindon, Wilts. SN1 1EL. Tel: 0793 28291.

ALLIED DUNBAR

PERSONAL FINANCIAL GUIDANCE

To: Bhari Jack, Retirement Planning Consultant, Allied Dunbar Assurance plc, Allied Dunbar Centre, Swindon, Wilts. SN1 1EL. Tel: 0793 28291.

☐ I would like a copy of your Retirement Planning Pack.

☐ I enclose a cheque for the full amount (£57.50 inclusive of VAT) made payable to Allied Dunbar Financial Services Ltd.

☐ Please invoice my company.

Please tick box if you require VAT invoice ☐

Name_____
Position_____
Company Address_____

Telephone_____

Please indicate tape format VHS ☐ Betamax ☐

Finance

Financial security is essential if life after work is to be lived to the full. The vast range of opportunities that suddenly become available – for travel, hobbies and leisure pursuits – can be seized only if there is sufficient income to pay for them in addition to meeting the continuing everyday living expenses such as rates, heating and lighting, food and clothing.

It used to be a maxim that people should start planning their retirement 10 years in advance. Now, it is never too early to begin because who knows when 'retirement' will come? Fifty years ago, boy school leavers starting a job could reasonably anticipate working to the age of 65, but this will be the exception rather than the rule for those who started work in the 1950s.

Early retirement and redundancy have introduced an element of uncertainty in many people's careers, especially if it comes late in middle age. So the need for planning is even more pressing because with ever-improving health care we are living longer and, if we finish full-time work earlier, a greater proportion of our lives will be spent in retirement.

Whilst it is never too early to start planning, neither is it ever too late. The first step is to have a complete understanding of everything that will make up your income in retirement, and to balance this against your anticipated requirements and expenses.

Income in retirement generally comes from three sources:
- *The State* Social security benefits have been paid for by you throughout your working life
- *Ex-employers* You may have also contributed for many years to one or more occupational pensions
- *Savings and investments* The sums accumulated over the years will now yield an income in the form of interest and capital growth.

Not everyone enjoys the benefit of income from all of these sources which are *all* taxable. The tax inspector does not lose interest in us once we have reached retirement age but is then a little less demanding.

Here the book will deal with each of these sources. The options available will be described together with the pros and cons to help you decide what is most appropriate for yourself. Worked examples are given for some real life situations to clarify some points.

All reported state payments and tax limits are current at the time of going to press. Adjustments will be made annually by the government, usually in April.

State pensions and other social security benefits

BASIC STATE RETIREMENT PENSION	27
Who qualifies	27
How you qualify	29
How your pension is worked out	29
What will you receive	29
Inflation protection	34
HOW TO CLAIM YOUR PENSION	35
HOW IT IS PAID	36
THE TAXMAN AND YOUR PENSION	37
ADDITIONS TO THE BASIC PENSION	38
For the spouse	38
For dependent children	40
Invalidity addition	40
Age addition	41
Christmas bonus	41
OTHER PENSIONS	41
Graduated pension	41
State Earnings Related Pension Scheme (SERPS)	41
Supplementary Pension	43
Invalidity Pension	43
MEDICAL SERVICES	45
Hospital in-patients	45
Other entitlements	45

EARLY RETIREMENT	45
Qualifying for unemployment benefit	45
DEFERRING YOUR PENSION	46
Maximum deferred pension	46
Cancelling your retirement	46
THE EARNINGS RULE	47
Married couples	48
RETURNING FROM WORK OVERSEAS	48
RETIRING ABROAD	49
WOMEN AND THE STATE PENSION	49
What is your entitlement?	49
The small stamp	51
Relying on your husband's contributions	52
Divorce	52
Separation	53
Widows	53
HOW TO FIND FURTHER HELP	57
GLOSSARY OF TERMS	57
BIBLIOGRAPHY	60
References	60

Many people have reservations about applying for state benefits, feeling that there is some stigma attached. A hangover from the days of the Poor Law and the workhouse, this attitude should now be overcome. All state benefits available from the DHSS have been paid for by the National Insurance contributions you will have made during your working life. Like any other form of insurance, it will provide you with some income once certain conditions have been met. In the case of pensions this depends on you reaching a certain age and stopping full-time work.

The various state benefits that are available are described below. You will not necessarily be eligible for all of these; further information may be obtained from your local DHSS office.

Benefit	£ Per week
Basic retirement pension	39.50
Extra pension for spouse	23.75
Total for married couple	63.25
Extra pension for dependent child or children	8.05
Graduated pension (maximum)	4.45 (man)
	3.72 (woman)
Additional pension (SERPS) (approx maximum)	21.00
Invalidity addition (maximum)	8.30
Age addition	0.25
Christmas bonus	10.00

BASIC STATE RETIREMENT PENSION

Who qualifies?

In general, a pension is paid to anyone who has been in regular employment or self-employment, and has been earning more than the minimum level at which National Insurance contributions should be paid. These people will have a full record of contributions. If you have had periods of unemployment or illness, your contributions record will not have suffered provided you registered as unemployed or claimed

QUALIFYING YEARS

The percentage of the full basic pension that is paid by number of qualifying years and length of working life.

YEARS OF WORKING LIFE

WL → QY ↓	31	32	33	34	35	36	37	38	39	40	41	42	43	44	45	46	47	48	49
6	31	Nil	Nil	Nil	Nil	Nil	Nil	Nil	Nil	Nil	Nil	Nil	Nil	Nil	Nil	Nil	Nil	Nil	Nil
7	26	25	25	Nil	Nil	Nil	Nil	Nil	Nil	Nil	Nil	Nil	Nil	Nil	Nil	Nil	Nil	Nil	Nil
8	30	29	28	27	26	25	Nil	Nil	Nil	Nil	Nil	Nil	Nil	Nil	Nil	Nil	Nil	Nil	Nil
9	34	33	32	30	30	29	28	27	26	Nil	Nil	Nil	Nil	Nil	Nil	Nil	Nil	Nil	Nil
10	38	36	35	34	33	32	31	30	29	28	28	27	27	26	25	25	25	25	25
11	41	40	38	37	36	35	34	33	32	31	31	30	29	29	28	27	27	26	25
12	45	43	42	40	39	38	37	36	35	34	34	33	32	31	30	30	29	28	28
13	49	47	45	44	42	41	40	39	38	37	37	36	35	34	33	32	31	31	30
14	52	50	49	47	46	44	43	42	40	39	39	38	37	36	35	35	34	33	32
15	56	54	52	50	49	47	46	45	43	42	42	41	40	39	38	37	36	35	35
16	60	58	56	54	52	50	49	48	46	45	45	44	43	42	40	40	39	38	37
17	63	61	59	57	55	54	52	50	49	48	48	46	45	44	43	42	41	40	39
18	67	65	63	60	59	57	55	53	52	50	50	49	48	47	45	44	43	42	41
19	71	68	66	64	62	60	58	56	55	53	53	52	50	49	48	47	46	45	44
20	75	72	69	67	65	63	61	59	58	56	56	55	53	52	50	49	48	47	46
21	78	75	73	70	68	66	64	62	60	59	59	57	56	54	53	52	50	49	48
22	82	79	76	74	71	69	67	65	63	62	62	60	58	57	55	54	53	52	50
23	86	83	80	77	75	72	70	68	66	64	64	63	61	59	58	57	55	54	53
24	89	86	83	80	78	75	73	71	69	67	67	65	64	62	60	59	58	56	55
25	93	90	87	84	81	79	76	74	72	70	70	68	66	65	63	61	60	59	57
26	97	93	90	87	84	82	79	77	75	73	73	71	69	67	65	64	62	61	60
27	100	97	94	90	88	85	82	80	78	75	75	73	72	70	68	66	65	63	62
28	100	100	97	94	91	88	85	83	80	78	78	76	74	72	70	69	67	66	64
29	100	100	100	97	94	91	88	86	83	81	81	79	77	75	73	71	70	68	66
30	100	100	100	100	97	94	91	89	86	84	84	82	79	77	75	74	72	70	69
31	100	100	100	100	100	97	94	92	89	87	87	84	82	80	78	76	74	73	71
32		100	100	100	100	100	97	95	92	89	89	87	85	83	80	79	77	75	73
33			100	100	100	100	100	98	95	92	92	90	87	85	83	81	79	77	75
34				100	100	100	100	100	98	95	95	92	90	88	85	83	81	80	78
35					100	100	100	100	100	98	98	95	93	90	88	86	84	82	80
36						100	100	100	100	100	100	98	95	93	90	88	86	84	82
37							100	100	100	100	100	100	98	95	93	91	89	87	85
38								100	100	100	100	100	100	98	95	93	91	89	87
39									100	100	100	100	100	100	98	96	93	91	89
40										100	100	100	100	100	100	98	96	94	91
41											100	100	100	100	100	100	98	96	94
42												100	100	100	100	100	100	98	96
43													100	100	100	100	100	100	98
44 OR MORE														100	100	100	100	100	100

REPRODUCED WITH THE PERMISSION OF THE CONTROLLER OF HER MAJESTY'S STATIONERY OFFICE

sickness or invalidity benefit from the DHSS. Free contributions are credited to you for such periods, even if you were not entitled to unemployment benefit.

If you have not made sufficient contributions for a full basic pension you will receive a reduced pension that will be based on the number of *qualifying years* you have accumulated in your *working life*. The table opposite will help you to assess how much pension you are entitled to.

How you qualify

To qualify for the *Basic Retirement Pension* all the following conditions must be fulfilled:
1. You must be aged 65 years for a man, 60 for a woman
2. You must have genuinely retired from full-time work
3. You must have paid sufficient National Insurance contributions or been credited with them during periods of sickness or unemployment

So if you retire early for whatever reason you must wait until you reach the State retirement age to qualify for the pension. However, if you reach retirement age but carry on working you cannot draw your State pension until you do give up work.

How your pension is worked out

The Department of Health and Social Security (DHSS) calculates your basic State retirement pension on the basis of *qualifying years*. These are all the years in which you have paid sufficient contributions. To obtain a full basic pension you need to have acquired qualifying years equivalent to roughly nine-tenths of your *working life*.

What will you receive?

The single person
The basic retirement pension of £39.50 will be paid to anyone with the requisite number of qualifying years on reaching retirement age provided they give up full-time work.

The married couple
A married couple who have *both* earned a full basic pension will *each* receive £39.50, a total of £79 a week between them. Where the wife does not qualify for a pension an extra pension of £23.75 is paid to her husband in addition to the basic £39.50. Once she is 60 the £23.75 becomes her pension in her own right.

NATIONAL INSURANCE CONTRIBUTIONS

An employee automatically pays Class 1 contributions which are deducted from the salary by the employer in the same way that income tax is paid under PAYE. (See below for details on the rates.) Class 2 contributions are made by the self-employed. The most convenient way of doing this is by direct debit through a bank account. You may also make voluntary contributions (Class 3) so that, in certain circumstances, your contributions record is maintained in order to safeguard your State pension rights. Class 4 contributions are paid only by the self-employed and do not count towards any benefit – it is, in reality, a further tax.

Contributions Protection

National Insurance contributions should have been credited during:
- Periods of unemployment (provided you signed on)
- Spells of unpaid sick leave (provided sick notes were sent to the DHSS)
- Periods in which you received maternity allowance, invalid care allowance or unemployability supplement
- Any course of approved training which you undertook

You can also receive NI credits if you have had to stay at home to look after someone (see *Home Responsibilities Protection* opposite).

Current National Insurance Rates

Weekly earnings (£)	Employee contributions (% of gross salary)	
	Contracted in (p. 41)	Contracted out (p. 44)
39	1.95 (1.50)	1.95
59	2.95	2.52
64	3.20 (2.46)	2.66
94	6.58	5.40
99	6.93 (3.81)	5.64
139	12.51	10.36
149	13.41	11.04
150	13.50 (5.78)	11.11
200	18.00 (7.70)	14.54
285	25.65	20.36
295 or more	26.55 (11.36)	21.05

Examples of the married women's reduced rate contribution are given in brackets.

Voluntary Contributions

Class 3 contributions may be paid in order to maintain your record for periods when you are not liable to pay National Insurance, for example if your income falls below the lower earnings limit. This is more likely to be appropriate for the self-employed with fluctuating incomes. The contributions are paid at a flat rate (currently £3.75) regardless of income levels and protect only the basic pension.

These voluntary contributions cannot be used to 'buy back' pension rights (that is, to fill gaps created previously) in a belated attempt to improve the pension. If these gaps are recent then you may be allowed to remedy them, but paying at current rates instead of those existing at the time of omission.

If you defer your retirement, you will not be able to make Class 3 contributions in order to improve the pension.

Home Responsibilities Protection

Staying at home to look after someone is likely to reduce the number of qualifying years you would otherwise need for a full basic pension. For each complete year after April 1978 for which you were
- getting child benefit for a child under 16
- receiving supplementary benefit while not working in order to care for an elderly or sick person at home
- spending at least 35 hours every week looking after someone who was receiving attendance allowance or constant attendance allowance

you will have the same number of years deducted from the number of qualifying years you would otherwise need for a full basic pension. You will then get the full pension *provided the number of qualifying years remaining after the deduction is not less than 20*. In that case, you will qualify for a reduced pension. (Note. Women who elected to pay the small stamp are not eligible for home responsibilities protection.)

Certificate of Age Exception

Once you have passed 65 (60 for a woman) you no longer have to pay National Insurance contributions. As these are on a graduated scale, the weekly saving can vary considerably. Currently it will mean around £9 a week more for those earning around £100 a week and up to £26.55 a week for those on top earnings. By giving your employer a *Certificate of Age Exception* deductions from your salary for National Insurance purposes should cease. If deductions have already been made following your 60th or 65th birthday you are entitled to ask for a refund.

Similarly the self-employed do not have to pay Class 2 or Class 4 contributions after reaching retirement pension age.

WILL YOU RECEIVE A STATE PENSION?

What is your working life?

For the DHSS the *working life* starts from the age of 16 and ends at the state retirement pension age. So that the working life is 49 years for a man and 44 years for a woman. For a full basic pension you need:

$(49 \times 90\% = 44.1)$ qualifying years as a man and
$(44 \times 90\% = 39.6)$ qualifying years as a woman

WHAT ARE MY BASIC PENSION PROSPECTS?

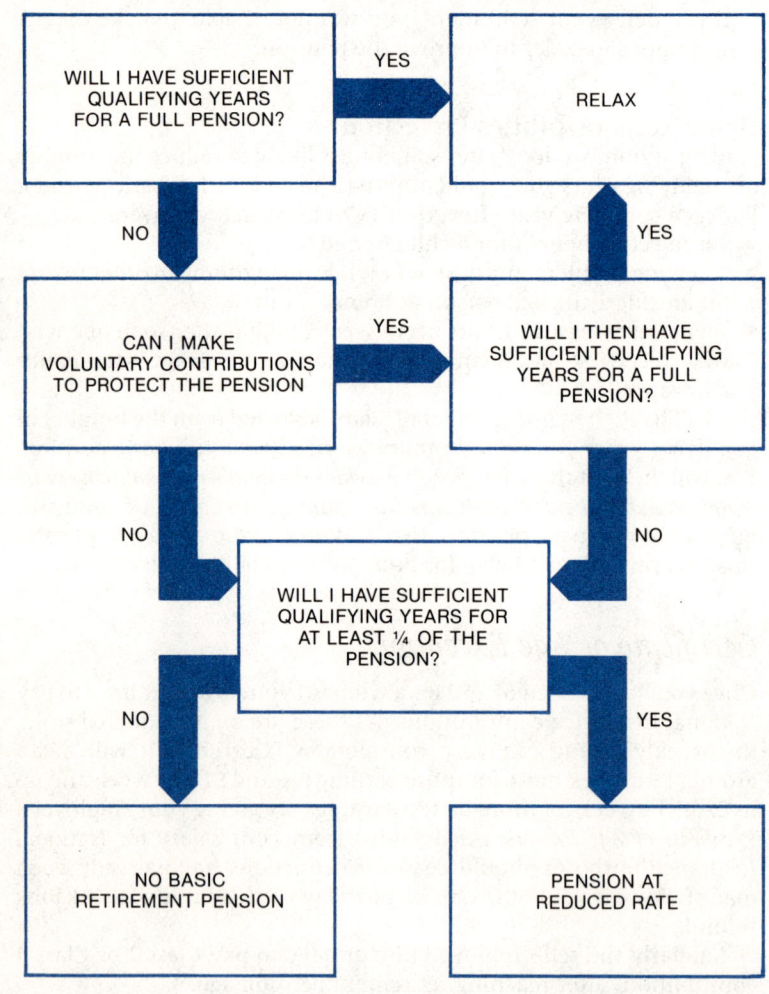

As the DHSS does not deal in fractions, you need full contributions for 44 years (man) or 39 years (woman). The former married woman's *small stamp* does not qualify towards a basic pension (see p. 50). If you have made fewer contributions your basic pension will be reduced.

What is a qualifying year?

Between July 1948 and April 1975 you needed to make 50 flat rate contributions in a year for it to qualify towards your pension. Since April 1975, National Insurance contributions have been related to earnings and for each of the following three years you needed to pay contributions on earnings equal to at least 50 times the weekly lower earnings limit (see opposite). However, from April 1978 contributions on earnings of at least 52 times the weekly lower earnings limit have been required. At present the limit is £39 a week, but this changes each April.

If you were over 16 in 1948

Your pension will depend largely on whether or not you were previously insured for pension purposes. At that time not all employment was insurable, nor was it necessarily continuous. If you were insured your *working life* is deemed to have started at the beginning of the tax year in which you last entered insurance or in April 1936, whichever is later. Those who left insurable employment before 1948 were granted a period of *free insurance* but if a new insurable job was not taken up by the end of the free period then the benefit of *all* previous contributions was lost.

At July 1948 only those in insurable employment or in a period of free insurance were able to move their previous contributions into the new scheme. If you were not in either category then your working life is considered to have begun in April 1948.

A simple method for discovering whether you will be entitled to a full basic pension is to work out your years of working life and deduct 5 from the total if it is more than 41 years, or 4 if it is 40 or less. This gives the number of *qualifying years* you will need for a full pension.

Example

A man reaching State retirement pension age in 1987 would have been 26 in 1948. Assuming he was not insured for pension purposes before that date his working life will be considered to have begun in 1948. Thus his working life will span 1948 to 1987, or 39 years, and the number of qualifying years needed for a full pension is $(39 - 4 = 35)$ years.

The growth of the State retirement pension since 1971.

Year	Pension (£)		
	Husband	Wife	Total
1971	6.00	3.70	9.70
1972	6.75	4.15	10.90
1973	7.75	4.75	12.50
1974	10.00	6.00	16.00
1975	13.30	7.90	21.20
1976	15.30	9.20	24.50
1977	17.50	10.50	28.00
1978	19.50	11.70	31.20
1979	23.30	14.00	37.30
1980	27.15	16.30	43.45
1981	29.60	17.75	47.35
1982	32.85	19.70	52.55
1983	34.05	20.45	54.50
1984	35.80	21.50	57.30
1985	38.30	23.00	61.30
1986	38.70	23.25	61.95
1987	39.50	23.75	63.25

Inflation protection

The basic pension, graduated pension, SERPS and supplementary pension (p. 41 and p. 44) are protected against inflation. From April 1987 they will go up each year in line with price rises over the preceding 12 months, taken from December to November. Benefits that are not protected against inflation are age addition and Christmas bonus.

The effects of inflation on pension upratings. The changes in the value of a pension for a married couple are given from 1976 to 1985 with adjustments to the spending power of 1985. (Source: Department of Health and Social Security.)

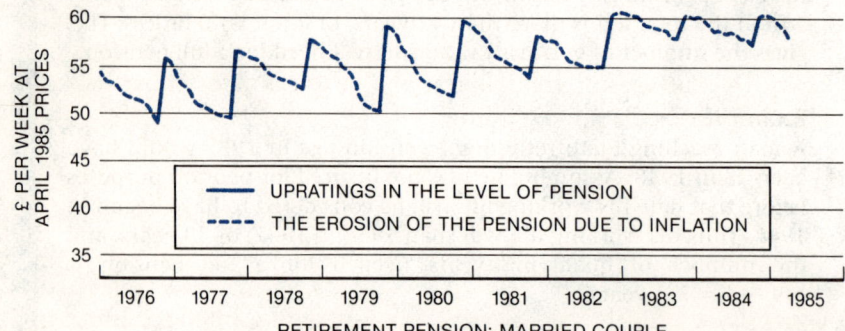

RETIREMENT PENSION: MARRIED COUPLE
REPRODUCED WITH THE PERMISSION OF THE CONTROLLER OF HER MAJESTY'S STATIONERY OFFICE

Inflation protection of State pensions was introduced in 1971 at the start of the worst period of inflation in recent times. This has resulted in pension rises from £9.70 for a married couple in 1971 to £63.25 by 1987 (see table opposite).

After each uprating the value of the State retirement pension declines steadily as inflation eats into it. This is shown for a married couple in the chart opposite.

HOW TO CLAIM YOUR PENSION

1. Get your claims form
Some four months before you reach retirement age the DHSS should send you a claim form. If you do not receive one, ask for it. Even if you intend to carry on working full time you should complete and return the form in order to establish your right to a pension ultimately. Married women should apply for their own pensions and for any graduated pension or SERPS to which they may be entitled.

2. Fill in details of when you will retire
The retirement date you should give on the claim form is the day after you stop work, or the date of your 65th birthday if you have already stopped working. You will be paid from the first pension pay day of retirement and, if possible, it is best to make that the date your retirement starts. So as the pension pay day is normally a Monday, it is convenient to retire on the preceding Friday or Saturday.

If you will continue working and wish to defer your pension, tell the DHSS. They will automatically send you a Certificate of Age Exception (see p. 31). You will have to notify them subsequently when you decide finally to retire.

3. Put in your claim
Any delay in completing the form and claiming your pension can result in loss of benefit. If you delay without good reason you will not receive pension for more than the three months immediately preceding your claim. Even with a good reason you will not be able to claim for more than 12 months before the date of claiming.

4. Wait for confirmation
Once you have claimed your pension, the DHSS will write to you. They will tell you how your pension is made up, what you must do if you disagree with the decision, and give you the name and address of whoever is responsible for paying you any guaranteed minimum pension (see p. 64).

HOW IT IS PAID

If you live in Britain and your pension amounts to more than £1 a week you can choose how it is paid.
1. By credit transfer into
   - your bank
   - a National Girobank account
   - an account with a building society
   - your National Savings bank account
   paid every 4 or 13 weeks at the end of each period.
2. By using a book of orders. Each order represents one week's pension which you can cash at a post office of your choice from one week in advance to up to three months after the date shown on it. If it is not

Specimen page from a pension book.

COUNTERFOIL RETAINED IN BOOK BY PENSIONER

TWO WEEKS' ALLOWANCE
(THESE SECTIONS ARE REMOVED BY THE PAYING OFFICE)

PENSIONER'S NUMBER

DATE DUE

PAYING OFFICE STAMP

AMOUNT PAYABLE

PENSIONER SIGNS HERE

PAYING OFFICE STAMP

REPRODUCED WITH THE PERMISSION OF THE CONTROLLER OF HER MAJESTY'S STATIONERY OFFICE

cashed within three months, a new order must be applied for, and if it is not cashed within 12 months the pension due on it may be lost altogether.

Many choose the second system believing that they need the book of orders to prove that they are entitled to the concessions that are available to the retired, such as reduced fares or free travel in some areas. This is not so. If you write to the **DHSS Central Pensions Branch** asking for form BR464 you will receive a pink card attesting that you are entitled to a National Insurance retirement pension.

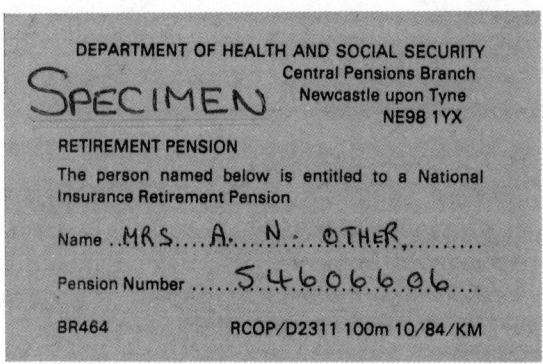

REPRODUCED WITH THE PERMISSION OF THE CONTROLLER OF HER MAJESTY'S STATIONERY OFFICE

THE TAXMAN AND YOUR PENSION

Most of the retirement benefits, including the basic, additional (SERPS), graduated pensions and the dependent spouse allowance (p. 27), are taxable income and should be included in your tax returns. Only one benefit escapes the tax net, that is the invalidity pension.

If you are under state retirement age then you will have a personal allowance which is tax free. Currently this is £2425 a year for a single person and £3795 for a married couple. However, for people of 65 and over this is replaced by an age allowance which is currently £2960 for a single person and £4675 for a married couple even if only one of them is 65. For those aged 80 and over, the age allowance rises to £3070 (single person) and £4845 (married couple). (See *Taxation* p. 179 for the rules governing this allowance.)

Although basic pensions fall within the limits of personal and age allowances, other sources of income, such as an occupational pension and interest from savings, are added to your pension when your tax liability is assessed (see p. 181 for examples).

Single person: £39.50 × 52 = £2054
Married couple (including extra for spouse):
(£39.50 + £23.75) × 52 = £3289

ADDITIONS TO THE BASIC PENSION

Extra pension for the spouse

Where the wife is not of retirement age and has not been working, a pension of £63.25 will be paid to the husband. This consists of £39.50 (basic) and £23.75 earned from his national insurance contributions for his wife. The £23.75 will become *her* pension once she reaches 60.

When the wife reaches retirement age before the husband
A wife reaching 60 years who does not qualify for a pension based on her own contributions must wait until her husband qualifies for his pension before she can get her pension as a spouse. So a woman who marries a man five years younger than herself would have to wait until she was 70 before receiving this pension.

Those who have made sufficient contributions for a small pension of their own will receive this at the age of 60 even if the husband is not 65. Once he reaches that age and retires, then she can choose to give this up and take the one earned by her husband's contributions.

Note: Although comparatively rare in practice, a wife supporting her husband is also entitled to the extra for a dependent spouse if she has earned a basic pension. The conditions for this are very stringent; for example, an invalid husband so incapacitated as to be incapable of earning a living.

WORKING WIVES

The payment for a dependent spouse under retirement age will be lost if they earn more than £31.45 a week. In this case earnings include any company pension from a previous employer. So wives doing part-time work for relatively small remuneration should examine this situation carefully.

Consider Mr Jones, Mr Brown, Mr Smith and Mr Green who are all 65 and retired. Their wives are all under 60 and each decides to carry on working.

Mrs Jones spends a couple of mornings a week typing, which brings in £28. Mrs Brown does much the same for a slightly more generous employer who pays her £32. While Mrs Smith's few hours of filing work earns her £30 a week and she receives £5 by way of a small occupational pension entitlement from a previous employer. Mrs Green however, reckons that now her husband has retired she needs every penny of the £50 she is paid for helping out at meal times at the local school five days a week. Who is going to be better off? The table below shows how much income each couple receives.

	Wife's earnings	Wife's occupational pension	Husband's basic pension	Extra for wife	Total family income
Jones	£28	nil	£39.50	£23.75	£91.25
Brown	£32	nil	£39.50	nil	£71.50
Smith	£30	£5	£39.50	nil	£74.50
Green	£50	nil	£39.50	nil	£89.50

Mrs Jones, who earns the least, fares best. Mrs Smith's occupational pension has pushed her earnings over the limit when added to her small income, so she and Mrs Brown would do well to knock off half-an-hour earlier each day and persuade their employers to grant them a small reduction in salary. Unluckily Mrs Green will have to squeeze another £1.75 out of the local education authority if she is to keep up with the Joneses.

So working wives earning just below the £31.45 limit should bear this problem constantly in mind. A pay rise could have unfortunate consequences for the total family income.

However, once a wife reaches 60, then the extra that her husband can claim becomes her pension. Mrs Smith will be glad to know that then her occupational pension will no longer count as earnings. However, if she continues to work, the pension she is receiving on her husband's contributions may well be affected by *The Earnings Rule* (see p. 47).

Extra pension for dependent children

An additional £8.05 may be claimed on the retirement pension for each child you have living with you and for whom you are receiving child benefit. However, this addition will not be paid if your income, including any occupational pension, is above a set limit related to the number of children (see table below).

To qualify for extra pension for a dependent child your income must be below the given limits for the number of children specified.

No. of children	Income limit (£) per week
1	85
2	95
3	105

Invalidity Addition

If you are receiving an invalidity allowance with *invalidity benefit* (see *Glossary*, p. 58) at any time within eight weeks and one day of reaching retirement pension age, the allowance will be automatically and permanently added to your pension entitlements. However, the amount will be reduced penny for penny by any additional pension (SERPS) or guaranteed minimum pension (see p. 64) that you receive, and it is quite possible for the invalidity addition to be completely extinguished in these circumstances.

Whereas before pension age, the invalidity allowance is tax free, when it is paid together with a retirement pension it becomes taxable. Alternatively the invalidity pension can be taken which is tax free (see p. 43).

There are three rates of invalidity allowance dependent on the age at which you become ill (see table below – the younger receive the higher weekly rate and the older, the lower one.

Rate of invalidity allowance with age at which you become ill.

Age	Invalidity allowance (£)
below 40	8.30
40–49	5.30
Women 50–55 Men 50–60	2.65

Men who fall ill after they have reached 60 (55 for women) do not qualify for invalidity allowance but may receive an invalidity pension.

Age Addition

This is something to look forward to once you reach 80, but it is not a lot, amounting to 25p a week. It has remained at that rate since it was first introduced in 1971. Had it kept pace with inflation this would now be about £1.17.

Christmas Bonus

Customarily this is £10 which is paid to everyone who receives the basic pension, graduated pension, additional pension, invalidity benefit or some other State benefit. It is an addition to the normal pension payment which is paid usually early in December. This, too, was first paid in 1971 and would now be worth £46.68 if it had kept pace with inflation.

OTHER PENSIONS

Graduated Pension

From 1961 to 1975 a graduated pension scheme was in operation in which each £7 paid by a man and £9.50 by a woman bought a pension unit worth 6d (old pence) per week. Each unit is now worth 5.17p (new pence) a week. The maximum number of units that could have been built up during the life of the scheme was 86 by a man, which is now worth £4.45 a week, and 72 by a woman, which is now worth £3.72 on top of the basic pension.

State Earnings Related Pension Scheme (SERPS)

SERPS began to operate in April 1978 but is now undergoing a period of change. It was designed to pay better pensions to higher earners who pay for it with higher contributions. The entitlement depends on the earnings on which National Insurance contributions have been paid since April 1978.

The DHSS uses a complex formula to arrive at your entitlement, which is known as *additional* pension, and is based on your earnings between set limits. This scheme is to continue unchanged for those who will reach retirement age this century, but because of the enormous cost anticipated, it is to be amended after that. Under the current arrangements it will attain its maximum value in 1998, 20 years after it started, and already it is paying worthwhile sums, around £21 a week, to those whose earnings were at the maximum levels of the scheme.

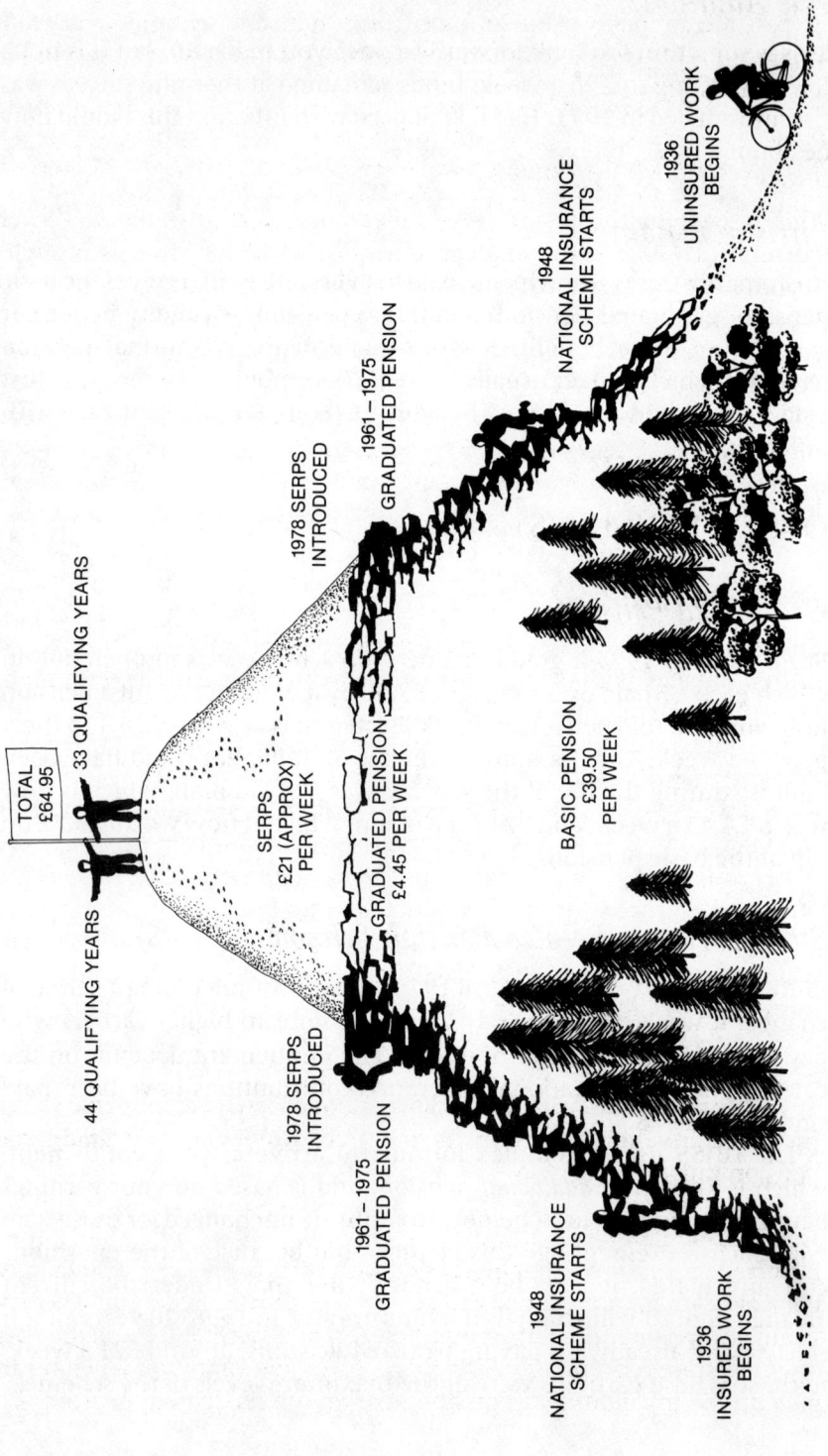

Contracting out

If you are or have been in a company pension scheme which has *contracted out* from SERPS then you can find further information in the chapter on *Occupation Pensions* (p. 61).

Supplementary Pension

This is paid to those whose incomes fall below a minimum level, currently at £38.65 for a single person and £61.85 for a married couple. If your total income in retirement falls below these figures, supplementary pension will be added to bring you up to the minimum level. Additionally, your rent and rates will be paid or, if you own your home, you may get help towards mortgage interest payments.

To qualify you, or you and your spouse together, should not have more than £3000 in savings. However, the first £4 of earnings from a part-time job is not counted against you when your income is assessed. Both husband and wife are entitled to this £4 allowance.

Invalidity Pension

This can be paid to those receiving invalidity benefit once they reach retirement age. It is tax free and may be taken instead of the retirement pension for a maximum of five years.

The rates are the same (£39.50 for a single person, £23.75 for a dependent spouse). If the pension is the sole source of income then it makes no difference which pension is taken as the sum will not be sufficient to incur tax. However, with additional income you may be better off taking an invalidity pension. Generally, the higher the income the greater are the benefits of doing this. If your total income after deducting personal allowances is above £17,900 a year then you will begin to pay tax at 40%. Taking the invalidity pension could then increase your income by up to £1315.60 a year.

SERPS

SERPS can be received as an additional invalidity pension which, like the basic invalidity pension, is tax free. However, any graduated pension must be given up.

Deferred pensions

Deferred pensions will not increase in value if you receive the invalidity pension since this is regarded as a benefit (see above). However, you may change to receiving a retirement pension at any time up to five years after the state retirement pension age. After five years you will have to give up the invalidity pension and take up the retirement pension.

BENEFITING FROM THE INVALIDITY PENSION

Mr Wright is 65 and will receive an occupational pension of £10,000 a year from his former employers. His wife, aged 58, will not have her own pension and must rely on her husband's contributions. The couple's savings yields an annual income of around £1200. Their total income is then £14,489 which after tax is £11,601.62.

Source of income	Amount of income (£)	
Occupational Pension	10,000	
Interest from savings	1,200	
Retirement pension	3,289	
Total income	14,489	14,489
Less personal allowance		3,795
Taxable income		10,694
Tax at 27%	2,887.38	2,887.38
Net income	11,601.62	

However, Mr Wright can take the invalidity pension instead of the retirement pension and the £3289 would not then be included. So for tax purposes his income would be about £12,489.65

Source of income	Amount of income (£)	
Occupational Pension	10,000	
Interest from savings	1,200	
Total income	11,200	11,200
Less personal allowance		3,795
Taxable income		7,405
Tax at 27%	1,999.35	1,999.35
Net income	9,200.65	
Plus tax free pension	3,289.00	
Total	12,489.65	

The saving of £888 in tax could be even greater if you are also entitled to an *invalidity allowance*. This is also not taxable if added to an invalidity pension rather than a retirement pension, in which case it would be taxable. This would mean a further increase of between £137.80 and £431.60 a year for Mr Wright.

MEDICAL SERVICES

Hospital In-patients

Your retirement, invalidity and widow's pensions and the age addition will all be reduced after eight weeks of stay in a hospital. The reduction is related to the number of dependants you have at home. Similarly, any extra pension you get for a dependant will decrease after he or she has spent eight weeks in hospital.

There are other rules to cover really long periods of hospitalisation.

Other Entitlements

- Reduced charges for medical prescriptions, dental treatment and glasses.
- Free prescriptions. Simply fill in the back of the prescription before handing it to the chemist.
- Free NHS dental treatment and glasses to those who are on a low income or receiving supplementary pension. Even if your income is above the level at which these services are provided free, you may get help towards the cost.

EARLY RETIREMENT

Although you will not get your State pension until you reach retirement age, you may receive unemployment benefit for up to one year. If you have retired voluntarily there will be a 13-week delay before payment starts and you may get it for only nine months.

The current rates of benefit are £31.45 plus £19.40 for a wife, providing she is not earning more than that sum. Your benefit will also be cut if you receive an occupational pension of more than £35 a week. For every £1 of occupational pension above this your unemployment benefit will be reduced by £1. Thus an occupational pension of more than £66 a week means no benefit.

Qualifying for unemployment benefit

To qualify for benefit you must be willing and available to accept reasonable offers of work. If this is not the case and benefit is not paid, either for this reason or any other reason, your insurance contributions will be credited automatically. Once you have registered as unemployed you need not go to the unemployment office to sign on regularly.

If you are available for work, it is worth signing on regularly as that entitles you to other benefits, such as for sickness, should you subsequently require them.

DEFERRING YOUR PENSION

If you decide not to retire you will not receive a State pension, but the pension you subsequently get when you do retire will be enhanced. This may rise by approximately $7\frac{1}{2}\%$ per year for the period of deferment based on the pension current at the time of taking *not* the time of deferment.

Example
If a man, or woman, entitled to a full basic pension of £39.50 puts off retirement for three years during which the pension level rises to say £42, the result would be:
$$£42 \times 7\frac{1}{2}\% \times 3 = £9.45$$
This is additional to £42, so the total pension is £51.45.

These percentage increases also apply to SERPS, a guaranteed minimum pension and the wife's pension. However, for any period in which you receive another social security benefit during the time you defer retirement you will not be entitled to the increase. The extra pension for the spouse is similarly affected if they receive a social security benefit during this period.

Maximum deferred pension

You can defer retirement for a maximum of only five years which would increase the pension by 37.5%. So when a man reaches 70, or a woman 65, they are regarded as retired and entitled to their State pensions even if still working and regardless of what they may be earning.

Cancelling your retirement

If you retire at pension age but later change your mind, you may tell the DHSS that you wish to cancel your retirement, but you can do this only once your State pension and the extra for your wife will then stop. So your wife has to provide written agreement to the cancellation and, if she is entitled to a lesser pension on her own contributions she may revert to this. However, this is a benefit and it will mean that there will be no annual increment to the pension her husband has earned for her, which she may wish to take again when he finally retires.

THE EARNINGS RULE

Although you must genuinely retire from your employment in order to qualify for the State pension, you may also work to enhance your income. This may be either on a part-time basis for your previous employer, for example, or something completely different.

Only if you *earn* more than £75 gross a week is your basic State pension affected. However, the following items are deductible.
- Trade union subscriptions
- Fares to work
- Necessary clothing such as overalls
- Up to 15p off the cost of a meal per day
- Reasonable costs for care of someone at home while you are working.

Money from investments, occupational pensions, strokes of good fortune with premium bonds, or more speculative forms of gambling are not considered.

The Earnings Rule is one reason for deferring retirement. For the first £4 above the £75 limit you lose £2 from your pension, but above that level your pension will be reduced by the amount that you earn. The earnings rule does not affect any graduated pension or additional pension.

Earnings (£)	Pension deduction (£)	Remaining pension (£)	Total income (£)
75	nil	39.50	114.50
79	−2	37.50	116.50
100	−23	16.50	116.50
116	−39	0.50	116.50

The effect of earnings on your pension.

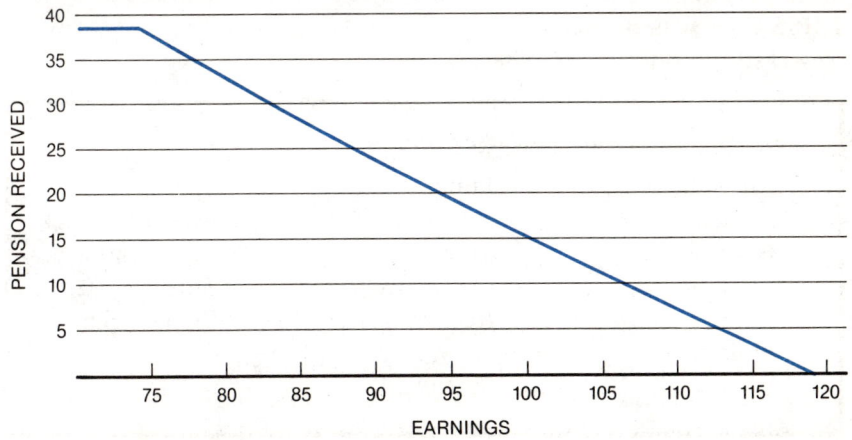

So it is impossible to raise your combined earnings and pension above £116.50 if you are earning more than £79 and less than £116.50. Clearly anyone earning at, or above, that level should defer taking the pension and reap the benefit of the 7.5% annual increase. However, those earning between £75 and £116 should consider how necessary it is to achieve a total maximum income of £116.50. If it is not, is it worth making do with less now in the realisation that every year of deferment may add about £3 a week (at current values) to the pension when it is finally taken?

Married couples

The married couple's pension is also affected, and if earnings exceed £138 they will eliminate the whole sum, except if the wife is 60. Then the husband's earnings will have no effect on her pension, whether earned by her own or his contributions. Her pension is affected only by her own earnings as described above. Conversely, her earnings will not affect her husband's pension.

While it is possible for a husband and wife to each receive their full pensions entitlement and to earn £75 a week when they are both over pension age, if one person earns more than £75 and the other less, they cannot do a balancing act on the basis that the joint earnings amount to £150 or less.

RETURNING FROM WORK OVERSEAS

Social security contributions made while working in Northern Ireland, the Isle of Man, an EEC country, or any other country that has a reciprocal agreement with Britain will count towards your pension. However, the terms of the individual agreements do vary and to be absolutely certain of your own situation you should contact:
DHSS Overseas Branch
Newcastle-upon-Tyne NE98 1YX

Countries with reciprocal agreements

Australia	Jamaica	Spain
Austria	Jersey and Guernsey	Sweden
Bermuda	Malta	Switzerland
Canada	Mauritius	Turkey
Cyprus	New Zealand	Yugoslavia
Finland	Norway	
Israel	Portugal	

RETIRING ABROAD

Normally it is not difficult to arrange with your DHSS office for your pension to be paid to you in a foreign country, but you may lose the inflation proofing of your pension and the increases when levels are reviewed annually. This depends entirely on the country of residence. You should, however, get the increases in an EEC country or any country that has a reciprocal agreement with Britain covering this point (see table opposite).

EEC member countries		
Belgium	Greece	Luxembourg
Denmark	Ireland	Portugal
France	Italy	Spain
Germany	Netherlands	United Kingdom

The main countries in addition to those in the EEC		
Austria	Israel	Sark
Bermuda	Jamaica	Switzerland
Cyprus	Malta	Turkey
Gibraltar	Mauritius	USA
Guernsey		Yugoslavia

If you live abroad temporarily and remain ordinarily a resident of the United Kingdom you may still get the increases in pension and receive them in the form of arrears when you return. If you are going overseas for less than three months you can simply allow your pension to build up during your absence as three months is the limit for cashing a pension book order.

WOMEN AND THE STATE PENSION

What is your entitlement?

If you have been in continuous employment for the whole of your *working life* or have acquired sufficient number of *Qualifying Years* then you will be entitled to the full pension for a single person or married couple. (See previous sections for further information.)

Here we will deal with the benefits available to those who have had an interrupted career.

SMALL STAMP OR FULL RATE CONTRIBUTIONS?

Mrs Grey is 45 and her husband is 50, so they will both reach their respective retirement ages together. For six years before her marriage, Mrs Grey paid full contributions but has since paid only the reduced rate. At present, she earns £60 a week and intends to carry on working until she is 60. So should she continue paying the small stamp or pay full contributions?

Mrs Grey is currently paying 3.85% of her gross pay at the reduced rate. This would increase to 5% if she pays full contributions, totalling an additional £538.20 payment for the period until she retires (see table below).

If her salary increases this difference will increase, but Mrs Grey will have added another 15 qualifying years to the six she has accumulated before her marriage, making a total of 21.

As Mrs Grey's working life is 44 years, six qualifying years do *not* earn a pension but 21 qualifying years will earn a pension of 54% the full rate.

However, Mr Grey will also be on the point of retirement then and his contributions will entitle his wife to a pension of around 60%.

	Contributions (£)	
Option	Per year	Over 15 years
Full rate @ 5%	156	2340
Small stamp @ 3.85%	120.12	1801.80
Additional	35.88	538.20

Salary @ £60 pw = £3120 pa.

Graduated pension

Many women who did not work for long periods and others who were poorly paid, were unable to build up many units, so graduated pension payments of only a few pence will be made in some cases. This is paid when a woman reaches 60 regardless of her entitlement to a basic pension. However, if the graduated pension is small, i.e. less than £1 a week, it will be paid on an annual basis and will be in addition to any other pension.

SERPS

Some married women may be entitled to SERPS when they reach 60 without being entitled to the basic pension because, for example, they may only have paid full National Insurance contributions in recent

Assuming that Mr Grey will be entitled to the full basic pension Mrs Grey should not make the change.

Although it seems that the higher the salary the less reason there is for changing to full contributions there are other factors to consider.
1. Paying the full rate would qualify her for sickness and unemployment benefits.
2. SERPS could be a welcome addition to the retirement income if there is time to build enough earnings related contributions.

But this should be balanced against the increase in contributions which can rise to 9% at the top level and may mean paying as much as £26.55 a week.

Mr and Mrs Brent are both 45, so that when Mrs Brent reaches 60 years she will have to wait at least five years for the spouse's pension. Like Mrs Grey, she has paid full contributions for six years, but has paid reduced contributions since her marriage. If Mrs Brent pays the additional £538.20 what could she expect? The payments at full rate for 21 qualifying years entitles Mrs Brent to 54% of the full pension, which is a weekly payment of

$$£21.33 = £39.50 \times \frac{54}{100}$$

This is an annual income of £1109.16, totalling £5545.80, over five years.

Mrs Brent will be more than £5000 better off and, assuming her husband will receive the full pension at 65, she can still exchange her pension for the slightly higher spouse's pension at 60% full rate.

The benefits of changing to full contributions are even greater for anyone who is older than her husband when each year of age difference increases the income by £1109.16. As the wife's personal allowance is £2335 this sum is effectively tax free.

years. However, as with the graduated pension, this will be paid on top of the basic pension based on their husbands' contributions.

The small stamp

In the past, married women who were working could pay a reduced rate contribution. But since 1978 newly married women and those who have been away from work for at least two consecutive tax years can no longer choose to pay this. However, some are still entitled to continue this and do so. In time all working women will be paying the same rate as men.

NB. Reduced rate contributions do *not* count towards qualifying for the State pension.

Whether it is worth changing to the full rate for those who can still make contributions at the lower rate depends on
(a) age
(b) how long you intend to continue working
(c) if you have paid full contributions in the past, say, before marriage, and
(d) if your husband will be entitled to the full basic pension.

Ask the DHSS for your record of contributions before making any calculations or taking decisions on your pension.

A pension based on a spouse's contributions is roughly 60% of the entitlement. If a full pension has been earned then 24 qualifying years are needed to better the amount received which includes any years before marriage (see p. 33).

If you are *less than five years your husband's junior*, it is worth while building your own entitlement to even a small pension which will be paid when you are 60. This may then be exchanged for the larger amount when your husband reaches 65 and retires. This arrangement is more important *if you are older than your husband*, and is increasingly so with increasing age difference.

Relying on your husband's contributions

If you are relying on you husband's contributions you will receive a maximum of £23.75. The amount you receive will depend on the pension that your husband will be entitled to, and is 60% of his entitlement. This pension will be lost if you earn more than £31.45 per week.

If you are under 60 when your husband retires, the allowance is included in his pension, but when you reach 60 or if you are 60 or above it will then become your own pension. This is independent of any entitlement to a graduated pension, SERPS or other occupational pension. (See pp. 41–44 for further details.)

Divorce

The effects of divorce on your pension will depend on
(a) the time of life at which the marriage ends and
(b) what you do afterwards.

If you divorce before reaching retirement age, on reaching 60 you may still take the pension you have earned yourself or one based on the contributions made by your ex-husband *up to the time of divorce* plus any contributions you have paid yourself since then. Since the pension based on your former husband's contributions no longer depends on his age, or even on whether he has died or remarried, then you can opt for the better pension at 60.

But if you remarry *before* 60 you lose all claims on your former husband's contributions and must rely instead on those of your new husband. All his contributions will be considered not just those he makes after the marriage even if he, too, is remarrying after divorce. In that case, with the aid of the State, he may be supporting two women on his contributions:
(a) his first wife from contributions to the time of divorce, and
(b) his second benefiting from his total contributions.
If you are over 60 when your marriage ends then you may rely entirely on your former husband's contributions, even if you remarry.

Similarly, a man can rely on his ex-wife's contributions up to the time of the divorce if it will yield a better pension.

Divorce has no effect on a person entitled to a full basic pension. Neither does it affect SERPS and graduated pensions which are based only on personal contributions.

The effects of divorce and remarriage on the source for your spouse's pension.

Age at divorce	Status		
	Single	Remarried under 60	Remarried over 60
Under 60	Ex-husband	Present husband	Ex-husband
Over 60	Ex-husband	—	Ex-husband

Separation

If you are separated then you are still treated as a married woman. Your husband will be entitled to the extra allowance on his pension at 65 if he is supporting you financially, but once you reach 60 you will be entitled to this amount as your pension. If you claim this or a superior pension based on your own contributions, the DHSS will cease paying the extra to your husband. If you reach 60 before your husband is 65, then you have to wait until he retires for your spouse's pension.

Widows

If you are widowed before 60
A new widow is entitled to the widow's allowance. This is currently £55.35 per week and is paid for the first 26 weeks after death. A claim form for this benefit will be sent by the DHSS after they have been supplied with the certificate given on registering his death.

After the first 26 weeks the widow may receive a widow's pension which is age related, the older the widow, the higher the pension. (See

Widow's pension according to the age at which widowhood began.

Age (years)	Pension (£ per week)
under 40	nil
40	£11.85
41	£14.62
42	£17.38
43	£20.15
44	£22.91
45	£25.68
46	£28.44
47	£31.21
48	£33.97
49	£36.74
50–60	£39.50

table above.) Unless they have children under 18, widows under 40 years do not qualify for a widow's pension once the 26-week widow's allowance finishes.

Widows do not progress in the scale as they grow older. So, a woman who is widowed at 44 will receive £22.91, but after her next birthday she will not receive the £25.68 applicable to age 45. Although the pension will rise annually with inflation, it will be based on the age at which she became a widow.

Widows with dependent children A widowed mother's allowance is available instead of a widow's pension. This is £39.50 a week with £8.05 for each child. When the children are no longer dependent, this payment stops. Then, if she is over 40, she will get a widow's pension based on her age at the time her children ceased being dependent. But there is nothing if she is still under 40.

If you are widowed after 60

Women who are widowed after 60 do not get a widow's allowance. Instead, a retirement pension is paid in the normal way. This may be based on your own and/or your late husband's contributions. (See table opposite.) You can receive a pension based on a combination of both your own and your husband's contributions up to a maximum basic pension of the standard rate for a single person. There is also an upper limit to the SERPS pension which is no more than that received by someone retiring at the time you were widowed, who had contributed to the scheme at the upper earnings limit from its inception in 1978.

Widows of working husbands will be better off with the widow's allowance as this is £53.55 per week rather than the £39.50 of

STATE PENSIONS & SOCIAL SECURITY BENEFITS

State benefits available for those who are widowed after 60.

Widow's status	Husband's status before death	
	Working	Retired (and over 65)
Working	Widow's allowance then husband's pension entitlement	Husband's pension(s)
Retired	Widow's allowance then your own or your husband's pension entitlement	Husband's pension(s)

maximum basic pension. You may also keep any SERPS or graduated pension due. If you are working then you can receive these pensions without having to retire yourself.

Widows approaching 60

If you are a widow approaching 60 you have three options:
1. Take a retirement pension and give up the widow's pension
2. Keep the widow's pension until you actually retire, or until 65
3. Defer the retirement pension and give up the widow's pension.

If you do not work or intend to retire at 60, then you should take Option 1 since the retirement pension that replaces the widow's pension will be of at least the same value. Although a retirement pension based on the husband's contributions will be the same as the widow's pension you can add to this any retirement pension earned from your own contributions to the limit of a single person's pension.

If your retirement pension does not look too good, then the basic pension may be improved by juggling with your contributions and your former husband's. The DHSS will do this for you, basing your pension on your own contributions and substituting to your advantage your husband's contribution record for either *all* of the years of *your* working life to the time you are widowed, or the years of your working life *from the beginning of your marriage* until the end of the tax year in which you were widowed. Men who become widowers before they are 65 may use their wives' contributions in a similar fashion.

If you intend to carry on working after 60, Option 2, your widow's pension will not be affected by your earnings. But at 65 you will be regarded as retired by the DHSS and your widow's pension will be replaced by the retirement pension as in option 1.

The third option requires careful thought and, as a general rule, is not to be recommended. The object is to secure a better retirement pension at 65, but to achieve it, the woman has to give up her widow's pension and forego the retirement pension until she stops work.

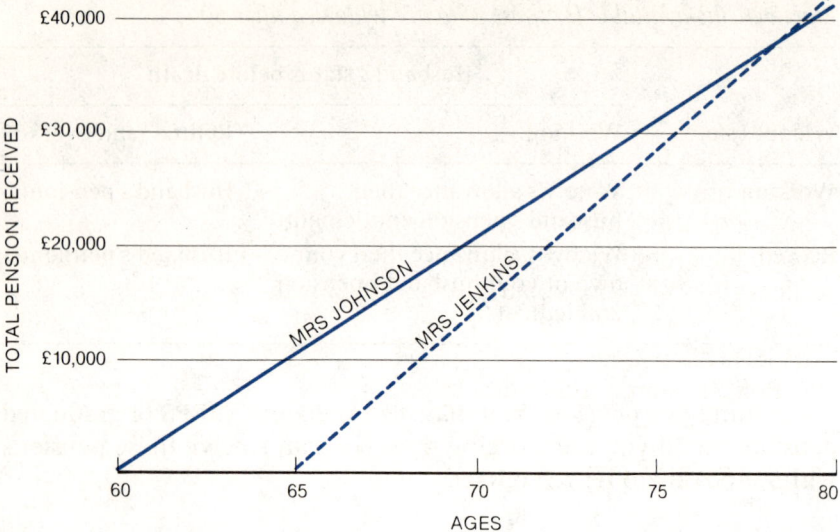

Example Both Mrs Jenkins and Mrs Johnson lost their husbands a couple of years ago and they are consequently receiving a widow's pension at the top rate of £39.50.

Mrs Jenkins decides to give this up so that for every year that she defers taking her pension it will be increased in value by about 7.5% which, over five years comes to 37.5% (see *Deferring your pension* p. 46). What difference does this make? The table below shows how much money Mrs Jenkins will give up over five years and the increase in the weekly pension as a result.

	Widow's Pension (£)		Retirement Pension (£ pw)
	pw (pa)	5 years	
Mrs Jenkins	—	—	54.31*
Mrs Johnson	39.50 (2,054)	10,270	39.50
Difference			14.81

* Includes increase of 37.5%

Even assuming that Mrs Jenkins pays standard rate of income tax, the net value of the pension given up would be about £7,500. Then if she escapes tax liability when she finally retires (which is unlikely) it will still take more than nine years for her to break even.

If she does not need the money while working she would do better to take it and put it into a savings account or, better still, into investments where it would earn interest and increase in capital value. It might have been a different story, had the widow's pension been quite small.

STATE PENSIONS & SOCIAL SECURITY BENEFITS

HOW TO FIND FURTHER HELP

Your local DHSS office will be listed in the telephone directory under Health and Social Security. To use their freephone advisory service, dial 100 and ask the operator for Freefone DHSS. When contacting your DHSS office it is helpful to give your National Insurance number or your pension number.

Most of the leaflets on benefits (including those given below) are obtainable from local DHSS offices, and some are also available at post offices and in libraries. You may also obtain them by writing to:

DHSS Leaflets Unit
PO Box 21, Stanmore, Middlesex HA7 1AY

GLOSSARY OF TERMS

Additional pension Also known as *SERPS* (State Earnings Related Pension Scheme), this was introduced in 1978 to give better state pensions to higher income earners but because of the high cost to the State, this is to be amended for those who reach retirement age after the end of this century.

Age addition Paid as an extra benefit to the over 80s, this is currently worth 25p a week.

Age allowance This replaces the personal allowance that may be set against gross income for tax purposes. It is higher than a *personal allowance* and may be claimed by single people at 65 or jointly by a married couple when one person reaches that age. There is a higher level of age allowance for those aged 80 or more.

Attendance allowance A benefit paid to those who, through disability, need a great deal of lookng after.

Basic retirement pension Payable at 65 (for men) or 60 (for women), this pension is based on the *National Insurance* contributions made during your *working life*.

Benefit Any form of social security payment.

Certificate of age exception This is provided by the *DHSS* to men of at least 65 and women of at least 60. It shows employers that they should no longer make deductions from a salary to pay *National Insurance* contributions for those employees as they are no longer liable to pay these.

Christmas bonus Paid annually to those receiving basic pension or some other benefits. Customarily £10.

Class 1 contributions The type of National Insurance contributions paid by employees; the sum is deducted from the salary by employers.

Class 2 contributions National Insurance contributions paid by the self-employed.

Class 3 contributions Sometimes called *Voluntary Contributions*, you may pay these in order to maintain your contributions record and protect your basic pension entitlement at times when you are not liable to pay National Insurance e.g. if your income falls below the *lower earnings limit*.

Class 4 contributions Paid by the self-employed but not counting towards any benefit.

Constant attendance allowance A higher level of *attendance allowance* paid to those more severe disabilities, through industrial or war injury.

Contracted out Employers who decided not to take part in the State Earnings Related Scheme are said to be contracted out, and so are their employees. (See *Guaranteed Minimum Pension*.)

Contributions Sums paid to the State *National Insurance* scheme by employers, employees and the self-employed, and on which qualification to most benefits depends.

Credits These are added to your record of National Insurance contributions at times when you are not obliged to pay, for example, during sickness or periods of unemployment.

Credit transfer A system by which your pension entitlements may be paid by the *DHSS* directly into your bank, building society, national savings or girobank account.

Deferred pension An enhanced State pension that is subsequently paid to those who do not take their pension at the ages of 65 (men) or 60 (women).

DHSS Department of Health and Social Security.

Earnings related Applied to National Insurance contributions that vary in size according to income.

Earnings rule Regulates the amount by which your pension will be reduced if, while receiving it, you earn more than a stipulated weekly amount (currently £75).

Graduated Pension scheme A State pension scheme that ran from 1961 to 1975. The pension is dependent on the contributions made.

Graduated retirement benefit Paid to those who were in the State *Graduated Pension scheme*.

Gross income Income before tax and other deductions have been made.

Guaranteed Minimum Pension This is paid to retired employees by employers who *contracted out* of the *State Earnings Related Pension Scheme*. It ensures that you receive a pension at least equivalent to that which you would have been entitled to from the State had your employer not contracted out of *SERPS*.

Home responsibilities protection A system designed to improve the State pension entitlements of those whose opportunity to make National Insurance contributions is curtailed by having to stay at home to care for a child or aged or infirm person.

Invalidity addition An *invalidity allowance*, paid as part of an *invalidity benefit* to those who qualify for this before retirement age, is added to the pension entitlements on reaching retirement pension age, subject to certain conditions.

Invalidity allowance An extra sum paid on top of the *invalidity pension*; the amount depends on the age at which the incapacity began.

Invalidity benefit This is made up of *invalidity pension* and *invalidity allowance*, and is paid in place of *statutory sick pay* or *sickness benefit* if you are still incapable of work after 28 weeks.

Invalidity pension (See *invalidity benefit*.)

Lower earnings limit This is the level of income at which you become liable to pay National Insurance contributions.

National Insurance The State system through which you pay, from your earnings, for benefits when in need, e.g. sickness and unemployment, and for your State pension entitlements.

Net income The sum at your disposal after tax and other deductions have been made from gross income.

Order The order to pay your pension in cash which you may present at a post office.

Pension book This contains the individually dated *orders* on which the pension, when due, is paid weekly to those who prefer to receive it in cash from a post office.

Personal allowance This is the sum that may be deducted from your gross income before tax liability is assessed.

Qualifying years Years in which you have made sufficient National Insurance contributions to qualify towards pension entitlement.

Reciprocal agreements Agreements entered into between various countries to protect the benefits and contributions of those working, or retiring abroad. The degree of protection depends on the individual agreements which are not uniform.

Reduced pension The benefit paid when insufficient *qualifying years* have been accumulated to earn a full *basic pension*.

Reduced rate contribution Often known as the *small stamp*, married women used to be able to elect to pay the lesser National Insurance payment which does *not* qualify towards pension. Some women still have the right to make this reduced payment, but it is being phased out.

SERPS State Earnings Related Pension Scheme. (See *Additional pension*.)

Sickness benefit This is a tax-free benefit fo those unable to work because of illness or disablement and who do not qualify for the statutory sick pay (e.g. the self-employed or unemployed). It is paid for 28 weeks and then replaced by *invalidity benefit*.

Small stamp (See *Reduced rate contribution*.)

State pension Generally used to describe all the components that go to make up your State retirement entitlements.

Statutory sick pay This is paid by employers for up to a maximum of 28 weeks to employees who are unable to work because of illness, provided the employee has paid National Insurance contributions (the married woman's *reduced rate contribution* does not count for this purpose). For illnesses longer than 28 weeks, see *invalidity benefit*.

Supplementary benefit For those whose incomes and savings are below a minimum level.

Supplementary pension Paid to those in retirement, and similar to the *supplementary benefit* for those below State pension age, it brings a pension up to a minimum level.

Unemployment benefit A weekly payment to those who would normally work for an employer but are out of a job.

Units These were bought by series of contributions under the old *Graduated Pension Scheme*. Each unit has a set value and the total entitlement is dependent on the number of units accumulated.

Voluntary contributions (See *Class 3 contributions*.)

Widowed mother's allowance This is paid instead of a *widow's pension* to widowed mothers with a dependent child or children.

Widow's allowance This is paid for 26 weeks to newly widowed women under 60 and to those over 60 provided the husband was not drawing his State retirement pension at the time of his death.

Widow's pension An age-related benefit paid to women of at least 40 after 26 weeks of widowhood, although women aged over 60 at the time of losing their husband do not qualify and are paid retirement pension instead.

Wife's earned income relief A married man may add his wife's earnings, up to a specified limit, to the *personal allowance* that is deducted from gross earnings before tax liability is assessed.

Working life A period stipulated by the *DHSS* when calculating your pension entitlements; it spans the years 16 to 65 for a man and 16 to 60 for a woman.

BIBLIOGRAPHY

Your Rights. Age Concern, 60 Pitcairn Road, Mitcham, Surrey CR4 3LL.

Useful leaflets that are free from the local DHSS offices include:

Christmas Bonus	(NI.229)
Earning extra pension by cancelling your retirement	(NI.92)
Fares to Hospital	(H.11)
Going into Hospital	(NI.9)
Invalidity Benefit	(NI.16A)
Looking after someone at home? How to protect your pension – Home Responsibilities Protection	(NP.27)
Married women – your national insurance position	(NI.1)
NHS Dental Treatment	(D.11)
NHS Prescriptions	(P.11)
NHS Vouchers for Glasses	(G.11)
NI guide for divorced women	(NI.95)
National Insurance Contribution Rates	(NI.208)
National Insurance for People with small earnings from self-employment	(NI.27A)
National Insurance for self-employed people	(NI.41)
National Insurance voluntary contributions	(NI.42)
Retirement Benefits for Married Women	(NP.32B)
Retirement Pensions and Widow's Benefits – Payment direct into bank or building society accounts	(NI.105)
Retiring?	(FB.6)
Social Security Abroad	(NI.38)
Social Security benefit rates and earnings rules	(NI.196)
Unemployment benefit and your occupational pension	(NI.230)
Widows – guidance about NI contributions and benefits	(NI.51)
Your Benefit as a Widow for the first 26 weeks	(NP.35)
Your Benefit as a Widow after 26 weeks	(NP.36)
Your Retirement Pension	(NP.32)
Your Retirement Pension if you are Widowed or Divorced	(NP.32A)

References

Social Trends No. 16 HMSO, London.
Your Retirement Pension (NP. 32) HMSO, London.

Occupational Pensions

CALCULATING YOUR COMPANY PENSION	62
GUARANTEED MINIMUM PENSION	64
WOMEN AND PENSIONS	65
ADDITIONAL FEATURES	66
Protection against rising prices	66
Widow's pension	68
Death-in-service provision	70
Early retirement	71
When is the pension paid?	72
Lump sum benefits	72
Additional voluntary contributions	77
Late retirement	78
PENSIONS FOR THE SELF-EMPLOYED	79
Personal pension plans	79
With-profits policies	81
Unit-linked policies	82
Pension for your spouse	82
Choosing a scheme	82
PENSIONS FROM PREVIOUS JOBS	83
HOW TO FIND OUT MORE	84
WHERE TO FIND A PERSONAL PENSION PLAN	84
GLOSSARY OF TERMS	88
BIBLIOGRAPHY	93

An occupational pension makes all the difference, for most of us, between living in relative poverty on what the State provides and managing to maintain a lifestyle similar to that we have enjoyed throughout our working lives. More than 11 million men and women, almost half the total workforce of the country, belong to an occupational pension scheme of one kind or another and it is probably the best investment they have ever made.

So if you are a member of such a scheme and are approaching retirement, it will pay you to look closely into your company pension provision and calculate the income you will receive.

You should start by examining your pension scheme booklet with care. It was no doubt given to you when you joined the scheme, but if you cannot find it ask for another from your pensions department. If it is a small company the company secretary will probably be responsible for this.

CALCULATING YOUR COMPANY PENSION

Near the beginning the document will say something like:

Your pension will be one sixtieth *of your* final pensionable pay *for each year of* pensionable service.

It might say 'eightieth' rather than 'sixtieth' and these are known as the *pension fractions*. The sixtieth is more generous than the eightieth and it enables you, after 40 years of service, to qualify for a pension equal to two-thirds of your final salary. An eightieth fraction, however, could achieve only a half-pay pension.

Example

Let's assume you have a salary of £15,000 a year, that you are a member of a scheme based on sixtieths, and that you have been a member of the scheme for 40 years. Your pension would be:

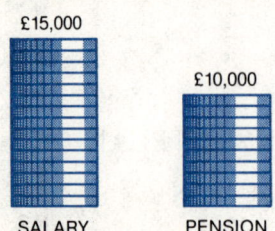

£15,000 ÷ 60 × 40 = £10,000

If the scheme is based on eightieths the pension would be:

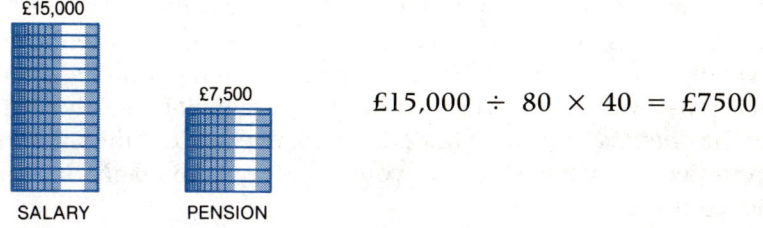

£15,000 ÷ 80 × 40 = £7500

If your final salary was £25,000 the same calculation would be:
$$£25,000 \div 60 \times 40 = £16,666$$
or
$$£25,000 \div 80 \times 40 = £12,500$$
But what if you had served for only 30 years with the same company? Then the man earning £25,000 would get:
$$£25,000 \div 60 \times 30 = £12,500$$
or
$$£25,000 \div 80 \times 30 = £9375$$
Since a woman normally retires earlier and therefore is less likely to be able to achieve a 40 years contribution record most women will receive lower pensions but the calculation is exactly the same.

It is important to know the meanings of various expressions used in calculating your pension. For example *final pensionable salary* might sound as if it can only mean one thing, but that is not necessarily so. It might mean
(a) the salary you are receiving on the day of your retirement
(b) the *average* of the last three or even five years of your working life
(c) even the average of the best consecutive three in the last five (or ten) years of your working life.
Check this out or your first pension payment might be a nasty shock.

You should check on the meaning of *salary* as well. It might mean
(a) your basic salary alone
(b) your basic salary plus overtime payments
(c) your basic salary plus overtime, plus commissions and any other payments.

Also check your *normal retirement age*. Most companies still fix 65 as the normal retirement age for men and 60 for women, but some have lower ages.

Another meaning to check is *pensionable service*. This may include
(a) all the years you have spent with the firm, or
(b) only those years during which you have been a member of the scheme.
They are not necessarily the same, because often employees have to stay with a company for a certain length of time before they are eligible

to join the scheme. Sometimes there is a lower age limit which may have ruled you out when you first started work.

Also look out for the way in which the scheme is affected by the State retirement pension. Some schemes pay the company pension in addition to the State one, but some discount part of your pay on the grounds that this part will be replaced by the State pension. It is usually referred to as the *deductive item* and it underlines the need to read the small print of your pension just as closely as you would read the small print of any other contract.

Some companies may send you a statement each year explaining what your pension will be, based on your present pay. But if you have any difficulty working it out, go to whoever is responsible for the pension scheme and ask for help. In working out a retirement budget it is obviously important that your basic calculations are based on accurate figures.

GUARANTEED MINIMUM PENSION (GMP)

This applies only to those who have been in what is called 'contracted out' employment at any time since April 1978. (See the *Glossary*, p. 88, for a definition of 'contracted out'.) If you are a member of an occupational pension that is *contracted out* from the State Earnings Related Pension Scheme (SERPS), your employer must pay you a guaranteed minimum pension at least equivalent to what would have been your SERPS entitlement. You and your pension scheme will be told what this amount is when you reach pension age. If you have left contracted-out employment during your career, then your right to the guaranteed minimum pension will have been

(a) *frozen* by that employer who will pay it when you retire
(b) transferred to your new employer if his scheme is also contracted-out
(c) transferred by the employer back into the State scheme on payment of a premium
(d) transferred to an annuity contract purchased by the employer from an insurance company.

Whatever course has been followed, you are guaranteed a minimum pension either on its own or in combination with any entitlement due from the State scheme, which will always be as much as or more than the inflation-proofed *additional pension* you would have earned had you never been in contracted-out employment. Since SERPS is protected against inflation then so too is the GMP. If you have moved between *contracted-in* and *contracted-out* jobs, you will be entitled both to a State additional pension and a guaranteed minimum pension, though both of smaller amounts.

WOMEN AND PENSIONS

In law men and women must be treated equally by employers so far as admission to pension schemes is concerned. The way in which benefits are calculated for women is also generally the same as for men. So, if a woman is a member of an occupational pension scheme for 40 years she will be entitled to a pension of two-thirds her final salary if it is a scheme using a pension fraction of sixtieths. In practice women are different in several important respects.

- Women usually retire at an earlier age than men, 60 instead of 65, so it is harder for them to complete the 40 years' service necessary to receive a full pension.
- Since they retire earlier the final salary is lower than if they had worked on to 65, so their pension is smaller as a consequence.
- Women will give up less of their pension than a man when they commute for a cash lump sum (see *Lump Sum benefits*, p. 72). If a woman takes a lump sum of, say, £10,000 her pension will be reduced by just over £900 whereas a man taking the same amount of cash would have his pension reduced by a little over £1100. This is because women retire earlier and then live longer, on average, than men so their pension is worth more in cash.
- They do not always enjoy the same fringe benefits as men. Whereas it is normal for a man's pension scheme to provide a half-rate pension for his widow it is much less common for the same benefit to be awarded to a widower.

One important piece of legislation concerning women in employment comes into force during 1987 as a result of the case of Helen Marshall, who claimed she had been treated unfairly by her employers, a hospital authority, when they made her retire at 62. She appealed successfully to the European Court who ruled that women working in the Public Sector must be allowed to work on to the same age as their male colleagues. The *Sex Discrimination Act 1986* was then passed. This specifies that by November 1987 employers must settle an equal retirement age for both men and women. It does not specify what age this should be, only that it must be the same for both. This does not affect the age at which they can draw their State pension, though employers and pensions organisations have been pressing the Government to take a lead and decide on some equalisation of pension ages.

Without a Government lead it is widely expected that most companies will continue to work on retirement ages of 65 years for men and 60 for women. However, a woman who chooses to work on to 65 will be allowed to do so. Those who do can choose to

- take their pension rights at 60 as they do now without suffering any reduction as would happen in the case of a man who took a voluntary early retirement

- put off drawing a pension until they actually stop work and allow their pension rights to be increased by a factor of, say, 9% a year
- earn extra years' pension rights, if their employers agree, based on the higher salary they would be earning at their actual retirement.

Although men might argue that there is now an element of discrimination against them, since they don't have the same choice, it is unlikely that a man could make a similar appeal under the sex discrimination laws as long as the State maintains that 65 is the normal retirement age for a man.

The fact that women have equal rights of access to company pension schemes does not mean that they must use them. Surveys show that only 35% of working women belong to a company pension scheme compared to 62% of men. Part of the difference is due to many women being part-timers and frequently ineligible on that account. It is thought that often where married women have the choice they decide to rely on their husband's pension arrangements.

ADDITIONAL FEATURES

Other facts about your pension to know in advance are
- Will it be protected against rising prices in the years ahead?
- Is there a widow's pension?
- Is there a death-in-service provision?
- Is there an early retirement provision?
- When is the pension paid?
- Is there a cash lump sum available either automatically or as an option?

Protection against rising prices

Suppose that you are awarded a pension of £10,000 today and that during the next ten years inflation averages five per cent a year. In order to maintain your purchasing power your pension will need to increase in the same ten years to over £16,000. However, unless you are a member of a public sector scheme you are unlikely to have such a guarantee. Only governments feel wealthy enough to promise to keep pensions in line with inflation – and we all know where they get their money from.

Many people who retired on private sector pensions in the early 1970s saw what seemed, at the time, to be comfortable incomes rapidly reduced to subsistence levels by the runaway inflation of the time. Even when inflation topped 24% in 1975 few private schemes gave increases much in excess of 3–5%. Many did worse. The effects of inflation on a pension can be seen opposite.

THE EFFECTS OF INFLATION ON A PENSION

Consider a man retiring in early 1970 on a pension of £5000 (which would have been excellent at the time). The graph shows how his pension would have increased each year had it kept pace with increases in the cost of living, and how it would have fared if it had risen at only 5% and 3% a year.

Start of Year	Increases at		
	RPI	5%	3%
1970	5,000	5,000	5,000
1971	5,320	5,250	5,150
1972	5,820	5,512	5,304
1973	6,233	5,788	5,463
1974	6,806	6,077	5,627
1975	7,902	6,381	5,796
1976	9,815	6,700	5,970
1977	11,434	7,035	6,149
1978	13,241	7,387	6,333
1979	14,340	7,756	6,523
1980	16,261	8,144	6,719
1981	19,189	8,551	6,921
1982	21,472	8,979	7,128
1983	23,319	9,428	7,342
1984	24,391	9,899	7,562
1985	25,611	10,394	7,789
1986	27,173	10,914	8,023

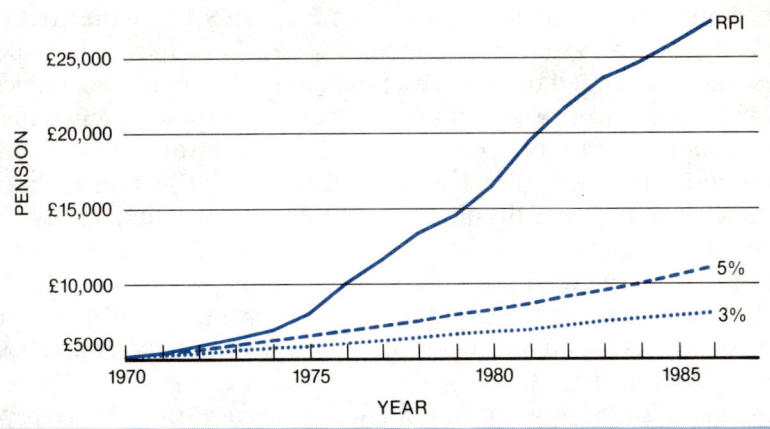

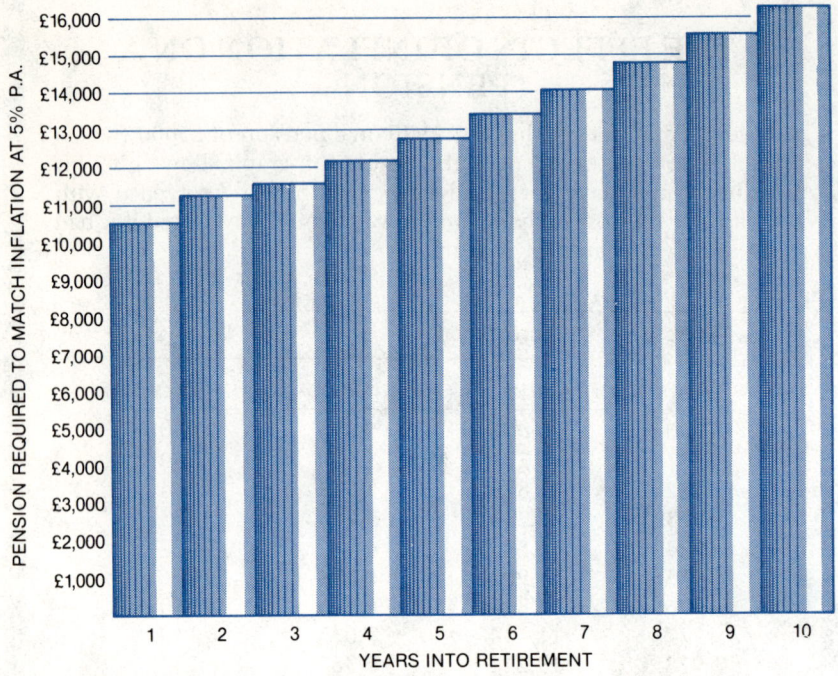

Although there is not much you can do to change this, it is worth finding out what increases have actually been paid in previous years to help you make your own estimates.

Widow's pension

Most schemes offer this automatically. Indeed, if your company has opted out of the State Earnings Related Pension Scheme (SERPS) they *must* offer it. The usual arrangement is for a widow to receive half her husband's pension if he dies. This is half of his *full* pension irrespective of whether he takes part of his pension as a lump sum. Many schemes also guarantee to pay the estate the equivalent of, say, five years' pension if the holder dies soon after retirement. This means that if a man dies after 12 months of retirement his widow would receive four years of pension as a lump sum (usually tax free) as well as the half-pay pension subsequently.

Unfortunately this same benefit is not often given to men whose wives have occupational pensions in their own right and who die before their husbands.

It may also be possible to enhance the pension available to your widow if you give up some of your pension from the start. On the face of

A WIDOW'S INCOME

June was widowed after her husband, Michael, had been retired for only three years. His salary of £22,500 had provided him with a pension entitlement of £15,000 a year which he commuted to give him a tax-free lump sum of £33,750 and a reduced pension of £11,250. How is June affected because her husband decided to take the lump sum?

June's widow's pension is not affected by commutation. Whether or not Michael had taken the lump sum she still gets half of his *original* maximum pension entitlement, not half of the reduced pension. She therefore gets a widow's pension of £7500 a year for life.

Michael's pension scheme also guaranteed to pay Michael's pension for five years, but this is at the *reduced rate* of pension after commutation. This is usually paid as a tax-free lump sum, so as he did commute June gets £22,500, two years' worth of his reduced pension.

Let us assume that June and Michael had spent the interest on their commuted lump sum but still had the capital intact. On Michael's death June would receive:

Interest on £22,500	£2587
Interest on £33,750	£3881
Widow's pension	£7500
Total	£13,968

But suppose Michael had not commuted. On his death June would receive:

Interest on £30,000 (twice full pension)	£3450
Widow's pension	£7500
Total	£10,950

So even if Michael and June had spent every penny of their commuted lump sum during his short retirement, June is no worse off because of his decision to commute.

Payments to the widow

Although most pension schemes give a guaranteed payment period and most make this payment as a lump sum there are some exceptions. Instead of the guaranteed pension being paid in a lump sum it might simply continue in payment.

A widow's pension might be paid in *addition* or it might be paid only at the end of the guaranteed period. Whatever the individual rules, it is unlikely that commutation will be disadvantageous to a widow. (In making these calculations we have assumed that interest on the capital is paid gross, though in the case of building societies or bank deposit accounts this would be paid net of tax. It makes little difference to the final totals since income tax would be levied on all the pension totals but it enables us to compare like with like.)

YOUR PENSION ON TAKING EARLY RETIREMENT

Jim, Eric and Bob each earn £20,000 a year and have been with the same company since they were 25. All three are 60 years old and if they work until their 65th birthdays each would be entitled to a two-thirds pension based on their salaries and 40 years' service.

However, Jim has been ill for some time and his doctor has recommended that he retire prematurely. Things are not good for the company either and it needs to shed staff. It is suggested to Eric that he might like to take early retirement. As for Bob, he's simply had enough and can't face another five years; he has gone to his manager and asked for early retirement.

This is how most pension funds are likely to handle the situation.

Since Jim is ill and his doctor recommends early retirement, the pension fund trustees are sympathetic and agree that Jim should receive the pension he would have received had he worked a full 40 years instead of only 35. He therefore retires with a pension of:

$$£20,000 \div 60 \times 40 = £13,333$$

It's less than he would have got if he had worked until he was 65 because, assuming pay rises averaging 5% a year, his salary would have increased to about £25,525 giving him a pension of £17,016. Nevertheless, it is generous and it is possible that being removed from the pressures of work his health may improve.

it the terms seem quite attractive. As an example, if you are entitled to a pension of £12,000 but agree to take only £10,800, the pension fund would guarantee to maintain your widow's benefit at the full pension on your death. You will need to make some fairly cold calculations about your relative survival prospects and you might like to consider this if you have married a younger woman and feel your health to be less than perfect. If she is a *lot* longer though, you would have to give up more of your own pension.

It pays to read the small print where widow's benefits are concerned. Some schemes *might* stop her pension altogether if a widow remarries.

Death-in-service provision

Most schemes provide for your death before retirement. There is often an insurance cover to pay the equivalent of one year's salary or more to your dependants, usually tax-free, plus a widow's pension typically fixed at half the pension you are expecting.

In Eric's case the company feels obliged to him in suggesting he goes early. So the pension fund trustees decide to split the difference in pension entitlements and assume he has completed $37\frac{1}{2}$ years instead of only 35. He is offered a pension of:
$$£20,000 \div 60 \times 37\frac{1}{2} = £12,500$$
He is not as well off as Jim, but he still has his health.

Bob is a different story. Since the company would otherwise have kept him on they see no need to be generous. They agree to let him go *but* the pension he is awarded, although based on 35 years with the firm, will be reduced by 30% to take account of the fact that his pension will be in payment for five years longer. As Bob's full pension after 35 years would be £11,666, the 30% reduction will reduce this by £3499.40, leaving Bob with just over £8166.

Now suppose Ellen, Ruth and Betty find themselves in much the same boat at the age of 55 years, since women retire at 60 as a rule and not 65. How would they fare assuming they were earning the same salary and pension at exactly the same rate as the men? Women inevitably get smaller pensions than men, because they can usually accumulate only 35 qualifying years instead of 40 and because the pension is expected to be in payment for longer. By using similar calculations they could expect to receive the following pensions:

Ellen retiring on health grounds:	£11,666
Ruth retiring by request of the company:	£10,833
Betty retiring at her own request:	£7000

Early retirement

Your scheme probably has a formula for dealing with early retirement which usually means leaving before 65 for a man and 60 for a woman. This may be for ill health, by invitation from your company, or a form of redundancy.

The pension is usually reduced by comparison with a pension paid at the normal date of retirement because it will be in payment for longer and, of course, it is based on a lower salary level, but this depends on your reason for leaving. If it is

(a) by your choice, the pension you have built up so far will almost certainly be reduced, perhaps by as much as 30% if you leave at 60 instead of 65.

(b) on grounds of ill health, you may receive the full pension based on your current salary

(c) by invitation or through redundancy, a similar arrangement, or one between the two might be paid.

How your pension is affected by taking early retirement is shown in the box above.

When is the pension paid?

Generally, payment is made on a monthly basis, and will probably go straight into your bank account in the same way that a salary is paid. But will the first payment be made on the very day after your retirement, at the beginning or the end of the next full month? It helps in budgeting to know if you have to wait for one or four weeks before being paid.

Lump sum benefits

This benefit arises from what is usually called *commuting*. The rules are simple. The Inland Revenue allows you to take up to one and a half times your final annual salary as a tax free lump sum in lieu of pension. (Under new rules, people joining schemes in future will have this benefit limited to a maximum of £150,000.) So if you earn £15,000 a year and have been in the scheme for 40 years, you can take up to £22,500 in cash. A man earning £25,000 could take £37,500 in cash. This option is normally available only to those in private pension schemes. If you are in the public sector then you are likely to receive a pension and a lump sum without the option.

Naturally your pension is reduced as a result. The formula for this varies from scheme to scheme but is generally about £9 cash for every £1 of pension for a man retiring at 65. For a woman retiring at 60 it is usually £11 cash for each £1 of pension.

Examples

If you are a man earning a final salary of £15,000 and you take the full £22,500 cash lump sum you would be giving up a pension of
$$£22,500 \div 9 = £2500$$
Assuming a two-thirds pension of £10,000 your final pension would be £7500 plus the lump sum payment.

If you are a man earning £25,000 and you take the full £37,500 cash sum you would be giving up a pension of
$$£37,500 \div 9 = £4166$$
Once again, assuming a two thirds pension of £16,666 you would be left with a pension of £12,500 plus the cash.

The number of years you have been in a pension scheme also affects the amount you can take as a lump sum. You can take three-eighties of your final salary for each year of pensionable service, which means you can take $1\frac{1}{2}$ times final salary only after completing 40 years with the scheme. It will be a different for women as they normally achieve fewer years of membership in a scheme.

The effect of taking a maximum commutation on a pension for a man and a woman who have each completed 40 years' service and are each earning £15,000. (The maximum commutation is £22,500.)

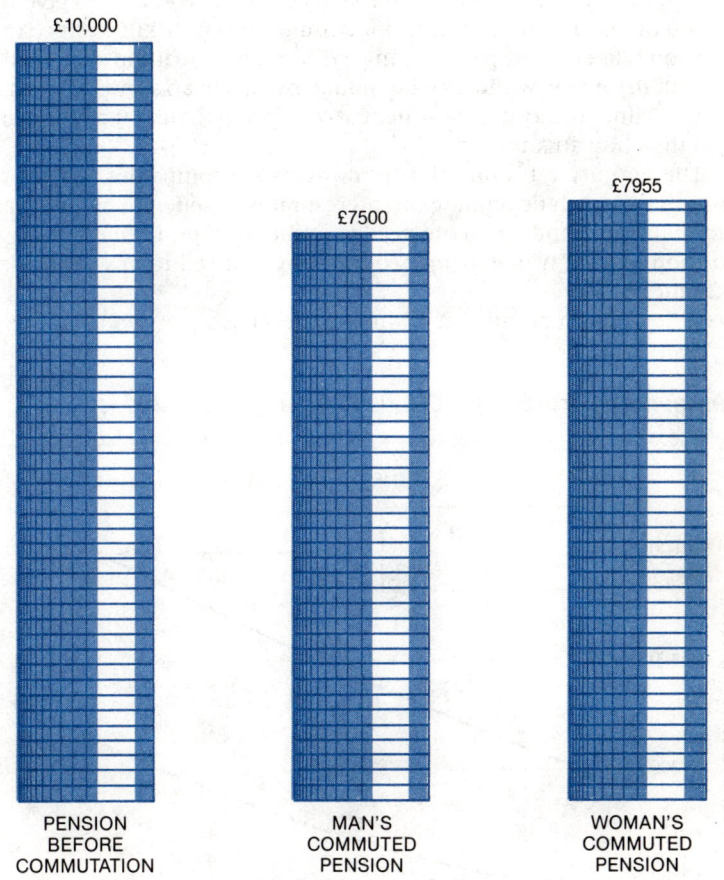

Examples

If you earn £25,000 and have been with the scheme for 30 years you can take

£25,000 ÷ 80 × 3 × 30 = £28,125

as a lump sum. However, a woman earning £25,000 a year would be entitled to a pension of £14,583. If she decided to commute as much as she could she would be entitled to

£25,000 ÷ 80 × 3 × 35 = £32,812

her pension would be reduced by

£32,812 ÷ 11 = £2983

leaving her with a pension of £11,600 plus the cash.

BUYING AN ANNUITY

George retired at 60 and decided to commute part of his pension into a cash lump sum. As he retired five years early, he was able to give up £1000 of his pension in return for a lump sum of £10,000 (since the pension is likely to be paid for longer). Normally the lump sum would be £9000. He now wonders if he should invest it in an annuity or put it in a building society or investment account at his bank for a few years and then buy an annuity.

The annuity rates on offer from insurance companies vary from month to month depending on interest rates in general and between companies depending on the need to attract savings. It therefore pays to shop around widely before committing yourself to any particular scheme. However:

- If he buys an annuity at 60 he may receive a pension of £1285 a year.

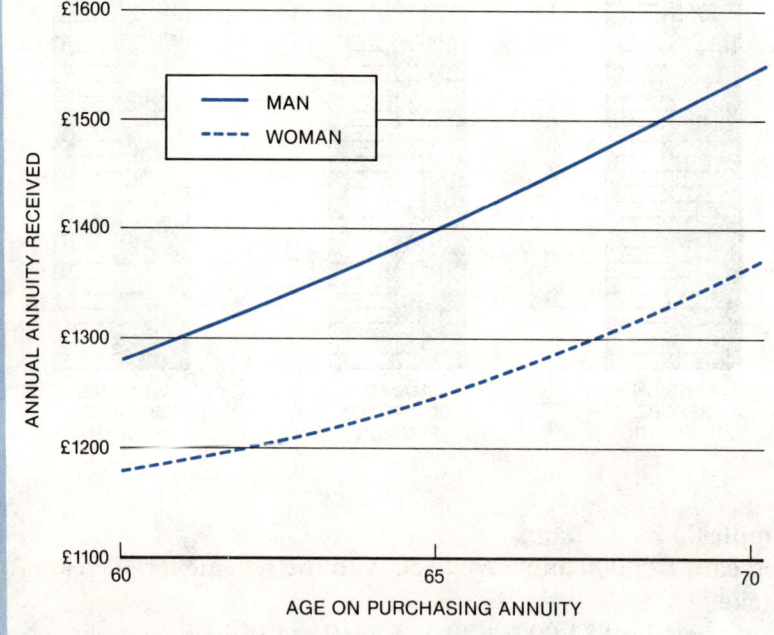

The annuity purchased for £10,000 according to age and sex.

You do not have to take the maximum lump sum. You can take as much or as little of it as you choose.

One thing that commutation does not usually affect is the widow's pension; this is generally half of the original pension that would have been paid if no part of it had been commuted.

- If he invests it for five years at a net interest rate of 8½% he could have a lump sum of £15,037 with which to buy a pension of say £2102 at age 65.
- If he invests it for a further five years he may have a lump sum of £22,610 with which to buy a pension of maybe £3511.

Myrtle is in a similar position, but the sums are slightly different. If she also took a £10,000 lump sum, for which she gave up £909 of her pension at the age of 60, then this is how Myrtle's annuity could grow over ten years:
- At 55 her £10,000 could earn an annuity of £1179.
- At 65 her £15,037 could earn an annuity of £1926.
- At 70 her £22,610 could earn an annuity of £3116.

What they should do is a matter of personal choice, but remember that if you put your money into an investment account with the intention of building up the lump sum, you will not have the income from either the interest or the annuity. Many people like to have control of a lump sum, but once you have put your money into an annuity, you cannot cash it in.

Annuity rates improve the older you get. Let's assume you want to invest £10,000 in an annuity at different ages. The return you could get according to age and sex is:

Amount invested (£)	Age (years)	Annuity (£) for man	Annuity (£) for woman
10,000	60	1285	1179
10,000	65	1398	1258
10,000	70	1553	1373

Annuity rates change with general interest rates. When interest rates are high you get a bigger annuity for your money, but the annuity is smaller when interest rates are low. So if you are keen on buying one, time it carefully.

One good feature of annuities is that you pay income tax on only that part which the taxman regards as the interest you are earning. For example on an annuity of £1285 for a 60-year-old man where the interest is £731, tax is paid on that sum not on the remaining £554 which is regarded as return of capital.

Should you take the lump sum?
The main pros and cons are:

The pros	The cons
• Freedom of choice	• You lose part of your pension
• You can provide a bigger income	• You miss out on upratings

Freedom of choice The idea of having a lump sum in the bank is very exciting and can mean anything from a world cruise to making gifts to your grandchildren. If the lump sum were substantial enough you could do both and still have cash left. In practice most of us spend a little and save a lot and, for the first year or so of retirement, while we are still sorting out our financial resources and needs, this is probably a wise thing to do. Nevertheless it is nice to have the choice.

You can provide a bigger income This is one of the best arguments for taking the cash and becomes more so the older you are. There are, of course, many ways to invest a lump sum both for income and capital growth and you will find much more on this in Chapters 5 and 6. You will probably be better off even if you do nothing more adventurous than buy another pension in the form of an annuity, though in that case it would probably pay you to invest the money in a building society for a few years first.

You buy annuities from insurance companies who will give you a quotation on request. But once you have bought it you cannot change your mind and get your cash back. (See page 74 for details of buying an annuity.)

Another case when taking the money is usually a wise decision is if your health is, frankly, poor and you do not expect to live to a ripe old age. Taking the money will not affect any guaranteed pension arrangement that your scheme may have, nor should it affect the widow's pension (see page 68). Your family will clearly benefit from having the cash in hand.

You lose part of your pension If the loss of income will leave you feeling the pinch in your day-to-day living then you need to work out very carefully how much extra income you can earn from your lump sum to make up the difference. Chapters 4, 6 and 7 on working out a budget, investment and taxation may help you with these calculations.

You miss out on upratings It is almost certain that your company pension scheme will exclude any pension that you have commuted when cost-of-living increases are awarded, usually each year. How serious a drawback this is depends on
- How serious the threat of inflation is for the future
- How generous you expect your company to be in making awards.

Obviously if you expect the rate of inflation to return to the frightening levels of the 1970s and your pension scheme has a good track record of keeping pension awards in line with the cost of living, then you will be loth to give up any part of your pension. On the other hand, if you feel that inflation is now more or less under control and your company scheme has not shown itself to be generous in the past, you may take the view that you are better off to take the money.

The true situation is somewhere in between for most of us.

Additional Voluntary Contributions (AVCs)

These are of special value to those people who have not worked long enough with their present employer to earn a full pension. Such people are in the majority. (It is estimated that only about five per cent of people work long enough with one employer to qualify for a full pension.)

AVCs allow pension fund members to make additional payments to 'top up' the company scheme. The company will not make any further contributions but your money, like all pension fund investment, is treated very favourably by the taxman. So payment into an AVC scheme at the rate of £1000 a year will cost you only £730 assuming income tax at the standard rate; it will cost even less if you are a higher rate taxpayer.

Example

Suppose a man of 55 takes out an AVC of £100 a month to boost his pension at the age of 65. The pension scheme will have had £12,000 to invest at a cost to him of only £8760 net, because of the tax relief he will get at 27% tax. By the time he retires this could have grown into a capital sum of around £26,000 which may be turned into a pension of about £3400 a year (or £283 a month). Even allowing for income tax at 27%, once the pension has been in payment for little more than $3\frac{1}{2}$ years the initial net outlay will have been fully repaid. Thereafter it is profit.

Most companies now have an AVC scheme; those that do not will have to introduce one by January 1988. As this is such a valuable investment you may also consider taking out an AVC through institutions other than your company. This is possible from October 1987 whereas previously you could take out an AVC only through your employer.

AVCs are the ideal retirement investment. It is worth taking out an AVC even with only a year or two to go to retirement, although you won't get so much. However, there is a limit to the taxman's generosity and in this case payments are tax free when your AVC payments plus the normal contributions to your company pension scheme do not exceed 15% of your gross earnings, which includes overtime.

The cash accumulated in your AVC account can (at the time of writing) also be commuted to a lump sum. Since your pension scheme will not include your AVC pension when it awards cost-of-living increases, it will pay you to cash in your AVC pension rather than your company pension for a lump sum. This way you ensure that you benefit as much as possible from any future rises. However, this facility is under review by the Government at present.

Late retirement

Fewer people are allowed to work on beyond normal retirement age these days, but occasionally people who specially want to do so and who are doing jobs which are valuable to the employer may be given the chance. There are special implications for these employees who are in line for an occupational pension and defer their retirement.

If they wish, they can usually take all their retirement benefits, including the pension and the lump sum at the normal retirement age and continue to work and draw their salary. They may be able to take the lump sum and put off taking the pension until they actually retire. Alternatively, they can simply put all the benefits due to them on ice until their retirement. The one thing they cannot do is to take the pension and leave the cash until they retire.

Taking the cash lump sum sooner rather than later could fit in well with whatever plans people have for their retirement. It is, of course,

---

LATE RETIREMENT AND YOUR PENSION

Peter was almost indispensable to the company accounts department and his imminent retirement was causing much concern despite the decision to computerise the accounts. Fortunately when asked if he would like to carry on beyond normal retirement age, Peter was very keen, but wondered what implications this might have for his pension. He had been looking forward to commuting part of it and taking his wife on a long cruise; he wanted to do that even if he did carry on his job for another five years.

If Peter retires now on a salary of £20,000, after 40 years with the company, he will be entitled to a pension of £10,000 and a lump sum of £30,000. If he wishes he can take both now *and* carry on working. But if he does so his annual income will suddenly rise from £20,000 a year to £30,000 which means he will be paying more tax.

If he prefers he can just take the lump sum, invest it, take the cruise as part of his annual leave and postpone taking his pension until he finally retires in five years' time. In the meantime his pension would increase in value at about 9% a year giving him a pension of approximately £15,380. If Peter decided to postpone taking the lump sum as well as the pension the lump sum would be worth £46,158 at age 70.

untaxed although any interest you earn from investing it will be taxed. But taking the pension while still working could be unhelpful to your tax position since your income, so far as the Inland Revenue is concerned, would be your salary *plus* your pension, and you would be taxed on the lot. Some, or all, of the extra may well be taxed at a higher rate than the rest of your income.

The good news about deferring taking your pension is that it will continue to grow even if you make no further contributions towards it. Most occupational schemes, recognising that they are going to be paying out the final pension for a shorter time, use an increase factor of about 9% a year. So a pension of £1000 a year would stand at £1090 if deferred for a year, at £1188 if deferred for two years and £1538 after five years.

A few schemes might let you earn extra pension rights for each year you put off retirement. So that instead of retiring at 65, say, on 40 sixtieths of your final earnings at that age, you could retire a year later on 41 sixtieths of your earnings at 66. But the taxman will not allow you to build up more than five years' extra rights in this way.

PENSIONS FOR THE SELF-EMPLOYED

Suppose you have no pension. If your firm does not have a pension scheme or you are self-employed, the only pension you will automatically receive is whatever the State provides. For those whose companies have no pension scheme this may be the State retirement pension plus the SERPS pension and perhaps the old graduated pension. For the self-employed it may very well be only the State retirement pension. This is clearly not sufficient to maintain a reasonable standard of living and research has found that a high percentage of retired self-employed people find their retirement income very disappointing.

Personal pension plans

If this is your situation consider a *personal pension plan* designed specially for you. Like other pension schemes they qualify for generous tax relief. The self-employed may invest up to $17\frac{1}{2}$ per cent of *relevant earnings* (which means their taxable profit for the year). Contributions are tax deductible and the interest earned by such investments is not taxed. From 4 January 1988, under new legislation, people over 50 will be able to invest even more of their income in a pension on a sliding scale up to $27\frac{1}{2}\%$ for those over 61. The self-employed will also be allowed to take their pensions from the age of 50 instead of 60 as at present.

Personal pension plans will become more important from April 1988 as the Government will allow people to opt out of occupational pension schemes and contribute to schemes of their own if they wish. Although this is unlikely to offer any advantages to men over 45 and women over 40 it may well attract younger ones and companies offering pension schemes will be doing all they can to attract business.

Another important benefit for the self-employed is that they are allowed to make retrospective provision for the previous six years by way of a single premium investment which will also attract tax relief.

On retirement the contributions are invested to provide a regular monthly income and you also have the option of a lump sum payment without any tax penalty. This is at least as valuable to the self-employed

SELF-EMPLOYED PENSIONS

Alan is a self-employed painter and decorator. He is nearly 50 and makes a profit of about £15,000 a year. He employs his wife, Joan, to look after his books, answer the phone and do general secretarial duties. For this, she is paid £1900 a year which just keeps her below the salary level at which he would have to pay National Insurance contributions for her.

So far Alan and Joan have been too busy running the business and raising a family to look too far ahead. But now they have some spare cash and they feel it is time to take out pension plans for both of them.

As he is self-employed, Alan's retirement plans are regarded favourably by the taxman. First he is allowed to make pension contributions for the previous six years as well as for the 15 years until retirement, a total of 21 years in all. He is also allowed the usual tax concessions on contributions up to $17\frac{1}{2}$%. After January 1988 he will be able to pay more than $17\frac{1}{2}$% and increase his contributions the closer he gets to retirement on the following scale:

Age (years)	%
Up to 50	$17\frac{1}{2}$
51–55	20
56–60	$22\frac{1}{2}$
61–75	$27\frac{1}{2}$

Alan opts for the maximum pension he can earn in the following 15 years. So for the preceding six years Alan can make a single payment of £13,000 (which is, in fact, a net payment of £9490 once he receives his £3510 tax rebate), and he decides to pay $17\frac{1}{2}$% of his future earnings into a personal pension plan. With a typical insurance company Alan can expect the gross £13,000 investment to grow into a

as the AVC scheme is to the employee, although buying a personal pension plan is slightly more complicated than joining a company pension scheme as you will have more decisions to take. Most companies will offer you two types of scheme: a *with-profits policy*, a *unit linked policy* or a combination of the two.

With-profits policies

With-profits policies are safe and sure. The company will invest your premiums and each year will declare a bonus which will be added to your fund. Once there it is there for good. It may not seem generous but with the various tax advantages the fund still builds up in a splendid

---

capital sum of approximately £75,843 by the time he celebrates his 65th birthday. (The assumed growth rate may seem high, but includes the tax benefits.) With this sum he can
(a) invest it to provide him with a pension of £10,562 a year, or
(b) take a lump sum of £18,960 and a pension of £7922 a year.

The annual payments from age 50 may accumulate as follows. It is assumed that Alan increases his earnings each year by 5% and he contributes 17½% of those earnings to the pension. The first year's contributions will total £1916 net which is worth £2625 with the tax refunds. At 65 he may have built up a capital sum of £145,848 which could earn him *either* an outright pension of £20,323 a year *or* a lump sum of £36,462 plus a pension of £15,235 a year. Therefore Alan would be entitled to two considerable options.

He could take two outright pensions totalling £30,885 a year *or* he could take two lump sums totalling £55,422 *plus* two pensions totalling £23,157.

If you want to relate these figures to Alan's income today, remember that we have made inflation and investment assumptions to work out what he will actually pay and receive. If his earnings increase by 5% a year then his earnings in his 65th year will have more than doubled to over £31,000. Unlike employees, the self-employed are not restricted to a maximum pension of two-thirds.

What about his wife, Joan? She is 45 years old and because she is an employee she cannot buy a pension for the previous six years as Alan did. In her case, pension experts may assume that her salary of £1900 a year will increase by about 8½% a year. Then Alan can pay an annual pension contribution on behalf of Joan which amounts to £1070. This is eligible for tax relief for the company. Assuming that she retires at 60, the same year as Alan, then Joan may have accumulated a capital sum in her pension fund of £39,880 which could provide her with a pension of £4480 *or* a cash lump sum of £6056 and a pension of £3977.

way. Recent surveys show with-profits policies have held their own with the unit-linked variety, though when the stock market has a good run their performance can look a little lack-lustre by comparison with unit-linked policies.

Unit-linked policies

Unit-linked policies do not guarantee returns but invest your money in unit trusts which *may* do very well; their record has been very good in recent years. On the other hand the value of unit trusts can also go down as the stock market fluctuates and you run the risk of the market being low when the time comes to cash them in and convert the proceeds to a pension.

It is possible to reduce this danger by transferring your unit-based policy to a with-profits policy a few years before retirement when prices seem to be good. Another option is to do both. As many self-employed people are not quite sure what their earnings are going to be from year to year, a with-profits policy based on a low income point, may be taken to cover them. At the end of the year when their profit for the year is known, any surplus can be invested in a one-off unit-linked policy.

Pension for your spouse

Those who employ their spouses in some paid capacity in the business (even if the salary is so low that National Insurance contributions are avoided) may purchase a valuable pension for them with the usual tax advantages. It is even possible to buy an *executive pension plan* for your spouse, which is highly adaptable and offers the opportunity to provide a good pension within a relatively short time.

Choosing a scheme

The personal pension market is already very competitive, both in that it pays to shop around and that many high pressure commission salesmen are seeking your business. Make sure that you take quotes from a variety of companies and try to get information which makes it possible for you to make direct comparisons (see p. 84 for addresses).

Most people looking for a pension plan look for a long-standing, reliable company they have heard of. But even within the circle of the big names there are many choices. Don't be rushed and remember that estimates of bonuses and ultimate pensions are projections which may, or may not, prove to be accurate. Remember also that what sounds a handsome pension today may not seem so in ten years time. Inflation at 5% a year will halve the value of your money in 14 years.

PENSIONS FROM PREVIOUS JOBS

Although a pension you may have earned from some previous employment may not be worth much, it is almost certainly worth claiming. Most of us will have changed jobs several times before we retire and this means we may have belonged to a number of pension schemes. In some cases it may have been possible to transfer one pension to another job. If not you may have been given the choice of
- taking a refund of your contributions, or
- accepting a deferred pension payable at retirement age.

Higher earners or people who had worked with the firm for five years or more would not usually have been given a choice. Their pensions would have been deferred and the benefit most likely *frozen* at the benefit level earned at the time. If you were previously a member of a non-contributory scheme to which the employer made *all* the financial contributions it would also have been automatically frozen. You might even have lost the pension altogether.

Write to all your previous employers asking if you are entitled to a pension. They are obliged to write to you anyway once their records indicate that you have reached retirement age, but unless they know where you live they might not be able to do so.

If you are entitled to even a small pension you might be glad of it and many frozen pensions are, indeed, very small. Sometimes they may be exchanged for cash as, under the Inland Revenue rules, the trustees of a pension scheme can pay a lump sum in lieu of a 'trivial' pension (i.e. a pension not exceeding £104 a year). A pension that small would not be significant if it were paid as £8.66 a month, but it is worth a lump sum of around £700. Thousands of these small pensions go unclaimed each year which is good for the pension funds but not for the person entitled to the money.

If a company you once worked for has now closed down or been taken over by someone else, it does not necessarily mean that your old pension scheme no longer operates. If you have difficulty tracing your old scheme you could start by approaching the local Citizen's Advice Bureau, Chamber of Commerce or Town Hall, or any former colleagues. You could also write to the Inland Revenue who have to approve all pension schemes. Failing all these write to

The Company Pensions Information Centre
7 Old Park Lane, London W1Y 3LJ
☏ 01-493 4757   or

The National Association of Pension Funds
12–18 Grosvenor Gardens, London SW1W 0DH
☏ 01-730 0734

HOW TO FIND OUT MORE

The Company Pensions Information Centre publishes a series of booklets on pensions matters. Single copies are available free of charge although they ask that you enclose a stamped addressed envelope measuring at least 9" × 7". The titles are:
- How to understand your pension scheme
- What pension terms mean
- How a pension fund works
- What is a pension fund trustee
- How changing job affects your pension

WHERE TO FIND A PERSONAL PENSION PLAN

The following insurance companies offer *with-profits personal pension plans*.

Avon
Tiddington Road
Stratford-upon-Avon CV37 7BJ
☎ 0789 204211

Britannic
Moor Green
Moseley
Birmingham B13 8QF
☎ 021-449 4444

Clerical Medical and General Life
15 St James' Square
London SW1Y 4LQ
☎ 01-930 5474

Colonial Mutual
24 Ludgate Hill
London EC4P 4BD
☎ 01-248 9861

Commercial Union
St Helens
1 Undershaft
London EC3P 3DQ
☎ 01-283 7500

Co-operative
Miller Street
Manchester M60 0AL
☎ 061-832 8686

Cornhill
32 Cornhill
London EC3V 3LJ
☎ 01-626 5410

Crusader
Reigate
Surrey RH2 8BL
☎ 07372 42424

Eagle Star
1 Threadneedle Street
London EC2R 8BE
☎ 01-588 1212

Ecclesiastical
Beaufort House
Brunswick Road
Gloucester GL1 1JZ
☎ 0452 28533

Equitable Life
4 Coleman Street
London EC2R 5AP
☎ 01-606 6611

Equity and Law
20 Lincoln's Inn Fields
London WC2A 3ES
☎ 01-242 6844

OCCUPATIONAL PENSIONS

Friends Provident
Pixham End
Dorking
Surrey RH4 1QA
☏ 0306 885055

FS Assurance
190 West George Street
Glasgow G2 2PA
☏ 041-332 2060

General Accident
Pitheavlis
Perth PH2 0NH
☏ 0738 21202

Gresham
2–6 Prince of Wales Road
Bournemouth BH4 9HD
☏ 0202 767655

Guardian Royal Exchange
Royal Exchange
London EC3V 3LS
☏ 01-283 7101

Hearts of Oak
Aviation House
Kingsway
London WC2
☏ 01-404 0393

Legal & General
Kingswood House
Kingswood, Tadworth
Surrey KT20 6EU
☏ 07373 53456

London Life
100 Temple Street
Bristol BS1 6EA
☏ 0272 279179

Manulife
Manulife House
St George's Way
Stevenage, Herts
☏ 0438 356101

MGM
MGM House
Heene Road
Worthing BN11 2DY
☏ 0903 204631

NFU
Tiddington Road
Stratford-upon-Avon CV37 7BJ
☏ 0789 204211

National Mutual
5 Bow Churchyard
London EC4M 9DH
☏ 01-236 1566

National Mutual of Australasia
National Mutual House
Serpentine Road
Poole BH15 2BH
☏ 0202 680666

National Provident Institution
PO Box 227
48 Gracechurch Street
London EC3V 0BB
☏ 01-623 4200

Norwich Union
Surrey Street
Norwich NR1 3NS
☏ 0603 22200

Pearl
High Holborn
London WC1V 7EB
☏ 01-405 8441

Provident Life
Provident Way
Basingstoke RG21 2SZ
☏ 0256 470707

Provident Mutual
25–31 Moorgate
London EC2R 6BA
☏ 01-628 3232

Prudential
Holborn Bars
London EC1N 2NH
☏ 01-405 9222

Refuge
Oxford Street
Manchester M60 7HA
☏ 061-236 9432

RNPF Nurses
Burdett House
15 Buckingham Street
London WC2N 6ED
☎ 01-839 6785

Royal
PO Box 144
New Hall Place
Liverpool L69 3EN
☎ 051-227 4422

Royal London
Royal London House
Middleborough
Colchester CO1 1RA
☎ 0206 44155

Save & Prosper
1 Finsbury Avenue
London EC2M 2QY
☎ 01-588 1717

Scottish Amicable
150 St Vincent Street
Glasgow G2 5NQ
☎ 041-248 2323

Scottish Equitable
28 St Andrew Square
Edinburgh EH2 1YF
☎ 031-556 9101

Scottish Life
19 St Andrew Square
Edinburgh EH2 1YE
☎ 031-225 2211

Scottish Provident
6 St Andrew Square
Edinburgh EH2 2YA
☎ 031-556 9181

Scottish Widows
15 Dalkeith Road
Edinburgh EH16 5BU
☎ 031-655 6000

Standard Life
3 George Street
Edinburgh EH2 2XZ
☎ 031-225 2552

Sun Alliance
1 Bartholomew Lane
London EC2N 2AB
☎ 01-588 2345

Sun Life
107 Cheapside
London EC2V 6DU
☎ 01-606 7788

Time Assurance
Central Gardens
80 Union Street
Oldham OL1 1DT
☎ 061-624 7299

UK Provident
United Kingdom House
Castle Street
Salisbury SP1 3SH
☎ 0722 336242

Wesleyan & General
Colmore Circus
Ringway
Birmingham B4 6AR
☎ 021-236 7894

Unit-linked policies are available from the following:

Abbey Life
Abbey Life House
PO Box 33
80 Holdenhurst Road
Bournemouth BH8 8AL
☎ 0202 292373

Albany Life
Station House
3 Darkes Lane
Potters Bar
Herts EN6 1AJ
☎ 0707 42311

Allied Dunbar
Allied Dunbar Centre
Station Road
Swindon SN1 1EL
☎ 0793 28291

Barclays Life
252 Romford Road
London E7 9JB
☎ 01-534 5544

Cannon
1 Olympic Way
Wembley
Middlesex HA9 0NB
☎ 01-902 8876

City of Westminster
Sentry House
500 Avebury Boulevard
Saxon Gate West
Milton Keynes MK9 2LA
☎ 0908 606101

Commercial Union
St Helens
1 Undershaft
London EC3P 3DQ
☎ 01-283 7500

Confederation Life
50 Chancery Lane
London WC2A 1HE
☎ 01-242 0282

Equity & Law
20 Lincoln's Inn Fields
London WC2A 3ES
☎ 01-242 6844

Gresham
2-6 Prince of Wales Road
Bournemouth BH4 9HD
☎ 0202 767655

Guardian Royal Exchange
Royal Exchange
London EC3V 3LS
☎ 01-283 7101

Hill Samuel
NLA Tower
Addiscombe Road
Croydon CR9 2DR
☎ 01-686 4355

Legal & General
Kingswood House
Kingswood, Tadworth
Surrey KT20 6EV
☎ 07373 53458

Lloyds Life
Administration Centre
Bretton Way
Peterborough PE3 8DQ
☎ 0733 262524

London and Manchester
Winslade Park
Exeter EX5 1DS
☎ 0392 52155

M&G
91-99 New London Road
Chelmsford CM2 0PY
☎ 0245 51651

NEL
Milton Court
Dorking
Surrey RH4 3LZ
☎ 0306 887766

Pearl
High Holborn
London WC1V 7EB
☎ 01-405 8441

Property Growth
Leon House
High Street
Croydon CR9 1LU
☎ 01-680 0606

Provincial Life
Stramongate
Kendal
Cumbria LA9 4BE
☎ 0539 23415

Save & Prosper
1 Finsbury Avenue
London EC2M 2QY
☎ 01-588 1717

Schroder Life
Enterprise House
Isambard Brunel Road
Portsmouth PO1 2AW
☎ 0705 827733

Standard Life
3 George Street
Edinburgh EH2 2Y2
☎ 031-225 2552

Sun Life
107 Cheapside
London EC2V 6DU
☎ 01-606 7788

Target Life
Target House
Gatehouse Road
Aylesbury
Bucks HP19 3EB
☎ 0296 5941

Trident Life
London Road
Gloucester GL1 3LE
☎ 0452 500500

Tyndall
Imperial House
15 Kingsway
London WC2B 6UN
☎ 01-240 9036

Vanbrugh
Vanbrugh House
41–43 Maddox Street
London W1R 9LA
☎ 01-499 4923

Windsor Life
Royal Albert House
Windsor
Berks SL4 1BE
☎ 0753 68144

GLOSSARY OF TERMS

Pensions experts, computer wizards and tax accountants all have one thing in common, they talk in a jargon that few others understand. You are likely to find some of these expressions in your pension handbook. Here is a glossary of the most common ones to help you understand what is meant.

Abatement This is a reduction in your pension. If you opt for a cash lump sum or a larger widow's pension than normal, your pension will be reduced or 'abated' to compensate for it.

Accrued pension Another name for the pension you are entitled to at any given time, though it is not paid until you actually retire.

Actuary A highly specialised expert whose job is to make forecasts about financial trends. These help pension funds to set aside appropriate funds for the payment of pensions. An actuary also calculates, based on ages, sex and health, the premiums for various kinds of policy.

Added years A person entitled to a higher pension than would be justified by the number of years served with a company will have *Added years*. This may arise from rights transferred from a previous employer or from additional voluntary contributions.

Additional Voluntary Contributions (AVCs) These are additional contributions which improve your pension if you have not been a member of a pension scheme long enough to qualify for a maximum two-thirds pension, or if your company scheme has a maximum below two-thirds. This is possible only if your pension scheme provides this option, which will be compulsory from January 1988. All the usual tax benefits are available for such payments to a total contribution, including contributions to your normal company scheme, not exceeding 15% of your gross pay.

OCCUPATIONAL PENSIONS 89

Administrator The name used by the Inland Revenue for the person responsible for the day-to-day running of a pension scheme. In your own company the administrator may be the pensions officer or company secretary.

Annuity Another name for a pension. It is most commonly used by the insurance industry where it is possible to pay a lump sum in return for a regular pension payment known as an annuity.

Approved scheme This is usually shorthand for 'exempt approved' schemes. This is the official recognition by the Superannuation Funds Office of the Inland Revenue and is necessary for the scheme to qualify for various important tax reliefs.

Assets The joint contributions by employer and staff are invested in a range of stocks and shares, unit trusts, property and even paintings. These investments are the scheme's assets. It is the interest and capital growth of these assets which ensures pension payments to retired members. The difference between capital growth and interest is explained in *Should you invest or deposit?*, p. 104.

Augmentation The payment of extra benefits that are sometimes awarded by the trustees of a pension fund.

Average salary scheme A scheme which bases pensions on the average pay throughout membership of the scheme. There are not many of these and most good schemes rely on *final salary*.

Cash option Also known as *lump sum* or *commutation*. It is the provision to take part of your pension, up to 1½ times annual salary, in cash. (See *Commutation*.)

Children's pension An arrangement whereby young children of an employee or a pensioner receive a pension after the member's death. It is usually paid until the age of 18 years or until full-time education has been completed.

Closed scheme A scheme which is not accepting new members and which will exist only until the death of the last member. It may relate to a company which went bankrupt or may have been replaced by a new scheme within the same company.

Commutation The usual name for taking a cash lump sum in lieu of part of your pension. It is possible to take up to 1½ times your final salary provided you have qualified for a full pension under the scheme. Your pension will be reduced as a consequence at the rate of about £100 a year for every £900 you take in cash if you are a man. If you are a woman then the cash sum is £11 for every £1 given up. If you are a public servant then the chances are your scheme will include a cash lump sum automatically, without offering you the option.

Continuation option The opportunity some schemes offer ex-employees to take out life assurance cover on commercial terms without having to undergo a medical. Life assurance cover for members still at work is a part of many pension schemes, but the cover often ends when people change jobs or retire.

Contracting out Under the State retirement scheme there are two types of benefit, the flat rate retirement pension and the additional pension derived from the State Earnings Related Pension Scheme (SERPS) in which premiums and benefits are related to income. Companies which offer pension benefits to staff which are at least as good as (and usually better than) the SERPS pension can be exempt from contributing to the state scheme.

Deductive item Sometimes also called a *Disregard*, it is that part of a member's salary that is discounted when calculating his benefit. This is on the grounds that the discounted slice is already covered by the State scheme.

Deferred pension (annuity) A pension for which a member has qualified but which will be paid in the future. This may be because an employee does not retire at the normal retirement age, so payment of the pension is postponed. Alternatively, it may be a pension earned with a previous employer, on which payment is postponed until the former member reaches retirement age. This is also known as a 'frozen' pension.

Dependant's option The choice to give up part of your pension at retirement in return for a pension to be paid to a specified dependant if you die. At that point it becomes a *Dependant's pension*.

Dependant's pension (See *Dependant's option*.)

Disregard (See *Deductive item*.)

Dynamism The process of increasing your pension on a regular basis. Sometimes it may be in line with the cost of living, in which case it is likely to be called *Inflation proofing* or *Index linking*. Other alternative names are *Escalation* or *Expansion*. Many schemes have some policy of increasing pensions annually, but very few in the private sector guarantee to match the rate of inflation.

Early retirement Giving up work and taking a pension before the normal age specified by your pension scheme. It might be for health reasons or because you have been offered early retirement by your company.

Endowment A form of insurance policy which can be used to fund a private pension arrangement. When it matures at retirement age it will be used to buy an annuity.

Escalation (See *Dynamism*.)

Ex gratia pension A pension which has been awarded without any contractual obligation.

Expansion (See *Dynamism*.)

Final salary The basis on which most pensions are calculated. This might be the actual salary you earn on the day of your retirement; the average for that year; the average of the final three or five years of your employment; or even the best year of the final five or ten years.

Fluctuating emoluments Earnings from bonuses, overtime or commission which are extra to your basic salary. They may or may not be included in pension calculations according to the fund rules.

Frozen pension Usually a pension earned with a previous employer which will be paid once you have reached retirement age. Although legislation now protects some of them against inflation to some degree, unfortunately most are *frozen* at the level of entitlement on the day you left. They are not increased at all.

Funded schemes Normal pension schemes in which contributions from employer and employee are lumped together to buy investments are known as *funded* schemes. They contrast with 'pay as you go' schemes in which pensions are paid from profits (in the case of companies) or from taxes (as with the State retirement pension which is not a funded scheme despite your contributions to it).

Guaranteed minimum pension (GMP) This is the pension guaranteed by your employer when you retire from a company which is contracted out of the State Earnings Related Pension Scheme (SERPS). It is roughly in line with the entitlement you would have earned had you belonged to the State scheme during the same period and, like the State scheme it is inflation protected.

Index linking (See *Dynamism*.)

Inflation proofing (See *Dynamism*.)

Insured scheme This generally refers to a scheme which is administered and financed on behalf of an employer by an insurance company. This is a popular option, particularly for smaller companies who do not have the skills or numbers to justify their own pensions department. It can also refer to a direct insurance company scheme to provide a pension in return for a lump sum or premium payments.

Late retirement If you continue working after normal retirement date, you have two main options: to take the pension as well as your salary, or to postpone the pension until you finally retire in which case your pension will be increased. (See page 78.)

Lump sum (See *Cash option*.)

Managed fund Commonly operated by insurance companies acting on behalf of a number of employers who do not manage their own pension funds. Contributions by the companies are pooled for investment purposes.

Money purchase scheme A scheme where a fixed sum of money is paid into the pension fund on a regular basis. The level of pension is then calculated on how the fund grows.

Normal retirement Starting your retirement at the age specified as normal for your pension scheme. The State scheme specifies 65 years for men and 60 years for women; although there is an increasing trend for occupational pension schemes to offer retirement at earlier ages, 65 and 60 are still widely accepted as normal.

Occupational pension A pension available as a result of working for a particular employer which is additional to any pension you receive from the State. Nearly half of all employees in Britain belong to an occupational scheme (11,100,000 out of a workforce of about 23 million). Many more have self-employed or other personal pension schemes.

Paid-up pension A pension which no longer accepts fresh contributions and from which a pension will be paid in the future. It may be preserved from a previous employment or a ceased *personal pension*.

Past service pension This may be offered to older employees of a company when a new pension scheme is introduced. Usually benefits under a pension scheme have to be earned by length of service and contributions, so when a scheme is introduced for the first time or is substantially improved, employees with only a few years till retirement may have little to gain from them. In these instances benefits may be offered (possibly on a reduced scale) for earlier non-pensionable service.

Pay-as-you-go-pension When pensions are paid from current income, which comprises profits in the case of companies and taxes in the case of the State. The State retirement scheme is one of these. The pensions are not paid from a fund of invested contributions.

Pension Also known as an *Annuity* or *Superannuation*. It is a regular payment made to former employees who no longer work and can be regarded as a form of deferred salary.

Pension fraction Most schemes calculate your pension entitlement on the basis of paying a sixtieth or eightieth of your salary for each year of service. This is the pension fraction.

Pensionable earnings The level of earnings taken into account for both the payment of pension when you retire and the calculation of contributions while you are at work. Some schemes allow all earnings to be taken into consideration including overtime, bonuses and commissions; others will consider only the basic salary.

Pensionable service The number of years you have worked for your company which will be taken into account in calculating your pension.

Personal pension Normally this refers to the sort of pension bought by self-employed people or employees whose company has no occupational scheme for them to join. It will take on a slightly different meaning after April 1988 when employees will be allowed to *contract out* of their company scheme and/or SERPS and take out their own *Personal pension*.

Preserved pension This is usually a pension earned during a previous employment which is held in a preserved or *frozen* state for you until it is due for payment at normal retirement age. (See also *Frozen pension*.)

Purchased life annuity A pension which can be bought with a lump sum and has better terms as you get older. It has different tax standing from most pensions as the pension which is usually paid by an insurance company, is regarded by the Inland Revenue as being part refund of your capital, which is not taxed, and part interest on that capital, which is.

Reversionary annuity. A pension which is not paid until the death of someone else. The most usual example is a widow's pension which, obviously, will not become payable until the death of the husband.

Salary sacrifice When an employee agrees to forego part of their salary in return for their employer paying an equal amount for pension or death benefits on their behalf.

Self-administered scheme A scheme which is run by the employer who probably employs some pensions staff.

Superannuation Another name for a pension.

Surrender value A value which will be paid back if you cancel an insurance policy prematurely. It is rarely an advantage particularly in the early days of a policy.

Tax relief The means by which payments into a pension scheme are larger than the deductions from net salary. The main features are:
- Contributions are deducted from your salary *before* income tax is deducted.
- Your employer's contributions are also allowed as a deduction against Corporation Tax which is levied against company profits.
- Money invested in the pension fund is free from income tax, corporation tax or capital gains tax.
- Any lump sum payable on death or as part of your retirement benefit is usually free of tax.

Top hat scheme A pension scheme designed mostly for the benefit of senior executives who are often given special treatment because they tend to be recruited late in their careers. This means they will be latecomers to a pension scheme and therefore have little hope of earning a full pension without help.

Transfer club The name given to those schemes which have agreed with each other to allow pensions to be transferred from one to another. Most public sector pension schemes are members of the *Club*.

Transfer value The lump sum that can be moved from one scheme to another when an employee changes jobs.

Transferability The right to transfer your benefits from one scheme into another when, for instance, you change job. In the past, employers have been accused of being recalcitrant over transferability maintaining that there are considerable administrative and financial difficulties involved. However, since January 1986 you have had the legal right to transfer your rights, provided your next employer or an insurance company agrees to accept them.

Trivial pension This is likely to be a

preserved or frozen pension from a previous employment which is worth less than £104 a year (as at March 1987). The Inland Revenue will allow the pension scheme to convert the whole of a *trivial* pension into cash for the benefit of the holder without tax penalty.

Trust deed This is the legal document under which the scheme is established and recognised by the Inland Revenue. Every scheme must have one.

Trustees Those who administer the pension fund. They may include representatives of employees or the trades union representing them, and they have ultimate responsibility for implementing the rules of the fund.

Unfunded scheme Another name for a *pay-as-you-go scheme*.

Unit-linked scheme A scheme where the pension benefits depend on how well or badly the investment of contributions has gone. Personal pensions are often linked to unit trusts.

Vested rights Your guaranteed rights to pension benefits even if you have left a particular employment.

Waiting period Many pension schemes have a waiting period of six months to a year before new employees may join. It is designed to save unnecessary administrative work involved in dealing with an employee who moves on quickly. Sometimes there is also a minimum age qualification.

Widow's option The chance to increase a *widow's pension* by accepting a lower pension from the start of your retirement.

Widow's pension A pension paid to a widow after the death of her pensioner husband, which is often at half the full rate due to the husband. It may also be paid after his death while still in full-time work.

Widower's pension A pension paid to a widower whose wife had been a full member of a company pension scheme. It is the same principle as for a widow's pension but is much less common.

BIBLIOGRAPHY

Gartland, Peter (ed.) (annually, in October) *Executive Pensions Handbook*. Financial Times Business Publishing Ltd, London.

Oldfield, Maurice (1987) *Understanding Pension Schemes*. Fourmat Publishing, London.

Rudinger, Edith (ed.) (1985) *What Will my Pension Be?* Consumers' Association, Hertford.

Managing your money

BUDGETING	96
SHOULD YOU PAY OFF THE MORTGAGE?	102
What happens if I die first?	102
PUTTING YOUR MONEY TO WORK	102
How deposits work	103
When should you invest?	104
Investing for income or growth	104
SHOULD YOU INVEST OR DEPOSIT?	104
How investments work	108
The effect of tax	108
Assessing the risks	106
SPENDING YOUR CAPITAL	109
Estimating your money needs	109
Planning your spending	110
Your home as capital	111
Bequests	111
ADVICE ON ADVISERS	112
Where to go	112
Is it truly independent?	112
What are the risks?	117
Useful addresses	117
BIBLIOGRAPHY	120

Retirement is *not* a retreat from worldly affairs, a gentle relaxation far from the rat race and the shedding of all responsibilities. It is a time when most of us stop working for an employer and start working on our own behalf to secure our survival in society. While inflation is nobody's friend, to the person no longer earning a salary it can be a deadly enemy. It is a challenge to anyone contemplating, or already in, retirement to minimise the effects of inflation on their finances and maybe improve their position.

Although the State pension is protected against inflation, the majority of company pension schemes are not and the annual increases that may be made are rarely sufficient to keep pace with rising prices. Therefore, you need to make a realistic assessment of the situation and plan how you will use your resources.

BUDGETING

It is essential to draw up a budget sheet to compare your income against your anticipated expenditure. (A typical budget sheet is shown opposite.) For those already retired the figures are real, but the exercise is equally valid however far off retirement may be. As long as you are working, you may expect your income to at least keep pace with inflation. Since company schemes are based on your final salary, then if your pay rises match inflation, today's buying power will be the same when you retire. Similarly with the State pension. So, bearing in mind the percentage of pensions you will be entitled to, imagine that you are retiring tomorrow.

Using Chapters 2 and 3 you can assess your income from:
- the State and/or company pension(s)
- commuting part of a pension
- lump sum payments, e.g. maturing endowments
- investments and savings

We can then estimate our outgoings which are likely to differ in retirement. For instance, there will be no need to travel to work.

Once you know the relative balances between income and expenditure, you can start your financial planning for the future. Quite possibly, the situation is not as alarming as you thought it might be. Almost certainly gross income will have gone down, but your net

Estimating your budget.

INCOME			EXPENDITURE		
	WORKING	RETIRED		WORKING	RETIRED
SALARY (GROSS)			TAX		
COMPANY PENSION			NATIONAL INSURANCE		
PERSONAL PENSION (SELF EMPLOYED)			COMPANY PENSION		
STATE BASIC PENSION			PERSONAL PENSION		
			INSURANCE FOR HOME		
GRADUATED PENSION			INSURANCE FOR LIFE		
SERPS PENSION					
OTHER STATE PENSIONS			INSURANCE FOR CAR		
INTEREST FROM BANK			INSURANCE FOR OTHER		
INTEREST FROM BUILDING SOCIETY			RATES		
			WATER RATES		
INTEREST FROM OTHER DEPOSITS			MORTGAGE		
INVESTMENT DIVIDENDS			RENT		
			TELEPHONE		
INCOME FROM LETTINGS			ELECTRICITY		
			GAS		
OTHER INCOME			OIL		
			HOUSE REPAIRS		
			HOUSE DECORATIONS		
			CLEANING MATERIALS		
			FOOD AT HOME		
			FOOD OUT		
			CLOTHES		
			DRY CLEANING		
			TOILET REQUISITES		
			CAR TAX		
			CAR MAINTENANCE		
			PETROL AND OIL		
			FARES		
			HOLIDAYS		
			HOBBIES		
			PAPERS/MAGAZINES		
			SUBSCRIPTIONS		
			THEATRE/CINEMA		
			TV/VIDEO RENTAL		
			TV LICENCE		
			TOBACCO		
			DRINK		
			STATIONERY		
			GREETINGS CARDS		
			CHRISTMAS/ BIRTHDAY GIFTS		
			POSTAGE		
			DONATIONS		
			OTHER		
TOTAL INCOME			TOTAL EXPENDITURE		

NET INCOME IN RETIREMENT

When Mr Smith retires at 65 he will receive a company pension at half his salary, and qualify for the full State basic pension. His wife does not

The change in net income on retirement for those currently earning £8000, £12,000, £20,000 and £25,000.

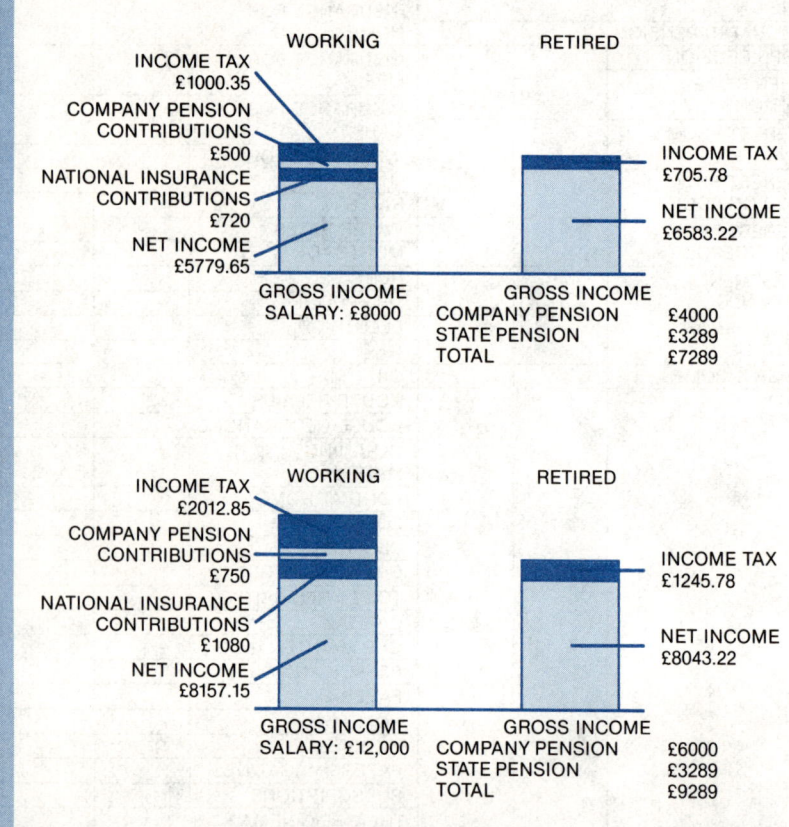

income may not be greatly different as you will be paying less tax and no contributions to National Insurance and company pensions. The deficit between income at work and in retirement progresses the higher the salary. Once the retirement income is at the level shown in the third bar chart (above), the benefit of age allowance will be lost. (For a full explanation of age allowance, see page 181.)

Even if you have a reduced net income, there are significant reductions in expenditure too. For example, with a lower income you

work and they have no other sources of income. The change in net income for the Smiths is shown below for a final salary of £8000, £12,000, £20,000 and £25,000.

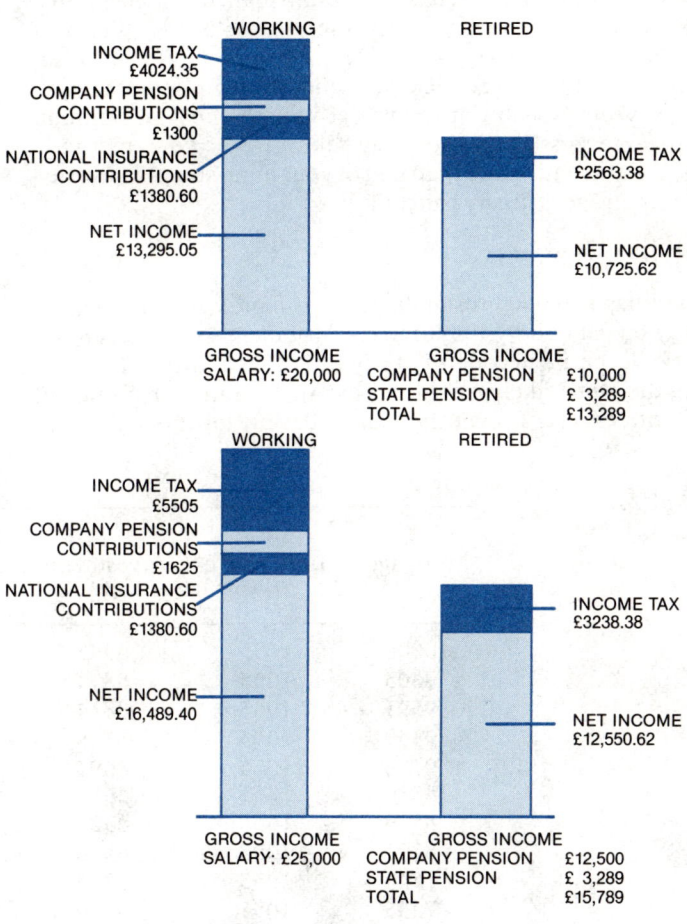

will be liable for less tax, and once you are 65 you will be entitled to the age allowance. You will probably spend less on food and drink outside the home with no restaurant lunch bills or rounds of after-work drinks in the pub with colleagues. Fares, or perhaps petrol costs, should go down when you stop commuting daily. However, caution is wise as heating and lighting costs may well rise, particularly if the house used to be empty during the day. Once you have worked out what your own circumstances are, you may be agreeably surprised.

THE COST OF EXTENDING YOUR MORTGAGE

Early in 1987 building societies were lending at an interest rate of 12.25%. With Mortgage Interest Relief at Source (MIRAS) a loan will actually cost only 8.7% in interest. If the sum loaned were deposited in an instant access account at a net interest rate of 8%, then you would be losing money at the rate of 0.7% a year. However, an investment in unit trusts can yield dividends from 5.6% net improving over the years probably at an average growth of 6% per annum. Thus it is quite possible to not only take care of your mortgage liabilities, but also have more than half of your lump sum still invested when the mortgage is finally paid off.

Example

Mr Howard has £10,000 outstanding on his mortgage at retirement which may be paid off by the lump sum payment from his pension scheme. However, he negotiates to pay this off in a further 20 years. Assuming the worst likely conditions for Mr Howard, a high rate of mortgage interest (12%) over the term with only low tax relief with

Table 2.
Mr Howard's assets over 20 years.

	Start of year		
Mortgage (£)	Deposit a/c (£)	Investment (£)	Total assets (£)
10000	1055	8945	10000
9805	1055	8893	9948
9591	1055	8834	9889
9359	1055	8768	9823
9106	1055	8694	9749
8830	1055	8612	9667
8529	1055	8520	9575
8201	1055	8416	9471
7844	1055	8300	9355
7455	1055	8170	9225
7030	1055	8025	9080
6567	1055	7862	8917
6063	1055	7680	8735
5513	1055	7476	8531
4914	1055	7248	8303
4261	1055	6993	8048
3548	1055	6708	7763
2772	1055	6388	7443
1962	1055	6030	7085
1004	1055	5629	6684

*Total assets = Dividends + sums realised from sale of total investment†

†Sales of shares are at 6% discount on value, this is the average difference between the bid and offer prices.

tax at 25%, then 9% net interest is payable and the monthly repayments are £91.29 or £1095.48 a year. To enable him to meet these he intends to deposit £1055 in an account which is expected to return a modest 7% net interest per annum. This will help him break even at the end of the year as he will not get 7% on the whole amount due to the monthly withdrawals.

The balance of the £10,000 is invested to produce net dividends of approximately 5.6% pa and capital growth of about 6% pa. In each subsequent year Mr Howard will collect his dividends and sell some of his investments in order to deposit the amount of money needed to cover the mortgage repayments over the next year. The charges in his assets are shown in the table below.

After 20 years he will still have more than £5000 of his original capital invested. The final figure will depend on:
(a) the mortgage lending rate
(b) the performance of his investment.

If the mortgage lending rate rises, then so does the borrowing rate. However, if the stock markets went into decline and investments took a hammering then he will be in a position to make an instant decision to pay off the balance of the mortgage after the first couple of years.

Year	Capital growth (£)	Total investment (£)	Dividends (£)	Total assets* (£)	Shares sold (£) Actual	Value†
1	537	9482	501	9414	554	589
2	534	9427	498	9359	557	593
3	530	9364	495	9297	560	596
4	526	9294	491	9227	564	600
5	522	9216	487	9150	568	604
6	518	9130	482	9064	573	610
7	511	9031	477	8966	578	615
8	505	8921	471	8857	584	621
9	498	8798	465	8735	590	628
10	490	8660	458	8598	597	635
11	482	8507	449	8446	606	645
12	472	8334	440	8274	615	654
13	461	8141	430	8083	625	665
14	449	7925	419	7868	636	677
15	435	7683	406	7628	649	690
16	420	7413	392	7360	663	705
17	402	7110	376	7059	679	722
18	383	6771	358	6723	697	741
19	362	6392	338	6346	717	763
20	338	5967	315	5924	—	—

SHOULD YOU PAY OFF THE MORTGAGE?

If you are expecting a cash lump sum from e.g. your pension or an endowment, you may wonder about paying off a mortgage. While that monthly commitment may be a worry it is worth considering what your situation would be if you did pay it off with a lump sum.

Pros	Cons
• Freedom from a monthly commitment • Ease of mind through absence of a large debt	• Loss of tax relief on interest • Loss of control of cash lump sum

The great disadvantage you face if you pay off your mortgage is that if you subsequently need to raise capital, any loan you take will not have the tax advantage enjoyed by mortgages, unless you move home and buy another property. Tax relief is allowed only on loans for the purchase of property or its improvement, such as making an extension.

For many there is a psychological barrier of feeling that it is vaguely immoral to be in debt. However, your major consideration should be 'Is it in my best interests to get rid of the mortgage or could I put the cash to better use?' The options are

(a) pay off the mortgage;
(b) ask the lender to re-schedule your mortgage for another term. If you can show that you can meet the repayments, banks and building societies are happy to do this.

By choosing Option (b) your lump sum can then be invested to yield an income that can help you meet the payments for the next term. If you are going to move house at any time during your retirement then you might also consider taking a mortgage on your new property.

What happens if I die first?

In that instance, the mortgage will be paid off from your estate. The inheritance tax payable is then less than it might have been because the estate passed on will be smaller, so that your beneficiaries will probably not lose as much as you spend.

PUTTING YOUR MONEY TO WORK

Capital in the form of redundancy, commutation and other lump sum payments, accumulated savings or sums from maturing insurance policies can be invested to protect it from erosion by inflation and to enhance your income. Deposit accounts keep the *nominal* value of your money, but inflation affects its real value so that often its purchasing power diminishes. However, with a genuine investment there is a risk that your initial capital might decline.

When should you invest?

The earlier you can invest the better. Sound investments, probably with the emphasis on growth rather than income, can give you a very sound

PROTECTING YOUR CAPITAL

Mr Jones retired at the beginning of 1986 and calculated that his sources of income from the company and State pensions were going to fall about £2000 short of the annual total he would like to have at his disposal. However, he commuted part of his pension and with an endowment maturing he had a total of £30,000 with which to generate that extra income. Mr Jones put all the money in an NS Investment account which is simple, secure and pays an attractive gross interest of around 11.25% per annum. He reckons that by leaving the money intact for 12 months the interest earned would be £3375 and he would draw only £2000 to pay the major bills.

However, Mr Jones found reality was less favourable due to income tax on the gross interest and the effects of inflation which, by the end of the year, had raised the cost of living by 3.7%. To keep pace with inflation, the real value of his cash on deposit must also increase by 3.7% so that its earning capacity is the same in the following year. The total needed in the account at the start of next year is then £31,110. However, his actual performance left him needing another £646.25. In reality, only £1353.75 of the gross interest should have been spent which represents only about 4.5% on his original £30,000. Moreover, if the company pension is not inflation-proofed, some of the interest should be used to remedy the effects of inflation on its purchasing power, ideally by adding to his savings and increasing their income earning capacity.

Table 3. *Mr Jones' savings balance after one year.*

	Income (£)	Debits (£)
Investment	30,000	
Gross interest @ 11.25%	3,375	
Tax on interest @ 27%		911.25
Withdrawal		2,000
Balance	30,463.75	

base from which to launch into a comfortable retirement. Once you are retired your needs may change and income may then be more important than the need for growth. However, you may prefer to do nothing with your capital other than put it in a building society, National Savings or bank deposit account until after a year in retirement. This gives you time in which to experience your retirement needs and to calculate your income requirements in real terms rather than make suppositions. You can also take some time to decide what you will want to do.

However, the first year in retirement is often the most expensive as people understandably rush to do all the things they have been looking forward to – visiting the family who emigrated to Australia, the long anticipated world cruise, or the erection of a greenhouse. All of these will come largely out of your capital thereby diminishing the sum on which you will rely for at least part of your income in the future.

Investing for income or growth

The uses to which you put your capital will vary with your life-style and a continuing interest in your own financial position and prospects is important. While you are working, any spare cash would be better invested mostly for growth, to increase the size of your capital, than for high income. If your income is more than sufficient to meet your needs then any increase in it only adds to your income tax liability. With unit or investment trusts specialising in growth rather than income your capital has a chance to keep pace with, and possibly outrun, inflation.

On retirement, your regular income will surely have decreased and may then need topping up. This is the time to reassess your situation and perhaps convert part of your capital to a higher interest investment or deposit. If either you or your spouse are 65 you will have the advantage of the higher rate of age allowance to set against income before tax.

SHOULD YOU INVEST OR DEPOSIT?

The rewards of using your capital are related to the risks involved, the higher the risk, the greater the rewards. The options you may consider are to place your money in a deposit or to invest. Which option suits you best depends on how much capital you have, your commitments and your aims.

How deposits work

Deposits usually involve handing your money over to another body, like a bank, in return for an interest payment. The nominal value of

Figures are taken from Money Management. *An interesting feature is the performance of the investment trusts and unit trusts which have both done rather better by comparison with the* Financial Times *All-Share index.*

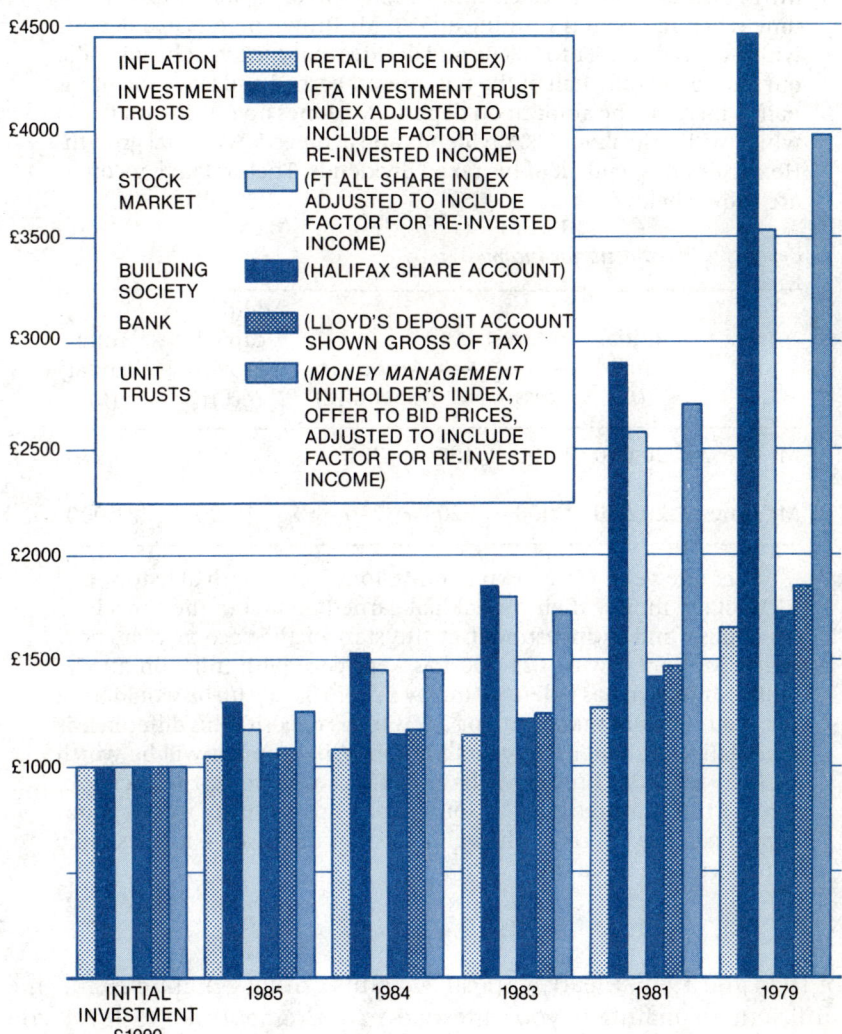

every £100 you hand over will be secure however long you choose to leave it. However, inflation will have affected its real value. For example, £100 placed in a bank account in 1974 had a purchasing power of £69, in 1976. Even with the interest added to the initial capital so that it, in turn, attracted interest, this did not counteract the inflation

DEPOSIT V INVESTMENT

Mr Brown and Mr Jones each have £20,000 of capital to invest at a time when inflation is running at 5%. Mr Brown invests in a deposit with a gross interest of 10% pa and decides that each year he will take out and spend only half of the net interest earned and leave the other half to increase the amount on deposit. Mr Jones invests in unit trusts which will yield about 5% dividends and achieve 5% annual growth. He decides to spend all of his taxed dividends. Their relative incomes are shown below.

Deposits v Investments for income.

	Initial capital (£)	Interest (£) Gross	Interest (£) Net	Amount to spend (£)	Addition to capital/ growth (£)	Total capital (£)
Mr Brown	20,000	2,000	1,460	730	730	20,730
Mr Jones	20,000	1,000	720	730	1,000	21,000

After one year, Mr Brown and Mr Jones were both able to spend £730 of the money their capital had earned them, but the sums held on deposit and in investment at the start of the second year, now differ. Mr Jones, with £21,000 has kept pace with inflation at 5%, while Mr Brown has fallen behind by £270. To keep up he would have to spend no more than £460, or 2.3% of his deposit. This difference is cumulative and after five years Mr Jones' investment will be worth £25,525 while Mr Brown will have £23,925 on deposit, a difference of some £1600. Moreover Mr Jones does not have to worry about capital gains tax because the value has not increased – it has simply kept pace with inflation.

of 1974 and 1975. Clearly deposit accounts cannot generate an income sufficient to maintain your lifestyle in retirement at the level you achieved while you were at work.

How investments work

When you make an investment you buy a tangible asset, from a share in a company to a diamond ring. Some forms of investment pay interest or a dividend while some will not. But all can go up or down in value. So if you invest £100 in a company share, it might be worth £120 or £80 a year later depending on the fortunes of the company. This may seem to

The graph below illustrates how the gap widens until after 10 years, Mr Brown, with some £28,620 is more than £3900 behind Mr Jones who has done no more than keep his capital in line with inflation.

Mr Brown's savings growth compared with that of Mr Jones.

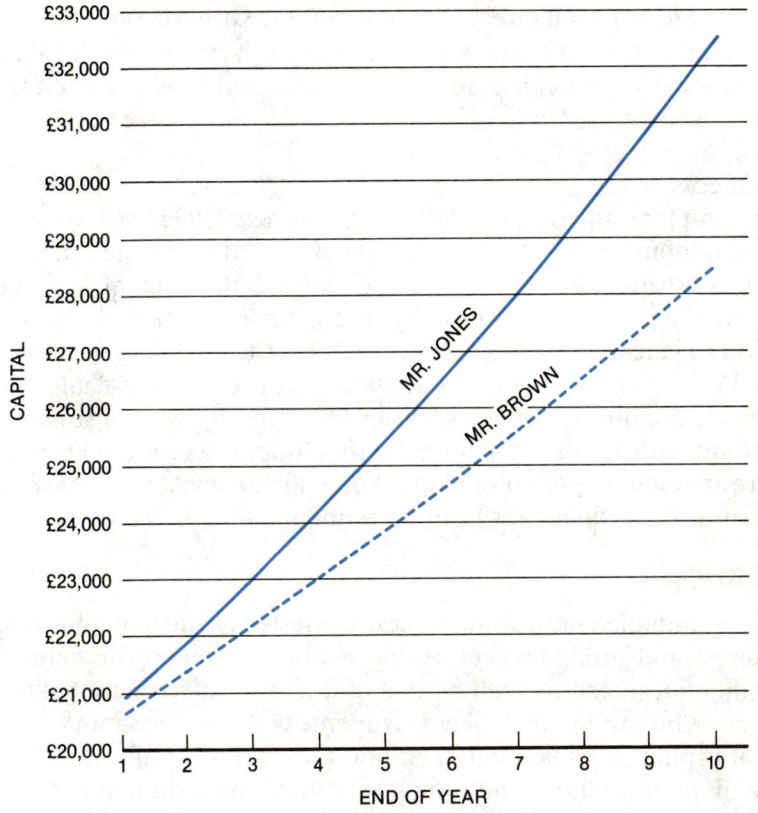

be somewhat risky in comparison with the safe and sound income you could derive from a deposit. However, it is worth remembering that while investments are a greater risk than deposits they also offer greater opportunities to generate some income while preserving, or even enhancing, the value of your capital so that it may go on earning interest at the required level in the years ahead, however severe inflation might be. The graph opposite shows how £1000 invested in various ways would have performed by 1 December 1986 if invested for 1, 2, 3, 5 and 7 years previously. You will see that investments have far out performed the 'deposits' over each period selected but all schemes did better than keep pace with inflation.

The effect of tax

The Inland Revenue treats investments differently from deposits which is one reason why investments can achieve significant capital growth.

Deposits

All interest from deposits is taxable, regardless of whether you spend it, save it or even draw out only part of the interest earned in order to keep your capital in line with inflation. On practically every deposit except some National Savings, *composite rate tax* is deducted *before* the interest is credited to you.

Investments

Only if your investments grow faster than the *Retail Price Index*, which is a measure of inflation, will you be liable for capital gains tax. Even if growth outstrips inflation you will be exempt from capital gains tax provided it is below a certain level that is reviewed at each Budget. Currently it means you pay no tax on the first £6600 per annum of realised gains. Above that tax is at 30%. This tax becomes liable only when you dispose of the asset, either by giving it away to someone other than your spouse or selling the investment in order to keep the cash, re-invest or deposit elsewhere. You will, however, pay *income* tax on the interest or dividends from investment.

Assessing the risks

Our over simplified illustration has assumed steady and matching rates of interest and inflation over a long period. However, the value of investments can fall as well as rise and is also affected by political changes. Who can say that all governments will take the same view of rates of capital gains tax and exemption levels? It is important to be aware of all possibilities and to invest with a long term point of view so that you can ride out periods when holdings may decline and wait for them to recover.

For many, a mix of savings in investments and on deposit is the most suitable solution and, although the sums of money involved will vary considerably from case to case, it is always essential that you *avoid being over-invested*. Always keep sufficient money available at short notice to cover unexpected emergencies. Approximately 40% of your total capital might be kept in deposits for this purpose, otherwise you may be in the unhappy position of having to sell investments at a time when the market is not favourable.

If you do not have much money then a deposit is probably the right home for it. Investment is likely to be more rewarding over the long term but carries risks of varying degrees.

SPENDING YOUR CAPITAL

Many people have been brought up to think it unwise to spend capital but that it is all right to take the interest. However, if you wish to remain as well off next year as you are this then you must let your capital grow in line with inflation. This means that you cannot take all of the interest; but is this really so?

If you were to take this philosophy to its logical conclusion you would die leaving a great deal more money than you began with at the start of your retirement. Maybe you have family and friends to whom you wish to leave all you can, but with some acute financial planning you may be able to do this whilst having a more comfortable lifestyle than you might otherwise have had.

Estimating your money needs

The use of Life Expectancy Tables (opposite) will help in your planning. These show what the Government Actuary thinks are our longevity prospects based on averages taken over the whole population in the UK. On average a 65-year-old man will live for another 13.04 years, i.e. until he is 78, and a woman can expect to live for another 16.98 years, or well into her 82nd year. As these are *averages* you may have a different expectation and to ensure that your finances are on the safe side you should assume that you will live twice as long as the average person. So if you are a 65-year-old man you can look forward to

Table 1. *The number of years your capital will last according to the net interest and amount withdrawn annually. If the percentage of capital withdrawn does not exceed the net interest on capital, then you can continue to do this indefinitely.*

Capital withdrawn annually* (%)	Net interest on capital (%)					
	5	6	7	8	9	10
5	—					
6	32	—				
7	23	28	—			
8	18	21	25	—		
9	15	17	19	20	—	
10	13	14	15	18	20	—
11	11	12	13	14	15	18
12	10	10	11	12	13	14

Note: Annual compound interest assumed.
*First withdrawal is at the end of year 1.

YOUR LIFE EXPECTANCY

The older you are the longer you can expect to live – this is backed up by the Government Actuary. Looking at the table below you will see that a 65 year old man can expect to live to 78, but once he is 78 the tables show he can still expect another 6½ years.

	Life expectation (years)	
Present age (years)	Men	Women
60	16.39	20.84
61	15.69	20.05
62	14.99	19.27
63	14.32	18.49
64	13.67	17.73
65	13.04	16.98
66	12.43	16.24
67	11.83	15.51
68	11.24	14.80
69	10.68	14.09
70	10.13	13.40
71	9.61	12.73
72	9.10	12.07
73	8.62	11.43
74	8.16	10.82
75	7.72	10.21
76	7.30	9.63
77	6.89	9.06
78	6.50	8.52
79	6.13	7.99
80	5.79	7.49

Source: Interim Life Tables, Government Actuary's Department (1981–83)

another 26 years. Alternatively, you can look at the ages at which your parents and grandparents died and add on a few years to allow for advances in medical care.

Planning your spending

Table 1 shows how long your capital will last for given net interest rates against various spending rates.

Example

Mr Williams is 65 years old and has £25,000 in various accounts earning net interest at 7% a year. If he wishes to spend his capital in equal sums over the next 25 years then he can afford to do so at the rate of about 8% a year, or £2140. While Mr and Mrs Collins who are already 70 years old will have different expectations.

Mr Collins has a life expectation of 10.13 years and may well live for another 20 years. His capital is getting a better rate of interest, 9%, and over the next 20 years he could afford to remove about 10% of his capital of £25,000 annually. As Mrs Collins can expect to live another $13\frac{1}{2}$ years on average she should plan for 27 years. If her money earns interest at only 6% pa she can afford to take out about 7% of her capital each year.

Your home as capital

The value of your home can also be taken into the equation as you could sell it at some stage and move into rented or sheltered accommodation. It is also possible to raise substantial sums of cash on your home and continue to live there rent free for the rest of your life (see page 100).

Bequests

Making your bequests during your lifetime is less traditional, but you probably help a lot more and may get more gratitude for it. Many children starting out in life may well be able to make better use of anything you intend to leave them now rather than in 20 years' time. It is possible to do this in annual instalments as part of your planned invasion of capital without incurring tax liabilities (see *Taxation*, page 180). Alternatively, you could arrange for a portion of your money to be completely locked in to provide an inheritance.

Example

If you want to leave half your £25,000 capital sum to a child you can place half aside for the bequest. If it is earning interest at a net rate of 8% then you will get £1000 in the first year. If you want to protect the bequest against inflation at, say, 5% a year, you would need to leave £625 to swell the capital which leaves 3%, or £375, for you to spend.

You can also calculate how long the other half of the capital will last to find your total income. If you have an average lifespan of 10 years and earn interest at 8%, then you can spend it at the rate of 10% a year, £1350, and you therefore have a total of £1725 a year to spend from the two capital sums whilst leaving the bequest intact.

ADVICE ON ADVISERS

Financial packages that are unsuitable may become difficult, and sometimes costly to escape from. Good financial advice is invaluable, but the question is 'Where can I go and how can I be sure that it is truly independent?'

Where to go

Members of the *Financial Intermediaries Managers and Brokers Regulatory Association* (FIMBRA) are governed in the conduct of their business by rules designed to protect the investor against negligence and fraud. Random checks are made in an effort to ensure that the advisers and managers are behaving properly.

FIMBRA was formed by the amalgamation of the *National Association of Security Dealers and Investment Managers* (NASDIM) and the *Life Insurance and Unit Trusts Intermediaries Regulatory Organisation* (LUTIRO). It was set up with the intention of being one of the new regulatory bodies required under the *Financial Services Act 1986*. There is a considerable degree of protection for the investor who deals with a FIMBRA member, but this does not remove all risks from investment. This will always be present as there is no protection for anyone against market movements.

Is it truly independent?

Even the *Financial Services Act 1986* which aims, among other things, to regulate the advice-giving industry, will not provide a wholly satisfactory answer, although advisers will have to be authorised or be members of and answerable to a regulatory body. However, there are some guidelines to help you evaluate the advice.

Evaluating financial advice
1. *Has the adviser found out everything about you?*
   This must be a personal interview, not just completing a questionnaire. Your adviser should insist on knowing the full extent of your capital, income, liabilities, state of health, dependants and ambitions. The examination should have been searching, maybe embarrassingly so, because without such knowledge the adviser is not in a position to offer comprehensive, considered advice.
2. *Have you been given the advice in writing and does it include a tax computation?*
   Never act on verbal advice. No competent adviser would ask you to do so because it is open to misunderstanding at the least and

misrepresentation at the worst. The tax computation should set out precisely the income you may expect to receive and what you will have to pay to the Inland Revenue.
3. *Has the adviser told you what he will gain if you follow his advice?*
You should know. If an adviser is to act for you, particularly by managing your money there must be absolute trust on both sides.
4. *Have the terms of business been set out?*
This should have been done in writing before giving you advice, using headed notepaper indicating membership of a regulatory organisation or stating that he/she is a licensed manager or dealer in securities.
5. *Have you been offered a banker's reference?*
The names of referees should ideally be given with the terms of business so that you can take up references as you wish.
6. *Does the adviser have professional indemnity insurance to cover the giving of financial advice?*
The holding of such insurance is obligatory to those operating under the regulatory bodies and should also be declared in the terms of business. It must be related to financial advice and not solely to activities as an accountant or lawyer under which you might have no redress.
7. *Who keeps the documents proving ownership, the adviser or you?*
Giving someone absolute discretion to manage your money is one of the easiest routes to fraud so if you are thinking of taking this option you should be more stringent in your testing.
8. *Have you checked on his standing with the professional body to which he belongs?*
Even if absolute discretion is not being suggested this is valuable.
9. *What have you learned from the adviser?*
How long has he been operating? How long has he been at his present business address? Do you really understand the advice given? Has the reason for this choice of investment been satisfactorily and adequately explained to you? All these questions are important in your evaluation.
10. *How much do you trust the adviser?*
After all the other questions have been answered, this is the one that really matters, and only absolute trust will give you peace of mind.

Evaluating the adviser
Although every person who is authorised to advise you financially stands to make money through it, sound advice may be obtained just as readily as good service from your lawyer, accountant, architect or doctor. Nevertheless, the range of service you may expect will vary.

INVESTOR PROTECTION

Once the *Financial Services Act 1986* is fully operational the framework for investor protection is likely to be like that shown.

At the start of 1987 the Securities and Investments Board (SIB) was waiting for power to be transferred to it by the Secretary of State for Trade and Industry. As the proposed regulatory bodies complete the drawing up of their rules it is expected that progressively each would be empowered to control its own sector of investment. One of the most important facets of this framework will be to ensure that those in the investment business put their clients' interests first when giving advice. Spot checks on records will be an important part of the policing role and any client who is dissatisfied with the service may complain to the appropriate regulating body.

The Securities and Investments Board (SIB)

The SIB will lay down the rules of conduct, and will authorise and supervise the self-regulating organisations in the different sectors. The rules of each organisation may not be identical to those of the SIB as they will be designed to suit the spheres over which they have control, but they will offer equivalent protection.

The SIB aims to ensure that those offering financial advice are competent, solvent and carry suitable insurances. Even individuals who work for one company selling only its own products, e.g. the insurance salesman, will come under its jurisdiction. Its powers will range from private or public reprimand to civil action to obtain restitution of clients' funds, and ultimately the suspension or disqualification of an offender. It will be a criminal offence to carry on business without the Board's sanction which could mean a maximum of two years' imprisonment and the invalidating of any contracts made when outside the scope of authorisation.

The Financial Intermediaries, Managers and Brokers Regulatory Association (FIMBRA)

FIMBRA will offer several levels of membership for those who act as independent advisers and offer management services in the spheres of life assurance and unit trusts.

The Life Assurance and Unit Trust Regulatory Organisation (LAUTRO)

LAUTRO will be concerned with insurance companies and friendly societies that devise investment schemes involving life assurance and with unit trust managers.

The Securities Association (SA)

Formed by the merger of the Stock Exchange and the International Securities Regulatory Organisation, the SA will be responsible for firms dealing in and giving advice on securities of all kinds: equities, international bonds, stock options etc.

The Association of Futures Brokers and Dealers (AFBD)

AFBD will regulate those firms dealing and broking in futures and options other than individual stock options.

The Investment Management Regulatory Organisation (IMRO)

IMRO will cover those who concentrate on investment management at the corporate level, including the operation of regulated unit trusts, investment trusts and pension funds.

Recognised professional bodies

Recognised professional bodies, such as the Law Society and the Royal Institute of Chartered Accountants may apply for recognition from the SIB to cover those members who give investment advice and make financial arrangements for clients incidental to their main activities. If the professional bodies do not apply, or fail to gain recognition, the individual members wishing to continue such activities will have to join the appropriate self-regulating organisation or seek authorisation from the SIB itself.

YOUR RIGHTS UNDER THE *FINANCIAL SERVICES ACT 1986*

Cold calling

Selling by unsolicited visits or telephone calls will be outlawed, save for a couple of exceptions. Any transactions resulting from such activity will be unenforceable by the investment company.

Cooling off

The exceptions to the ban on cold calling are likely to be life assurance and unit trusts. Any customer who enters such a transaction as a result of an unsolicited approach will have 14 days in which to reconsider the matter and pull out.

Disclosure

Customers will be entitled to know much more about the investment schemes, particularly in the field of life assurance, e.g. the surrender value of policies and the commission earned by their salesmen. They must also be told whether they are dealing with a representative of a company tied to its range of products, or an independent intermediary acting as the agent of the customer.

Compensation

It is intended to establish an industry-wide compensation scheme, operational from early in 1988. This will remedy losses incurred when an authorised person, or firm, holding investors' money, goes into liquidation.

Some advisers you may approach, or indeed who may approach you, are tied to one range of products, insurance salesmen employed by one company for example, and those products are all they have to offer. Even the bank manager owes loyalty to his own employers and it would be surprising if one of the bank's own products was not recommended. This does not mean that the products are not excellent, but will they suit you? If you are unsure then you should seek independent advice about it.

'Independent' advisers are paid by commissions from insurance

Private investors

The private investor will be covered completely for sums up to £30,000. The next £20,000 will be covered to the extent of 90% which means that the top limit of compensation under this scheme will be £48,000.

Stock Exchange

The Stock Exchange already has a compensation scheme but the new Securities Association will be embraced by the SIB scheme. However, the Stock Exchange *may* retain a 'top up' scheme to cover individual investors up to a level of £250,000, which is in line with the current scheme.

Insurance companies

The *Policy Holders' Protection Act 1975* provides for a levy on all insurance companies to meet up to 90% of the liabilities of any authorised insurance firm that fails. Liabilities under insurance that is compulsory by law, such as third party risk for motorists, will be fully (100%) covered.

Unauthorised insurance companies are obliged by law to disclose their status, or lack of it, before accepting your business. If you have any doubts the Department of Trade or the British Insurance Association can confirm the status.

companies, unit trust managers and the like. This is based on the cash you invest or which you allow them to manage for you. But remember, it is *your* money so never be hustled into a hasty decision and never hesitate to ask questions, however searching. 'No' may be one of the hardest words to say, but don't say 'yes' unless it is to good advice that will put your capital to its maximum use in the safest possible way. Major considerations before acting on advice or handing over your money for management are commission, over-investment, guarantees and switching.

Commission
This is paid only to advisers when you act through them and you will gain nothing by acting on your own. The commission will still be deducted from your investment but it will not be rebated to you. Continuing good advice is needed to protect your capital for the future and it is worthwhile using a known good source.

Over-investment
This may happen if the adviser was carried away by the idea of increasing the commission income by encouraging you to invest to the maximum. Never lock into an investment money that you might need in an emergency as you might have to sell on disadvantageous terms which could result in an actual loss. There are no blanket rules in this matter, but if you have been advised to place more than 60% of your capital in investments it should at least sound a warning bell.

Guarantees
How often has your adviser used the word 'guarantee'? Sadly, there is only one valid guarantee that an adviser can make, to do the best he can. Neither levels of income nor rates of growth from investments can be guaranteed in a fluctuating financial world. The past performance of stocks and shares, unit trust funds and insurance-orientated investment is no guarantee of future prospects. It is perfectly legitimate to point out how well an investment has done in the past, but any attempt to project that past performance into the distant future, sometimes producing quite ridiculous figures, should be viewed with suspicion. Even if they turned out to be accurate in the long run, the effects of inflation may well take off the bloom.

Switching
One of the advantages of allowing your adviser to manage your money is that it should ensure that more often than not it is in the right investment at the right time. Sometimes it is necessary to move your money from, say, one unit trust fund to another that promises better performance. As each time a switch is made your investment manager may earn further commission, you should ask if any of this commission will provide a discount for you.

Excessive switching, called *churning* in the trade, should be watched. During a time of market buoyancy you may finish a year quite satisfied with the increased value of your holdings, but if you were to take into account the commission earned from them, they could have been worth even more had they been left in the original funds. You can, however, limit activity by insisting that you are consulted before any alteration is made.

What are the risks?

The rules designed to protect individual investors against misbehaviour by financial advisers and intermediaries (see page 114) and the compensation funds planned to reimburse consequent loss (see page 118) do not remove all risks from investment. If shares in a company, or units in a unit trust fund go down, or if a company in which you have invested collapses and goes out of business making your holding worthless, that is a risk that you will have to bear. All investment carries some degree of risk and the SIB sums it up very neatly:

The existence of SIB no more removes the need for investors to pay attention to where they place their money than the existence of the Highway Code removes the need to look before crossing the road.

No legislation, no regulatory or controlling bodies can protect the individual from his own greed. The allure of high returns can blind a greedy investor to the realities of the risks. Without that human failing, far fewer people would fall victim to the outright fraudster or the incompetent adviser. That is no excuse for those who seek to take advantage of this human weakness, but in the final analysis your common sense is your best defence against them. However, the conscientious and competent adviser has always operated in accordance with the principle that the client's interests come first. Such a person is invaluable to help you invest for reasonable gain at an acceptable risk. This principle is enshrined in the *Financial Services Act 1986* which imposes on authorised advisers a legal obligation to act in this way.

Useful addresses

Association of Futures Brokers and Dealers
Cereal House, 58 Mark Lane
London EC3R 7NE
☏ 01-488 0898

British Insurance Association
Aldermary House, Queen Street
London EC4N 1TP
☏ 01-248 4477

Department of Trade and Industry
1–19 Victoria Street
London SW1H 0ET
☏ 01-215 7877

Financial Intermediaries Managers and Brokers Regulatory Association
22 Great Tower Street
London EC3R 5AQ
☏ 01-929 2711

Investment Management Regulatory Organisation
45 London Wall
London EC2M 5TE
☏ 01-256 7261

Life Assurance and Unit Trust Regulatory Organisation
Aldermary House, Queen Street
London EC4N 1TP
☎ 01-248 4477

Securities Association
Stock Exchange
London EC2N 1HP
☎ 01-588 2355

Securities and Investments Board
3 Royal Exchange Buildings, Cornhill
London EC3V 3NL
☎ 01-283 2474

Stock Exchange
London EC2N 1HP
☎ 01-588 2355

BIBLIOGRAPHY

The Which? Book of Money (1984) Consumers' Association, London.
The Which? Book of Saving and Investing (1983) Consumers' Association, London.
Dibben, Margaret (1986) *The Guardian Money Guide* Willow Books (Collins), London.
Goff, T. G. (1986) *Theory and Practice of Investment* Heinemann (William) Ltd, London.
Hardman, Roger (1986) *Stocks and Shares* Daily Telegraph Publications, London
O'Shea, Daniel (1987) *Investing for Beginners* Financial Times Business Information Ltd, London.
Taylor, Felicity (1986) *How to Invest Successfully* Kogan Page, London.

Instant access and deposit accounts

INSTANT ACCESS SERVICES	123
Current accounts	123
High interest cheque accounts	125
Special services	125
Credit cards	126
BANK DEPOSITS	126
Ordinary deposit accounts	126
Term deposit accounts	126
Offshore accounts	127
BUILDING SOCIETY DEPOSITS	127
Deposit accounts	128
Ordinary share accounts	128
Premium interest accounts	128
Term shares	128
Fixed term, fixed interest accounts	129
Notice accounts	129
Regular savings accounts	129
Expatriate accounts	129
NATIONAL SAVINGS	130
Taxable savings	130
Tax-free savings	134
Tax-free prizes	138

OTHER TYPES OF DEPOSITS 139
Local Authority bonds 139
Insurance companies income bonds 142
Money and deposit funds 142
Useful addresses 142

The 1980s have seen a change in the services offered by banks and building societies with each entering the areas traditional to the other. The *Building Societies Act 1986* has done much to lift the previous restrictions faced by these organisations. Now as both banks and building societies can offer easy access to money deposits, insurance, mortgages and investment schemes, amongst other services, it is worthwhile looking around to find *the* company that can offer the services you need. The various options available are described here.

INSTANT ACCESS SERVICES

Current accounts

Most banks now offer 'free banking' for personal current accounts which do not become overdrawn. Even if this happens you may still escape bank charges if the average bank balance over the period has been above a certain level, generally £500. If you feel that you may be overdrawn from time to time then consult your bank manager who can advise you on the best way to handle these situations.

Bank charges
Charges may be made for:
(a) withdrawals
(b) deposits and withdrawals
The charging period may be:
(a) for the period you are overdrawn
(b) for 1 month
(c) for 3 months
The shorter the charging period the better as charges will be applied to all transactions in that period. The longer the charging period, the more transactions there will be which will lead to a significant increase in charges as a result of only a short period of being in the red.

Example Mr Simmons went into debit for a day or so in one 3-month period but did not maintain a sufficiently high average balance to escape charges. On average he writes 15 cheques a month, pays two direct debits and four standing orders, and uses the cashpoint three times. His charges on a monthly basis may amount to £6 compared with £21–£23.88 on a 3-month period.

Some banks give a notional credit if you have paid in cheques which have not yet cleared before your withdrawal and charge only for the days you are in debt.

Where to cash cheques
Avoid cashing a cheque at any bank other than your own. You will face charges ranging from 50p to £2 per cheque by going elsewhere depending on:
(a) the bank you go to for money
(b) the bank which holds your account
(c) the day of the week.
If you do need money on Saturdays, consider applying for a card for use in a cash-dispensing machine.

Cash-dispensing cards
Many banks, building societies and other institutions are now linking up to provide a better service for their customers. The main groups are:
(a) the National Westminster, Midland and Clydesdale banks offer a network with nearly 3000 machines; the Trustees Savings Bank will join this in 1988.
(b) Lloyds, Barclays, The Royal Bank of Scotland and Bank of Scotland.
(c) The Halifax has more than 400 dispensers.
(d) the Link-shared teller network comprises American Express, the Cooperative Bank, National Girobank, Western Trust & Savings, and the Abbey National, Britannia, Chelsea, Dunfermline, Eastbourne, Gateway, Nationwide, Newcastle, Sussex County and Yorkshire Building Societies. There are many other members and it is still expanding.
(e) the Matrix network serves the customers of the Alliance and Leicester, Anglia, Bradford and Bingley, Bristol and West, Leeds Permanent, National Provincial and Woolwich building societies.

One drawback is that if your cash card is lost or stolen and money is dishonestly drawn from your account, there is no legal obligation to reimburse you. However, some banks regard all debits which occur before you report the disappearance of the card to be your responsibility, although there may be a ceiling on your liability. As they can act at their discretion in this area policies vary from bank to bank. Banks also prefer to rely on their sophisticated technology rather than on your memory when you are debited with a withdrawal which you believe you did not make.

High interest cheque accounts

Minimum deposit   £1000–£2500

Access   Instant. Some schemes require a minimum sum to be withdrawn (generally £200).

Interest   The nominal interest may vary within 1% and may also differ according to the size of the balance in your account.

Should the balance fall below the minimum then a lower interest is paid. Some accounts have special conditions, e.g. a restriction on the number of cheques and the value that may be withdrawn without incurring charges. For example, Lloyds requires a minimum balance of £2500 from which you can draw up to £300 a day from cashpoint machines, have a special cheque book and arrange for standing orders and direct debits to be paid through the account. However, only three withdrawals of any nature are free in one quarter, thereafter you pay 50p per withdrawal. So if you have a large number of small amounts to withdraw then making three withdrawals as lump sum transfers to your current account and paying your bills by cheque, standing order or direct debit from that source is probably best.

The Cooperative Bank's *Cheque and Save Account* allows as many transactions as you wish but imposes a fixed monthly administration charge (£3 at the start of 1987).

Special services

Some banks have identified those over 55 years as a distinct market group and offer services which may be available elsewhere although not as a tailored package. Some of the benefits include loans of £2000–£10,000 for home improvement on a mortgage interest repayment only basis. Examples of services to those who are 55 plus are:

(a) *A New Beginning* from the Midland Bank which provides plenty of encapsulated sound advice on retirement generally.
(b) *The Golden Years Club* at the Bank of Ireland which requires a minimum balance of £500. This pays interest at a higher rate than an ordinary deposit account and gives free banking on a current account even if that goes into debit. Travellers cheques can also be obtained commission-free which saves about 1% which is charged on the value of your cheques. Withdrawals may be made on demand but you lose all the benefits if your balance falls below £500 and your account will be treated as a normal deposit account.

Credit cards

Sensibly used, credit cards are convenient and reduce the necessity for carrying large sums of money. They are best used by the customer who settles the entire sum outstanding each month. This gives you free credit. Once you start paying interest it is a very costly method of borrowing money, as 2% per month works out at a rate of 26.8% per annum.

BANK DEPOSITS

Banks display the current rates of interest in their branches, and most of them are also given on the financial pages of national newspapers. However, changes in the bank rate, which means changes in the interest paid on deposits, are always well publicised. All banks offer deposit facilities and you can choose to have:
- a deposit account
- a term deposit account
- an offshore account

Ordinary deposit accounts

Minimum deposit/balance	£1
Access	Immediate or 7 days' notice for withdrawal without loss of interest
Interest	Modest. Paid half-yearly

This type of account is ideal for holding small sums for use when there are unexpected demands on the current account. Money can then be transferred fairly quickly to avoid an overdraft situation.

Term deposit accounts

Minimum deposit	Usually £2500
Access	Money is deposited for a fixed term of, e.g. 1, 3 or 6 months or 1 year.
Interest	The rate will be fixed for the term of your investment and will vary according to the length of the term.

This type of account could be good or bad, depending on whether interest rates generally rise or fall. If you think the rates will go down and you are offered nominal rates of 7.13% for one month, 7.81% for three, 7.88% for six and 8.06% for twelve months, then you will probably elect the final offer. But if the reverse is likely, it may be wise to commit your money for only one month, taking lower interest in the short term and reserving the option to take advantage of any rises.

If you have at least £10,000 to deposit, there is more flexibility and you can receive fixed interest for any period from seven days to five years. Alternatively the interest rate may be adjusted in line with the money market at a notice period specified by you varying from one week to six months. For substantial sums of £100,000 or more you may be able to negotiate better interest rates with the bank manager.

Offshore accounts

Most banks, including all the major ones (Barclays, Lloyds, Midland and Nat West), have offices in the Channel Islands and/or the Isle of Man where interest on deposits is paid before deduction of composite rate tax. Such accounts provide a refuge for the non-taxpayer but if you are liable for tax the income should be declared in your tax return. The variety of accounts available is similar to those on the mainland but the best rates of interest are paid on higher deposits of £10,000 or more. It would not really be worthwhile placing less than £2000 in any offshore account.

BUILDING SOCIETY DEPOSITS

There is enormous variation in the rates, conditions and terms relating to building society deposits. Some of the smaller societies frequently offer higher rates than the giants with no greater risk to your money. However, the conditions for withdrawal may involve loss of interest. For example, a society offering 10% pa but which demands three months' notice of a withdrawal and stipulates that no interest will be paid during those three months, would be giving only 7.5% interest on a 12-month investment in the year of withdrawal. Free advice on all aspects of building society deposits may be obtained from **The Building Society Shop** (see page 142). There are a number of types of account available from building societies including:
- a deposit account
- an ordinary share account
- term shares
- a fixed term, fixed interest account
- notice accounts
- regular savings accounts
- an expatriate account.

Deposit accounts

Minimum deposit   £1

Access   Instant

Interest   Normally credited annually.

Now little used by individual savers because interest rates are unexciting, the advantage of this account is that, if the society runs into financial difficulty, the depositor has priority over other customers and is assured of getting his money back. But this is a remote possibility these days.

Ordinary share accounts

Minimum deposit   £1

Access   Instant

Interest   Credited either half-yearly or annually

This is ideal for smaller sums of money as you can pay in and draw out whenever you choose.

Premium interest accounts

Minimum deposit   Normally between £100 and £250

Access   Instant

Interest   Higher than the ordinary share account. May be credited monthly, quarterly, half-yearly or annually.

A development of the ordinary share account but, for the advantage of higher interest, requires a minimum level of deposit to be maintained.

Term shares

Minimum deposit   £500 with some societies; higher with others

Access   Conditions vary for fixed terms of 1–5 years

Interest   There is generally a guaranteed premium of 2.25–4% above the *ordinary share account* rate.

This pays a higher rate of interest than any other building society account.

Fixed term, fixed interest accounts

Minimum deposit   £500–£2000

Access   Access to your money is possible only at the end of the agreed period which is usually 6 months or 1 year.

Interest   The rate is guaranteed for the agreed term of 6 months or 1 year.

Notice accounts

Minimum deposit   Usually £500; higher with some societies

Access   7 days' to 6 months' notice required for withdrawal. Immediate access is possible with loss of interest on the sum withdrawn.

Interest   The interest rate is determined by the length of the notice period; the longer this period is the higher the rate will be.

Regular savings accounts

Minimum deposit   From £1 per month, but more usually around £50

Access   Instant, but varying conditions offered by individual societies

Interest   Higher than ordinary share accounts, usually credited half-yearly or annually

These accounts require a commitment to regular monthly deposits. Some societies will allow one or two withdrawals a year to be made without affecting the status of the account. Others will allow only total withdrawal, thus closing the account.

Expatriate accounts

The interest rates for these accounts are often better than those on *offshore accounts*. It is intended for those who are no longer resident in the UK and to whom interest may be paid without the deduction of tax, a declaration confirming non-resident status in the UK and stating the actual place of residence has to be made in order for exemption to be possible.

NATIONAL SAVINGS

National Savings are not only suitable for those on comparatively low incomes, but as there are a number of schemes where the returns are completely tax-free they are well worth considering by even the highest income earners. Most schemes have various attractions for small savers and those on low incomes can avoid taxation altogether with the investment account. The interest on the investment account, income bonds, indexed-income bonds and deposit bonds is paid gross so that you will pay tax only if your income exceeds the allowances that may be set against it.

> ## WATCHING BRIEF
>
> National Savings make it easy for you to take an interest in your savings with a 24-hour Ansafone service in addition to the announcements made in newspapers of changes that are made from time to time. The Ansafone numbers are:
>
> | | |
> |---|---|
> | Southern England | 01-605 9483/9484 |
> | Northern England | 0253 723714 |
> | Scotland | 041-632 2766 |

The schemes that are available are:

- an investment account ⎫
- an ordinary account   ⎪
- income bonds   ⎬ taxable saving
- indexed income bonds   ⎪
- deposit bonds   ⎭

- savings certificates   ⎫
- index-linked certificates ⎬ tax-free savings
- yearly plan   ⎭

- premium bonds   tax free prizes

Taxable savings

Investment account

Minimum deposit £5 (maximum £100,000)

Access 1 month's notice for withdrawal. No penalties. Payment by warrant to be cashed through a bank or Post Office.

INSTANT ACCESS AND DEPOSIT ACCOUNTS 131

Interest — Variable. Interest is calculated on a daily basis and is credited gross annually on 31 December. If the interest earned pushes your total above the maximum, you may still keep it in the account.

An account can be opened at any Post Office.

Ordinary account

Minimum deposit — £1 (maximum £10,000)

Access — Up to £100 may be withdrawn on demand from any Post Office; up to £250 on demand from a named Post Office by which you are regarded as a *regular customer*. Larger amounts may be withdrawn by warrant with only a few days' notice.

Interest — Lower than an investment account. There are two fixed rates depending on the amount deposited (in 1987 these are 3% and 6% pa). Interest is credited annually on 31 December and is paid on each whole pound deposited for a complete calendar month. The first £70 (£140 for a joint account) of interest is tax free each year.

The interest rates are normally announced in November and are fixed for the following year starting on 1 January. However, while the

The graph illustrates the disproportionate effect that a short term withdrawal to below the £500 level has on the interest earned over a longer period. It assumes that £20 is taken out of the account in the last week of February and restored in the first week of March.

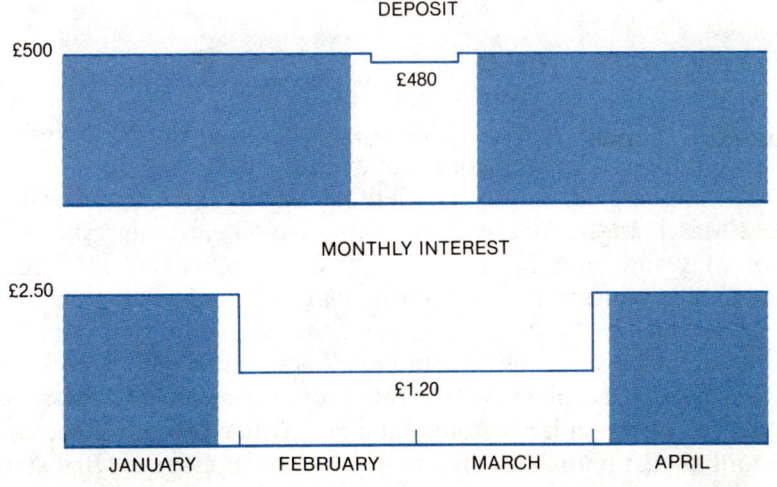

INVESTMENT ACCOUNT VS ORDINARY ACCOUNT

How valuable is the tax exemption for the first £70 earned in an ordinary account? At the beginning of 1987 the investment account variable interest rate was 11.75% against the 6% fixed top rate for the ordinary account. If £1000 were deposited in each by people liable for basic rate tax then, assuming no change in the investment account rate, the net value of both deposits by the end of the year would be as shown in the table below. The investment account interest rate would have to be 3.5% lower for the net interest to equal that of the ordinary account. The discrepancy between the accounts widens if the interest on the ordinary account exceeds £70 (at an interest rate of 6%, you would exceed this with £1166) and the net results on deposits of £2000 are:

Investment account   £2171.55
Ordinary account   £2106.50

So although the ordinary account may be convenient, the investment account gives a better return on your money.

Comparative performance of an ordinary deposit account vs an investment account.

Account	Deposit (£)	Interest (£)	Interest (%)	Tax (£)	Net balance (£)
Ordinary	1000	60.00	6	Nil	1060.00
Investment	1000	117.50	11.75	31.72	1085.78
		82.50	8.25	22.27	1060.23

government is committed to this rate for the 12 months there is no obligation for you to keep your money in the account.

As interest is paid only on complete calendar months, a deposit made on 14 March and withdrawn on 28 July would earn interest only for April, May and June. In order to receive the higher rate you need to have an account for a complete calendar year and the higher rate is then paid for each complete calendar month in which there is a minimum balance of £500 (see p. 138). Otherwise you will receive the lower rate. So December is the ideal month for your first deposit.

To become a regular customer at a Post Office you need to hold an account at that branch for six months before applying for that status.

This allows you to withdraw up to £250 without surrendering your account book temporarily. Otherwise the book must be surrendered temporarily for any withdrawal of more than £50.

You can also pay regular standing orders at no charge but you have to keep sufficient money in the account to cover the following month's payments. Bills for items such as electricity, rates, road fund tax and TV licence up to a total of £250 may be paid directly through the account by filling in a withdrawal form for the appropriate amount and handing it over at the Post Office with the bills and your bank book, which will be returned to you.

Income bonds

Minimum deposit	£2000 (maximum £100,000) multiples of £1000
Access	3 months' notice. Withdrawals in multiples of £1000 with a minimum of £1000.
Interest	Rates variable at 6 weeks' notice. Credited on the fifth day of each month and paid on the nearest working day, the interest begins immediately the deposit is received. At the start of 1987 the interest rate was 12.25% which on £5000 would yield an annual income of £612.50 paid at about £50 a month.

Available from Post Offices, these can give you an income yet preserve your capital, but although paid gross this income is liable for tax. Hence, for the non-taxpayer income bonds are particularly attractive, although they may also be attractive to the standard rate taxpayer in search of a regular income. Payment is made either directly into your bank, building society or National Savings bank account or by crossed warrant. Warrants up to £50 can be cashed at a Post Office. The full rate of interest is paid only after one year, and only half the rate from date of purchase to date of repayment is paid if you cash it in earlier. A deduction will be made from the capital returned to you to compensate for payments you will have received less the interest earned.

Indexed-income bonds

Minimum deposit	£5000 (+ multiples of £1000 to a maximum of £100,000)
Access	3 months' notice with no loss of interest after 1 year. If held for less than 12 months, half the interest between the date of purchase and the date of repayment is lost.

Interest	8% for the first year. Rates are then adjusted each year to match the increase in the retail prices index, and the new rates are guaranteed for the whole year to which they apply. The taxable interest is paid gross on the 20th day of each month and is calculated from the day of deposit.

Introduced in 1985 to give inflation-proofed income over a period of 10 years, the interest starts at 8% and it is that that is inflation-proofed rather than the capital. So when you cash your bonds you will get back only the amount that you put in.

The Government may withdraw an issue from sale at any time and bring out a new one with a revised initial interest rate. All subsequent adjustments for inflation will be based on that. If you already hold the maximum, you have to cash in at least some to buy into a new issue but you may also hold £100,000 worth of ordinary income bonds.

This may be appropriate only for those for whom a secured income is the overriding consideration.

Deposit bonds

Minimum deposit	£100 (in multiples of £50 up to a maximum £100,000 which may be exceeded by the addition of interest)
Access	3 months' notice for withdrawal of a minimum of £50. If repaid within 12 months of purchase only half the interest for the relevant period is received.
Interest	Rates may vary at 6 weeks' notice. At the start of 1987 it was 12.25%. The taxable gross interest is added to the capital 12 months after purchase.

These are available from any Post Office and if you wish to go for deposit bonds, do so only with the intention of leaving your money there for a considerable period. On each anniversary of purchase, and after a part repayment, the Deposit Bond Office will send you a certificate showing the current value of the bond. This should be included with your application for repayment which should be made at the Post Office.

Tax-free savings

Savings certificates (32nd issue)

Minimum deposit	£25 (maximum £1000 per issue)

Access   You can cash them at any time with 8 working days' notice but if you do so in the year of purchase you simply get your money back.

Interest   Tax free. Rate guaranteed and compounded over 5 years. The 32nd Issue, current early in 1987, will pay 8.75% compound interest over 5 years.

These are ideal for the long term saver and to secure maximum benefit you need to hold them for a minimum of 5 years. The increasing scale of interest is an inducement to hold for the full term.

In order to keep the interest rates in line, new certificates are issued from time to time and sale of the earlier ones is stopped. You cannot transfer earlier issues to the new ones so if the new interest rate is an improvement, you need to judge whether it is worth cashing in what you hold and starting again, or to leave your certificates to mature and use further capital to buy the new issue. If you wish to hold on to the certificates after five years you will earn further tax-free interest at the *general extension rate* which is varied in order to keep it competitive.

Example £5000 worth of 32nd Issue certificates bought in 1987 will pay £2605 interest in 1992 at 8.75% compounded over five years. The table below shows the gross yield that tax payers in the various tax bands would have had to achieve to match the tax-free £2605 and the percentage gain this would represent on a £5000 investment. While this

The gross income equivalent to a net of £2600 according to the tax band.

Rate of tax (%)	Gross equivalent (£)	% gain over 5 years
Nil	2606	52.1
27	3570	71.4
40	4343	86.9
45	4738	94.8
50	5212	104.2
55	5791	115.8
60	6515	130.3

form of saving becomes more favourable with increasing rate of tax, for the non-taxpayer the investment account may be better. Assuming it averages 11% interest over the five years, the £5000 would grow to £8425 in the time the certificates become worth £7606.

USING SAVINGS CERTIFICATES TO DERIVE AN ANNUAL INCOME

Mr Jones bought 200 certificates of the 32nd Issue at £25 each and planned to take a regular amount from these every year and yet have his original capital at the end of 5 years. The income he can receive is about £400 a year which requires him to sell his certificates as shown in the table below. However, the value of his capital is reduced by inflation. (The 32nd Issue of certificates was withdrawn in the first half of 1987 and replaced by the 33rd Issue which imposes a purchase ceiling of £1000. However, those holding the 32nd or any earlier issue certificates are entitled to re-invest up to £5000 of them in the new issue making a maximum holding of £6000 at a compound rate of 7% if held for five years.)

The effect on capital of using savings certificates to derive an income

End of year	Interest (%)	Value per certificate (£)	Certificates cashed		Balance	
			No.	Value (£)	No.	(£)
0						5000.00
1	6.52	26.63	16	426.08	184	4899.92
2	7.51	28.63	15	429.45	169	4838.47
3	8.66	31.11	14	435.54	155	4822.05
4	9.90	34.19	13	444.47	142	4854.98
5	11.23	38.03	11	418.33	131	4981.93

Taxable income needed to match tax-free yield of certificates.

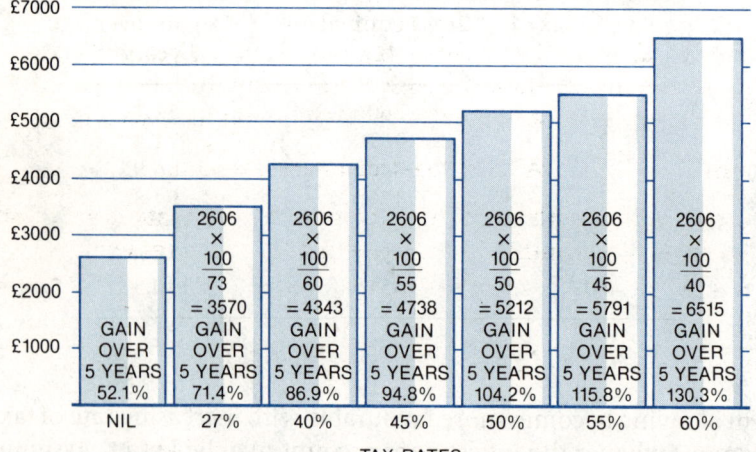

Index-linked certificates

Minimum deposit — £25 units (maximum £5000)

Access — 8 working days. You can cash these within the first 12 months at the original purchase price by applying to most banks or Post Offices.

Interest — Modest compound tax-free interest is paid and, linked to the Retail Prices Index, your capital is protected against inflation. At the beginning of 1987 the interest was equivalent to 4.04% compounded over 5 years. This means that on £5000, if there was no inflation, you would get back your original capital plus tax-free interest of £1095. With inflation, your capital will be increased in line with RPI and the interest will also be greater because it will be based on a larger capital value. After 5 years inflation-proofing continues and interest will be paid at variable rates.

Available from most Post Offices and banks, originally these 'Granny Bonds' could be bought only by older people, but that restriction no longer applies.

Yearly/Plan

This scheme allows you to buy a certificate over 12 months by standing order instalments.

Minimum deposit — £20 per month (in multiples of £5 to maximum of £200 per month) by standing order

Access — Payment by warrant 14 days after application. You may cancel your standing order in the first year and receive back what you have paid in.

Interest — A fixed tax-free interest is paid.

The rate varies with the length of time a certificate is held, and is calculated on a monthly basis. Early in 1987 the rates were:

Year	1	2	3	4	5
Rate	6	6.64	7.56	7.68	8.84

The variable general extension rate applies after 5 years.
In 1987, a certificate costing £2400 would be worth £3530.10 at the end of five years.

Tax-free prizes

Premium bonds

Minimum deposit £10 (maximum £10,000 in multiples of £5)

Access At least 8 working days

Interest None

National Savings premium bonds are really a gamble because the only way to avoid a fall in the value of the money you spend on them is for Ernie (Electronic Random Number Indicator Equipment) to draw your number. It is for fun only, for money that you do not need to provide income for you and that you can afford to allow to depreciate.

If you do not buy any premium bonds you will certainly not win the monthly £250,000 jackpot or any of the other prizes ranging from £100,000 down to £50. However, there are no rules or formulae to apply to luck which is the sole determining factor for these bonds. If you had bought £100 worth of bonds in 1975, you would have needed to have won £250 in prizes in the following ten years just to stay even with inflation. If you had not had a win at all, your £100 would by 1985 have been worth less than £37.

Comparative yields from various forms of National Savings over an identical 12-month period.

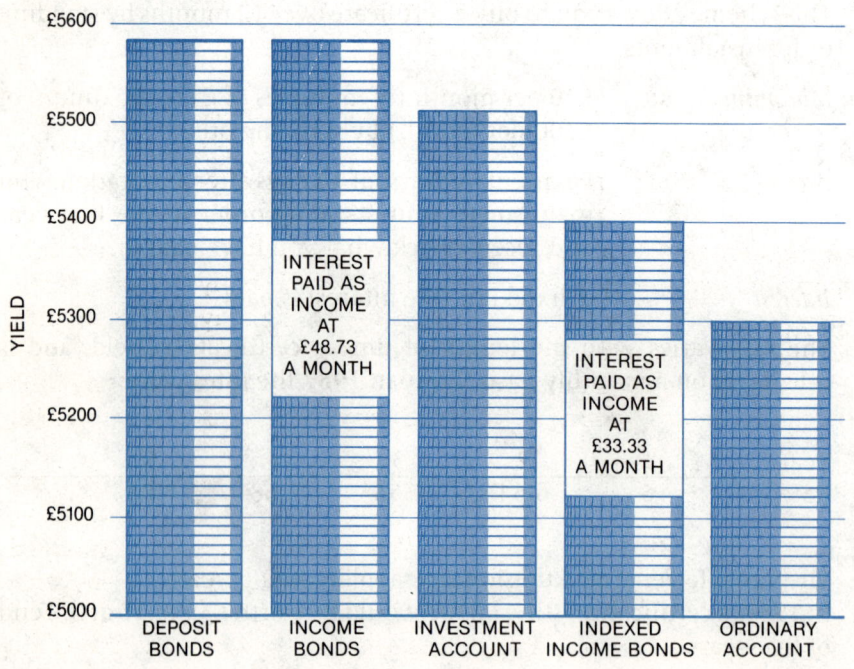

INSTANT ACCESS AND DEPOSIT ACCOUNTS

Premium bonds may be bought at most Post Offices or banks and can be cashed through the same sources. Although sales are in multiples of £5, each £1 gives you one chance in every draw once they have been held for at least three calendar months. All prize money is tax free. The figure on p. 138 shows the comparative yields from the various forms of National Savings over an identical 12 month period. Deposits that offer increasing benefits for longer term holding have been excluded from this analysis.

OTHER TYPES OF DEPOSITS

Deposit facilities are also offered by:
- Local Authorities
- Insurance companies
- Money funds
- Deposit funds.

Local Authority bonds

Minimum deposit Most authorities require £500 although one or two may accept £250.

Access Money is deposited for a fixed term of 1–10 years and may not be retrieved before expiry without penalty.

Interest The rates are competitively fixed for the term of your deposit, and generally the longer the term the higher the rate. Interest is paid net and normally half-yearly.

Although some local authorities seem to be in a precarious financial position, any money you lend to them is protected by the law conferring trustee security status to such loans. Their repayment is the first charge on local rates. This is an attractive form of saving for those seeking a reliable, steady income with the usual caveat about the declining value of your capital in real terms so long as inflation is with us.

A list of authorities offering savings bonds can be obtained from the **Chartered Institute of Public Finance and Accountancy (CIPFA)** (see page 142) for a fee of £2.50. By writing to them enclosing a stamped addressed envelope of not less than 9 × 4 inches, you will receive a list of those currently seeking loans giving the terms and rates of interest applicable.

IS THE INTEREST WHAT YOU THINK IT IS?

When you decide to place savings on deposit, apart from considering the level of interest on offer you should also think about:
- How long you have to leave the cash on deposit to gain the full interest
- How frequently interest is paid, or added to the deposit
- Whether the interest rate is fixed or variable. If variable, is there any penalty if you want to get your money out quickly to invest elsewhere on better terms?
- Are you paying tax unnecessarily?

Compounded Annual Rates (CARs) and Composite Rate Tax (CRT) can greatly affect your savings, sometimes unnecessarily so.

The effect of Compounded Annual Rate (CAR) on your income

The true return on a deposit is related to the number of times in the year that interest is calculated and added to the original capital to increase its earning capacity. If one deposit yields 6% per annum with interest added annually, while another pays 6% per annum with interest calculated half yearly, then the second will be paying more interest. What you will get will be 3% after the first six months and a further 3% on your capital including the first six months' interest, at the end of the year. This is a CAR of 6.09%.

Example

Mr Andrews has £10,000 to invest and has the choice of four investment homes each offering 6% pa interest. However, one makes the interest calculation monthly, the second quarterly, the third half yearly and the fourth annually. The table opposite shows what he ends up with after 1 year.

Composite Rate Tax (CRT)

This tax is levied on interest from deposits in places such as banks and building societies. It is deducted before the interest is paid out or reinvested in the account, and you cannot recover it, even if your gross income (including the tax) is less than your personal allowance. This makes the collection of tax simpler for the authorities but whether this is a just system may be debatable. Certainly it is hard on those with low

	£10,000 invested at 6% pa with interest (£) calculated			
Month	Monthly	Quarterly	Half-yearly	Annually
January	50.00			
February	50.25			
March	50.50	150.00		
April	50.75			
May	51.00			
June	51.26	152.25	300.00	
July	51.52			
August	51.78			
September	52.04	154.53		
October	52.29			
November	52.26			
December	52.82	156.85	309.00	600.00
Total	616.77	613.63	609.00	600.00

incomes and their choice of a suitable deposit is restricted to National Savings where interest is still paid gross. However, it is a slight bonus for those who pay tax. Once CRT has been deducted the tax is deemed to have been paid at the standard rate, although the actual rate of CRT is less than the standard rate, and from April 1987 it is 24.75%.

Financial magazines, such as *Money Management*, *Planned Savings* and *The Savings Market*, and the financial pages of newspapers may show you where the best return for money on deposit may be achieved. Banks, building societies, National Savings, local authority bond and other deposits are covered to show not only the nominal rate of interest but the annual percentage rate net for taxpayers in the various bands.

Shopping around

Some people have a loyalty to their bank or building society and will not consider changing. However, the world of finance is increasingly competitive as the demarcation lines between the various institutions become more blurred. As banks expand their mortgage business and as building societies secure the right to lend to borrowers for other than the purpose of house purchase or improvement, you may like to shop around for the best terms possible.

Insurance companies income bonds

Access — Your capital will be returned at the end of a fixed period. Surrender terms are not generous and it is expensive to get out early.

Interest — Income bonds provide a guaranteed level of income for the fixed period and your original capital may then be repaid or, if you wish, used to purchase an annuity. (Normally the cash option is better.)

Insurance companies offer bonds on either:
(a) a single premium endowment policy, the guaranteed bonus additions being used to provide the income which is free of tax to the basic rate taxpayer, or
(b) a series of single premium policies which are cashed throughout the term of the bond.

This form of income raising will be more attractive to the person paying basic rate tax than to one paying a higher tax rate. It is worth consulting a good insurance broker or financial adviser.

Money and deposit funds

Deposit facilities are also offered by secondary banks and finance houses dealing in hire purchase. These usually give a slightly better rate of interest because their lending rates to borrowers are also higher. However, they also accept a greater degree of risk in their business as will you if you use them.

USEFUL ADDRESSES

The Building Society Shop
Advanced Business Centre
Maid Marian Way
Nottingham NG1 6BH
☏ 0602 472595

CIPFA Sterling
65 London Wall
London EC2M 5TU
☏ 01-638 6361

Investments

STOCKS AND SHARES	145
Types of shares	147
How do you buy shares?	147
How much money is needed?	148
How do share values grow?	152
Keeping track of share values	152
Selecting your shares	154
GILTS	154
Types of gilts	155
How to buy and sell gilts	155
How does the value of gilts change?	156
Keeping track of the value of gilts	157
Tax advantages	157
Risks	158
UNIT TRUSTS	159
Types of trust	159
How to buy and sell	160
How does the value of unit trusts change?	162
Monitoring performance	162
Taxation	163
Risks	163
Further information sources	166

INVESTMENT TRUSTS 166
Split capital trusts 166
Buying and selling shares 167
How does the value of shares change? 168
Monitoring performance 168
Tax 168
Further information 168

PERSONAL EQUITY PLANS 169
Types of schemes 169
Buying and selling 169
Tax benefits 170
Risks 170
Choosing a plan 171

HIGH RISK INVESTMENTS 171
Traded options 171
Unlisted Securities Market (USM) 172
Third market 172
'Over the counter' market 172

OTHER TYPES OF INVESTMENTS 172
USEFUL ADDRESSES 173
GLOSSARY OF TERMS 173
BIBLIOGRAPHY 177

The philosophy behind investments and how to approach them has already been covered in the chapter *Managing your Money* (page 95). This chapter explains in further detail the types of investment available.

When forming an investment plan it is vital to consider the risks involved in the investments as well as their potential rewards. The table below summarises these risks which are discussed further in the individual sections below.

Conventional and specialist investments.

Conventional	Specialist
• Stocks and shares	• Commodities
• Unit trusts	• Financial futures
• Investment trusts	• Traded share options
• Gilts	• Unlisted securities market
• Whole-of-life assurance investment bonds	• Third market shares

STOCKS AND SHARES

In the early 1980s the private investor on the Stock Exchange was widely regarded as a dying breed, and in 1983 it was estimated that about two million people owned 25% of all shares in British companies compared with 54% twenty years earlier. Yet in 1987 it is estimated that the number of private shareholders in Britain is now eight million. This increase may be put down to three main factors:
- The privatisation by the government of industries such as British Telecom and British Gas
- The 'Big Bang' or deregulation of the Stock Exchange in the autumn of 1986 which reduced stockbrokers' commissions on larger deals and encouraged them to actively look for new private customers
- The increasing trend for companies to reward staff with shares or the option to buy shares in their own company at advantageous rates.

Now small investors, even the 'safety first' investors, are interested in Stock Exchange investments. A recent survey showed that more than 50% of those with investments in British Telecom thought their money

THE STOCK EXCHANGE

How the Stock Exchange works

The Stock Exchange is the market place in which stockbrokers buy and sell shares of publicly-owned companies for clients at the best price they can get. The prices are fixed by the *market makers*, previously known as *jobbers* until the Big Bang, and they deal only with stockbrokers. Technically there is now only one type of member of the Stock Exchange, the broker/dealer who can register with the Stock Exchange to be a market maker or a broker. Both operate under strict codes of practice and even if they work for the same stockbroking company there is a requirement for secrecy between the two departments to protect investors.

There are 356 stockbroking firms whose broking staff are entitled to trade in the shares of *public limited companies*. These are paid by commission charged to both the purchaser and the seller.

How big is the Stock Exchange?

In 1986 there were 2685 companies listed with the Stock Exchange and most of the share prices are quoted daily in *The Financial Times*. Other papers print selected lists of companies. In order to be listed, a company must have a five-year trading record, provide the Exchange with a great deal of detailed financial information and agree to continue to provide all information in future which might affect the share price.

Another major listing of companies is the Unlisted Securities Market. Companies can apply to join this listing with only a three year trading record and need to provide rather less financial information.

The sizes of the stock markets at the end of 1986.

Market	Total share value (km)	Number of companies			
		Quoted	New	Removed	Promoted
Full listing:					
UK	320,671	2,101	136		
Irish	3,389	72	0		
Overseas	818,962	512	36		
Total	1,143,022	2,685	172	69	—
Unlisted	4,900	368	94	4	28*

*Promoted to full listing

was as safe as if it were in a building society, but Stock Exchange investments are fundamentally *risk* investments, which means that in theory you could lose everything you have invested.

Types of shares

There are two main categories of non-government shares, ordinary and preference shares.

Ordinary shares

Ordinary shares are often referred to as *equities* and ownership of these makes you a part-owner of the company concerned. As such you are financially liable to the limit of your shareholding and you will share in any profits. If the company has a poor year the dividend may be reduced or even abandoned and if it goes into liquidation then the assets are used to pay, in preference order:
- The Inland Revenue and customs
- *debenture* holders and owners of *preference shares*
- trade creditors

Preference shares, debentures and convertible loan stock

Such investments in companies receive a fixed rate of interest *provided* the company makes a sufficient profit to pay. Debenture trustees also have the power to sell off some of the company assets in order to do this. Preference shareholders may not necessarily get the interest promised each year, but if the company is unable to pay one year the interest may be added on to the payment due the following year.

The price for such shares depends on the level of interest rates generally. If other interest rates are high the demand for fixed interest stocks may be depressed, but if interest rates fall their relative value will rise and it is possible to make a capital gain by selling them.

How do you buy shares?

Most people who bought shares in British Telecom, TSB or British Gas will have simply filled in a coupon and sent off a cheque. Normally you need to buy or sell through a bank or stockbroker.

Banks

Most banks have an investment advisory service for customers. Your manager will put you in touch with them if you require investment advice. Straightforward buying and selling of shares can be done by giving your instructions over the counter or by phone. The transaction will be carried out the same day. However, as the bank is an intermediary this is likely to be more expensive than going to a broker direct.

Stockbroker

You can register directly with a stockbroker who will offer services ranging from simply carrying out your buying and selling instructions to a full advisory and discretionary management service for sufficiently high sums. Few brokers are interested in small transactions, although several made special arrangements to handle one-off sales of some of the recently privatised companies. This is the cheapest and quickest way of buying and selling shares and with the new computerised trading techniques your deals can be done within minutes of your picking up the phone, with settlement required 10 days after the end of the Stock Exchange account.

Finding a broker Several stockbrokers have a network of regional offices and a list of brokers interested in taking on private clients may be obtained by writing to **The Public Affairs Department** (see page 173).

How much money is needed?

Investment levels

Brokers offer three main types of service, each of which has a minimum requirement (see table below).

The average requirement for brokerage services.

Service	Average
Execution only	£10,000
Portfolio advice	£25,000
Discretionary	£25,000

Execution-only service You decide when to buy and sell shares, and telephone your instructions. You may ask your broker to buy or sell at the best possible price, or only at a set price or better. A broker will take a holding instruction to sell or buy at some time in the future when a pre-set price is reached.

Portfolio advisory service Knowing the details of your financial situation and your investment objectives your broker will offer advice and make some recommendations. You then have to give instructions and approve all investment decisions.

Discretionary service Once again the broker will consult you about your objectives and your financial situation, but control on the investment

A typical contract note.

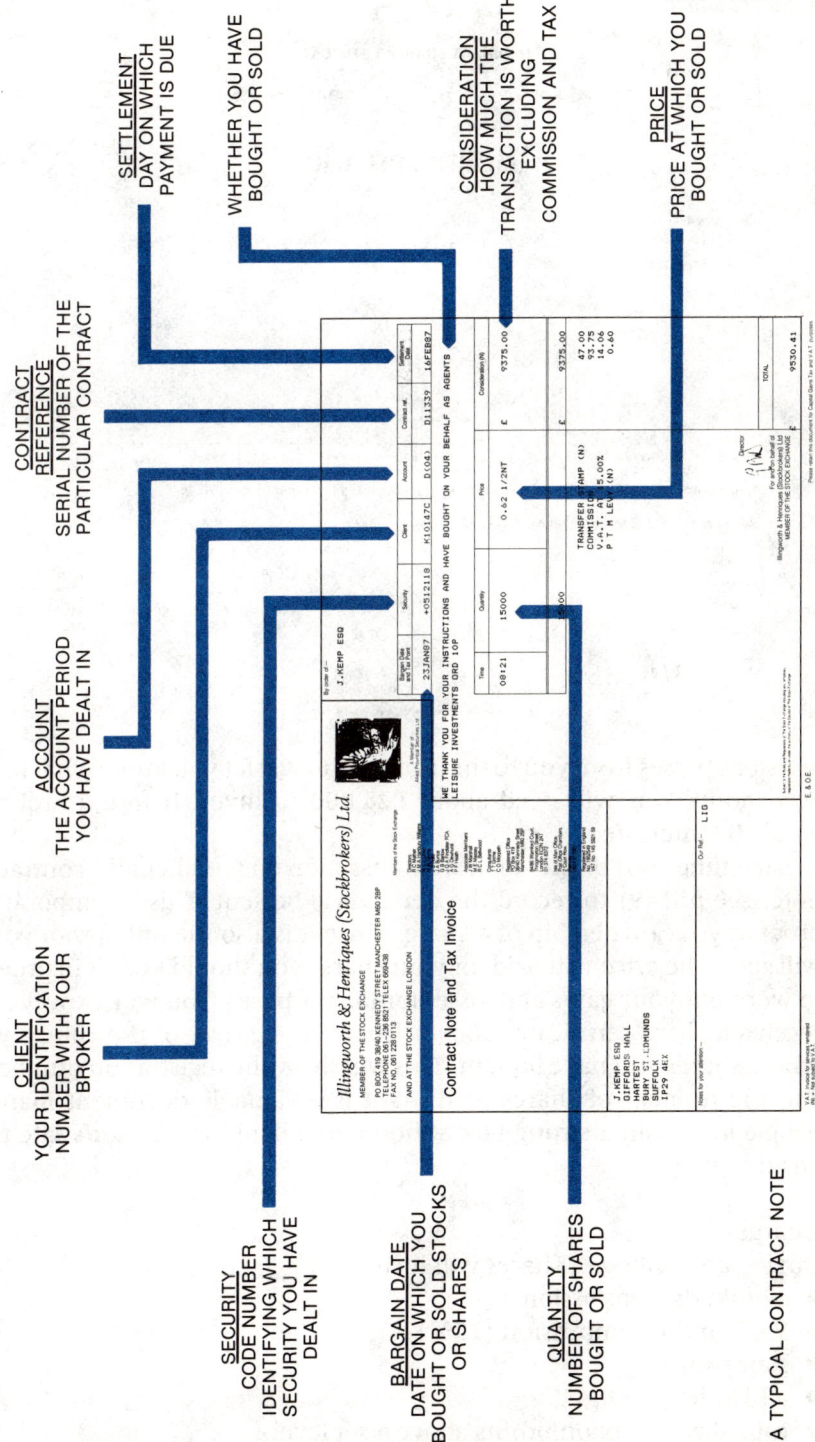

A TYPICAL CONTRACT NOTE

A typical share certificate.

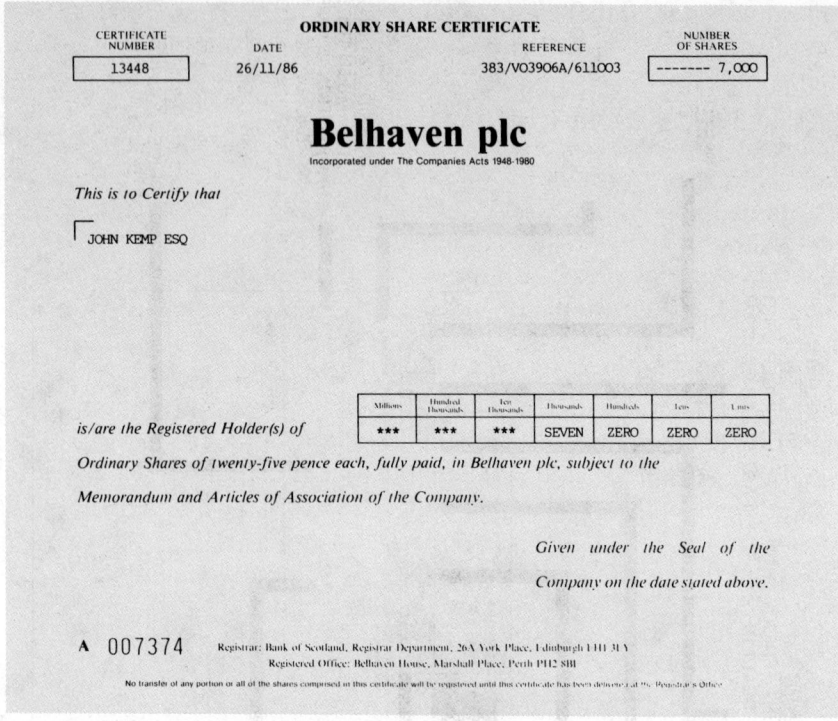

decisions passes from you to the broker who will let you know what has been done. You will need about £25,000 to invest before a broker would be interested.

Each time your broker makes a transaction on your behalf a contract note (see p. 149) to record the details will be sent. This is temporary proof of your ownership of a share. Since it is also the only proof you will get of the price you paid for your shares you should keep it in order to work out your gains and losses for tax purposes. You will, however, receive a share certificate (above) from the registrar of the company whose shares you have bought. This will show the registration number and the number of shares held. As it is a valuable document many people keep it in a strong box at home or a bank or solicitor's safe to ensure safety.

Charges
Buying and selling of shares will incur:
- a broker's commission
- VAT on the commission (15%)
- stamp duty
- a PTM levy
- capital gains tax on profits above a set level.

The broker's commission Although fixed commission charges were abolished as part of the 'Big Bang', most smaller investors will find the commission charges are around 1.5–1.65% on transactions under £7000 and about 1.25–1.5% on larger transactions.

Stamp duty This is levied only on purchases and was reduced to $\frac{1}{2}$% by the Government at the time of 'Big Bang'. Where it exceeds £3, it may be rounded up to the nearest pound.

The PTM levy This finances the work of the Panel on Takeovers and Mergers and is paid at a flat rate of 60p on all transactions which exceed £5000.

Capital gains tax The capital gain or profit you make on selling a share is free of tax up to a limit of £6600 a year. Above that level you are liable to tax at a flat rate of 30%. If your total sales realise more than twice the tax-free limit, full details will be required. Any losses can be offset against the profits and there is also an inflation allowance (see *Taxation* on page 179).

THE COST OF BUYING SHARES

The greater your investment the smaller proportionally the charges you will face. Consider the purchase and sale of two transactions worth £1000 and £10,000. The charges incurred are shown in the table below.

So the charges involved in buying and selling shares are 2.4% and 1.9% on £1000 compared with 2.02% and 1.5% on £10,000.

Charges incurred on buying and selling shares at £1000 and £10,000.

	Value of transactions (£)			
	£1,000		£10,000	
Charges	Buying	Selling	Buying	Selling
Commission (1.65% up to £7000; 0.55% above £7000)	16.50	16.50	132.00	132.00
VAT on commission (15%)	2.47	2.47	19.80	19.80
Stamp duty	5.00		50.00	
PTM levy	Nil		0.60	0.60
Total	23.97	18.97	202.40	152.40

How do share values grow?

Shares can increase your assets by:
(a) the payment of dividends
(b) increasing in value.

Dividends
Dividends have to be approved by the shareholders at an annual meeting and are usually paid twice a year as an *interim dividend* paid halfway through the company's financial year and as a *final dividend* paid at the end of the trading year. Compared with a building society or National Savings these are usually modest and it is not uncommon for a dividend to be little more than 2% or 3% per year after tax.

Increases in the capital value
An investment in *ordinary* shares is unprotected so the value of your investment can go up and down on a daily basis. This is both the attraction and the danger of share ownership. Shares bought today for 100p per share may be selling tomorrow for 110p, a 10% profit, or 90p, a 10% loss. For this reason you should invest only money you will not have to call on at short notice.

Share perks
Some companies give their shareholders a bonus to their dividends in the form of discounts on the company's goods. Some companies find this easier than others but a wide range of perks are on offer. These are mostly in the form of discounts on hotel bills, cleaning bills, ferry travel, wines and restaurant meals. They are not in themselves a good reason to buy a particular share.

Keeping track of share values

You can keep an eye on how well or badly your shares are doing by looking at daily Stock Exchange prices published in the *Financial Times* and most of the quality daily newspapers. The various indices of share prices are given in:
- the *Financial Times* All-Share Index which covers 739 selected shares
- the *Financial Times* 30-Share Index
- the *Financial Times* Stock Exchange 100-Share Index (more commonly referred to as the FT-SE100 or 'Footsie')

Watching the main indices will give you an indication of how the Stock Market is moving in general and how your particular shares are doing by comparison. If they are beating a rising market, fine, but if they are doing worse than most enquire why and perhaps adjust your shareholding accordingly. If you have chosen shares which pay a relatively

INVESTMENTS 153

The presentation of share values in a newspaper.

GROSS YIELD
THIS IS A LITTLE MORE COMPLICATED. THE FIGURE GIVEN REPRESENTS THE DIVIDEND PAID BY A COMPANY, DIVIDED, IN TURN, BY THE SHARE PRICE AND EXPRESSED IN PERCENTAGE TERMS. IN OTHER WORDS, IT IS THE DIVIDEND EXPRESSED AS A PERCENTAGE OF THE SHARE PRICE AND PROVIDES AN ACCURATE INDICATION OF HOW MUCH A SHARE IS ACTUALLY YIELDING IN INCOME TERMS. FOR EXAMPLE: IF A COMPANY PAYS A DIVIDEND OF 10p PER SHARE AND ITS SHARE PRICE IS £1.00, THEN ITS GROSS YIELD IS 10%.

PRICE/EARNINGS RATIO
THIS IS THE SHARE PRICE DIVIDED BY THE MOST RECENT YEAR'S EARNINGS PER SHARE (THE NET RETURN EARNED BY A COMPANY DIVIDED BY THE NUMBER OF SHARES ISSUED). FOR EXAMPLE, A COMPANY WITH A QUOTED SHARE PRICE OF £1.00, WITH EARNINGS OF 10p PER SHARE, WOULD HAVE A P/E RATIO OF 10 TO 1. PRICE/EARNINGS RATIO IS A MEASURE OF THE PRICE WHICH AN INVESTOR HAS TO PAY FOR A GIVEN INCOME FROM HIS SHARES.

TYPE OF SHARE
LISTED SHARES ARE DIVIDED, FOR CONVENIENCE, INTO A NUMBER OF SECTORS – FOR EXAMPLE ENGINEERING OR ELECTRICALS, BRITISH GOVERNMENT SECURITIES OR INVESTMENT TRUSTS. SOME SECTORS – SUCH AS MINING – ARE BROKEN DOWN STILL FURTHER INTO SUB-GROUPS SUCH AS TIN, DIAMOND AND PLATINUM

1987		Company	Price		Ch'nge	Gross div p	Yld %	P/E
High	Low		Bid	Offer				
		INDUSTRIALS A - D						
329	273	AAH	326	328	..	11.1	3.4	18.4
230	163	AGB Research	217	224	+1	9.3	4.2	33.1
185	128	AIM	177	182	+2	7.9	4.4	18.3
705	573	APV	673	677	●+3	26.0	3.9	12.9
152	86	Aaronson	143	145	..	5.8	4.0	40.9
318	226	Adwest	308	312	●-5	11.8	3.8	15.7
527	372	Alexandra W wear	520	528	● ..	10.6	2.0	22.7
298	200	Alumasc	295	300	+5	8.0	2.7	19.0
453	303	Amber Ind	445	460	+10	11.9	2.6	21.0
237	63	Ang-African Fin	230	240	●+5	2.5	1.1	14.9
37	24½	Anglo Nordic	31	33	-1	..	..	43.2
248	206	Appledore	228	235	-4	8.2	3.5	13.7
76	53	Arenson	72	75	●+6	1.7	2.3	12.2
58	44	Armour	52½	54	-½	0.6	1.1	20.6
545	390	Ash & Lacey	540	550	● ..	32.9	6.0	11.7
94	37	Ashley	83	85	● ..	0.7	0.8	..
450	248	Ass Br Eng 8%	330	350	..	11.0	3.2	..
109	76	Aurora	102	104	● ..	2.4	2.3	15.1
370	226	Avis Europe	368	370	+15	10.4	2.8	20.1
597	363	Avon Rubber	567	570	+3	8.9	1.6	15.4
76	44	Ayrshire Metal	57	60	+1	0.7	1.2	68.6
199	132	BBA	195	198	●+5	3.4	1.7	24.5
263	225	BET Ord (aa)	260	264	s+4	11.6	4.4	19.0
155	80	BETEC	123	126	..	3.0	2.4	11.4

DIVIDEND
THIS TELLS YOU HOW MUCH PROFIT A COMPANY RETURNED TO ITS INVESTORS, FOR EACH SHARE THEY OWN AT THE LAST DISTRIBUTION DIVIDENDS ARE LISTED EITHER AS GROSS FIGURES (BEFORE DEDUCTION OF TAX AT THE STANDARD RATE) OR NET FIGURES (AFTER TAX HAS BEEN DEDUCTED).

PERFORMANCE RECORD
THIS COLUMN SHOWS THE HIGHEST AND THE LOWEST PRICES AT WHICH THE STOCK HAS BEEN TRADED DURING THE YEAR TO DATE

STOCK NAME
THIS COLUMN LISTS THE NAME UNDER WHICH THE STOCK IS TRADED.

PRICE
THESE COLUMNS SHOW FIRST THE 'BID' PRICE (THE PRICE TO SELLERS) AND THE 'OFFER' PRICE (TO BUYERS) AT THE END OF DAY'S TRADING. THE BLOBS SHOW SHARES ARE OFFERED EX-DIVIDEND.

PRICE MOVEMENTS
THIS COLUMN TELLS YOU HOW MUCH THE ROUGH PRICE OF A SHARE HAS RISEN OR FALLEN ON THE PREVIOUS DAY'S CLOSING PRICE. IT'S A GOOD SHORT TERM INDICATOR OF WHETHER A SHARE PRICE IS ON THE WAY UP OR DOWN.

Taken from Industrials A–D table, The Times, May 4th 1987. © Times Newspapers Ltd 1987.

high dividend they may not keep pace with the market leaders for growth.

Checking prices in the daily papers can be slightly confusing at first. *The Times* gives the purchase and sale prices of shares separately not just the mid price. This can be interpreted as shown on p. 153.

Selecting your shares

The shares available through the recent 'privatisation' issues were readily available and each was priced very conservatively, presumably to ensure success. Investors in British Telecom could have easily doubled their money by selling at the right time. TSB buyers could have made a fairly quick profit of 40–50% and although early trading in British Gas offered a profit of only 10p to 15p this represented a profit of 20–30% on the 50p partly-paid shares. This improved significantly after a few weeks. However, once you start to make your selections from the 7000 stocks and shares available to you on the Stock Market immediate success is not so certain and stock market trading should be regarded as a mid to long term investment.

GILTS

These are fixed interest stocks offered by the Government and are popular among people looking for a safe investment. These stocks offer a steady and known rate of interest and repayment of capital at a fixed date in the future.

Types of gilts

Gilts are classified as longs, mediums or shorts according to the length of time before they mature.

Type	Maturity period
Longs	Stock with a life in excess of 15 years.
Mediums	Stock with a redemption date of between 7 and 15 years ahead.
Shorts	Stocks within 7 years of redemption. As these are so close to maturity they tend to be fairly stable and their price is much closer to face value.

Sometimes stock has a variable redemption date such as 1995–98 which the Government can redeem at any time between those years; it is usual for repayments to be made later rather than sooner. There are some stocks with no redemption date at all, indeed one of them, Consols 2½%, was first issued in 1752 and is still actively traded.

Index-linked stocks
Index-linked stocks are a fairly recent introduction and are unique in having interest rates and face values linked to the cost of living. The level of return and face value are fixed on the date of issue and are increased every year in line with inflation. These are the most certain form of gilt as both your investment and the interest it earns will have the same value on redemption as at the start.

How to buy and sell gilts

Gilts can be bought either through a stockbroker or bank and the various features are shown in the table below. A limited range can also be bought through Head Post Offices. A list of stocks on offer through this source is given in *Buying Gilts on the National Savings Stock Register*, a leaflet available from the Post Office. Buying from the Post Office is cheapest but as it is a postal transaction, the actual price paid will not be known until after the event. There is, however, a maximum of £10,000 that may be invested in any one stock, though there is no limit to the total amount of stock you may hold.

Features of buying gilts from a stockbroker/bank or Post Office.

Stockbroker/Bank	Post Office
• Immediate transaction	• Postal transaction
• Known cost	• Unknown cost
• Unlimited quantity	• Limited quantity
• Net interest paid	• Gross interest paid

If you buy gilts through a stockbroker, they are registered with the Bank of England and cannot be sold through the Post Office. Similarly if you buy through the Post Office they are registered on the National Stock Register and cannot be sold by a broker, though he will be able to provide you with the necessary forms for a sale.

Costs of buying and selling
The costs incurred between sources vary and the most appropriate outlet depends on the size of your investment (see table on p. 156). For example, it would be cheaper to buy £1000 worth of gilts through the Post Office but it is better to go to a broker when dealing with £10,000 worth (see p. 156).

Charges incurred in buying and selling gilts according to source.

Charges	Broker	Post Office
Minimum	£10	10p for each £10 worth sold up to a maximum of £100 £1 for purchases up to £250
Additional	0.25% on £5000–£15,000 0.05% on £15,000 +	50p for each additional £125

Comparison of costs of buying £1000 and £10,000 worth of shares.

Investment	Post Office	Broker
£1000	£1 on £250 + 50p on each additional £125 = £3	£10
£10,000	£1 on £250 + 50p on each additional £125 = £39 Total = £40	0.25% on £10,000 = £25 + 15% VAT = £3.75 + levy = 0.60p Total = £29.35

How does the value of gilts change?

Government stocks always have a nominal value of £100 which is what the Government will pay back on the maturity date, but that is not necessarily what you will pay to buy one.

Example
If gilts are paying 10% interest a year at a time when other interest rates were higher, £100 worth of stock may be bought for a good deal less than £100 because of the unattractive interest rate. But if interest rates in general then began to fall, the gilt would become more attractive and you may be able to sell your stock for rather more than you paid, perhaps more than the face value. It also works in reverse which means timing is critical.

It is just as easy to lose money buying and selling gilts as it is to make it, so some degree of expertise is necessary and professional advice is strongly recommended. An average of nearly £1400 million worth of gilts are bought and sold on the Stock Exchange every day. As with most things on the Exchange, prices tend to move in *expectation* of a change in interest rates rather than waiting for it to happen.

In recent years, even some of the cleverest manipulators of the market who invest unit trust funds in gilts have underperformed practically every other sector and it has been a nightmare for them.

THE ART OF GILT DEALING

The classic scenario for a dealer in gilts is to buy stock when its interest rate is relatively unattractive in the expectation that the other rates will fall thus making the gilt become more attractive. The dealer can then sell the stock and invest in other forms of interest-paying investment until interest rates rise to depress the price of gilts. The cycle can then be repeated. You can think of it rather like a see-saw. When interest rates generally go up then the price of gilts goes down. When the rates fall again the price of gilts goes up.

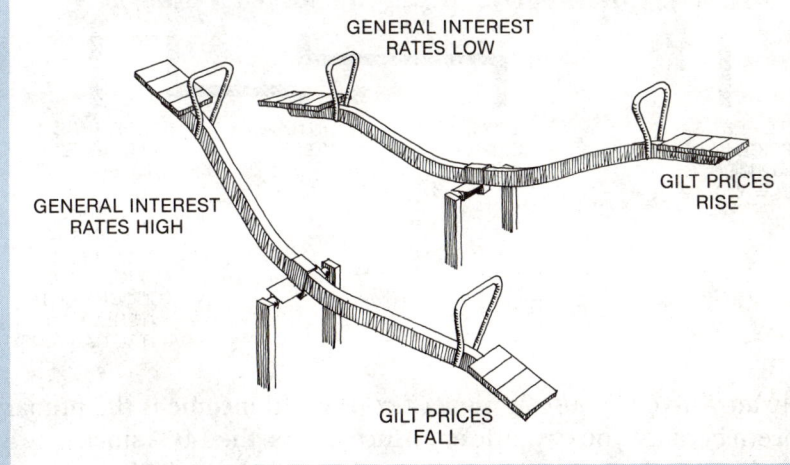

Keeping track of the value of gilts

The value of gilts may be found on the financial pages of a newspaper under *British Funds* with a typical entry such as that shown on p. 158. (Tradition dictates that the pound is split into fractions rather than pence.) With this stock it would have been best to buy at £92 and sell it at £98 or even £107.

Tax advantages

Interest payments on gilts are subject to income tax in the same way as any other income, but any capital gain on gilts is free of tax. So with a range of stock available including Treasury 10pc 1992 selling at £98 (mentioned above), Treasury $14\frac{1}{2}$pc 1994 selling at £$119\frac{1}{2}$ with a yield of 12.13% and Treasury $6\frac{3}{4}$pc 1995–98 selling at £$77\frac{3}{8}$ with a yield of 8.73%, choosing the last option takes greatest advantage of the capital gains tax exemption since, when it is redeemed at £100 much of the profit is a capital gain which will not be taxed. This option is increas-

Finding out the value of gilts.

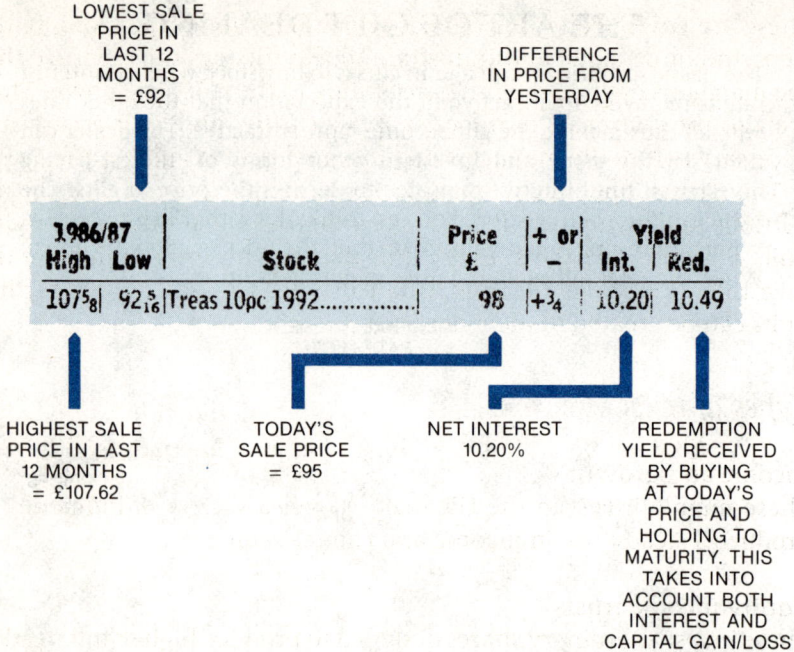

ingly attractive to those at higher tax levels. If income is the primary concern because you pay little or no income tax, the 14½% stock may be better despite the fact that you will have to pay above the face value to get it.

Risks

Although they pay a reliable level of interest and a known sum on maturity, gilts are negotiable. You are free to sell yours to anyone else who in turn is free to sell. This means that their price varies according to how attractive the interest rate happens to be at the time. The loan is repaid on a fixed *maturity* date at a fixed rate of interest which is referred to as the *coupon*. This stems from the time when stock certificates had little tear-off coupons on which to send in your claim to interest. A 'low coupon' stock is one paying a low rate of interest.

Interest

The interest returns on gilts are on the face value of the stock so that if you paid £95 for £100 worth of stock paying 9% interest, the interest on your investment is rather better than 9% at £9, which is 9.47% on your capital. If you hold it to redemption date then you have a capital gain of £5 as well.

UNIT TRUSTS

These are governed by trust deeds which have to be approved by the Department of Trade and Industry and the trustees must ensure that the managers operate the funds according to the rules laid down. They are also the guardians of the cash and securities and their approval is necessary before the managers can vary investments within the Trust.

The Trusts operate by making investments to form a balanced portfolio and invite the public to take a share in the portfolio by buying units from the managers. Every unit then has an interest in *all* of the investments made by the fund. Unit trusts are open-ended and further units can be created to meet demand.

Types of trust

Income and growth
These mainly invest in the UK market over a variety of industries to produce a steady rise in income and capital value.

Equity income trusts
These invest in ordinary shares designed to produce higher and steadily increasing income.

Gilt and fixed interest trusts
These endeavour to produce high, secure income from investment in government securities and corporate bonds although some (gilt and fixed interest growth trusts) go for capital appreciation.

Growth
These often include overseas investments while some concentrate on specialised fields such as small companies and recovery stocks where share prices are low and there is greater scope for improvement.

Overseas funds
Their names indicate where they are invested:

North American USA and Canada, some with a general spread across those markets; others concentrating in new technological development or recovery stocks.

Far Eastern Trusts Japan, Hong Kong, Malaysia, Singapore, Australia, New Zealand. These generally aim for growth.

Japanese Concentrating in that country, usually seeking growth.

Australian trusts Again the emphasis is on growth.

European These are invested in markets in various European centres for either income or growth.

International trusts These are spread over various markets throughout the world thus reducing risk but they are unlikely to produce the level of income achieved by investment in the UK market.

Commodity and energy trusts
Unit trusts may not invest directly in commodities but are allowed to buy the shares of companies involved in the production of raw materials, such as oil.

Financial and property trusts
There can be no direct investment in property by unit trusts but they can buy shares in property companies. This sector also takes a stake in financial institutions such as banks and insurance companies.

Investment trust units
Investment trusts are themselves invested in the shares of a wide variety of companies so these unit trusts rely on income and growth from companies that are seeking the same thing from stock markets worldwide.

Fund of funds
A fairly recent innovation is the *unit portfolio managed* fund launched by several companies, each with a number of other trusts under their management. Each trust must, by law, be independent of the others, but this new system creates a 'fund of funds' which can buy units in its own sub-funds. The advantage is that switches can be made by the managers between the sub-funds without the transactions becoming liable to capital gains tax as they would be if the individual investor made the switch and achieved a profit in excess of the exemption limit.

How to buy and sell

Units are bought at an *offer* price which is always higher than the current *bid* price – this is the price the managers will pay to buy back units. The managers are obliged to buy back units from those who wish to sell. These prices are usually calculated daily and held for 24 hours although some may be changed more frequently in times of active markets. The difference between the two is known as the *spread* and is usually of the order of 5.5–7.5%, although it could expand to about

12% or 13%. You will only start to gain when the bid price becomes greater than the offer price you paid. The *offer-to-bid* situation is the most important feature, as the greater the spread the more leeway you have to make up before your investment starts to show a profit. The spread is likely to be greatest in trusts which invest overseas or in highly specialised investment areas. The offer-to-offer or bid-to-bid comparisons that are sometimes advertised do, however, show the rates of growth of funds from which you may make assumptions as to how long it will take you to break even.

Minimum purchases
Investments of less than £250 in a unit trust are rare and even at that level your choice of trust would be fairly restricted. The more you are prepared to invest, the wider the choice until at £1000 there should be no difficulty in buying units of any fund you wish.

Regular payment schemes
Many trusts cater for the small investor by offering a savings scheme whereby a regular monthly sum, usually a minimum of £20, may be put into the scheme and the money used by the managers to buy units in their fund. This has the advantage of levelling out the price you pay for your holding in the long term if the value of the units fluctuates; when the offer price rises your regular savings sum will buy less of them and when it falls your money will buy a larger number of units.

Some schemes allow irregular increases to the monthly contribution while others allow you to make small, irregular payments once the first contribution has been made. You can stop at any time without incurring a penalty unless it is covered by a life assurance plan. But if your contributions have not been sufficient to meet the minimum investment required by the trust the managers may ask you to sell the units you have bought.

Availability Unit trusts do not always advertise these savings schemes but this does not mean they do not operate them. If you are interested in investing in a particular trust by such a method, it is worth asking the managers.

Proof of ownership
Once you have bought your units you will receive a contract note giving details of the purchase and some time later a unit certificate. This is vital for when you wish to sell either all or part of your holding as it must be sent to the managers. If you lose it you will not be paid until you have provided the managers with a costly indemnity against having to pay out twice.

The cost of buying and selling

The bid and offer prices are based on the value of the underlying securities and include the initial charge on the total invested which may vary between around 5% and 8% and incorporates:
- dealing charges
- stamp duty
- VAT
- commission (3%)

Additional payments include:
- annual management fees (0.75–1.25%)

As these charges are included in the bid price of the units, calculating your profit is quite straightforward.

How does the value of unit trusts change?

As units can be created to meet demand and reduced when demand falls, the value of the units is based on the value of the shares held by the trust, which are governed by the laws of supply and demand. The income earned by units in the form of dividends from the underlying securities will either be paid to you or used to purchase more units on your behalf. This is done automatically under accumulation units.

Monitoring performance

The performance of your units can be found in the financial pages of some national daily newspapers. This appears typically as shown below. For this company you would have paid 50.0p for each unit, an increase of 0.3p on the previous day and received 46.5p for each unit sold. The expected level of income from your investment would be 5.0% over the next 12 months.

A typical way of presenting the performance details on unit trusts.

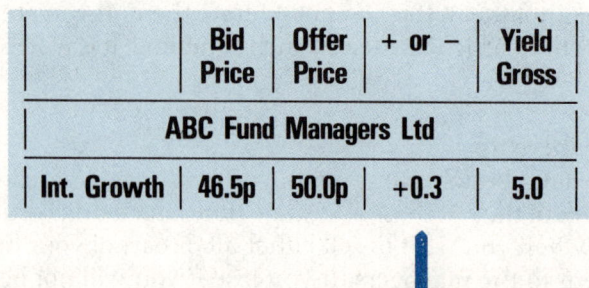

	Bid Price	Offer Price	+ or –	Yield Gross
ABC Fund Managers Ltd				
Int. Growth	46.5p	50.0p	+0.3	5.0

INCREASE IN OFFER PRICE OVER PREVIOUS DAY

Example

If you invest £1000, the anticipated income will be:

$$£1000 \times 5\% = £50$$

As you will have bought 2000 units, each unit will be earning 2.5p gross income. If the next day something drastic happened to capital values in the markets and the offer price fell to 40p per unit the yield for purchasers at the new price would have improved, rising by 1.25% to 6.25%. This is because the same £1000 now buys 2500 units each of which will still produce an income of 2.5p. The investment is then worth £62.50, which represents 6.25% on your £1000 investment. Similarly, if the units had risen in price and you received fewer units for your money, the yield would have gone down.

Taxation

The income earned by units in the form of dividends from the underlying securities will either be paid to you or ploughed back to purchase more units on your behalf. It is ploughed back automatically under accumulation units.

Any dividends earned on unit trust investments are regarded as taxable income once they are distributed by the Trust regardless of what happens to them. Thus it is the net income that is paid to you or added into the Trust. As the trusts themselves are not liable for capital gains tax, the managers can move investments about as much as they like but the unit holder is liable for any gain made on sales subject to the indexation allowance and the exemption in force at the time (see page 186). However, any real losses can be offset against any real gains for tax purposes.

Risks

Unit trusts should be regarded as a fairly long-term investment. To just break even could take 12 months or more as you will also have to make up the difference between the bid and offer prices, but over a period unit trusts have proved themselves ideal for producing both income and growth for the longer term investor. In order to minimise the risks involved, it is important to know when to buy and sell.

When to buy and when to sell

The best time to buy is when more people are selling than buying because the managers may then be selling shares to raise cash and the prices of units may be suppressed by, say, 6% below the true bid prices of the underlying securities. However, only when the trend is reversed with more buyers than sellers will the offer price of units reflect the true offer prices that the managers are having to pay for the underlying securities. This accordingly raises the bid price for the seller. The public are frequently invited to deal directly with the managers through advertisements but this is not always the best time for you to make purchases in this fund.

An expanding unit trust is best and it is wise to seek sound financial advice before committing your capital. Timing is all important as there is nothing to be gained, and perhaps a great deal to be lost, by investing at a favourable price in a contracting fund, especially if it goes on contracting.

Similarly, there is no point in selling at a profit from an expanding fund unless you believe that the expansion is coming to an end and that some other trust, or a different form of investment, will offer you better prospects.

Gains on a £1000 investment in unit trusts. Realisation value of £1000 invested 5, 10 and 15 years ago, with net income. (Figures as at 1 January 1987.)

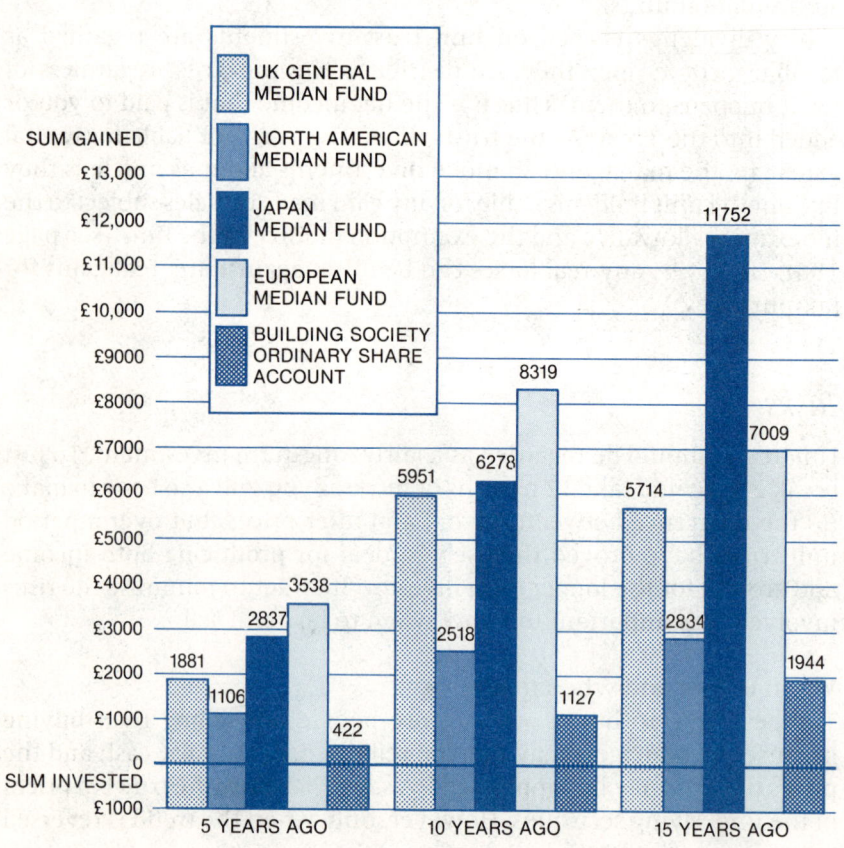

Choosing your trusts

There are more than 1000 unit trusts in Great Britain offering an enormous variety of investment opportunity. Some concentrate on investment in UK companies, others in Europe, America or the Far East. Some aim to produce a high income, others to achieve growth with little emphasis on income, and there are some trusts that strive to create a balance between the two. Some concentrate on narrower, specialised fields such as commodities and property shares but these lose the advantage of spreading money over a wide area to reduce risk.

A trust will always state its objective, whether principally for income or growth. Those seeking high income are likely to invest in UK ordinary shares, and perhaps gilts and fixed interest stocks. They will rarely invest overseas – a happy hunting ground for trusts in search of growth. It is wiser to choose a trust or trusts that will give you an interest in both home and overseas markets as growth funds are more

Increasing income from the equity income median fund. A graph comparing the income from an original investment of £1000 in the Equity Income Median Fund and Building Society ordinary share account. (Figures as at 1 January 1987.)

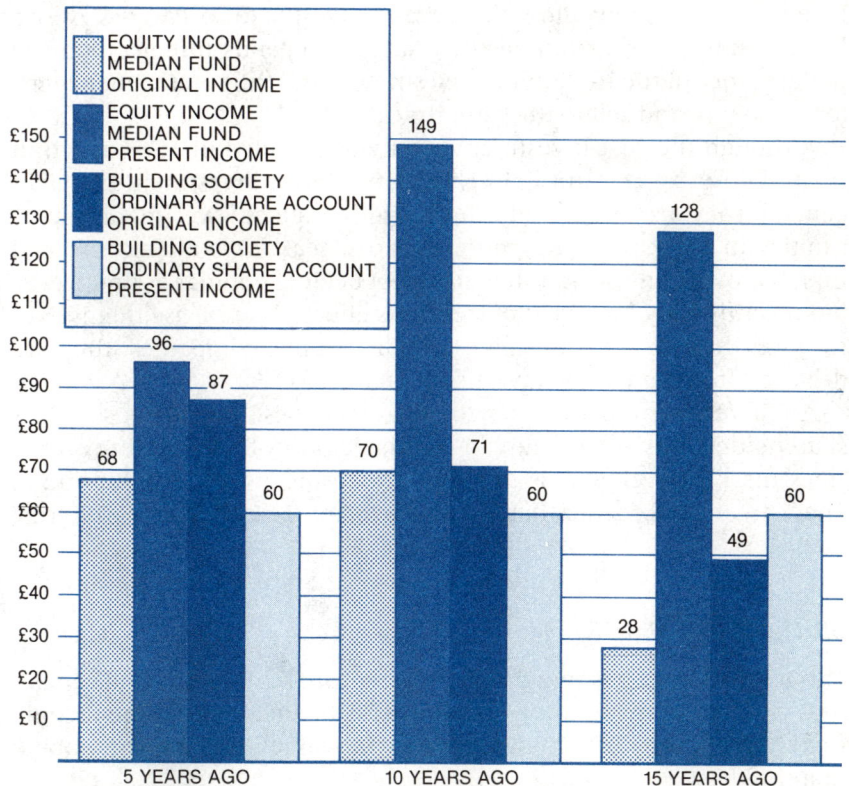

speculative, some being positively volatile. By doing so you spread the risk and level out the troughs in one market while chopping the peaks of others. The movement of international currencies also affects the prices of trusts invested overseas.

Further information sources

The **Unit Trust Association** (see page 173) provides an information service in this area for the public and also produces informative booklets, among them *Explaining Unit Trusts* and the rather more detailed *Everything You Need to Know about Unit Trusts* which lists the trusts and outlines the investment opportunities they individually offer. Both booklets are free when requested singly, but a charge may be made for multiple orders.

INVESTMENT TRUSTS

Investment trusts are companies that buy, sell and hold shares in other companies in the UK and/or internationally. They tend to specialise, some seek capital growth, some income and others a balance of both. Like unit trusts, they allow the smaller investor to spread risk over a large number of shares, and their success depends primarily on the performance of the underlying investments and thus on the managers' ability to buy and sell at the right times.

Although the first investment trust was founded in 1868 and unit trusts did not appear until 1931, there are fewer investment trusts. In general, they are larger and offer a wide range of investment opportunities in the United Kingdom and overseas for both income and capital growth. In the past they have not been as popular as unit trusts, but recently they have made strenuous efforts to publicise themselves through their Association. Like all other public companies, they are debarred from generally advertising their shares.

An investment trust aims to make the best possible use of its shareholders' cash to build up a profitable portfolio by trading on the stock markets in the areas to which the terms of the trust confine it. These are much broader than the restricted range available to unit trust managers.

Split capital trusts

This form of trust has two distinct types of shares, income and capital. As a rule, all of the income to the trust is divided among the income shareholders and all of the growth in value goes to the capital shareholders.

These trusts have a potentially limited life after which the income shares are repaid *at par*, the price at which they were first sold, and the remaining assets are divided among the capital shareholders. As the income is divided among those who hold the income shares, it is naturally at a higher rate than if it was distributed to all shareholders. But at the end of the day the income shareholders will get back only the nominal value of the shares on the winding up of the trust. For example, a 50p share may be valued at 80p because it is offering a high yield, but it may have a potential life of only five or six years. So, before you decide to invest in income shares, you have to weigh the likely value of the interest to be derived in those remaining years against the actual loss that will inevitably be incurred if the shares are held to the end of their lives.

People with no dependants may find income shares a useful way in which to bolster income and a modest investment in these trusts will greatly improve net income from a general portfolio of investments. However, there is an art to moving from trust to trust in order to avoid winding-up dates.

The capital shares are more volatile because the potential value of the total assets to be divided at some future date is harder to gauge. The Stock Market view of this potential varies from time to time leading to fluctuation in the prices.

Risk
It may be unwise to make this type of investment when markets are high because the potential for loss is greater than one might find in other forms of investment. Yet there are also chances of exceptional gain when markets are low.

Buying and selling shares

Unlike unit trusts, investment trust shares are traded on the Stock Exchange and are bought and sold through a stockbroker, either directly or through your adviser. They are *closed funds*, that is there is a fixed number of shares on issue and the directors cannot create more to meet a demand for them. Investment trusts may borrow money to buy more shares for their portfolios. This is called 'gearing'. Naturally, interest has to be paid on the borrowed money, but as long as the markets are improving at a rate that more than covers the loan repayment a loan is of benefit to the trust and its investors.

Minimum investment
There is no real minimum, but the smaller your investment the greater the charges are likely to be proportionately. In general, for a reasonable

investment of £1000 or more for which you simply give an instruction to buy specific trust shares, you might expect to pay 2.4% for stockbroker's commission and stamp duty. However, if you require additional services such as advice on the trust that will best suit your requirements and whether now is a good time to buy, you may pay more.

How does the value of shares change?

Investment trust shares are subject to the laws of supply and demand when traded in the stock market and quite often they trade below the value of the underlying shares. Then you are buying a stake in those underlying shares at a *discount*. In effect, you will have more assets working for you than you would have had, had you bought the underlying shares direct, or even through a unit trust. A discount of, say, 25% means that for £100 placed in the investment trust you are acquiring an interest in underlying shares to a value of £133 (£100 being about 75% of £133). Occasionally discounts can be as great as 30% or 40%. When the price of the investment trust shares is greater than the value of its underlying assets, they are said to be trading at a *premium*. As premiums and discounts change it is advisable to have professional help when dealing in this market.

Monitoring performance

Investment trusts are listed among the companies quoted on the Stock Exchange. The information given in the financial pages of the press is similar to that for unit trusts but there are more columns to cope with. The *Financial Times* gives the most information on these.

Tax

Like unit trusts, investment trusts are not liable internally for capital gains tax, but *you* would become liable should your real gain exceed the exemption limits when you disposed of your holding. Dividends are paid net but with the benefit of tax credits.

Further information

The **Association of Investment Trust Companies** (see page 173) will answer general inquiries from the public and produces a free explanatory booklet *More for Your Money*. Also available is a guide *How to Make It* giving details of each individual trust and a considerable amount of statistical information.

A typical way of presenting the performance details on investment trusts.

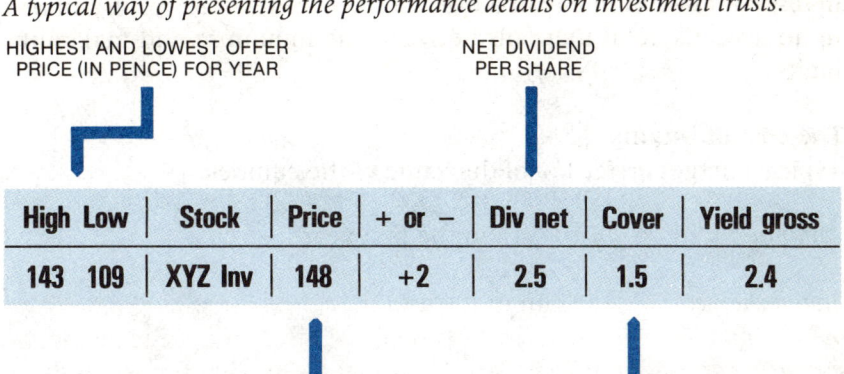

PERSONAL EQUITY PLANS

Personal equity plans were introduced in the 1986 Budget as an extension of the Government's strategy to encourage more people to take a stake in British industry through the stock market and to widen share ownership. Ironically, although they may attract the small and first time investors, the tax advantages offered by the scheme, which began to operate at the start of 1987, appear to be of more benefit to those on high incomes who already have substantial holdings.

Types of schemes

Fairly typical of the earlier schemes were those marketed by the major banks. The Midland produced two schemes:
(a) one that included some proposed investment in the USM;
(b) one that would devote a proportion of investment to its own unit trust income fund and the remainder to sound UK equities.

Lloyds Bank produced a managed scheme and another scheme which enables the client to select his own investments within the plan from a selection of shares and unit trusts.

Buying and selling

Method of payment
The appeal to the small investor is the instalment nature of the plans. You may invest between £20 and £200 monthly in a personal equity plan, or from £240 to £2400 a year. Regular instalments are not

necessary so you can pay in a lump sum or make varied contributions up to a yearly total that falls between the minimum and maximum limits.

The cost of buying
Typical charges are at 1% of the value of the equities.

Minimum	£10–£15 in the first year
Initial charge	5% on unit trusts
Annual charge	0.75%
Brokerage fees	0.2%

Tax benefits

Provided the investment is maintained for a further year and dividends from it are reinvested, the income and any gain is completely free of tax. Once you have established your exemption from income and capital gains tax in a plan, you retain it whether you dispose of your holding immediately or many years later. This tax exemption is also available for those who pay tax at the top rate. It offers the opportunity to increase the capital gains exemption allowed to everyone by whatever gain the £2400 annual investments have attained by the time they are disposed of.

The new small investor is highly unlikely to achieve rapidly gains that match inflation and exceed the capital gains exemption level even if investing the annual maximum of £2400 (see *Taxation*, page 179). However, the exemption from income tax is attractive to anyone who pays tax, the only drawback is that the dividends cannot be used as income, it has to accumulate in the plan.

Risks

The plans are managed by authorised dealers who may invest money from them in UK ordinary shares and unit trusts. During 1987 they do not have to invest your money immediately if they think it is not a good time to be buying stock. In that case, your cash will be held on deposit, earning tax-free interest until the time is judged right to invest it in shares or units. From 1988, however, the money will have to be continuously invested. As with unit and investment trusts, you have the advantage of professional management of your investment, but pay for that expertise.

There is no track record to help would-be investors when choosing between the plans on offer. But to gain some idea, it is reasonable to assume that there will be a 10% annual compound growth in the Stock Market and that the shares will yield 5%. In that case, you would almost double your money five years after completing the first subscription year, that is, six years after paying your first instalment. The charges on that, including VAT, might be in the region of £200. If your strategy is to invest £2400 every year, for the five years prior to retirement with the intention of then converting all your holdings into a lump sum, you could expect your £12,000 investment to increase by about 50%. In this case freedom from capital gains tax is of no value unless you have other investments which you intend to dispose of in the same year and which would take you beyond the exemption limit.

Choosing a plan

A variety of plans were being offered at the outset by the banks and other money managers. As with unit and investment trusts, the main difference in choice was in the type of investment. Better for the small investor are those which put their money to work in blue chip companies with a proportion also in investment trusts and unit trusts. This proportion can be as high as £420, or 25% of the total invested, whichever is the greater. A seasoned investor, seizing on the chance to make tax-free capital gains, might be more inclined to go for plans that include more risky, but potentially more rewarding, investments such as the unlisted securities market.

HIGH-RISK INVESTMENTS

Traded options

These are a specialised field of investment within the Stock Market and offer the opportunity to speculate on the future movement of shares. You deal in either *call options* or *put options*. Call options are the right to buy a share at a fixed price at a specified time in the future and are an advantage if share prices rise. *Put options* are a right to sell a share on a set date at a fixed price and are advantageous when share prices fall.

The price agreed is the *exercise price* which will depend on the price at negotiation and the time period chosen, which can be three, six or nine months. If the price rises past the exercise price, then you make a profit either by buying the shares and selling them, or by selling your option to someone else. Most traded options are never exercised as investors generally aim to make their profit by trading in the options themselves, and are likely to take their money or cut their losses before expiry by selling the options back to the market. A good deal of experience is needed before dabbling in either of these.

Unlisted Securities Market (USM)

Not every company qualifies for a full listing on the Stock Exchange, but one may want to offer its shares for sale to the public nevertheless. Such a company may qualify for admission to the *Unlisted Securities Market* which enables its shares to be traded in the same way. There are about 370 companies in this market. Fortunes have been made and lost in buying the shares of a young but growing company. In general USM shares are more volatile than those on the main list and therefore greater care should be taken in buying their shares.

Third Market

Launched in January 1987, this is a third tier for trading in the shares of companies that are too small, or too new for either a full or USM listing. They are often small or privately-owned companies that wish to offer a few of their shares for sale but do not want either a full or USM listing. Shares are placed with selected brokers who will place them with suitable purchasers. Sometimes companies specify no sales to institutions or, alternatively, to private purchasers.

'Over the counter' market

Companies trading on the *Over-the-counter (OTC) market* are not connected with the Stock Exchange at all. Dealings on this market are conducted by licensed dealers in securities, rather than stockbrokers. This market is not nearly so well regulated as the Stock Exchange and is consequently more risky.

OTHER TYPES OF INVESTMENTS

Unusual areas for investment are:
- Works of art
- Stamps
- Antiques
- Coins
- Carpets
- Fine wines

Collecting valuable items is for experts and is not recommended for the beginner anxious to enlarge a commuted pension or redundancy lump sum. Although anything that may become more valuable with time and for which there is a market, either by private sale or public auction, may be regarded as an investment, extracting any income while you are holding them could be difficult.

INVESTMENTS 173

USEFUL ADDRESSES

Association of Investment Trust Companies
16 Finsbury Circus
London EC2M 7JJ
☎ 01-588 5347

The Bonds and Stock Office
Blackpool
Lancashire FY3 9YP
☎ 0253 697333

Unit Trust Association (Head Office)
16 Finsbury Circus
London EC2M 7JP
☎ 01-638 3071

Unit Trust Association (Information Office)
Buckingham House
6–7 Buckingham Street
London WC2N 6BU
☎ 01-930 4241

The Public Affairs Department
The Stock Exchange
London EC2N 1HP
☎ 01-588 2355

GLOSSARY OF TERMS

The world of finance has developed its own language and some of the terms have very specific meanings. Here, some of the terms used on the Stock Market are explained

Account Normally the two-week period (sometimes three weeks) during which share trading takes place. There are 24 trading periods during the year and settlements must take place within 10 days after the end of each of them.

Account dealing Buying and selling within the two-week account period means you do not have to put up the cash for the shares you buy. So you can buy shares on the opening day of the account at, say, 100p and sell them a week later at 110p for a 10% gain or at 90p for a 10% loss. Then on *settlement day* you will either be paid your profit or pay your losses. It is also possible to operate this technique in reverse, selling shares that you don't already own at the start of the account hoping they will fall in value, so that you can buy them at a lower price thereby making a profit. If they rise in value then you lose. This form of dealing incurs only one set of commission.

Annual General Meeting Every company must have a meeting each year to present an annual report to shareholders and to elect or re-elect executive directors. This is an opportunity for shareholders to question the chairman and directors about the affairs of the company. In special circumstances, e.g. in a crisis or to change the constitution of the company, an *Extraordinary General Meeting* might be called at some other time during the year. Shareholders unable to attend in person at either type of annual meeting can vote by proxy.

Bargain Any transaction to buy or sell shares that is carried out by your broker.

Bear Someone who sells shares hoping they will go down in value. A profit is made by buying them back at a lower price.

Bear market A period when prices of stocks and shares generally are falling.

Bear raid A co-ordinated attempt by *bears* to reduce the value of a share by large scale selling.

Bid price The price at which a broker is prepared to buy back your shares. It is always slightly lower than the *offer price* at which he is prepared to sell you the same shares.

Big Bang The de-regulation of the Stock Exchange with the abolition of the distinction between *broker* and *jobber*, the abolition of fixed commission charges, the removal of various restrictions on the ownership of stockbroking companies and the introduction of computer trading on the Stock Exchange.

Blue chip shares The shares of leading companies; these are regarded as safe and reliable, and they are companies such as ICI, Marks & Spencer and GEC.

Broker A dealer in stocks and shares, and a member of a recognised Stock Exchange. Individuals who buy stocks and shares either use the services of a broker directly or, if their resources are limited, approach someone like a bank manager who will use the bank's broker to do the deal.

Bull Someone who buys shares in the expectation that they will rise in value enabling him to sell them at a higher price.

Bull market A period during which prices of shares generally are rising.

Call option An option to sell a share at a future date.

Chinese Wall An imaginary wall which divides the share dealing department of stockbrokers from the *market making* department which is responsible for offering shares at particular prices.

Churning the portfolio A broker's practice of selling a client's shares and buying new ones more with the object of making commission than acting in the client's best interests. It has always been frowned on and is now illegal.

The City Shorthand reference to the City of London, the small area of London in which the Stock Exchange, the Bank of England and most of the financial institutions of the country are based.

Commission The fee brokers charge for their services. It is now open to negotiation with individual clients, but is generally around 1.65% of the value of the deal either for selling or buying. Clients who are able to deal in larger sums of money will be able to negotiate a better commission rate than people dealing in small sums.

Compensation fund A fund maintained by the Stock Exchange to recompense investors should a member firm fail to meet its obligations. It does not offer protection against a bad investment.

Contango Day The day on which an investor can arrange, for a fee, to defer settlement until the next settlement day. This is not usually available to small investors.

Contract note Instructions between broker and client are usually verbal but the broker always sends a contract note as confirmation of the bargains struck on your behalf. If you give a broker *discretion* to act on your behalf he may buy and sell your shares without prior reference to you and the contract notes are your record of his activities.

Coupon Generally refers to the rate of interest on a fixed interest security. It arose from the fact that some securities have a tear-off coupon which is exchangeable for dividends.

Debenture A loan to a company on a fixed interest and fixed repayment date. Debenture holders have a prior claim on the assets of a company.

INVESTMENTS

Discretion Clients may give their brokers *discretion* to manage their portfolio of stocks and shares on their behalf. The broker then has the authority to buy and sell your shares without prior reference to you, but you can set limits to their activities relating either to specific shares or to the sums involved. A broker may also be given the authority for *account dealing* on your behalf. This is not a licence to make money as brokers can also get it wrong and make losses as well as profits.

Dividend Company profits are divided between the company needs for future development and resources, and *dividends* to the shareholders. Dividends are usually paid twice yearly as an interim dividend at the six months' stage and as a final dividend at the end of the trading year. They are usually expressed as pence per share held.

Equities Another name for the ordinary shares of a company.

Ex-dividend If you buy shares within about six weeks of the payment of a dividend you will probably have to forego the right to receive that dividend payment.

Extraordinary general meeting (See *Annual general meeting*.)

Fixed-interest securities Otherwise known as *stocks*, these are investments in companies which give a fixed return calculated as a percentage of their nominal value, usually £100, thus a 7% stock would return £7 a year. The market price for such stock changes according to the prevailing interest rates.

Flotation The name used when a new company comes to the Stock Market to offer its shares for sale. There has been a rash of these in recent years including several flotations of former nationalised industries.

Gilt-edged stocks Usually referred to as *gilts*, they are fixed-interest investments in government securities. The principle is the same as for *fixed-interest securities*. They became known as gilts because in the early days the paper they were printed on was edged with gold leaf. They have become synonymous with safety, having the full financial resources of the State behind them.

Government shares Generally known as *gilts*.

Institutions In the context of finance, refers primarily to the large financial groupings of the city including insurance companies and pension funds which, between them, provide the City with most of the money available for investment in stocks and shares.

Investor Anyone who buys stocks or shares.

Jobber Before their abolition in 1986 *jobbers* fixed the prices of stocks and shares. They were replaced by *market makers*.

Market maker The new name for *jobber*. They fix the buying and selling prices of shares.

Middle price This is the average of the day's buying and selling prices, and is the one usually published by newspapers the following day although some, like *The Times*, have recently taken to showing both the buying and selling price.

Offer price The price at which shares are offered for sale on a particular day. It is always slightly higher than the relative *bid* price at which a broker is prepared to buy back shares.

Options This is another way of speculating on the rise and fall of share prices. Investors can purchase options to buy or sell shares at some future date. A *call* option enables him to sell a share which he hopes will later have risen in price. A *put* option enables him to buy a share he hopes will later have fallen in price. They are a useful hedging instrument which enables you either to lessen or increase the risks of a particular investment.

Penny shares Refers to the shares of companies that are either new to the Stock Market or in a recovery position. These shares may be bought for a few pence, enabling a large amount of stock to be bought for a relatively small sum. With inflation the *penny share* now refers to any share up to about 60p. Despite the widespread advertising and increasing numbers of advisers in this area, you can lose money on penny shares just as easily as on any other, and it pays to take professional advice or, at least, to keep your investment modest.

Portfolio The collective name given to your spread of investments.

Put option An option to buy a share at a future date.

Quoted company This is a company which is quoted on the Stock Exchange.

Recovery stock A company that has seen hard times but is now tipped to do well. Their shares are therefore likely to rise quickly in value. Some investors and unit trusts specialise in watching out for recovery stock as a means of making substantial profits on investments.

Rights issue When a company needs to raise extra capital, e.g. for an investment programme, it can offer new shares to its shareholders in proportion to the number of shares already held, such as one new share for each four currently held. They are usually offered to shareholders at a discount and if they are not all taken up they may be offered for sale through the Stock Exchange at the best price available. Their name comes from the fact that existing shareholders have first rights to them.

Scrip Issue If a company wishes to reduce the value of its individual shares, perhaps to make them more marketable, this can be achieved by giving away extra shares to existing shareholders. Thus, if every holder of a company share worth 100p was to receive a scrip issue on a one-to-one basis, they would all end up with twice as many shares worth 50p each.

Securities An all embracing name for stocks and shares. They are a useful form of security if you wish to borrow money from a bank since the bank will usually accept them as their guarantee against loss.

Settlement day The day on which each two-week account must be settled. If you have bought shares you must send a cheque to the broker by this date. If you have sold shares or made a profit on *account dealing* then he must pay you.

Share Ordinary shares in a company are also known as *equities*. Each has a face value, which is technically the legal limit of your liability in the case of a company becoming insolvent, but they seldom trade at that value on the Stock Exchange. The price can rise and fall according to the performance of the company. Each share earns a proportion of the company's profits in the form of a *dividend*.

Share perks The practice of some companies which give perks to their investors in the form of a discount on their goods or services.

Shareholder Someone who owns shares in a company.

Speculator Someone who buys shares in the hope that they will rise rapidly in price in order to sell them again for a profit.

Spread The difference between the buying and selling price of a share.

Stag Anyone who buys shares in a new company in the expectation that they will quickly rise in value to produce a quick profit.

Stamp duty A tax levied on share

transactions. Since the *Big Bang*, it has been halved to ½%.

Stocks An investment which pays a fixed rate of interest. The purchase price is redeemed on a fixed date at some time in the future. Used in the singular it refers to an investment in shares or stocks in general.

Take-over bid When one company endeavours to buy another by offering the shareholders a sum for their shares which the purchaser hopes will be more attractive to them. Investors often have much to gain from such a bid because the value of the shares usually soars when such a bid is made. Some investors make a speciality of looking out for companies that are likely take-over targets.

Third Market Companies that are too small or too young to gain admission to either the main Stock Exchange listing or the *Unlisted Securities Market* may be admitted to the *Third Market*, which was introduced only in January 1987.

Unlisted Securities Market This consists of companies that wish to raise cash by offering their shares for public sale, but that cannot fulfil the requirements of the Stock Exchange Council for a full listing on the Stock Exchange. These can sometimes gain admission to the USM which is a second-tier market in which shares are bought and sold in the same way as the main Stock Exchange. It is generally accepted that although you may make a substantial profit by picking the right company on the USM your risks of losing everything are also greater.

Yield The annual rate of interest or dividend produced by a stock or share.

BIBLIOGRAPHY

Buying Gilts on the National Savings Stock Register (1987) Department for National Savings, London.

Everything You Need to Know about Unit Trusts (1986) Unit Trust Association, London.

Explaining Unit Trusts (1987) Unit Trust Association, London.

How to Make It (annual) Association of Investment Trust Companies, London.

More for your Money (1987) Association of Investment Trust Companies, London.

Taxation

INCOME TAX	180
How tax is paid	180
Your level of tax	180
CAPITAL GAINS TAX	185
What is a capital gain?	185
Inflation	186
How tax is paid	186
Reducing your tax liability	186
Selling your business	187
INHERITANCE TAX	188
What is your liability?	189
GIFTS	189
Capital gains tax	190
Inheritance tax	190
Declaration of gifts	190
Covenants	190
TAXES ON SAVINGS	191
Tax paid at source	191
BIBLIOGRAPHY	192

Of the various taxes levied by the Government there are three which are particularly important as you approach retirement. They are:
- Income tax
- Capital gains tax
- Inheritance tax.

INCOME TAX

This is levied on income from most sources but only after various allowances have been deducted. The tax year starts on 6 April of one year and ends on 5 April of the next.

How tax is paid

Those who have paid tax under the Pay-As-You-Earn scheme (PAYE) will continue to have tax deducted by the former employer once they have retired. However, the tax authorities, who instruct the former employer about the scale of tax deductions, will include the level of State pension in that calculation. Since your State pension is paid gross (i.e. no tax is deducted) and your occupational pension is paid net, income tax will be deducted not only in respect of your occupational pension but also on your State pension. So if you retire before the official retirement age, you will see a significant increase in the tax deduction from your occupational pension once you begin to receive your State pension.

Your level of tax

The levels at which tax rates change are known as the *tax thresholds*. If you happen to be on a threshold then it may be worth considering ways in which to invest your money. For example, if you have a taxable income of almost £17,500 and you are thinking of paying off your mortgage or putting a lump sum into a high interest deposit account you will almost certainly end up paying 40% tax. If you aimed for capital growth instead you may end up paying no extra tax at all. For most of us income tax is a fairly straightforward business, but if you find yourself in the situation described above it will pay you to seek advice from an accountant or tax expert.

How much will you pay?
The age allowance gives a significant tax advantage to people over the age of 65 whether or not they are in full time work, provided their total gross income does not exceed £9800. The allowance is given to single people starting in the tax year during which they reach 65, irrespective of sex, and is given to married couples once one of them does so. An additional age allowance goes to those who reach 80 under the same conditions.

Status	Age (years)	Allowance (£)	Net income (£)
Single	55	2425	7808.75
	65	2960	7953.20
	80	3070	7982.90
Difference*	55/65		144.45
	65/80		29.70
Married	55	3795	8178.65
	65	4675	8416.25
	80	4845	8462.15
Difference*	55/65		237.60
	65/80		45.90

Income = £9800; tax at 27%.
*The difference in net income due to the increased allowance for age.

If your income exceeds £9800 Those who benefit from age allowance will have that reduced at the rate of £2 for every £3 by which the gross income exceeds that sum. The benefit of age allowance is lost entirely once a married couple's income exceeds £11,120 (£10,602.50 for a single person). For example, suppose you are married and have an income of £10,400 in retirement. This exceeds the age allowance limit of £9800 by £600 and the age allowance is therefore reduced by:
$$£600 \div 3 \times 2 = £400$$
Your new age allowance is therefore £4275. As an income of £11,120 exceeds the age allowance limit by £1320, the age allowance is reduced by £880, which brings it to £3795, the same as for younger people, but it won't be reduced any further.

Just as there is a danger of inadvertently pushing your income over one of the tax thresholds by investing for income, there is a similar risk to your age allowance. For every pound you earn from investments in this way you will be taxed at an effective rate of almost 45%. So it is

INCOME TAX

Taxable income

- Salary while in full time work
- Occupational pension (whether retired or not)
- State pension
- Part-time earnings
- Income from rents
- Income from investments

The basic allowances for 1987–88

- Single person's allowance £2425
- Married man's personal allowance £3795
- Wife's earned income relief £2425
- Single person's age allowance £2960(3070)* ⎫ where total income
- Married couple's age allowance £4675(4845)* ⎭ does not exceed £9800

*For those over 80

The *Wife's earned income relief* is a valuable allowance that is usually added to the allowance of a husband whose wife is working. This allowance continues into retirement and the husband can claim it against:
- his wife's income from a job
- her occupational pension
- her own State pension earned in her own right.

Additional Allowances

- Blind person's allowance 540
- Housekeeper's allowance 100
- Widow's bereavement allowance 1370
- Dependent relative's allowance 100(man) 145(woman)
- Child's service allowance 55

The *Blind person's allowance* is paid to the registered blind.
The *Housekeeper's allowance* is available for widows or widowers who have someone living with them to act as housekeeper.
The *Widow's bereavement allowance* is designed to help widows over the difficulties of bereavement and adjustment. It begins at the time of

death and continues until the end of the *following* tax year, as long as the widow does not remarry before then. In theory, therefore, it could last for almost two years.

The *Dependent relative's allowance* is paid to a man or woman who is not married or not living with her husband. This is applicable only if you are supporting a dependent relative whose only income is the State retirement pension.

The *Child's service allowance* is given for a son or daughter who is maintained by you and lives at home because of your dependence on them due to old age or infirmity.

Non-taxable income

- Supplementary benefits paid for reasons other than unemployment
- Industrial injury benefits and war disablement benefits
- Invalidity benefit
- Attendance and mobility allowances
- War widow's pension
- Christmas bonus
- Interest on National Savings Certificates
- Voluntary payments made to you by relatives, unless covenanted
- First £70 of interest from ordinary deposit accounts with the National Savings Bank (husbands and wives are each entitled to this)
- Occasional winnings on lotteries, premium bonds and football pools
- Redundancy payments not exceeding £25,000
- Maturity payments from endowment policies
- Lump sums commuted from your pension

Qualifying mortgage interest and premiums for deferred annuity contracts taken out by the self-employed or those in non-pensionable employment are deductions from income not allowances and so are removed from gross income before allowances are assessed.

Tax rates for 1987–88

Taxable income (£)	Rate (%)	Maximum tax on this portion (£)	Total maximum tax (£)
1–17,900	27	4,833	4,833
17,901–20,400	40	1,000	5,833
20,401–25,400	45	2,250	8,083
25,401–33,300	50	3,950	12,033
33,301–41,200	55	4,345	16,378
Over 41,200	60		

YOUR HIDDEN INCOME

Mary and Roger have a taxable income of £9400 at present. They also have a cash lump sum of £5000 which they are thinking of investing in a building society deposit account offering a return of 8% net. Roger reasons that £5000 at 8% gives an interest of £400 which, added to their present taxable income of £9400, gives a total income of £9800, just escaping the abatement of age allowance. However, the Inland Revenue does not view that building society interest as £400 but as £547.95, which is the interest before the building society has deducted tax at the basic rate. This is known as *grossing up*.

As far as the Inland Revenue is concerned, therefore, Mary and Roger have a gross taxable income for the year of £9400 + £547.95 = £9947.95 which affects their age allowance, cutting it back by £98.63. Their age allowance is now £4576.37 instead of £4675, a reduction that has cost an extra £26.63. So that extra £147.95 of income has been taxed by a total of £66.58, an effective tax rate of 45% which is an expensive oversight.

Roger and Mary could have avoided this by investing only *some* of their cash in a building society and putting the rest into a tax-free interest bearing investment such as National Savings Certificates, an ordinary deposit account with the National Savings Bank yielding low interest but where the first £70 is free of income tax, or unit trusts invested primarily for capital growth rather than income. (For more information on the difference between investing for income rather than growth see page 104.)

particularly important to beware of the words 'net of tax' or 'tax free' in advertisements for investments. There may be circumstances, therefore, when you will be better off by investing for capital growth rather than for income. For instance, a deposit in a building society or high interest bank deposit account produces income all of which will be taxable. This will therefore be taxed at the rate applicable to you, but if your total gross income is pushed over a *threshold* it makes a great deal of difference for you to consider again what you should do with your money. By investing for capital growth such as in a unit trust paying virtually no interest at all, or low interest bearing Government stock (see page 154) then most of your benefit will come via the capital growth of your investment. Provided your profit is modest, you will pay no tax on it at all.

Those over 80 will lose the additional age allowance if the income exceeds £11,375 in the case of a married couple and £10,767.50 in the case of a single person.

CAPITAL GAINS TAX

Allowance £6600 (single or married)
Tax rate 30%

What is a capital gain?

All that you own, with certain important exceptions, that can be sold at a profit is capable of making a capital gain. These are *chargeable assets*. By far the most important exclusion is your home, but only your *principal private residence*. If you also own a country or seaside home which you subsequently sell at a profit then you will have to pay tax if the profits exceed £6600. However, if you sell your present home and move into the second property you will probably escape any CGT charge on that provided you stay 'put' for some time.

CAPITAL GAINS TAX

Goods liable for Capital Gains Tax

- Stocks and shares
- Unit trusts and investment trusts
- Land
- Property (other than your own home)
- Jewellery
- Antiques
- Gold and silver

Exclusions from Capital Gains Tax

- Your main residence
- Motor cars
- Government stocks
- Certain other tax-free investments such as National Savings
- Small possessions regarded as 'chattels' by the taxman including antiques and jewellery worth less than £3000 per item (an item can be a pair, etc)
- Winnings on lotteries, including premium bonds
- Gifts between husband and wife
- The proceeds of maturing endowment policies
- Gains made in Personal Equity Plans

People who move house and subsequently have difficulty in selling their previous home may have problems but the last year of ownership does not count anyway and the Inland Revenue may extend that period provided it can be shown that continuous efforts have been made to sell the previous main residence. People who allow a dependent relative or relatives to live *rent free* in a property they own will also be able to claim exemption from the tax when they eventually come to sell the house.

Inflation

Capital gains on items acquired on or after 31 March 1982 may be compared with the rise in the retail prices index over a similar period. Only gains exceeding the rise in RPI will count as capital gains. Articles that improve in value by less than the rise in the RPI will have made a loss. For things acquired before 31 March 1982, an allowance is calculated by adding a value, based on RPI rises, on that date to the original value when acquired.

Example
An article acquired for £200 in 1970 is worth £1000 on 31 March 1982, but the RPI rose by 25% in that time so £250 is added to £200 and gains or losses are calculated from a base value of £450.

How tax is paid

A virtue of capital gains tax for the investor is the fact that the tax does not have to be paid until December of the year in which the tax year ends. So if you sell shares on 6 April 1987 you can invest your profit elsewhere before paying tax on 1 December 1988, which is some 20 months later.

Reducing your tax liability

By far the most common reason for incurring capital gains tax is by the sale of stocks and shares (including unit trusts). If you have invested well and are liable to capital gains tax you can make arrangements to limit your liability. If you do not *need* the money you can sell only part of your shares so as to keep within the £6600 allowance selling the rest in another tax year, which is the same as that for income tax. So if you have a share success at the end of March, you can sell enough of your shares to realise a £6600 profit and sell more to make another £6600 on 6 April. You will pay no tax unless you make further profitable sales before 5 April of the following year.

WHAT IS YOUR CAPITAL GAINS TAX LIABILITY?

John, Gerry and Jack each invested £10,000 in unit trusts of their choice. Six months later the units have all increased in value and they would like to sell and take their profits. John's units are now worth £15,000, Gerry's did rather better and are now worth £17,500 and Jack made a really inspired selection and doubled his money.

What tax would each pay?

During the same period the RPI went up by 2% so they all have a base value of £10,200 from which to calculate their capital gains. Thus John's shares increased in true value by £4800. As he made no other capital gains during the year, he has no tax to pay.

Gerry's shares increased in true value by £7300, which exceeds the £6600 allowance by £700. He must pay tax of £210, so his net profit is therefore £7290, including the £200 inflation allowance.

Similarly Jack made a true gain of £9800 of which £3200 is liable to tax amounting to £1960. This leaves him with a net profit of £9040.

Selling your business

Capital gains tax may be levied on businesses just like any other asset which is bought and sold, but since many self-employed people rely on selling their business enterprise to fund their retirement they can benefit from a special concession of £125,000.

The first £125,000 of gain is exempt provided you are 60 or over, have worked in the business for at least 10 years and own at least 25% of the shares, or own at least 5% with at least 50% owned by you and your family.

The rules are varied slightly where several members of the same family have been associated with the business, but the same concessions may apply provided that between them, they and the estate owner have owned 50% of the business.

People who sell up before age 60 because of ill health may also be treated more leniently, while if you pass on your business to your children it is likely to come under the aegis of *inheritance tax*. Immediate tax liability will not necessarily be incurred in this case and there may be further conditions which help to limit liability. This is one area where it will pay you to take professional advice.

INHERITANCE TAX

This replaced Capital Transfer Tax in the 1986 Budget and is a tax on the estate you leave on your death. It is therefore a problem for your heirs and successors rather than for you except that you can limit how much is paid and make provision for its payment.

INHERITANCE TAX

Tax bands

Inheritance (£)	Rates (%)	Total maximum tax (£)
0– 90,000	Nil	Nil
90,001–140,000	30	15,000
140,001–220,000	40	47,000
220,001–330,000	50	102,000
Over 330,000	60	?

Tax exemptions

- Wedding gifts up to £5000 to any of your children
- Wedding gifts up to £2500 to any grandchild
- Wedding gifts up to £1000 to anyone else
- Any number of gifts to other people not exceeding £250 each
- The first £3000 in any one year in addition to the above conditions
- Gifts to charities
- Gifts to political parties
- *Normal expenditure* gifts out of income which do not affect the standard of living of the donor

Inheritance tax abatement rates

Survival period (Years)	Portion of tax payable (%)
Up to 3	100
3–4	80
4–5	60
5–6	40
6–7	20

MINIMISING YOUR LIABILITY

Alan and Edith have an estate valued at around £150,000 which includes a house worth £100,000 that they own jointly. At present they plan to leave everything to each other and then leave it to their two children equally. If one of them dies then the other will inherit everything without having to pay inheritance tax. But if the survivor then dies, having made no plans for passing the estate on but leaves everything to be shared equally between the two children, then the tax bill will be £19,000. Professional advice can help you limit your liability. For instance, any of the following options would reduce the tax bill faced by the beneficiaries.

1. Alan and Edith can take out special insurance policies in the name of the children to cover the likely tax bill taking inflation into account.
2. After providing for Edith, Alan could leave part of the estate to the children when he died. Provided it does not exceed £90,000 there would be no tax to pay.
3. Alan and Edith can change the ownership of their house from joint ownership to owners as 'tenants in common'. Under this arrangement they are each deemed to own exactly half the house. The first to die can then leave their half to the children rather than to their spouse, so reducing or even eliminating the ultimate tax bill. An arrangement can be made in this case for unfettered occupancy of the house, or a substituted house, during the life of the survivor.

What is your liability?

Many people may look at the figures at which inheritance tax becomes payable and think that it will not affect them. However, the estate you leave behind is not just money but also the cash value of everything you possess including your house, car, furniture, jewellery, stocks and shares. With a modest semi-detached house in London and the Home Counties often fetching close to £100,000 these days, it is very easy to pass on a substantial tax bill to anyone but your spouse. The tax will eventually be paid when the survivor dies.

GIFTS

Gifts are also subject to tax and are liable for capital gains tax or inheritance tax with the exemptions as stated on pages 185 and 188.

Capital gains tax

Gifts of shares, diamonds or property are subject to tax which is levied against the *giver* by the taxman making his own assessment of the gain, which may be negotiable. If the *receiver* of the gift agrees, the tax can be levied against him at such time as the gift is subsequently disposed of.

Inheritance tax

The introduction of inheritance tax was felt by many experts to be no more than a re-introduction of estate duty which was replaced by capital transfer tax (CTT) in 1975. Under CTT gifts made to other people were liable to tax if they exeeded certain limits but that is no longer the case.

A gift (or transfer) made today will not be liable for inheritance tax provided you and your spouse are excluded from benefit and you survive the transfer by more than seven years.

If you survive by fewer than seven years the value of the gift will be added to your estate and taxed. There is, however, a sliding scale of tax abatements depending on how long you survived the gift.

There are many gifts which can be made without attracting tax, and if you have an estate which is likely to amount to around £100,000 or more you should seek the advice of your accountant and solicitor. They can help you make or revise your will suggesting how you can reduce the likely tax bill to your heirs and help them to pay it.

Declaration of gifts

As the taxman does not know about your gifts, you are required by law to declare them. Since inheritance tax will be paid on gifts by the receiver they must declare the gifts after your death, otherwise your estate will be expected to pay. You should take care to go into this thoroughly when making gifts or your surviving spouse may be caught for the tax bill.

Covenants

You can greatly increase the value of gifts to charities, children, nieces, nephews and grandchildren, if you agree to make your payments on a regular basis and sign a legally binding covenant to do so. The benefit is that the receiver, provided they are not themselves liable to pay income tax, can claim back the tax at basic rate, which you are deemed to have paid on the gift. You should make covenants only if you pay tax, otherwise you may face a bill from the tax office.

Example
If you wish to donate £100 a year and sign a covenant promising to do so, the recipient can claim back the tax you have already paid on that £100. So instead of receiving £100, the recipient will receive £136.99, £36.99 being the tax payable on £136.99 at 27%. Alternatively, if you want the benefit to be £100 in total you can send a cheque every year for £73 and the recipient could claim an extra £27 from the Inland Revenue as a tax refund.

Maximum rebate
Tax is returned to the beneficiaries of covenants only at the basic rate of tax, even if you pay at higher rates. If you do pay at higher rates you can recover the additional tax yourself in your annual tax return, but this is possible only if your covenant is to a charity.

Using building societies and banks
The interest from building society and bank deposit accounts is available for covenanting. Although *you* cannot recover the tax, the beneficiary of the covenant can.

How to make out a covenant
It is often worthwhile arranging a covenant for a student child or grandchild. Your solicitor or accountant can sort it out in minutes. Alternatively you can write to
The National Union of Students
461 Holloway Road, London N7 6LJ
☏ 01-272 8900
for a covenant form and helpful leaflet. Most charities will send you covenant forms if you ask for one.

TAXES ON SAVINGS
Some forms of investment pay interest gross, and you will have to declare it and pay tax when you make your annual tax return. Gilts bought through the Post Office and interest from National Savings Investment Accounts come into this category. However, tax is sometimes paid for you by other bodies.

Tax paid at source
Dividends and interest received from stocks and shares, and unit trusts are paid after tax has been deducted at the basic rate. If your income is sufficiently low that you do not need to pay income tax you can reclaim

the tax. If, on the other hand, you are liable for tax at higher rates then you will get a demand for the extra in due course.

Composite rate tax
This is another way in which tax is paid at source and applies to interest on building society and bank savings accounts. Notionally tax has been deducted at the basic rate in the same way as for dividends on shares, but in this instance if you are not liable for income tax you *cannot* reclaim the tax. So people with an income below the income tax threshold should *not* put their money into such accounts as 27% of the interest is lost unnecessarily. Higher rate taxpayers will, however, get an additional demand so they are usually better off looking for capital gains rather than interest of any kind. Personal Equity Plans (see page 169) may have a particular appeal as even capital gains tax is avoided.

BIBLIOGRAPHY

The Daily Mail Income Tax Guide (July 1987) Publications Department, Associated Magazines, Carmelite House, London EC4Y 0JA.

Tax Saving Guide Consumers Association, 14 Buckingham Street, London WC2N 6DS.

Insurance

PROPERTY INSURANCE	195
What is the right level of insurance?	195
Penalties of underinsurance	196
How to work out rebuilding costs	198
What does property insurance cover?	199
CONTENTS INSURANCE	199
Cost of insurance	199
What is covered?	200
Accidental damages	201
Not covered	201
Other features	201
Making a claim	201
Working out the value	204
Discounts	204
MOTOR INSURANCE	208
What kind of policy	208
Special policies	209
LIFE ASSURANCE	209
Whole life assurance	209
Term assurance assurance	213
Endowment assurance	213
Annuities	214

Optional features	215
USEFUL ADDRESSES	215
REFERENCES	216

Insurance of all kinds is probably more important on the approach to retirement and beyond than at any other stage of life. We are likely to own more than at any earlier age and as our earning days are coming to an end, we have less opportunity to recover the situation should disaster strike. Insurance impinges on most areas of our lives but the areas to look at in middle age are:
- Property insurance
- Contents insurance
- Motoring insurance
- Life insurance

PROPERTY INSURANCE

There is probably more confusion over the right level of insurance for the fabric of our homes than any other form of insurance. It is important to get the level of insurance right because:

(a) if you are underinsured the insurance company will refuse to meet your claim in full
(b) if you are overinsured you are spending money on premiums needlessly.

What is the right level of insurance?

Insurance companies expect you to insure your home for the cost of replacing it should it be destroyed. For instance, a fire which got out of control during your absence from the house and which so badly damaged the property that it was declared unsafe and would have to be pulled down. You must therefore estimate the rebuilding cost covering:
- clearing the rubble away
- employing an architect to redesign it
- finally rebuilding it.

It is important to bear in mind that the rebuilding cost is not necessarily the same as the purchase or sale value, particularly if you live in the London area where housing is expensive, or in some of the provincial areas where housing is still relatively inexpensive.

Example

Compare a four-bedroomed detached house in the suburbs of London with a similar one in a small town in rural Yorkshire. Both are well-built structures erected during the inter-war years with a total floor area, upstairs and down, of about 1350 sq ft. Towards the end of 1986 such a house in London would cost just over £100,000 to buy while in Yorkshire the same property would cost a little over £41,000. The costs of rebuilding would also differ.

Using the tables provided by the **Association of British Insurers**, London builders would charge about £52.50 per square foot, a total of £70,875 for the house, while in Yorkshire a local builder would charge only £41.50 a square foot, which is a total of £56,025 to rebuild. These are therefore the correct insurance values for each house, excluding any extra costs which might need to be added to cover the value of garages or other outbuildings.

If both householders decided to insure their homes for the purchase price (at a cost of £1.80 per £1,000) the Londoner would have been substantially overinsured, paying premiums of about £180 a year, instead of the £127 he needed to pay; but the Yorkshireman would have been underinsured to the tune of £15,025 which is approximately 25% of the rebuilding cost of his house.

The purchase prices and rebuilding costs are compared for two similar houses, one in London and the other in Yorkshire.

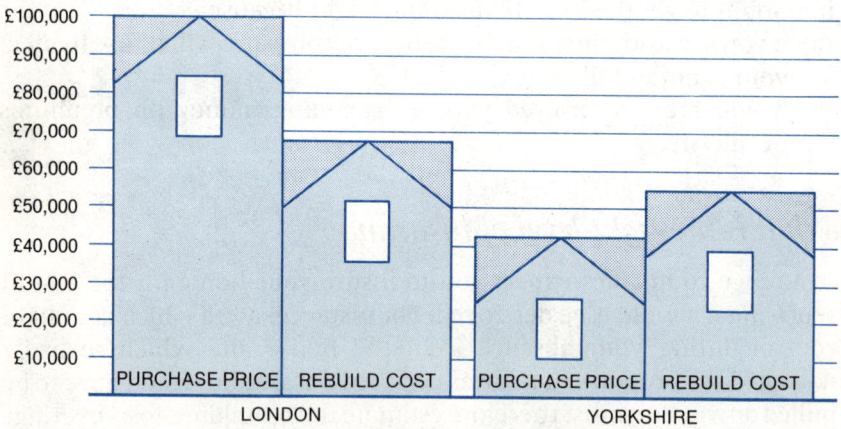

Penalties of underinsurance

The overinsured Londoner would not get any extra for paying a higher than necessary premium but would receive only the rebuilding cost, while the underinsured Yorkshireman is likely to be heavily penalised for being underinsured. This will affect *all* claims.

INSURANCE 197

A guide to choosing your building insurance level. (Reproduced with the permission of the Association of British Insurers.)

Regions

1. **London Boroughs**
2. **South East and North West England**
   Bedfordshire, Berkshire, Buckinghamshire, Essex, Hampshire, Hertfordshire, Kent, Oxfordshire, Surrey, East Sussex, West Sussex, Cheshire, Greater Manchester, Lancashire and Merseyside.
3. **Scotland, Wales and Northern England**
   The whole of Scotland and Wales and Cleveland, Cumbria, Durham, Northumberland, Tyne & Wear.
4. **East Anglia, East Midlands, West Midlands, South West, Yorkshire & Humberside and Northern Ireland**
   All other counties.

NOTES

1. This chart has been prepared by the Building Cost Information Service of the Royal Institution of Chartered Surveyors and the majority of householders have been catered for by providing rebuilding cost information on five different house types, with average quality finish, depending on their age, size and location. Of course, it is impossible to cover all circumstances and, for instance, the chart is unsuitable for certain types of property including the following:-
   (a) Properties which are not built mainly of brick.
   (b) Properties with more than two storeys (for three-storey houses, see 'Making your own estimate') or with basements and cellars.
   (c) Flats, because there are wide differences in construction and responsibilities for shared parts.
   (d) Houses with special design features or of greater sizes than those described in the chart.

2. **All the figures in the chart are based on houses of average quality finish and might need adjusting.** For example, if your house is of higher quality, with luxury kitchen and sanitary fittings, floor and wall finishes and double glazing, your final figure would need to be increased by up to 25%.

3. The figures in the chart are based on rebuilding your home to its existing standard using current materials and techniques available. If older houses are required to be reinstated in exactly their original style, a professional valuation is essential.

4. All the figures in the chart include allowances for full central heating (at an approximate cost of £2,200) and demolition costs and professional fees.

How much would it cost to re-build your home?
SEPTEMBER 1986 costings — £ per square foot (external)

		PRE 1920			1920–1945			1946–DATE		
		LARGE	MEDIUM	SMALL	LARGE	MEDIUM	SMALL	LARGE	MEDIUM	SMALL
DETACHED HOUSE	Region 1	53.00	57.00	56.00	50.50	52.50	53.00	43.00	45.50	46.00
	2	46.50	50.00	49.00	44.50	46.00	46.50	37.50	40.00	40.00
	3	44.00	47.50	46.50	42.00	44.00	44.00	36.00	38.00	38.00
	4	41.50	45.00	44.00	40.00	41.50	41.50	34.00	36.00	36.00
	Typical Area ft²	3450	1700	1300	2550	1350	1050	2550	1350	1050
SEMI-DETACHED HOUSE	Region 1	51.50	52.50	52.50	54.50	52.50	52.50	39.00	41.50	44.50
	2	45.50	46.00	46.00	48.00	46.00	46.00	34.50	36.50	39.00
	3	43.00	44.00	43.50	45.50	44.00	44.00	32.50	34.50	37.00
	4	41.00	41.50	41.50	43.00	41.50	41.50	31.00	33.00	35.00
	Typical Area ft²	2300	1650	1200	1350	1150	900	1650	1350	1050
DETACHED BUNGALOW	Region 1				54.50	50.50	52.00	47.00	47.00	49.00
	2				48.00	44.50	45.50	41.00	41.50	43.00
	3	The chart does not cover pre-1920 bungalows, as few such properties were built.			45.50	42.00	43.00	39.00	39.50	41.00
	4				43.00	40.00	41.00	37.00	37.00	38.50
	Typical Area ft²				1650	1400	1000	2500	1350	1000
SEMI-DETACHED BUNGALOW	Region 1				56.50	57.00	50.50	45.50	46.00	47.50
	2				49.50	50.00	44.50	40.00	40.00	42.00
	3				47.00	47.50	42.00	38.00	38.00	39.50
	4				44.50	45.00	40.00	36.00	36.00	37.50
	Typical Area ft²				1350	1200	800	1350	1200	800
TERRACED HOUSE	Region 1	56.00	55.00	54.50	54.50	54.50	54.00	39.50	42.50	47.00
	2	49.00	48.00	48.00	48.00	47.50	47.00	34.50	37.50	41.50
	3	46.50	45.50	45.50	45.50	45.00	45.00	33.00	35.50	39.50
	4	44.00	43.50	43.00	43.00	43.00	42.50	31.00	33.50	37.00
	Typical Area ft²	1650	1350	1050	1350	1050	850	1650	1300	900

Example

If the roof was blown off in a gale and would cost £2000 to repair, the insurance company could argue that since only 75% of the rebuilding cost was insured, they would meet only 75% of the claim. The extra £500 would then have to be found elsewhere. Some insurance companies might revert to an *indemnity* settlement which means they would make a deduction for wear and tear (see page 204).

How to work out rebuilding costs

You will need to find out the total floor area of your house. This can be done by measuring the *outside* dimensions of the house in feet and multiplying the length by the breadth to get the total ground floor area. For a normal two-storey house this can be doubled to get the total floor area. The average rebuilding cost per square foot in your area can be found using tables devised by the **Association of British Insurers** (see page 215) and should be multiplied by the total floor area of your house. A suitable sum for your outbuildings should be added to give your rebuilding value for insurance purposes.

Your property insurance covers damage by all the ways shown.

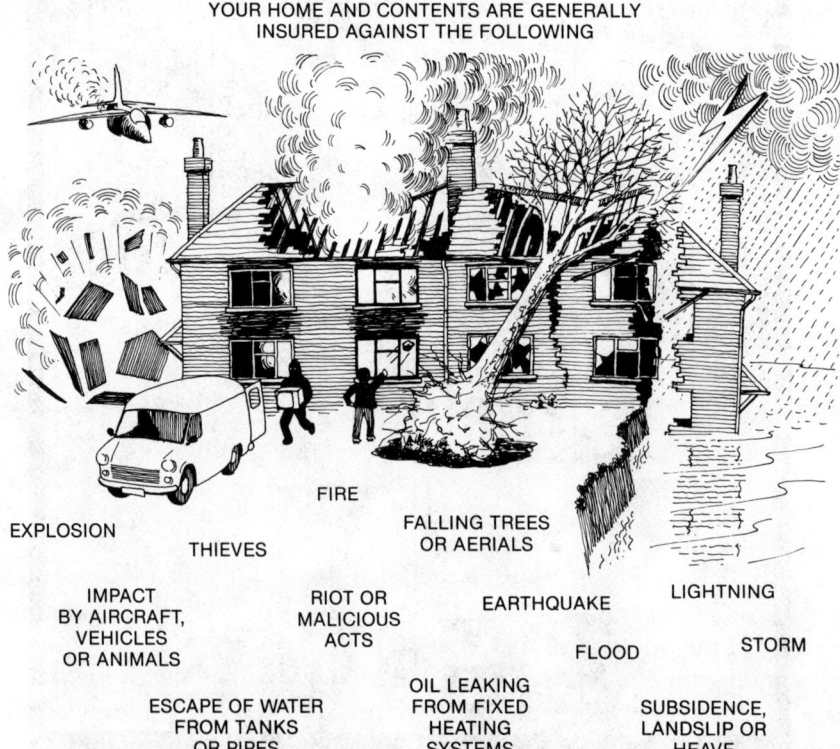

YOUR HOME AND CONTENTS ARE GENERALLY INSURED AGAINST THE FOLLOWING

FIRE
EXPLOSION
THIEVES
FALLING TREES OR AERIALS
IMPACT BY AIRCRAFT, VEHICLES OR ANIMALS
RIOT OR MALICIOUS ACTS
EARTHQUAKE
LIGHTNING
FLOOD
STORM
ESCAPE OF WATER FROM TANKS OR PIPES
OIL LEAKING FROM FIXED HEATING SYSTEMS
SUBSIDENCE, LANDSLIP OR HEAVE

What does property insurance cover?

Your property will be covered against damage by all the ways shown opposite. There is usually extra cover (typically 10% of the total cover) offering to pay for:
(a) alternative accommodation if your home is no longer fit to live in
(b) damage to underground pipes and cables, and glass in doors and windows.

In addition to the structure of the house most standard policies will cover permanent fittings such as baths, lavatories, sinks and kitchen and bedroom cupboards. Interior decorations are covered and policies usually extend to include outbuildings such as garages, sheds and greenhouses. Walls, fences, gates and paths may also be included in the cover but flood and storm damage will usually be excluded.

CONTENTS INSURANCE

There are nearly half a million burglaries from our homes every year and insurance company losses are running at well over £200 million a year from this cause. Yet this is probably the commonest area of underinsurance because it is so easy to get out of date and out of touch with the real value of your possessions. There are two ways to insure your contents:
- On an *indemnity* basis
- On a *replacement-as-new* basis

Indemnity insurance
In the event of a claim you will be paid the cost of repairing damaged items or of replacing them at their present value after allowing for age, wear and tear, and depreciation.

Replacement insurance
The insurance company will pay either the cost of repair or the full cost of replacing whatever has been lost or destroyed with equivalent new articles.

Cost of insurance

Insuring on an indemnity basis is obviously cheaper than replacement-as-new but most people insure their contents for replacement value because of the prohibitive cost of replacing carpets, furniture and other equipment which is perhaps five or ten years old, but perfectly satisfactory in all other respects. If you have not checked the value of your house contents for some years then you should do so now using the checklist on page 202. This is designed to help you remember everything, but only you can put a price on each item. You cannot afford to get this wrong because if you do you may risk having your claim reduced by the insurers. So the carpet you bought ten years ago for £200, may need to be valued at nearly £500 so that you are compensated for the effects of inflation since 1977 (see the table of inflation rises below).

RPI How inflation has increased prices in the last 20 years.

Year	%age rise in RPI during the year	Year	%age rise in RPI during the year
1966	3.9	1978	8.3
1967	2.5	1979	13.4
1968	4.7	1980	18.0
1969	5.4	1981	11.9
1970	6.4	1982	8.6
1971	9.4	1983	4.6
1972	7.1	1984	5.0
1973	9.2	1985	6.1
1974	16.1	1986	3.7
1975	24.2		
1976	16.5		
1977	15.8		

What is covered?

Insurance companies will cover your:
- cutlery
- food and drink
- furniture
- furnishings
- glassware and porcelain
- kitchen equipment and appliances
- mirrors and glass-topped tables
- personal valuables such as jewellery, books, records, sports equipment
- radios
- televisions and videos

against the same risks as they will insure your property.

The policy will also cover money up to stated limits and property such as fur coats, jewellery, cameras and sports equipment should you lose or damage them while using them out of the house.

Accidental damages

Most standard policies do not include *accidental damage* such as paint spillage, damage to your television or video because you have dropped it, or damages arising from the dog knocking over the dressing room table, e.g. a smashed mirror. If you want such cover you will probably have to ask for it and pay extra.

Not covered

The only things they are likely to refuse to cover on a replacement-as-new basis are clothing and bed linen which will usually be covered only on an indemnity basis. So when you are working out a value for them you must make allowances for age and depreciation.

Other features

Most insurance companies ask you to specify items above a certain value, say £500 or £800, which means that if you own works of art, antique furniture or other valuable pieces you should have them individually valued and provide the insurance company with this evidence.

An important additional feature of most contents policies is cover against accidental injury to other people or their property by you, your children, your dog or even a slate falling from the roof. This cover may be between £500,000 and £1 million.

Making a claim

If you suffer a theft for which you intend to make a claim, even if it is a small one, it is a condition of insurance policies that you inform the police. Depending on the size of the claim your insurers may accept a written declaration of the loss and pay up without quibble. Otherwise they may send one of their assessors to inspect the damage. This is when difficulty over the sum insured is most likely to arise. If the inspector sees a well-furnished home and apparently well-to-do occupants who have insured their possessions for a mere £10,000 he may well decide that you are underinsured and make his own assessment of how much you *ought* to have been covered for. If it is decided that you are, indeed, underinsured on your policy the insurance company has two options:
(a) they will apply *averaging*
(b) they will take *wear and tear* into account.

WHAT'S IT WORTH?

The following is a check list to enable you to estimate what you would have to pay to replace your house contents at *today*'s prices. In doing this exercise it is often helpful to take a new sheet for each room. The replacement value for each item should be entered so that you can then find the room total and house total. The Association of British Insurers will give further help in this area.

Sitting room

- Armchairs
- Books
- Bookcase and contents
- Briefcase
- Carpets
- Clocks
- Curtains
- Desk/bureau
- Electric heater
- Houseplants
- Lamp standards
- Mirrors
- Ornaments
- Paintings
- Piano/musical instruments
- Records
- Record/cassette player
- Rugs
- Settee
- Tables
- Television
- Video

Kitchen

- Blinds
- Chairs
- China
- Coffee percolator
- Cooker
- Cutlery
- Drinks
- Floor tiles/covering
- Food
- Food mixer
- Freezer
- Freezer contents
- Glassware
- Handbag/s and contents
- Kettle
- Microwave
- Pots and pans
- Pressure cooker
- Refrigerator
- Slow cooker
- Stools
- Table
- Television/radio
- Toaster/sandwich grill

Dining room

- Cabinet
- Candle holders
- Carpet
- Chairs
- Curtains
- Dining table
- Food trolley
- Lampshades
- Napkins, etc
- Ornaments
- Pictures
- Table cloths
- Table mats

Hall, stairs, landing

- Cabinets
- Carpets/floor covering
- Chairs
- Contents of linen cupboard (wear and tear value)
- Curtains
- Lampshades
- Occasional tables

Under the stairs

- Cleaning materials
- Suitcases
- Vacuum cleaner
- Wine

Utility room

- Dishwasher
- Garden shoes
- Ironing board
- Mops/buckets
- Outside clothes
- Tumble dryer
- Umbrellas
- Washing machine
- Wellington boots

Garage

- Garden tools
- Ladders/steps
- Lawnmower
- Paints
- Roof rack
- Sports equipment
- Tools

Bedrooms

- Bed
- Bed linen (wear and tear value)
- Bedside lamps
- Bedside tables
- Camera
- Carpet
- Clothing (wear and tear value)
  - ☐ Casual wear
  - ☐ Dresses
  - ☐ Furs
  - ☐ Hats
  - ☐ Jackets
  - ☐ Jumpers
  - ☐ Nightclothes
  - ☐ Overcoats
  - ☐ Underclothes
  - ☐ Shoes
  - ☐ Skirts/slacks
  - ☐ Sports clothes
  - ☐ Suits
  - ☐ Trousers
- Curtains
- Dressing table
- Easy chairs
- Fan heater
- Jewellery
- Radio
- Wardrobe
- Watches

Bathroom

- Carpet/floor covering
- Curtains
- Electric razor
- Make-up
- Medicine cupboard (and contents)
- Perfume
- Toiletries
- Weighing scales

Averaging

If there is an averaging clause in your insurance it means that if you make a claim while underinsured the insurer will pay out no more than a percentage of your claim. This is normally in line with the percentage cover you have taken.

Example If your television caught fire and damaged not only itself but the curtains behind it. The cost of replacing them may be £500. However, it is decided that although you had insurance cover for £20,000 it *ought* to have been for £40,000. So under the averaging rule the insurance company might pay only 50% of your claim, £250, since you are 50% underinsured.

Wear and tear

If there is no averaging clause they would be within their rights to take wear and tear into account. If the television and curtains are both seven years old and have a life of about ten, then only three tenths of the total claim, £150, will be paid.

Working out the value

In order to work out a realistic value of your house contents, you need to walk from room to room jotting down what is in there and what you think it would cost if you had to buy it new today. Don't forget to look in the drawers, cupboards, garage and shed as well (see page 202 for a checklist). It is sometimes easy to forget small items such as loose change, plants and trinkets, but they should all be included. The total may persuade you that you ought to get a burglar alarm at once, but there is no point in declaring a lesser value.

Most insurance companies offer an inflation proofing system whereby they will increase the amount of cover each year in line with the rate of inflation. However, if you buy something new you will need to increase the cover over and above that.

Discounts

An increasing number of insurance companies (e.g. Legal & General, Sun Alliance, Royal and Norwich Union) are now prepared to give premium discounts to householders who fit special locks on doors and windows, or who belong to *Neighbourhood Watch Schemes*. Some companies may give an additional discount for those who install alarm systems. As companies are showing an increasing interest it is worthwhile contacting your own insurers to find out if they offer similar savings.

BEAT THE BURGLAR

There are many simple things that you can do in order to make your home more secure. Apart from giving you peace of mind all of these measures are approved by insurance companies.

Doors

Which door is more important – the front or the back? Answer – all doors are equally important but the *door by which you leave* is the most vulnerable, because you cannot bolt it from the inside. All outside doors should have good quality locks which conform to BS 3621. Doors which you can lock from the inside should have, at the top and the bottom, bolts which preferably should be key operated. Double doors should have bolts at the top and bottom of both doors, as well as a lock. With aluminium sliding doors, fit an extra security lock.

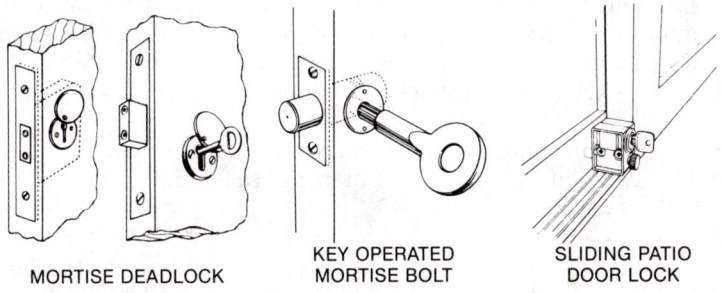

MORTISE DEADLOCK KEY OPERATED MORTISE BOLT SLIDING PATIO DOOR LOCK

Windows

- Shut them all whenever you leave the house – even if it is just to go round the corner. More thieves break in through windows than doors. More thefts occur during daylight hours.
- Fit security locks. All accessible windows (ground floor and those near drainpipes and flat roofs) should have these locks which are not expensive. Any inconvenience is well justified by the protection they give.

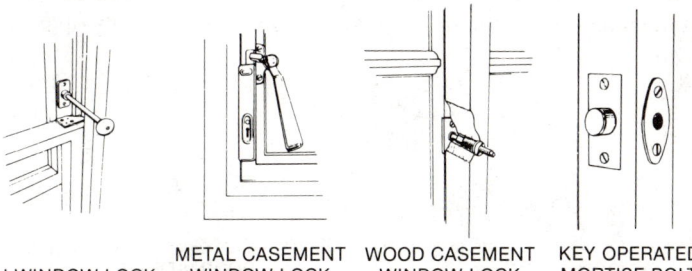

SASH WINDOW LOCK METAL CASEMENT WINDOW LOCK WOOD CASEMENT WINDOW LOCK KEY OPERATED MORTISE BOLT

Keys

- Always take care with keys – no lock has any value otherwise. Never leave keys in a lock – you should always carry them with you.
- Never leave keys in a 'secret' hiding place – under the mat or inside the letter box – thieves know all the hiding places. Leave a spare key with a trusted neighbour.

Moving house

Change all the locks and fit good quality replacements when you move house. Remember, there may be a number of people with keys to the old locks.

Going away

- Don't make it obvious that you are away from home – cancel the milk and papers. Make arrangements in person or by letter – don't leave notes which tell passers-by that you are away.
- Leave a key with a trusted neighbour and ask them to keep an eye on your house.
- Take jewellery and other valuables to the bank for safe-keeping.
- If you are going to be away for more than a few days tell the police.

Going out

- Always lock up and shut windows – however short a time you are going to be away. Most burglaries are by opportunists.
  Important – Keep garages and sheds locked. They often contain useful tools. Always chain and padlock ladders, or keep them in locked sheds or garages.
- If you are out for the evening leave a light on in a room, not the hall.

Callers

Check the credentials of all callers. Ask for some identification if they claim to be officials – don't be fooled by a uniform. Door viewers and door chains allow you to see who is outside without fully opening the door.

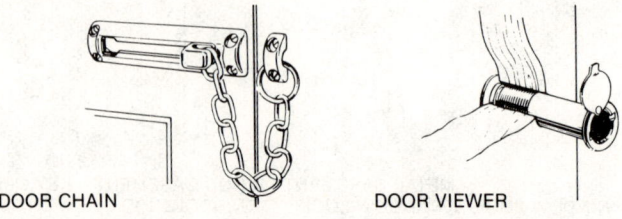

DOOR CHAIN   DOOR VIEWER

Know your own property

Keep a detailed description of your property. It will help you – (and the police) after a theft. Lack of an adequate description hampers the police in their work as items they believe to be stolen cannot be positively identified and the thieves prosecuted. It also means that much stolen property recovered by the police is never claimed because it cannot be identified by the owners.

Checklist

Use a checklist (available in the leaflet from the ABI), then keep it in a safe place. Note the serial numbers of items of domestic equipment. List other items with as many details as possible, including such distinguishing features as number, hallmarks or imperfections. Thieves often try to dispose of stolen goods in an area some distance away, so if you have a photograph or sketch which police can show to dealers, trade publications and other forces, you will have a better chance of getting your property back. You can take the photographs yourself – they do not need to be by a professional.

Ultra-violet marker pens can mark your property invisibly until put under an ultra-violet light. This helps identification if property is recovered. Just use your postcode, plus the number of your house.

Safes

If you own a lot of valuable property, such as jewellery, you may prefer the added security of a safe. Your insurance company surveyor or police crime prevention officer will advise you which type is best suited to your needs.

Alarms

Insurance companies recommend that installation of alarms is carried out by companies registered with the National Supervisory Council for Intruder Alarms (whose head office is at St Ives Road, Maidenhead, Berks).

Remember, most alarms only warn that someone has broken into your premises – your first priority should be to stop them getting there.

Reproduced with the permission of the Association of British Insurers.

Suitable locking systems
Discounts may be obtained for:

- fitting 5-lever mortise dead locks on doors (cost £11–12) ⎫
- fitting special window locks (cost £2–3) ⎬ 10% discount
- secondary double glazing system with interior locks ⎭

- membership of neighbourhood watch scheme   5% discount

The special window locks prevent a burglar opening a window even if he breaks the glass and can reach the window latch.

The neighbourhood watch scheme originated in America and is now gaining popularity here. The idea is that groups of residents in streets, on estates, villages or similar small areas get together to organise a 'lookout' for people and cars behaving in a suspicious way and report, where necessary, to the local police. The fact that signs are usually erected advertising the presence of the scheme is quite a deterrent in itself. You can find out more from your local police station.

MOTOR INSURANCE

Insurance companies like older motorists and many are prepared to offer special premiums to those over 50 whose experience, more relaxed temperament and lower mileage tends to keep them out of trouble on the road. As a result:
- premiums are lower than for younger motorists
- no claims bonuses are often guaranteed (so you don't lose them even if you have an accident)
- there are sometimes 'frills' on the policy offering you such bonuses as a free hire car if your own vehicle is off the road because of an accident.

What kind of policy?

According to the *Road Traffic Act 1972* in order to take a vehicle on the road you must be insured for liability against injury to other people, including your passengers. Damage to your vehicle or to any other vehicle or property is your responsibility. In practice few people are offered such policies. Full third party insurance is the minimum cover most insurance companies are prepared to offer. Although comprehensive cover is not essential under the law, two out of three motorists (and certainly most older drivers) have comprehensive policies. This covers them and any other authorised driver for fire, theft and accidental damage to vehicles, whoever is at fault. It also covers injury and damage to other people's property.

Special policies

If you have an inexpensive second car there are cheaper policies available. Some people like to keep vintage cars on the road and it is easy to find special policies which give preferential rates. There are some restrictions such as:
- limited mileage each year (e.g. 3000 miles)
- driving restricted to driver only or driver and spouse
- an agreed valuation may also be suggested.

Sometimes it is necessary to provide the insurance company with a written estimate of the value of the vehicle and good colour photographs of it.

Insurance schemes are often run by the clubs associated with famous marques like the MG, Jaguar or Austin Healey Owners' Clubs.

Insurance companies which have special deals on offer to older motorists are given at the end of this chapter. Other companies not offering special policies for people over 50 pointed out that older drivers gained an advantage in terms of premiums anyway since age was one of the factors built in to fixing a premium.

LIFE ASSURANCE

Life insurance is worthwhile even on the approach to retirement. If you die while still having dependants then your income or pension that is lost or reduced on your death may be covered by life assurance. There are four main types of life assurance:
- Whole life assurance
- Term or temporary assurance
- Endowment assurance
- Annuity assurance

Whole life assurance

Earlier in life you may have taken out a whole life policy as a relatively inexpensive form of assurance for your family in the event of your untimely death. Your family will still benefit from that cover even when you have retired but there is one important additional reason for taking out this *additional* cover, that is the implications of inheritance tax for your family (see page 188). For instance, if both you and your spouse died in an accident the beneficiaries of your will would inherit not only your estate but a tax bill to go with it. By insuring to cover the tax bill you can ensure that your children enjoy *all* that you intended them to have, not just the bit left by the taxman. To do this, your children have to be named as beneficiaries under such a scheme and both you and your spouse will have to take out similar policies.

TYPES OF MOTOR INSURANCE COVER AVAILABLE

Two out of three motorists hold comprehensive policies and the remainder, third party, fire and theft or third party only. It is extremely rare for a motorist to request 'Act Only' cover. The scope of the various policies is indicated below.

COMPREHENSIVE Sections 1 to 10

THIRD PARTY, FIRE AND THEFT Sections 1 to 6

THIRD PARTY Sections 1 to 5

ACT ONLY Sections 1 and 2

1. Liability for injuries to other people, arising from accidents caused by your car on public roads or elsewhere. Legal costs incurred with your insurance company's consent in connection with a claim against you will also be paid.

2. Liability for injuries to passengers in your car.

3. Liability of passengers in your car in respect of accidents caused by them – for example, the careless opening of a door causing injury to a passer-by or damage to his property.

4. Liability for damage to other people's property. For example, if you are involved in an accident which causes damage to another car, your insurance company will pay all or part of the cost of repairs to the other car, depending on the extent to which you are legally to blame.

5. Liability for injuries to other people or damage to their property caused by a trailer or caravan attached to your car.

6. Fire or theft but if your car is not normally kept in a locked garage at night your insurer may exclude theft, make theft cover subject to special conditions or charge an extra premium.

ACT ONLY

This type of cover is restricted to liability for injuries to other people, including your passengers, in traffic accidents on public roads. Act-only policies are limited to the minimum compulsory requirements of the Road Traffic Act 1972.

7. Accidental damage to your car but not wear and tear, depreciation, loss of use, mechanical or electrical breakdown and punctures. If at the time of the accident, your car is being driven by or is in the charge of someone who holds a provisional licence or has held a full licence for less than a year, or who is under 25 years old, you will usually have to pay for damage to your car up to a maximum stated in your policy. This 'excess' will generally be from £25 upwards.

8. Accidents to yourself and perhaps your wife or husband, resulting in death or loss of sight and/or limbs, up to stated amounts. This applies to all journeys in your private car or in any other car not belonging to you, whether you are driving or not. This benefit applies only to policies in the name of an individual.

9. Medical expenses up to a stated amount incurred by you or your passengers as a result of an accident involving your car.

10. Loss of or damage to rugs, clothing and personal effects up to a stated amount while they are in the car.

REPRODUCED WITH THE PERMISSION OF THE ASSOCIATION OF BRITISH INSURERS

Example

Joe and Madge are both 50. They have a house in the suburbs of London worth £100,000; furniture, car, caravan and other belongings at home worth around £40,000; a pension scheme with a guaranteed payment provision worth £45,000; and savings and investments worth another £10,000. The total estate is £195,000.

The first £90,000 is exempt but tax is levied on the remaining £105,000. With the top slice attracting tax at 40% the total sum due is a stunning £37,000. If they were killed in a car crash it would make a significant dent in the estate left to their children. However, if they had each taken out a life policy naming the children as beneficiaries for, say, £40,000 the tax bill would be easily covered for an annual premium between £40 and £50.

How whole of life assurance operates.

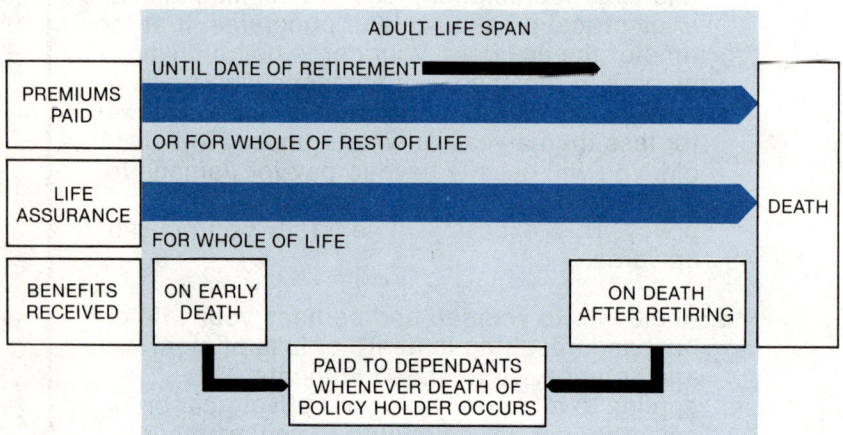

How a term assurance works.

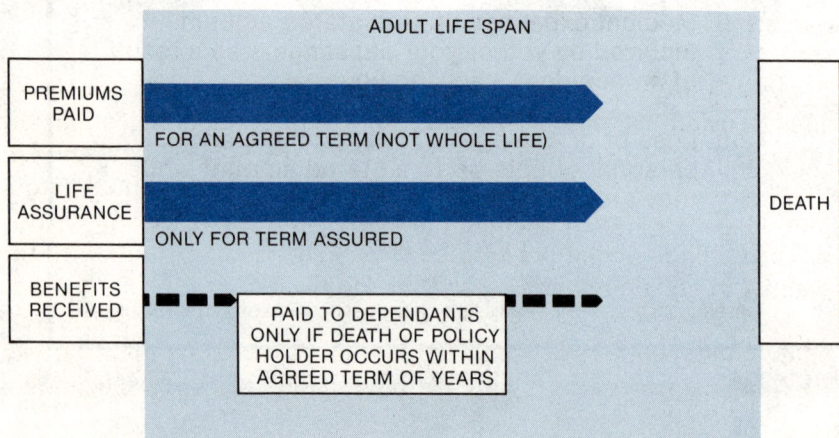

Term assurance

This is the life assurance you take out for a limited period to cover a specific risk such as the years during which the children are growing up, or a mortgage protection policy which covers you until you pay the final instalment on the house, or perhaps to cover a specific risk like an overseas journey.

Endowment assurance

This is a savings scheme combined with a life assurance cover and is often used by people wanting to plan ahead for cash lump sums later in life. The expected year of retirement is a popular maturity date for endowment policies. You can take them out at almost any age, but obviously the older you are the more expensive they will be. In practice it is unusual to take out an endowment for fewer than ten years and the majority are for longer periods than that. But a man or woman in their early to mid-fifties contemplating ways of saving for retirement could make effective use of an endowment.

Tax
Do not use an endowment as a substitute for a pension scheme. Life assurance policies no longer enjoy any tax relief on premiums, neither do the insurance companies enjoy tax relief on the invested funds. An endowment cannot, therefore, offer a growth rate that matches any personal pension plan or pension enhancement scheme such as additional voluntary contributions.

If your intention is to save money for a pension or lump sum for retirement then you should examine all the various pension schemes first of all to the maximum the Inland Revenue will allow. Only after that should you consider endowments or other savings schemes. Also, do not embark on an endowment unless you are sure you can complete the term as early surrender of your policy for cash may well be on terms that are not advantageous to you.

Example Godfrey is 50, has a job paying £17,000 a year and can expect a good pension. He is making the most he can by topping it up to the maximum level with additional voluntary contributions. He still has some spare cash to invest but doesn't want to dabble on the Stock Market. Nevertheless he likes the idea of unit trusts and discovers that he can combine the opportunities of high returns from units with the security of an endowment policy.

He decides to invest £40 a month for ten years in a 'unit-linked' endowment policy of which 97% is used for investment in unit trusts. His total investment during the ten years period will be £4800, and for

that he will receive:
- A guaranteed minimum of £3600 payable on death during the ten-year term
- A cash sum at the end which, assuming a steady 10% a year rise in the value of his units, will pay out more than £7000 on maturity.

How endowment assurance works.

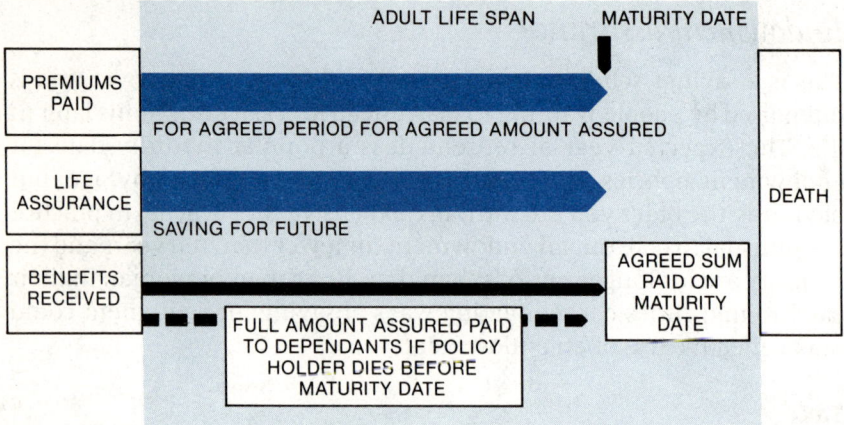

Annuities

The main difference between an annuity assurance policy and the other life policies is that instead of a single lump sum payment being the ultimate outcome in the event of the policy being claimed or maturing, the annuity offers a regular income. The annuity is a popular form of saving for retirement and there are two forms:
- regular premium payments
- lump sum investment.

Regular premium payments
You pay a regular premium to an insurance company for an agreed number of years to mature on your 65th birthday, or some other date agreed at the time. On maturity instead of a lump sum you receive the first of regular payments that will be paid for the rest of your life.

Lump sum investment
You invest a single lump sum into an annuity at any age after, say, 60, in return for a regular income for life.

Tax
It is important not to confuse an annuity with a normal pension scheme or a personal pension plan. It does *not* attract tax relief on the premiums

How an annuity works.

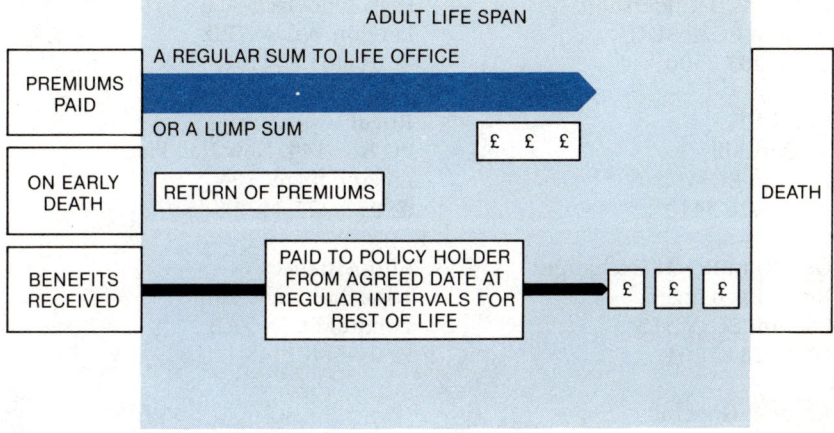

and, like an endowment policy, should be used as a means of providing income for retirement only *after* you have taken full advantage of any pension schemes open to you (see page 62 for further details).

Optional features

Whole life or endowment assurance may have an additional option of taking a straight 'no frills' policy or adding a 'with profits' bonus. The latter will cost more but it means that each year the insurance company will share part of its profits with you. Although the size of the bonus varies each year, once it has been paid it cannot be taken away. This means that the final sum you receive from the insurance company is not fixed, but it is certain to be larger than the basic sum assured. An alternative to a 'with profits' policy is a 'unit-linked' policy where your yearly bonuses are linked to specific investments made by the company through Stock Exchange investments. Your bonus will depend on how these perform during the year.

USEFUL ADDRESSES

The following insurance companies give some form of special deal to motorists over the age of 50. For details contact either your broker, the local branch or the head office of the company concerned.

Association of British Insurers
Aldermary House
Queen Street
London EC4N 1TT

Britannic
Moor Green, Moseley,
Birmingham B13 8QF
☎ 021-449 4444

Commercial Union
St Helens, 1 Undershaft
London EC3P 3DQ
☎ 01-283 7500

Cornhill
32 Cornhill
London EC3V 3LJ
☎ 01-626 5410

Guardian Royal Exchange
Royal Exchange
London EC3V 3LS
☎ 01-283 7101

Legal & General
Temple Court
11 Queen Victoria Street
London EC4N 4TP
☎ 01-248 9678

Pearl
High Holborn
London WC1V 7EB
☎ 01-405 8441

Royal
PO Box 144, New Hall Place
Liverpool L69 3EN
☎ 051-227 4422

Sun Alliance
1 Bartholomew Lane
London EC2N 2AB
☎ 01-588 2345

REFERENCES

Beat the Burglar Association of British Insurers, London.
Buildings Insurance for Home Owners (1986) Association of British Insurers, London.

Your will be done

WHY MAKE A WILL?	218
INTESTACY	219
HOW YOUR SOLICITOR CAN HELP	220
Cost of making a will	220
DIY WILLS	220
Revising your will	220
Witnesses	221
Executors	221
LETTERS OF ADMINISTRATION	222
KEEPING THE WILL	222
INVALID WILLS	222
Limited rights	222
Marriage and divorce	222
Commorientes	223
BIBLIOGRAPHY	224

It is easy to think that we will live forever, but as it is unlikely we should make a will to ensure that we bequeath no headaches to those we care about. Yet it's surprising how few people bother. In 1985 more than 590,000 deaths were registered but only 178,000 wills were recorded by the Probate Registry. Many people feel that it is tempting providence, but they do not have the same forebodings when they take out insurance on their cars, or against fire, burglary or some other disaster befalling their home. There are *no* statistics to prove that making a will accelerates death.

WHY MAKE A WILL?

So your will will be done
The primary reason for making a will is that it is the only way in which you can be certain that your wishes are carried out, provided, of course, that it is properly drafted. To be sure of that it is best to employ a solicitor.

It is easy to delude yourself with the comforting thought that everyone knows your wishes and will work it all out amicably if you do not make a will. However, bereavement is a time of enormous stress and the last thing your relatives and friends need is the added problems, and possibly disagreements, that will arise from trying to divine your intentions.

To avoid hardship for your dependants
People who do not make wills die *intestate* which means that what they leave is apportioned out in accordance with a laid down formula. It generally takes longer to sort out an estate where there is no will, so that dependants unable to get at much-needed cash to pay the bills that continue to flow in may get into real difficulty. This difficulty may occur even when there *is* a will and one way to avoid it is to have a joint bank account to which the survivor will continue to have access. Accounts solely in the name of the partner who has died will be frozen until probate, or letters of administration, are granted.

How an estate is apportioned in cases of intestacy.

	Net value of estate		
Beneficiaries	Up to £75,000	£75,000–£125,000	+ £125,000
Spouse			
with children	Everything	£75,000 + all personal chattels + life interest in ½ remaining estate (reverts to children)	£75,000 + all personal chattels + life interest in ½ remaining estate (reverts to children)
without children	Everything	Everything	£125,000 + all personal chattels + life interest in ½ remaining estate
Children	Equal shares†	Equal shares of ½ remaining estate	—
Others*	—	—	½ remaining estate

*Other beneficiaries are, in order of priority:
- parents of the deceased
- brothers and sisters of the deceased
- children of the siblings

†Only if there is no surviving spouse

INTESTACY

The table above shows how an estate will be apportioned should this situation occur. If the net value of the estate does not exceed £75,000, everything goes to the widow, or widower. If there is no surviving partner the estate is divided equally between the children. Where the net value exceeds £75,000, the spouse gets £75,000 and all personal chattels. The remainder of the estate is then halved and the spouse has a life interest in one half while the other half is divided among the children of the marriage. The portion of the estate in which the surviving partner has a life interest will ultimately go to the children on that partner's death.

If a couple have no children and the net estate does not exceed £125,000 everything goes to the survivor. If it is worth more than that figure, the surviving partner receives £125,000, all personal chattels and a life interest in half of the remainder of the estate. The other half goes to whoever is highest in a list of possible beneficiaries.

Common law spouses have no legal right to inherit anything unless it can be proved that they were being supported by their partners.

HOW YOUR SOLICITOR CAN HELP

A solicitor is useful not only to draw up an accurate will, but can also draw your attention to ways in which you can minimise inheritance tax liability. As solicitors charge for the work and time involved it pays not to waste their time by uncertainty and frequent changes of mind.

Before the interview, have all the necessary information at your fingertips, what your assets are, and the names and relationships of the intended beneficiaries. Do not keep secrets from your solicitor; if you were previously married and have children by that marriage, tell him. It is a good idea to jot it all down in advance. If it is a complicated will, your solicitor can act as executor for you.

Cost of making a will

Around £30 but there is *no standard fee* and you are within your rights to ask the solicitor how much he will charge before you put him to work.

DIY WILLS

Although you can draw up your own will it is often far more expensive to sort out the problems created by home-made wills than to pay to have them drawn up. It would be better to pay a modest sum at the outset and be sure that it is done properly than to risk the possibility that the value of what you leave may be considerably diminished by the legal costs of sorting out an error or ambiguity.

If you still wish to draw up one yourself a will form can be obtained from a stationers together with some simple instructions. It is important that when you have written your will you have two people to witness your signature to it. It is not acceptable to ask someone to sign if the will has already been signed by you outside of their presence. It is essential that you as the *testator* should sign in the presence of your witnesses, with the date alongside, and they should add their names immediately. It is useful also to include an *attestation*, or a statement, by the witnesses in the form:

Signed by the testator in our joint presence and then by us in his presence.

Although it is not a legal requirement, ask the witnesses to add their addresses and occupations in case they have to be traced in the future.

Revising your will

Never alter, amend or cross out anything from your will nor mark it in any way. Any alterations must be made by *codicil*, an addition, to your will and the procedure is precisely the same as for the making of the original, although you do not have to have the same two witnesses. If there are many amendments, it will probably be better to make a completely new will.

Having made a will you cannot forget it entirely as your circumstances may change as may the circumstances that affect you, e.g. the rules relating to inheritance tax. You should take the will out and look at it every three or four years just to make sure that it still serves the purpose you intend.

Witnesses

Anyone can act as a witness provided they understand what is happening, but if you ask a relative or friend, remember that they *cannot be a beneficiary under the will*. The will would not be invalid if you made a gift in it to a witness, but the gift would. The same applies to a legacy made to the husband or wife of a witness: they would not be allowed to inherit it.

Executors

Executors must safeguard the assets of the estate and, when probate is granted by the probate registry with authorisation for them to act, they must pay the debts and expenses, and then distribute the estate according to the provisions of the will.

Unlike witnesses executors *can* be beneficiaries under the will. They frequently are if a close relative is appointed to act in this capacity. You do not have to ask permission of anyone to make them your executor, but it is sensible to do so because they can refuse to act when the time comes.

It is sensible to have at least one younger person to act as an executor, as not only is there less chance that your executors will die before you, but at a time of high emotional stress the role may be an unnecessary additional burden for an elderly close relative. You may have as many executors as you wish, but probate will be granted to no more than four.

For complicated wills and estates you may wish to appoint a professional executor as well as non-professionals to act with him. This is rather expensive although invaluable in complex situations. For the average will, a couple of sensible friends or relatives should be able to cope without too much trouble, and at considerably lower cost. Banks also provide executor and trustee services and so will the Public Trustee. These base their fees on a percentage of the total value of the estate. All professional executors, with the exception of the Public

Trustees, require that provision is made in the will so that they may draw their fees from the estate. Further information may be found in leaflets from the high street banks and the Public Trustee will send details if you write to:

Stewart House
Kingsway, London WC2B 6JX

LETTERS OF ADMINISTRATION

Letters of administration are required when:
(a) there is no will
(b) a will has not appointed an executor
(c) the executors are unwilling or unable to take up their duties.
The Probate Registry issues these to enable an administrator to carry out the task. This generally causes delay in settling an estate because, while an executor can take some action before probate, an administrator can do nothing until the authority has been issued. It is not necessary to employ a solicitor to obtain probate or letters of administration. The Probate Registry is geared up to deal with people acting without professional advice.

KEEPING THE WILL

You can keep your will with a solicitor, bank or at home. Whatever you do, tell your executors where it is. If it is with your solicitor you should have a copy.

INVALID WILLS

Limited rights

Within reason, you can leave your money as you wish, but if you leave out your marriage partner, a child or indeed anyone dependent on you they can apply to the court for provision to be made for them from your estate. Anyone who has this sort of problem should certainly seek legal advice and have the will drawn up professionally.

Marriage and divorce

A will you have previously made is automatically revoked if you marry. The only exception is if the will was made specifically in contemplation of the marriage, and makes this plain in its wording. Again, a solicitor is advisable in such circumstances. If you marry and fail to make a new will you will ultimately die intestate.

Divorce does not revoke a will, but it does revoke the appointment of the former partner as an executor and any gifts made to him or her. It is always sensible to consider making a new will in these circumstances, although a former spouse may still have a claim on the estate.

Commorientes

This covers the situation of simultaneous death of a husband and wife, which is generally the result of an accident. Remote though this possibility is, as long as you travel together by land, sea or air it is wise to make provision for it in your will. Since it is often medically impossible to determine whether one person fractionally survived another in an accident, the law assumes that the younger one always survives the older. You can also cover it in your will be providing that if there is doubt, one shall be considered to have survived the other. You may also make a provision that requires a beneficiary to survive you by a period of say 28 days, in order to inherit.

Survival clauses

Does it matter? From a tax point of view it may well be important. Assume a husband and his younger wife make wills leaving everything to one another but including a 28-day survivorship requirement. If they die together alternative beneficiaries will inherit; these are normally the children. The husband's will provides that his assets will be dealt with as though the wife had died first and the wife's will is drawn up on the basis that her husband pre-deceased her. If these provisions had not been made and the couple had died together, the law would assume that the husband, who was the older, died first and that his wife inherited his estate. That would be added to her own assets and everything would then pass to the children. But by making these provisions in their wills the estates have been kept separate so the children would inherit not one large estate, but two smaller ones and both with the £90,000 exemption from inheritance tax.

In drawing up wills with clauses to cover simultaneous death it is important that the wording in the wills be precise.

Example A couple made wills leaving their estates to one another. Both made provision in the wills so that if they died together alternative beneficiaries would inherit so each named different beneficiaries in their individual wills. It is reasonable to assume that what they intended was that all of the beneficiaries named in *both* wills should receive the gifts specified. However, the circumstances of their deaths made it impossible to prove they died at the same moment or indeed, which of them died first. So under the rule of *commorientes* the wife, who was the younger, was considered to have survived her husband. His estate passed to her and was then inherited by the beneficiaries named in *her* will. Those named in his will got nothing.

BIBILIOGRAPHY

Wills and Probate (1983) Consumers Association, London.

Health and well-being

PHYSICAL HEALTH AND YOUR STATE OF MIND	228
EXERCISE AND FITNESS	230
Muscles and strength	230
Joints	231
Exercise programmes	232
LOOKING AFTER YOURSELF	233
Lung cancer	233
Coronary heart disease	234
Nutrition – facts and myths	238
CHECKING ON YOUR HEALTH	241
Regular health checks	241
Prevention and screening	242
SPECIAL PROBLEMS OF MEN AND WOMEN	244
Gynaecological problems	244
Bones	244
Breast cancer	245
Cervical cancer	245
The prostate	245
Further information	246
STRESS AND RELAXATION	246
Stress in retirement	246

    Treatment   247
    Learning to relax   247
    Relationships   251
    Problems of couples   251
    Family and friends   252
    Living alone   253
SEXUAL RELATIONS   254
    Sexual needs   254
    Sex and the menopause   254
    Loss of libido   255
SURVIVING BEREAVEMENT   256
    The progress of bereavement   256
    Facing up to death   257
    Help from others   257
USING THE HEALTH SERVICES   257
    The general practitioner   257
    Private treatment   260
    Chemists   261
    Dental services   261
    Optical services   262
    Hearing centres   262
    Fringe, alternative and holistic medicine   263
    Further information   263
OLDER RELATIVES – SUPPORT AND CARE   264
    Back-up care   264
    'Granny' flats   264
    Sheltered housing   265
    Surrogate homes   265
    The hospice movement   265
COMMON PROBLEMS IN LATER LIFE   266
    Vision   266
    Hearing   267
    Strokes and raised blood pressure   268
    Fluid intake   269

Warmth	269
Mobility	270
Memory and reflexes	270
Confusion	271
USEFUL ADDRESSES	271
BIBLIOGRAPHY	275
References	275

PHYSICAL HEALTH AND YOUR STATE OF MIND

Gloom, anxiety and depression are the harbingers of disease. Ebullience, *joie de vivre* and general well-being, on the other hand, make for enjoyment of life and good health.

That is my philosophy for a long and healthy retirement. There are, of course, some useful and sensible ground rules for promoting and maintaining physical health which will be discussed later, but the key to growing old gracefully is to promote a sense of general well-being. Many active, involved people do not tend to be ill.

If you face retirement, not as the end of life's road, but as the entry into new, unmapped, but exciting and interesting territory, then you are starting off on the right foot. Active, involved people have no time to be ill. It is only in recent years that the medical profession has really begun to understand the relationship between the state of our minds and the state of our bodies. We tended, in the past, to concentrate on the obvious physical problems without paying much attention to the mental problems that may be underlying cause. Identifying and treating the symptoms are easier.

Now our basic thinking about health and disease has moved to more constructive levels. We know now that how a person feels emotionally is reflected in the state of the body. If the mind is 'out of sorts' with the world then the body also is likely to feel 'dis-eased'. A person who is full of mental and physical vigour, on the other hand, is far less disposed to becoming ill or diseased. Your mind and body interract to determine the way we adjust to the demands of living and for many of us these demands are as much emotional as physical. As you approach retirement it is important to understand that

- You are as old as you feel and never mind what it says on your birth certificate.
- How you feel is very much under your control. If you spend the last ten years of your working life harbouring grudges because you were not promoted as far as you felt you deserved; or if you are pushed into retirement deeply resentful of the fact that you have to give up work, then you are half way to the state of dis-ease which can be so dangerous.

More of us retire at the age of 60 these days and if we are in reasonably good health we can look forward to another 20 years of

HEALTH AND WELL-BEING 229

active life – women can look forward to even longer. That is far too much time to spend with a long face. Indeed with that kind of approach your expectation of life must be substantially reduced.

Retirement is a shock to the system, as I know from personal experience. It can be just as difficult as the transition from school to the real world of earning a living, probably *more* so because your retirement has to be entirely self-motivated and has no fixed framework. Work provides the status, identity and association with other people around which we build our lives. So in order to promote a sense of well-being in retirement, we need to create a new identity for ourselves with a new network of associations and associates. It will not happen automatically. You have to go out and create this life for yourself. Building a new identity and maintaining, or even improving health, can be assessed under a number of headings and given a great deal of thought.

1. Accept that you now have 20 or so years of new and wide-open opportunity. You are not reaching an end but a new beginning.
2. Decide *how* you are going to spend your time.
   (a) do you want (or need) to take on a full or part-time paid job, or
   (b) will your activities be largely voluntary or recreational?
   It is critical that what you do will be stimulating and challenging. It is not enough to drift from one largely social or sporting activity to another. I believe that even if you don't need the money, paid work, even at a humble level, is likely to be more motivational, particularly for younger retirees. Professional people often have opportunities for consultancy appointments.

   Quite a lot of your time should be spent with, and for, other people in order to help create your new identity and provide status. Society needs this help and we all benefit from being wanted. At the end of this planning stage, there must be plenty of things in the diary and tomorrow must be worth getting up for.

   Another crucial decision to be made is how much time couples wish to spend together and how much separately. I recently spent a brief holiday with two friends in their cottage. They were on holiday and coming up to retirement. They each have different creative interests and to foster enjoyment and reduce potential conflict, they decided to spend alternate days together and the next doing their own thing. It worked splendidly for them.
3. You must decide where you wish to spend your retirement. You will find more about this in the Chapter on *Moving to Your Retirement Home*, but I mention it here because it has a fundamental bearing on your state of well-being and therefore your health.

   I don't want to sound dogmatic about this but I would suggest that moving to a new part of the country where you will be a stranger can, by breaking the rules of association, be dangerous.

Try to visualise what it will be like in 10 to 15 years' time when you are less active and possibly even alone. A safer bet might be to move to a suitable house in an area you know well.
4. Money. You may once have wondered how this subject could find a place in a chapter on health, but if you have followed my philosophy so far you will realise that undue anxiety about money can also predispose you to dis-ease.

Although husbands often take the initiative in sorting out the financial side of retirement it is often an unspoken cause of anxiety to wives that they are not *sure* what the financial future holds for them if they survive their husbands. Financial planning ought, therefore, to be a joint affair.
5. Remember that the state of your health is partly in your hands and anything you do now to improve your state of physical and mental fitness will pay handsome dividends.

EXERCISE AND FITNESS

> *"If I had known I was going to live so long,*
> *I would have taken more care of myself."*
> W. C. FIELDS

I believe you can invest in health just as soundly as in the building society, and it will pay you to do so. The younger you are the easier you will find this, but it is never too late. Getting fit to retire can, in physical terms prove a good investment. Middle age is a time for self-assessment and improvement.

Muscles and strength

Muscles must have regular use. Your muscles are made up of large numbers of thick, contractile fibres for strength and fewer thinner ones for rapid response, like sprinting in athletics or taking your hand away rapidly from a hot kettle. Both fibres degenerate with disuse but strengthen with exercise. Even a trained athlete, if confined to bed for several weeks because of injury, will not only lose a lot of his strength but take a considerable time to regain it. An older person, who makes little use of their muscles will suffer in the same way, but may *never* recover full capability. The older you are the more difficult it is to regain the strength you lose through inactivity.

Most of us, therefore, would benefit from more regular exercise, not to become athletes but to maintain our strength for daily living. Simple activities such as playing with grandchildren on the floor, walking up and down stairs or digging the garden all help. My gardener, a countryman for all of his 84 years, can still do a full day's physical work because this is what he has always done.

The heart

Your heart muscle works in just the same way although physiologically it functions automatically. In order to be fit, it needs to be exercised regularly to the point where you get out of breath. The increase of older people taking up aerobic exercises, jogging and even marathon running is highly desirable, in my view, and keeping your heart muscle fit will do much to reduce coronary heart disease (CHD). Sadly Britain is still near the top of the international CHD league, largely because of dietary indulgence, cigarette consumption and relative physical inactivity. The jogging cult in America has probably contributed significantly to their impressive CHD reduction.

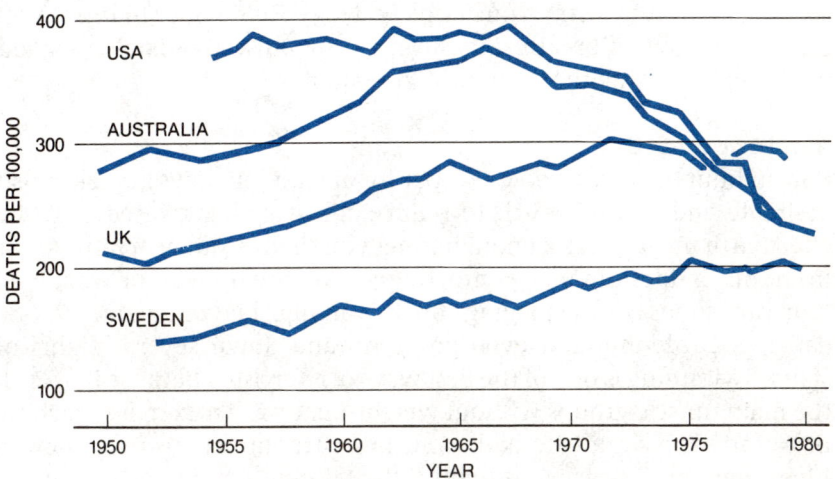

CHD MORTALITY RATES – INTERNATIONAL TRENDS OF CORONARY HEART DISEASE MORTALITY (MEN AGED 35 – 64, AGE ADJUSTED)

Joints

Arms, legs, back and neck joints also benefit from regular use. Like the hinges of doors or box lids, if you only half use them they will creak and be stiff when you try to use them fully. Use them fully at every opportunity and there will be no problem. Children are naturally active and fully use their joints but older people, particularly if they suffer from arthritis, tend not to and stiffen up as a result.

Reasonable (not excessive) physical activity is therefore a 'must' for successful retirement. There are two components to this
- A regular 'daily dozen' of mobility exercises
- Half an hour a day of brisk aerobic exercise.

Exercise programmes

The 'daily dozen'
This is a series of mobility exercises which put all your main joints through their full range of movements. They also help to strengthen the thinner muscle fibres. There are a number of books which give suitable exercises including publications from the Health Education Council (see the Bibliography, page 275).

Gentle exercise is normally quite safe at any age, but if you know that you suffer from high blood pressure or diabetes then it is best to check with your doctor first. Exercising should be enjoyable and you should find your best time of the day; this may be before breakfast or before lunch.

Always start an exercise session by warming up gently and slowing down at the end. Wear loosely fitting clothing and find an area large enough for you to swing your arms and legs. Remember to rest if you get tired or out of breath. Measuring your pulse rate is also a good method of ensuring that you don't overdo it.

Aerobic exercises
Half an hour of brisk aerobic exercise for at least four days a week is also desirable and will do much to reduce coronary heart disease. To be effective, it must be brisk enough to get you slightly out of breath. Apart from this, it does not matter much how exercise is taken or what it is. You can choose from jogging, brisk walking, playing active games, dancing, gardening and even going up and down several flights of stairs. Swimming is one of the best ways of exercising because it uses all the main muscle groups without weight-bearing. An exercise machine or a static bicycle in the bathroom or bedroom can also be a sound investment and is easy to use by all the family.

It is, however, essential to exercise regularly all through the year. It is no good being a fair-weather exerciser. If you wall yourself up for Winter, you will emerge in Spring weak and flabby like a hibernating hedgehog. Consider having a regular family outing in the fresh air at weekends or regularly exercise a medium-sized dog; it is good motivation and can be fun.

How safe is it?
If you have any medical doubts or get pains or undue breathlessness, have a medical check-up. Consult your doctor before starting any strenuous exercise programme, but don't assume that because you have a heart condition you will be told not to do it. Doctors no longer tell patients to 'take it easy'. Heart patients are encouraged to get out of bed as soon as possible and are then sent to a gymnasium for gradual

rehabilitation. Your body will look after itself and if you go too far becomes painful and gets out of breath. Provided you build up gradually not only will you come to no harm, but you will noticeably improve.

What if I'm disabled? If you have a disability, such as an arthritic joint or weak back, it is even more vital to keep up muscle strength. Special exercises may be prescribed by a physiotherapist if necessary. Not long ago *Choice*, the retirement planning magazine, put 50 readers with an average age of around 63, through a six-months' supervised gymnasium course. They enjoyed it enormously, their improvement was measurable and their well-being vastly improved. Even those with angina and raised blood pressure benefited. Everyone was motivated by the sense of being part of a team. So if you can find others to exercise with you, you may be encouraged to keep it up.

Exercise is vital for physical health, but a spin-off is that it also promotes liveliness and well-being. You will feel better, sleep better and *be* better for it.

LOOKING AFTER YOURSELF

Exercise is not the only ingredient of good health in middle life. There is plenty more you can do to improve your own outlook. This is because many of our major health problems are self-inflicted and related to our lifestyle. They are also, however, very much under our own control. You can, for example, choose:
- whether or not you smoke
- how much alcohol you drink
- how much you eat
- what sort of food you eat

all can be contributory factors in causing serious diseases such as lung cancer and coronary heart disease, as well as a host of other ailments.

Lung cancer

There is overwhelming and well-publicised evidence linking cigarette smoking with lung cancer (as well as other cancers such as the oesophagus) and coronary heart disease (see page 234). Obviously the earlier you give up smoking the better it is for your health prospects, but it is never too late. Retirement may well provide a very good opportunity for you to succeed in giving up as the pressures of work are lifted and the pattern of your lifestyle changes. For those who find it difficult to give up, there are many sources of help and therapy. (Further information can be found on page 272.)

Coronary heart disease

Coronary heart disease (CHD) is a common problem. A total of 354,000 new cases of CHD arise in general practice each year in England and Wales, of which 27% involve men aged 45–64 years. Four-fifths of deaths arising from CHD occur in persons over 65 years. Therefore, it is especially important that you try to minimise the risk of CHD.

Risk factors

The 'risk factors' for coronary heart disease are:
- genetic inheritance
- lack of exercise
- cigarette smoking
- overweight and an excess of animal fats (cholesterol) in the diet
- raised blood pressure
- stress.

By examining and questioning patients, doctors are able to apply a coronary risk rating against each of these factors using a scale of 0–2. How this is interpreted depends very much on the judgement of the

---

Simple formula for identifying individuals at high CHD risk.

---

7 × years of smoking cigarettes
plus 6.5 × mean BP (mmHg)
plus 270 if the man recalls a diagnosis of IHD
plus 150 if there is questionnaire evidence of angina
plus 85 if either parent has died of heart trouble
plus 150 if he is diabetic

Those scoring more than 1000 are in the top 20 per cent of the distribution of the risk score.

Source: Shaper, 1986.
BP = blood pressure
IHD = ischaemic heart disease

---

individual doctor. They will check medical background, take biochemical tests and use an electrocardiograph (ECG) to check heart function. Then they tell you whether you are at high or low risk of coronary heart disease (CHD). A perfect score of 0 is rarely achieved and so, fortunately, is a score of 11 or 12. If your parents are both over 70 or lived to be over 70, if you are reasonably active, do not smoke, are fairly lean and have no blood pressure problem, then the chances are that your score will be very low.

Obviously there is nothing you can do about your genetic background except that you can help by taking special care to minimise the

CORONARY HEART DISEASE – THE FACTS

Incidence of coronary heart disease, males and females by age, England and Wales 1981/82, rates per 1000 population.

	Males			Females		
Age	Acute myocardial infarction	Angina of effort	Other coronary heart disease	Acute myocardial infarction	Angina of effort	Other coronary heart disease
15–24	0.0	–	0.1	–	–	–
25–44	0.8	0.3	0.2	0.2	0.4	0.1
45–64	7.4	6.8	3.6	2.5	4.4	1.6
65–74	12.8	14.2	6.9	6.8	9.0	5.5
75+	13.9	14.4	8.4	9.2	9.5	6.8
All ages	3.4	3.3	1.8	1.9	2.6	1.4

Source: Royal College of General Practitioners, 1986.

CHD mortality patterns

One death in every three in England and Wales is due to heart disease but heart disease is a broad term embracing a wide range of specific disorders. Of these, coronary heart disease is the most significant. In 1985, it caused 163,104 deaths, that is 28% of the total for England and Wales in that year.

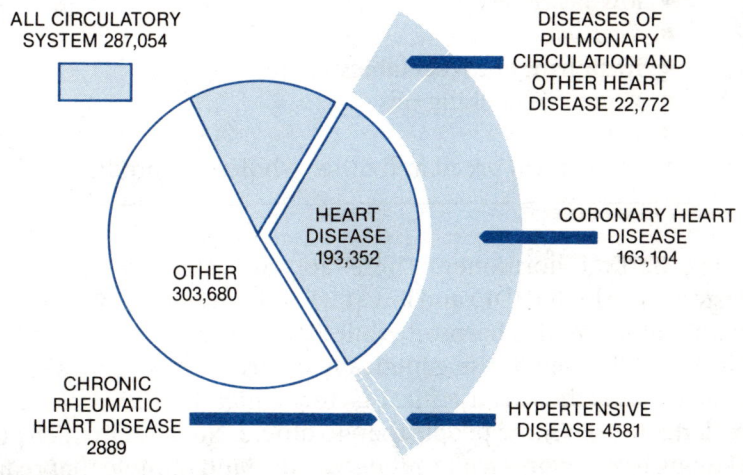

other risks. If you have a problem with raised blood pressure it is important that this should be monitored and treated if necessary (see *Checking on Your Health* page 241).

Reducing the risks of CHD

Coronary heart disease is due largely to deposition of cholesterol on the walls of the coronary arteries which are those arteries that supply the heart with blood. This 'furring up', known as arteriosclerosis, can lead to a blockage which deprives the heart of oxygen and nutrients resulting in a heart attack. Its severity is determined by the number of blood vessels cut off to the heart muscle.

Cholesterol itself is a package of blood fats. It is derived from the diet and is essential for making and maintaining nerve cells and for syn-

---

Foods containing potentially harmful cholesterol

- fatty red meat
- eggs
- butter
- cream
- animal fat cooking oil or lard
- full cream milk
- dairy cheese

Foods containing less harmful cholesterol include

- special margarines like Flora
- low fat cheese
- yoghurt
- fresh fruit and vegetables
- vegetable cooking oils
- fish
- wholemeal bread and other wholemeal products

---

thesising natural hormones. There are two main components to cholesterol, the high (HDL) and low (LDL) lipoproteins. LDL is obtained from animal fats and is harmful while HDL comes from vegetable fats and is useful. However, the genetically determined way in which the body deals with them is a critical factor, which is why cholesterol is more dangerous to some people than to others. No matter which group you belong to it is worthwhile adopting a diet and lifestyle that reduces the risk of CHD.

Diet If you have a cholesterol problem you will need to be particularly strict about your intake of animal fats in the form of butter, red meats and so on (see page 238). Even if you do not have a very high cholesterol rating it is probably sensible to at least cut down on these foods. Consider using meat mixed with soya meat substitute (available from health stores), change to skimmed milk and choose low fat cheeses such as cottage cheese rather than the high fat hard cheeses such as cheddar. Other changes of a more long-term nature are to cut down on red meat and to introduce more meatless meals. Recent work has shown that vegetarians have a lower rate of cardiovascular disease than meat eaters. Similarly, if you have raised blood pressure you may also need to watch your diet.

Cigarette smoking This is known to increase the level of LDL taken in the blood. The smoke contains carbon monoxide and an efficient inhaler (i.e. a smoker with good lung function) can take in higher carbon monoxide levels than are permitted in industry. This carbon monoxide damages the lining of the blood vessels and makes cholesterol deposition more likely, as well as causing mild anaemia by reducing the oxygen-carrying capacity of the blood.

Weight Apart from weight loss or gain due to specific diseases, there are two factors which determine our weight, our in-built metabolic rate and the amount we eat. Our metabolism controls the rate at which food is used by the body so that some people remain thin despite eating prodigiously while others put on weight very easily. The thin types (called ectomorphs) have limited energy stores and the good converters, called endo- or mesomorphs, burn up less energy and store the extra away as fat. If, on balance, we eat more than we need, the surplus is stored as fat. Reducing the calorie intake so as to draw on the reserves is the basis of all weight-reducing diets. If you are within 10–15% over your optimum weight then you are reasonably safe, providing your blood pressure is normal. Above this level then being overweight can be dangerous, causing a strain on the heart and joints, decreasing mobility and the capacity for beneficial exercise. By checking your weight against the table on page 238 you can decide if you ought to be doing something about it.

Lifestyle Changing your diet, cutting out smoking and getting your weight to within acceptable limits are the major moves you can make to reducing your risk of heart disease. Additional steps to take can include taking more exercise and reducing stress. Keep in touch with news on this area as the benefits you gain will make your life so much more pleasant than if you had CHD.

The average weight (in underclothes only) for different ages and heights is given, but the weight to aim for is that given for your height for a person under 30.

height	under 30	30–39	age (years) 40–49	50–59	60 plus
			men		
5ft 3	9st 8	9st 12	10st 1	10st 2	9st 13
5ft 4	9st 10	10st 2	10st 5	10st 6	10st 3
5ft 5	10st 1	10st 6	10st 9	10st 10	10st 6
5ft 6	10st 4	10st 10	11st 0	11st 1	10st 13
5ft 7	10st 8	11st 0	11st 4	11st 5	11st 2
5ft 8	10st 11	11st 4	11st 8	11st 9	11st 7
5ft 9	11st 2	11st 9	11st 13	12st 0	11st 13
5ft 10	11st 6	11st 13	12st 3	12st 5	12st 3
5ft 11	11st 11	12st 4	12st 8	12st 10	12st 8
6ft 0	12st 2	12st 8	12st 12	13st 0	12st 13
6ft 1	12st 7	12st 13	13st 3	13st 5	13st 4
6ft 2	12st 11	13st 4	13st 8	13st 10	13st 9
6ft 3	13st 1	13st 10	14st 0	14st 2	14st 1
			women		
4ft 11	8st 3	8st 9	9st 2	9st 5	9st 7
5ft 0	8st 5	8st 11	9st 4	9st 7	9st 9
5ft 1	8st 7	8st 13	9st 6	9st 10	9st 13
5ft 2	8st 9	9st 1	9st 9	9st 13	10st 2
5ft 3	8st 12	9st 4	9st 12	10st 2	10st 5
5ft 4	9st 1	9st 8	10st 1	10st 5	10st 8
5ft 5	9st 5	9st 12	10st 5	10st 9	10st 13
5ft 6	9st 8	10st 2	10st 9	10st 13	11st 0
5ft 7	9st 12	10st 6	10st 13	11st 3	11st 5
5ft 8	10st 2	10st 10	11st 3	11st 8	11st 10
5ft 9	10ft 6	11st 0	11st 7	11st 12	12st 0
5ft 10	10st 10	11st 4	11st 10	12st 3	12st 7
5ft 11	11st 0	11st 6	12st 0	12st 7	12st 11
6ft 0	11st 4	11st 10	12st 3	12st 11	13st 4

Nutrition – facts and myths

Diet concerns what we choose to eat, which is determined largely by what is locally available. Eskimos eat a high fat, high protein diet because they have no vegetables or cereals. In other parts of the world people eat a high fibre diet because there is little protein, fat or sugar available. They don't *choose* to consume what we now regard as a healthy diet – they just don't have the option. With the wide choice and plentiful supply of food that we have in developed countries there should be little danger of malnutrition. Nevertheless problems exist that are caused by either over-eating or consuming too much of the wrong things. As eating patterns are acquired from the family bad habits as well as good ones are perpetuated. No matter what stage of life you are at now it is well worthwhile changing those bad habits.

Basic needs

We actually *need* to eat relatively little in order to keep our bodies adequately supplied with energy proteins, vitamins and minerals so that survival is assured. What we know now, compared with 30 years ago, is that the various foodstuffs are much more interchangeable than we thought, in terms of their basic chemicals and energy constituents. We still talk about fats, proteins and carbohydrates, plus a few vitamins and minerals, but as far as the first three are concerned, they have less specific functions and can almost be regarded as alternatives.

'Over-nutrition'

Since the Second World War, people in developed countries have been suffering from a new syndrome of 'over-nutrition'. Many of us are seriously overweight, and we have also increased our risk of coronary heart disease (see page 234) by consuming vastly more animal fats as meat, butter, cream and milk products. The growth of convenience and 'junk' foods (such as cakes, prepared custards, ice cream, white sliced bread, some cereal products and potato crisps) has also contributed to this. Most of these foods, whether or not they have nutritional value, tend to be low in bulk and fibre and high in calories.

Digestion

Sensible eating habits should also take account of how our digestive system works. It can be described as working on a 'squeeze-through' basis, with food being taken in, pushed through the system and the residue discharged. During the 'push through' process, the food is 'digested', that is, broken down in absorbable fractions, absorbed and then used or stored by the body. For the digestive system to work efficiently, the food has to be bulky enough to be squeezed through – there has to be grist in the digestive mill. As we age, the digestive system becomes sluggish and tends to need more, rather than less, bulk to function at its best. This bulk is provided by the fibre content in our diet which can be easily obtained through eating wholemeal bread, fruit, raw vegetables such as carrots and celery, and dried fruits. (The *F-plan Diet* gives more information on how to introduce fibre to the diet.)

Food additives

A spin-off from the food industry, which is large and making lots of money, is the use of various complex chemical additives for flavour, colour and preservation. Many of these are suspected of being harmful or even carcinogenic (i.e. promotes cancer). Some of them may well turn out to be, but probably not many and it will take years to prove one way or the other. If you can possibly avoid them, then it is better for you to do so.

We also consume too much salt. In temperate climates we actually need little salt, but over the years we have become used to large quantities being added to everything from ketchup to bread. Attempts are now being made to reduce this because it is likely that at least some types of raised blood pressure problems are salt-related. As we don't actually need it, it seems sensible to cut down. This can be done by avoiding many prepared foods such as tinned goods, and also using far less in cooking. By cutting down gradually you may find that one day you no longer use it.

'Health' foods

Another modern phenomenon is the 'health food industry' which promotes organically grown foods as healthier than others. Although they are certainly more expensive, they are not necessarily better. For example, white sugar is purer than brown, but as far as the body is concerned they are chemically the same – neither can be said to be 'good' for you. Similarly, a cabbage is a cabbage no matter how it has been grown and the only variant may be the chemical insecticide sprays used to keep out the caterpillars. Since sprays are fairly carefully monitored, they are unlikely to have harmful effects. In terms of basic nutrition, such health foods have no scientifically proven advantage. In as much as health food shops do encourage people to take a closer interest in what they are eating, I have no criticism of them. But do bear in mind that many of their foods are to be found, a good deal cheaper, at other stores including the major supermarkets and chain stores.

Vitamins

Vitamins and minerals, like iron, are required in small quantities daily because the body cannot manufacture them. A reasonable, mixed diet contains more than you require and, despite advertising, there is nothing to be gained from buying extra vitamins. Scurvy and rickets are virtually unheard of these days. Rickets is caused more by being enclosed than by vitamin deficiency and if you get out into the sun occasionally your body will make enough vitamin D to satisfy your needs.

In today's climate of 'creative' advertising, it is prudent to maintain a sceptical approach to food fads. By eating a good mixed diet with a high fibre content and cutting down on animal fats, dairy products and salt, you should be eating quite healthily. There is no need to avoid any food religiously. An occasional sweet or biscuit is unlikely to be harmful, but if these feature regularly then consider how you can cut down.

CHECKING ON YOUR HEALTH

Regular health checks

Just as you have your car serviced to avoid it breaking down, regular health checks, e.g. once every two years, are important for your body to perform well. As with cars, older ones benefit from being serviced more than new ones. Obviously if there is any known disease or disability, this requires monitoring and possible treatment updated, but it is also worth having regular (not necessarily annual) checks on:

- hearing
- vision
- blood pressure
- urine
- teeth

as well as some simple blood tests. A health check need not be as detailed or expensive as those offered at BUPA centres, and such monitoring can be very reassuring, or can lead to preventative intervention. A valuable retirement present is a good basic health check to establish a baseline against which to measure your health.

A typical screening that you will receive at a BUPA centre will include a detailed computer-led cross examination on your medical background and present condition. You will also have an interview with a doctor for tests on heart and lung function; tests on blood and urine; a biochemical profile will check on cholesterol levels and other potentially harmful chemicals; checks on weight, hearing and vision; and an X-ray examination. For women there are also X-rays of breasts and a cervical smear. There are 19 BUPA centres in various parts of the country which you can find by looking them up in your local phone book or by contacting **BUPA** head office for details.

Many group practices now operate what are called 'age and sex registers' and offer simple screening on the items listed above to their older (70 plus) patients. If your practice does not offer this, ask for it taking the opportunity to also discuss any problems. Any symptoms, no matter how trivial, may be important so don't worry about 'bothering' the doctor. Self-examination techniques are also very important (see *Special problems of women*, page 243).

Prevention and screening

Obviously the more you can do to prevent illness, the better. Many of our health problems are to some extent self-inflicted and due to our lifestyle (see *Exercise and Fitness* (page 230) and *Looking after yourself* (page 233). For those that are not there are other measures that we can take to avoid health problems. For example, people with 'bad chests' from chronic bronchitis often benefit from regular small doses of antibiotics during the winter to keep down infection. Since older people are more vulnerable to influenza and its sequels there is also a strong case for a flu jab at the start of every winter.

Hypertension (raised blood pressure)

Hypertension is one of the risk factors in coronary heart disease (see page 234) and also the prime cause of strokes (see page 268). It is usually a long-standing disease which starts in middle life but it can be treated. Long-term trials have established that early diagnosis followed by long-term treatment with hypotensive drugs can considerably reduce the incidence of strokes. There is every good reason, therefore, to have regular checks on your blood pressure so that, if necessary, treatment can be given at an early stage.

Cancer

Cancer can be thought of as a condition of the elderly because it is a reflection of the breakdown of the mechanisms that control and co-ordinate groups of specific cells. It has a sinister reputation because it does kill. What is not generally realised is that at least half of all diagnosed cancers are successfully treated and cured, and many more can be contained if there is early diagnosis. Take advantage of the screening facilities available for certain cancers, notably breast and cervical cancer (see *Special problems of women* page 243).

Warning signals If you have any new symptoms which persist for more than a few days, present them to the doctor and get a diagnosis.

Common symptoms which come into this category are:
- any change in bowel habit: looseness, constipation or a mixture of both
- any non-explained change in weight
- loss of appetite
- thirst, frequency of passing urine or other urinary symptoms, particularly in men
- pain anywhere which comes on without obvious explanation. Naturally if you have a minor injury it will be swollen and painful but even this may be worth an X-ray

CANCER SURVIVAL RATES

The 'cure' rates for various forms of cancer are given below. The figures are based on patients first diagnosed as having cancer in 1978 in England and Wales and who survived for 5 years or more after treatment. Patients who died from causes other than cancer are discounted. The statistics, from the **Office of Population Censuses and Surveys** and the **Cancer Research Campaign**, relate to patients diagnosed in 'all stages' of the disease. Survival rates for patients diagnosed in the 'early stages' are invariably better.

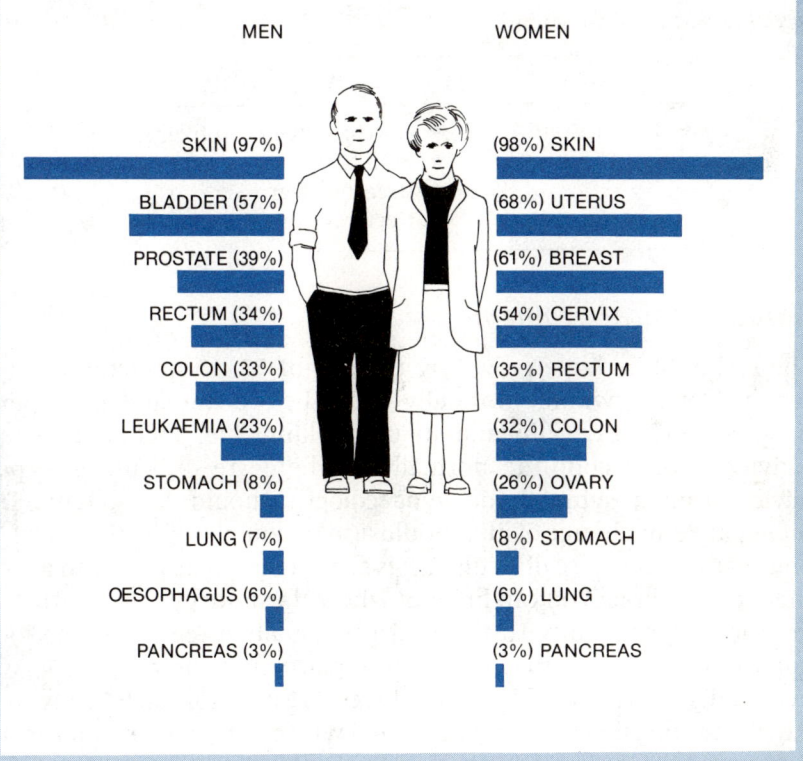

MEN	WOMEN
SKIN (97%)	(98%) SKIN
BLADDER (57%)	(68%) UTERUS
PROSTATE (39%)	(61%) BREAST
RECTUM (34%)	(54%) CERVIX
COLON (33%)	(35%) RECTUM
LEUKAEMIA (23%)	(32%) COLON
STOMACH (8%)	(26%) OVARY
LUNG (7%)	(8%) STOMACH
OESOPHAGUS (6%)	(6%) LUNG
PANCREAS (3%)	(3%) PANCREAS

- any bleeding or discharge from anywhere. Piles (haemorrhoids) are common and often bleed, but the bleeding may come from higher up and need investigation
- any change or increase in the symptoms of chronic digestive pain
- any new lump, bump or swelling in or under the skin. A mole or wart which becomes ulcerated, grows, changes colour or bleeds. Similarly any ulcer in the skin, particularly on the face, which fails to heal

- a cough, even if it follows a heavy cold, which lasts for more than a couple of weeks.

Remember, in achieving an early diagnosis the doctor can only begin to help if you present your symptoms for evaluation. Even if your symptoms turn out to be trivial, they should *still* be evaluated. Looking after yourself is prudence not hypochondria, and in medicine a 'stitch in time' may well save major surgery or more serious treatment later.

SPECIAL PROBLEMS OF MEN AND WOMEN

There are a number of problems which may affect specific sexes as they grow older. These are given in Table 3 below.

Special problems for the sexes.

Men	Women
- The prostate	- Gynaecological problems
	- Frail bones
	- Breast cancer
	- Cervical cancer

Gynaecological problems

These should be largely over by the age of 55. Hysterectomies (the removal of the womb) normally occur before this and if properly handled both surgically and in counselling, life, including sexual activity, should continue normally. If there are difficulties, expert advice from a sympathetic gynaecologist should be sought. The menopause, or change of life, should also be completed by the age of 55 and again, if there are difficulties it is sensible to get advice or to go to a menopause clinic. You can find out where these are by calling BUPA or your local Community Health Council, usually listed under the local authority. It may be that hormone replacement therapy (HRT) will eventually be prescribed and this will require monitoring. HRT involves supplementing the hormone oestrogen which falls off when menstruation stops. It helps to fool the body into thinking that menstruation still continues, and some doctors use it to help eliminate some of the problems of the menopause, such as depression and hot flushes.

Bones

In older people and particularly in women, the bones tend to get thinner leading to easier damage – it is very easy to fracture the neck of the femur (thigh bone) in a trivial fall. Ways are being sought both to identify vulnerable women and to prevent the calcium loss. Hormones are known to play a part in this and it may well be that HRT over a longer term will become more common in the next decade. Calcium and vitamin D supplements may also be advised. For the moment, however, the best protection seems to be to maintain reasonable physical activity. The bones seem to maintain their strength with use and active weight bearing. (Astronauts who are weightless for considerable periods of time lose a lot of calcium.)

Breast cancer

Cancer of the breast is still the commonest cause of death in middle-aged women, affecting about one in thirteen. However, the cure rate is improving and the degree of surgery required is decreasing. The outlook is good for cancers that are picked up early and malignant cells can be removed by a local operation called a 'lumpectomy'.

Early detection
Early detection is all-important in the successful treatment of cancers. Every woman should learn to carry out regular monthly, systematic self-examination of her breasts, from adolescence to the end of life. Any new lump, painful area or nipple discharge should be reported at once and investigated by surgery or needle biopsy. Breast lumps are common and only a small proportion turn out to be malignant, but all must be regarded as hostile until proved harmless. Once cancer has spread outside the breast, it is more difficult to treat successfully. The availability of breast screening is spreading, being offered by the nationwide BUPA Medical Centres. It is also available under the NHS – ask your GP. Screening may be by special low-intensity radiation X-rays, called mammograms, which can pick up lumps that cannot be felt, especially in large breasts.

Cervical cancer

Cervical cancer is not as common as breast cancer. However, unless there has been a total hysterectomy, cervical smear tests should be continued from your teens until you are over 60.

The prostate

The only commonly troublesome male organ is the prostate gland. This surrounds the outlet to the bladder and for no very understandable reason, has a habit of enlarging later in life. It is also prone to cancer which produces similar symptoms.

When the prostate enlarges it blocks the outflow from the bladder causing difficulties in passing urine. Symptoms vary from urgency to dribbling, from frequency to difficulty in starting and stopping. As the enlargement is progressive, it is sensible to seek advice early because this is easier to deal with than the pressure damage to bladder and kidneys that will occur with delay.

Treatment to unblock the drainage system is by surgery. This can now be done relatively simply using a 'magic telescope' which does not require opening the bladder. It entails only a few days in hospital. That the operation destroys sex life is entirely mythical. It may happen that the ejaculatory ducts which run through the prostate are damaged which will mean that ejaculation may not be complete. Instead it travels into the bladder rather than to the outside, but enjoyment should not be affected. It does cause sterility, however, but this may not be of major concern to you.

Further information

There are BUPA medical centres in most major regions that screen both men and women. Their addresses may be obtained by writing to the head office (see page 273). BUPA head office also publishes a series of leaflets covering most areas of preventive health care (see page 275).

STRESS AND RELAXATION

Stress is a much misused word and it is important to be clear as to what we mean when we say someone is 'stressed'. We all need challenge at various levels in order to maintain motivation and provide us with satisfaction. Thus, an individual who has to cope with a heavy load of work, responsibility or anxiety, is not necessarily stressed, though they may well be tired. However, when the challenge becomes too much for us we may become stressed. Stress is a personal reaction to a particular situation. Often it is a sign of the individual's inability to cope which results in a defensive reaction. The symptoms of stress are many and varied, some often being attributed to other causes (e.g. colds and other physical illnesses), and then it is difficult to identify stress as the primary cause. However, periodic reviews of your lifestyle and adaptations to enable you to relax more may help you to avoid this problem.

Stress in retirement

Retirement is a life-crisis and, like any period of change in our lives (e.g. getting married and moving home) it can bring its own problems and worries. This is why it is so important to plan ahead for our new lifestyle. 'Workaholics' are particularly vulnerable to stress if they lack other satisfying interests to take the place of work. Too little work can be just as stressful as too much and a person who is used to coping with a heavy workload may well feel lost without it. Unhappy or strained relationships with partner or family can also contribute to the stress level as can worries about the future, whether real or imagined.

Treatment

It is important to realise that stress is a condition that involves the whole person and as such requires treatment for the whole person, or *holistic treatment*. Worry from work influences our life at home and *vice versa*. We function and react as a whole and cannot cut ourselves up into separately functioning slices, much as we may like to. Ideally, treatment should help to readjust the balance between the individual and their environment. Talking through and defining problems will often do more than relieving the symptoms with pills.

Learning to relax

Tension is, in physiological terms, being all tense and screwed up. This tension may be exhibited as pain in the back, neck or other muscles. It may be the cause of abdominal pain or colic, even raised blood pressure. Such tension is wearing and lowers the stress threshold. Clearly if the person can be taught to relax, they are likely to be better able to cope. There are a number of relaxation techniques that can be learnt and built into daily living, with enormous benefit. The best known is probably Transcendental Meditation, derived from yoga. This is a form of autohypnosis by use of a personal mantra which, when repeated under quiet conditions, produces a semi-trance with consequent relaxation.

Other techniques include biofeedback, autogenic training and schedules of direct muscle relaxation. Many of these can be learned from tapes or at classes such as those run by **Relaxation for Living** who are also able to give individual advice and provide many useful books on the subject. Find the method and the teacher that suits you best. There is no universally successful system, most of them have good physiological and psychological bases to take off some of the strain. If you are a tense and anxious person, retirement may provide you with the opportunity to learn to relax – it could well help you to live longer. Remember too, that sleep is complete relaxation, and as anxiety and tension are a common cause of insomnia, one of these techniques could improve the quality of sleep and make life easier. Anything that calms the worried mind will be beneficial.

WHAT IS YOUR LEVEL OF STRESS?

Not long after the last world war an American psychiatrist called Richard Rahe analysed episodes of illness in relation to the commoner life crises such as getting married, moving house, losing a job and bereavement. Not surprisingly he found that illness and sick leave were higher at such times of crisis. Retirement too is a life-crisis and, combined with other crises such as moving house or losing a partner, it will make you vulnerable to stress. Some events are outside your control but others are not and exercising judgement on how many changes you will make to your life can make all the difference as to whether you feel stimulated or stressed. A shortened list of events and the stress factors associated with them that were determined by Rahe and his colleagues is given below.

Event	Stress factor
Death of spouse	100
Divorce	73
Separation	65
Imprisonment	63
Death of close family member	63
Personal injury or illness	53
Marriage	50
Dismissal from job	47
Marital reconciliation	45
Retirement	45
Change in health of family member	44
Pregnancy	40
Sex difficulties	39
Gain of new family member	39
Business readjustment	39
Change in financial state	38
Death of close friend	37
Change of job	36
Change in number of arguments with spouse	35

Coping skills

Another approach to this problem is to learn what are called 'coping skills'. Being able to consciously relax and be objective about causes of tension and anxiety is likely to be beneficial. However, many of us lack the degree of objectivity necessary to identify our own weaknesses and so we blunder on in spite of the tension. Coping skills have been

Event	Stress factor
Taking out large mortgage or loan	31
Foreclosure of mortgage or loan	30
Change in job responsibilities	29
Son or daughter leaves home	29
Trouble with in-laws	29
Outstanding personal achievement	28
Spouse begins or stops work	26
Begin or end school or college	26
Change in living conditions	25
Change in personal habits	24
Trouble with boss	23
Change in work hours or conditions	20
Moving home	20
Change of school or college	20
Change of recreation	19
Change in church activities	19
Change in social activities	18
A moderate mortgage or loan	17
Change in sleeping habits	16
Change in number of family get-togethers	15
Change in eating habits	15
Holiday	13
Christmas	12
Minor violation of law	11

If any of these life events have happened to you during the last six months you can work out the degree of stress you are under by adding up the values accorded to each. If you score below 60 then life is pretty free from stress; if you score between 60 and 80 then life is pretty normal; from 80 to 100 then you have been through higher than normal stress, perhaps because of a single significant event; over 100 then pressures have been piling up and you need to take active steps to combat the effects of stress.

developed largely in relation to business life but are equally applicable to daily living. They consist of:
- identifying the tasks or situations that are likely to be difficult
- thinking ahead and preparing for them.

In trying to identify your vulnerable points it is often helpful to talk things through with a friend. They may enable you to be more

LEARN TO RELAX

Learning to relax properly is harder if you are tired and worn out. You will learn better when you are fresh and alert. Try to minimise background noise and the obvious presence of other people. Do not try to rush through it. If you are worried about spending too long or falling asleep, then set an alarm. If at first you don't succeed *don't* try harder. Forget it for a couple of days and try again. Prepare yourself by

- choosing a quiet, comfortable place
- try to set aside 20–30 undisturbed minutes
- loosen any tight clothing and take off your shoes
- sit or lie as comfortably as possible
- close your eyes, uncross your legs and, if you are sitting, hold your hands flat, one on each knee.

The most basic exercises involve tensing each part of the body for a count of 10. Take a deep breath, feel the tension, then let the tension go as you breathe out and relax the muscles once again. Parts to be worked on in this way are, in order, your

1. *toes* Curl your toes towards you or down to the floor.
2. *calves* Point your toes towards your face.
3. *thighs* Tighten the large muscles of the thighs and press your thighs either together or outwards against the arms of your chair.
4. *buttocks* Push your buttocks hard against your chair, floor or bed, at the same time trying to make your body feel as heavy as possible.
5. *abdomen* Tense your tummy as if preparing to receive a punch in the stomach.
6. *arms and hands* Clench the fists and press the arms close against the body.
7. *shoulders* Shrug your shoulders as high as they can possibly go.
8. *throat* Use your chin to press your throat hard.
9. *neck and head* Press your neck and head against the backs of your shoulders.
10. *face* Pull a really ferocious face to tighten as many facial muscles as possible, including forehead, jaw, chin and nose.

When you can do this effectively you can find all sorts of times and places during the day when you can use the technique to relax tension be it sitting at your desk, or in the car as you wait for the lights to change.

objective. It is also a good idea, when analysing a situation, to make a list of options from which to choose your best way of tackling the problem. There is a feeling of great relief once you can act instead of thinking about a problem.

Learn to switch off tension by relaxation techniques, adopting a better posture and so on. Clearly, too, a period of tranquillity before a threatening situation must help to 'charge the batteries' and ease tension. A short break to get away from it all can help you to feel more ready to cope.

RELATIONSHIPS

Problems of couples

When you think about how much time a married couple actually spend together during the latter part of their working lives, it is often relatively little. A typical routine consists of one or both partners leaving the house well before 9 a.m., getting back tired around 7 p.m., eating and dozing through the evening and retreating to bed. Much of the weekend may also be spent separately – on the golf course or sailing. After retirement, all this changes. You may find yourself sharing each other's company 24 hours a day, seven days a week. Naturally, if you get on well together you will look forward to seeing more of each other but some people may, understandably, be worried about getting under each other's feet. No matter how you feel about the future together it is wise to cultivate activities which will bring you into contact with new people. No one person can provide *all* the needs another has for warmth, friendship and stimulation. People are multi-faceted and generally need diverse company as well as interests.

Outside interests
Obviously a good solution to this problem is to have some separate outside activities which will promote well-being and give you both more 'breathing space'.

Example Twenty years ago when we opened the first office of the Pre-Retirement Association in Clapham, a retired man walked in one day and asked if he could help in any way at all. It transpired that every morning around ten o'clock his wife turned him out of the house and told him not to come back until lunch time. His willingness to help out with anything soon made him part of the office family from which we all benefited.

Communication and sharing
Whatever your outside interests, however, there is still often a need to improve and work at your relationships. Many couples find that they have been leading such separate lives that they are not used to

discussing, planning and doing things together. This relationship may therefore seem fairly negative or even a source of frustration and conflict. In order to improve matters you need first to admit that there is a problem. Many people (and the British are particularly famous for this) adopt a relatively unemotional attitude to life which leads them to shy away from 'a good row' and continue to tolerate frustrating situations. Merely bottling things up in this way to avoid overt conflict is very harmful to your well-being and does nothing to improve matters. However, many problems and differences can be resolved by frank (but constructive) discussion, if necessary with the aid of a neutral counsellor.

Role changes
The roles which couples adopt during their working lives are usually determined by the extent to which either spouse works, or is involved, outside the home. When this pattern changes couples will need to adjust accordingly and perhaps rethink their domestic routine. In most cases retirement means that the man is now much more available and could take on more of the domestic load such as the cooking and ironing. A change of routine should be beneficial to both partners, but again this may require some discussion. You need to consider each other's roles in a new light and be prepared for give and take on both sides.

Family and friends

In retirement, particularly as it progresses into the last, say, 15 years of life, relationships become particularly precious to us. They are increasingly part of the framework of the status and identity on which well-being depends. The family is likely to be the centre of this network but it may need refurbishing and working at. It is important that our relationship with our children develops as we get older and that we relate to them *as adults* with their own lives to lead. It helps also to be tolerant of generation differences, such as how your grandchildren are brought up. Standards and attitudes change over the years.

Keeping up old friendships and making new friends needs to be worked at more positively in retirement, especially if you are single or have relied on work to provide most of your social contact. Your plans should include doing things with, as well as for, other people. We all need to be wanted and usually this has to be earned. Good relationships with your family, friends and neighbours will bring much satisfaction and provide stimulation. Hopefully, as we get older and frailer, people will keep an eye on us, not necessarily as a duty but because they enjoy doing so.

Living alone

Some men and women who live singly in retirement may have problems replacing the associations they enjoyed at work. Especially vulnerable are those who feel themselves to be loners, who don't fit into groups for whatever reason. They are often workaholics. Independence may be highly desirable, but after some time it can lead to unwelcome isolation. It is therefore important for a single person to plan their retirement with perhaps more effort than couples need to. Apart from thinking about where to live and how to spend your time, you should give priority to solving the problems of loneliness.

Example Several years ago I received an interesting letter from a lady who had read an article that I had written on this topic. She was living alone and getting older. She made two points which may be important to you, but about which you have not thought.
- as one gets older it is essential not to be too isolated from shops and other people who might help in a crisis. 'The remote cottage,' she said 'becomes a hazard.'
- there is a greater need to have your affairs not only in good order but also to have someone, a solicitor or relative, who knows all about you (and is known by others), who could move in and take over in a crisis or at death.

It is true that anyone living alone who dies suddenly can leave an estate or situation that is difficult for outsiders to clear up.

Community housing

Loneliness is often a trap that grows worse with time. This is particularly so as you become older, less active and less mobile. It is difficult to lay down hard and fast rules for avoiding these situations. Perhaps you could consider living with supportive people around you, either sharing your home with some friends, or perhaps live in a retirement development unit with sheltered back-up when you need it. Any way in which you can become more involved with other people helps. Those of this group (the majority of whom tend to be competent, well-organised women) who have been most successful in coping have usually gone out of their way to get involved with people.

Socialising

Many single people find it difficult to find social groups into which they fit easily. This also applies to widows and widowers. In many areas, there is a real need to set up special groups that can meet regularly. Such groups would not only become mutually supportive, but could also be a focus for retired people in general, to work towards the provision of better facilities in the area.

SEXUAL RELATIONS

Some conversations and media articles seem to indicate that there is a problem about sex in later life. In reality sexual activity should present no greater difficulties in later life than at any other time. Indeed, given the greater freedom and lack of fatigue after retirement, there could well be fewer problems and greater enjoyment than previously. Obviously, if there were problems before retirement these are likely to be carried forward and are unlikely to resolve automatically with the change. These should be dealt with in the usual way by expert advice or sex counselling.

Sexual needs

It is unwise to try to generalise about sexual needs, particularly in older people. They are very much a reflection of the individual personality, past experience and current needs as well as a reflection of the nature and dynamics of the relationship, and its needs. Couples who have always had regular intercourse are more likely to continue to do so in later life than couples with less need.

However, warm, close and affectionate relationships are perfectly possible without direct sexual activity. This is usually a natural demonstration of warmth and affection and much to be enjoyed. What is important is that throughout life there should continue to be some demonstration of this affection by word, touch and 'being nice' to each other. This benefits from being spontaneous and occasionally unexpected.

Attitudes to sex may include guilt or the view that intercourse is best confined to procreation, but it is the natural expression of love and affection, and age in itself is no bar to the active continuation of sexual intercourse. A satisfying sexual relationship and attraction still remains a major source of pleasure which holds relationships together.

Sex and the menopause

Women often experience a greater feeling of freedom after the menopause because precautions against pregnancy no longer have to be taken. However, although fertility decreases before the menopause, there is still a risk of pregnancy. As the monthly periods become irregular and taper off, it is sensible to continue precautions for several months. Medical advice should be sought about this.

Menopausal symptoms
Any significant menopausal symptoms must be treated and not tolerated as inevitable. This can be done either by your GP or at a

menopause clinic. The main post-menopausal symptom tends to be vaginal dryness which is easily dealt with by a simple lubricant or hormone cream. Any other symptoms, such as pain or discomfort, again need medical advice.

Loss of libido

Men, in particular, sometimes suffer a 'mid-life crisis' on the approach to retirement and any lack of confidence which arises, is likely to diminish libido. But this is *effect* and not *cause*. Usually your sexual urge in later life is a reflection of that in earlier life in terms of performance and frequency. Bodily systems tend to react to habit and demand, so that couples having regular intercourse now are more likely to have regular intercourse later than are those who have it only once a month or less.

Libido is very much a reflection of general well-being and varies from person to person and throughout life. Fatigue is the biggest enemy of libido, so it may well improve after retirement. Poor general health or mild depression can also reduce desire and it is well to remember the old but true adage that although alcohol heightens desire it limits performance.

There are drugs on the market which claim to improve libido, but they usually have little more than a placebo effect and fail to significantly improve performance. In general, clutching at such straws should be resisted.

New approaches
There might be an element, if not of boredom, at least of automatism for a long-married couple. To combat this thought has to be given to new approaches, different times and places, and so on. As the end of the day is often the time of most fatigue your main urge is likely to be to go to sleep. There is, therefore, a case for making love in the mornings, at weekends and on holiday instead. Co-operative imagination and some new excitement can be a help.

Problems
Difficulties occur when the needs and capacities of partners vary, so that one feels frustrated and the other guilty. This can clearly build up tension within a relationship and needs to be discussed. Sexual counselling or therapy is a relatively new area of expertise and well worth seeking out if there is a real difficulty. Help and information are available from **The Association of Sexual and Marital Therapists**, the **National Marriage Guidance Council** and the **Institute of Psychosexual Medicine**.

SURVIVING BEREAVEMENT

The word 'bereavement' means 'to be deprived of', and coping with bereavement involves re-adjustment to a heartbreaking deprivation. The loss of a close relative or lifelong partner is something that is likely to happen to all of us as we get older. Sometimes our British reluctance to express emotions hinders this process. It is essential to realise that grieving and mourning, expressing grief and working through memories, is a necessary and natural part of recovery. Don't be afraid of expressing your grief and remember that crying is a natural biological safety valve.

When we are in a crisis, it is easy to think that the situation is unique to us and that we have been picked out for this pain and suffering. But we must remember that bereavement is a situation which we will all, at some time, encounter.

The progress of bereavement

In terms of reaction and adjustment there are three phases to bereavement.

Stage 1
The initial reactions are shock, disbelief, numbness, anger that it should happen to you, maybe associated with some guilt that it is your fault and that you ought to have done more. This is accompanied by an inability to accept what has happened and the hope that actually it has not and that all will again be well. Sometimes the early stages of this phase may be easier and more realistic if you have been able to see and contact the body. Where terminal illness is concerned it also helps if the possibility of death has been openly admitted by the family rather than pretending that recovery is likely. With serious illness, the earlier the possibility of death is faced, the easier it is to accept. Obviously, if death is sudden and unexpected, it is much more difficult to cope with.

Stage 2
Realisation and acceptance follows, often with feelings of pain, recollections of old emotions and memories, happy times and sad times shared, feelings of guilt and remorse. There will be difficulties in eating and sleeping, and often in older people this leads to depression. Over a short period sleeping pills can be a help, but it is not good to take them for long because it is easy to become dependent on them. Brisk exercise outside can be a balm because physical fatigue helps both sleep and well-being. This stage can last a long time but should not be for more than a year. On the anniversary of the death, have a mourning session with your friends and then firmly step into the future. This is not

forgetting but re-starting, which is certainly what your partner would have wanted.

Stage 3
The final stage brings relief from pain and negative emotions. You become more positive and start to accept a new life. This will not be the same, but you have to make the best of it and start building up alternatives. You must struggle back into circulation. This can be very difficult for an older person, perhaps left entirely alone, but it can be achieved. No good is done by living in a fantasy world that is in the past. Life goes forwards, not backwards.

Facing up to death

Although this may sound gloomy, a family contingency plan, agreed in advance, can be a great help by adding some structure to a shapeless and seemingly empty existence. Some prior planning about what you would both like the other to do when there is only one of you left can be a comfort when it arises. It is easier to do this when you are both in good health, so don't avoid discussing this subject. It is better to face up to realities than to have nagging fears at the back of your mind. Moreover, the time of bereavement is rarely one when decisions are made well, it would be better to wait until you can think clearly about your situation.

Help from others

Many people are embarrassed by others' grief and shy away from a bereaved person. This attitude is very sad as at these times the person has an intense need for company and support. Make the effort to overcome this squeamishness and positively support your bereaved friends. Your own loss may well be easier to bear if you have had the experience of helping others through theirs. There are also organisations such as the country-wide organisation **CRUSE** which offers a support network for the bereaved. Contact with such groups can bring comfort and also help you to get back into circulation and restart your life with hope and purpose.

USING THE HEALTH SERVICES

The General Practitioner

Our present primary care system, the general practice, is based on the old Lloyd-George 'panel' system under which workers signed on a doctor's panel. In return the doctor received a modest capitation fee and the patient received free consultation. Under the National Health Service (NHS), which was set up after the last world war, doctors kept their independent status and did not become directly employed by the Government.

Each area of the country now has a Family Practice Committee (FPC) which employs the doctors using Government money, and pays them a capitation fee for every patient on the doctor's list. Everyone is entitled to register and the doctor's reimbursement is determined by a complicated sliding scale according to age of patient, practice allowances, mileages and so on.

Now as single-handed general practitioners are both discouraged and disappearing, group practices are appearing that are integrated into the local health and social services systems to provide a team of nurses, social workers and health visitors.

Registration

Registration is a two-way contract in which both parties have freedom of choice. This means that a patient can choose his or her own GP and that the GP is entitled to refuse a patient. There is also a limit to the number of patients who can be registered at any one practice, which depends on the size of the practice, and most practices have a geographical limit to reduce travel for visiting. Once registered the doctor has a statutory obligation to provide certain services, like 24-hour cover and home visiting, but locums may be used for night calls.

In an under-doctored or overcrowded area, the local FPC will allocate extra patients. Similarly, if *all* the doctors refuse registration to a difficult patient, the FPC will allocate that patient to a doctor regardless of like or dislike.

Choosing your doctor

Finding a doctor who provides a good service in adequate buildings, and who is also someone that is in rapport with you may be difficult. If you are not happy with your present GP you are perfectly entitled to 'shop around', either within the same practice, or by going elsewhere. Remember too, that all members of the family do not have to register with the same doctor.

Although practices are now being encouraged to provide descriptive leaflets about their facilities and lists of practices are available from information centres and the FPC, recommendation based on word of mouth by friends or neighbours is probably the best and most common way of starting an assessment. By going and looking at the surgery you can then make up your own mind about the receptionist, the facilities available and anything else you feel is important.

To change your doctor all you need to do is be accepted by a new one and fill in a form. (It is courteous, but not obligatory, to tell the old one why you are leaving.) Your medical records will then be transferred through the FPC, but this may take some time, particularly if you have moved to a new area.

Complaints
There are complicated rights of making a complaint which must be made within a specified time of the offence. The procedure can be established from either the FPC or the **Citizens' Advice Bureau**. Patients do have rights and can exert reasonable pressure to get a fair deal. There is also a **Community Health Council** that acts as a consumer watchdog over the local system

Getting a second opinion
Patients often don't realise that they are entitled to a second opinion. You can ask for referral to a specialist if you are still worried after consulting your GP. Even within a hospital it is legitimate to have a second opinion in cases of doubt or worry, and your GP can help you achieve this. There can be genuine doubt about some methods of treatment or the need for an operation, and it may well be worth getting a second opinion from another consultant.

Referral system
Access to hospital, except in emergencies, is via a referral from your GP, with whom the hospital communicates about you and their advice as to treatment. This may take time and can cause difficulties. The reason for this is that the GP is always technically in control of his patient and should know best who to refer him to, even though often it is automatically to the Outpatients Clinic rather than to a named consultant. Drugs are then supplied through the GP either directly or on specialist advice.

The doctor–patient relationship
At long last we are moving towards a more open doctor–patient relationship and the 'consumer' should not be timid about asking for information on and explanation of their illness and treatment. In my view, you should also question the prescription of drugs:
- Why are they needed?
- For how long should I take them?
- What alternatives are there?
- Are there any side effects?
- Will they react with any other drugs I am taking?

Some doctors still prescribe too many drugs and for too long. 'Do I still need them?' is another good question to ask if treatment goes on.

There is currently also a move to give patients access to their own medical records so that they know what is being said about them.

Though in many ways this is a desirable change, it is not without hazards as it may cause some patients undue worry about their health, rather like a house survey worries a buyer.

The practice should know about the waiting lists for various operations in different areas and be prepared to shop around to get you treatment as soon as possible. There is no reason why you *have* to be treated at your local hospital; if there is a bed available in London or some other part of the country you are entitled to use it. There may, however, be geographical limitations on such a transfer depending on the condition to be treated. The **College of Health** monitors this situation nationally and can advise you about this.

Later in life your GP should also be the focus for getting you access to the range of social services such as home helps, home nurses and even house modifications. You can also go direct to the social services department of your local authority for advice and information, particularly on cash and disability benefits.

Private treatment

For various reasons there are relatively few private GPs but numbers are increasing. Your NHS GP cannot take you on as a private patient, but it is possible to be on a GP's list and also go privately to another doctor. There are a few specialised procedures (e.g. certain vaccinations required for holiday trips, sick notes, life insurance examinations, industrial reports and cervical smears) for which any GP may charge a fee.

The network of independent hospitals is also growing and available in most areas. These hospitals provide a facility for specialist use so that admission is via a specialist or consultant. You cannot just present yourself at a private hospital and ask to be treated. Referral should be through your GP although some NHS doctors may be unhappy about doing this.

Cost of private treatment

Most private hospital treatment is paid for through insurance with organisations such as BUPA or PPP which hold 85% of the market between them (other providers of medical insurance include Western Provident, BCWA and Health First). This is often subsidised by an employer as part of a pay package and if you have had this, it is beneficial to keep it up in retirement. It may be expensive as older people tend to be a bigger insurance risk; being susceptible to more serious illnesses and needing treatment for longer.

If you do go privately and require surgery, it is wise to ask the full cost in advance and make sure that it is within your insurance cover.

Treatment in the private sector should be treated like any other major item or service.

Chemists

The nature of the chemist's shop has changed considerably in my lifetime. Gone are the old fashioned jars and range of potions. Chemists now dispense prepared drugs and no longer make up ointments, mixtures or pills. Their shops have become more like the American drug store.

Nevertheless, to dispense or supply drugs requires a legally qualified pharmacist, who may well know more about drugs, their alternatives and inter-reactions than the prescribing GP. Since this is so there is now a move to reduce the load on GPs for minor conditions by encouraging you to consult the pharmacists first and buy over the counter with their help. This is called 'self-medication' and can be sensible for minor ailments.

Chemists shops keep normal shop hours but in many regions there is a rota system by which each shop in a group takes its turn to open late and dispense prescriptions. For shops such as Boots only medicines are sold. You will find the rota displayed in the window or doorway of most chemists.

Prescription charges
The National Health Service drugs bill for 1986/87 in England alone was £1.79 billion, of which £145 million (roughly 8%) was recovered in prescription charges. Nevertheless, now that prescription charges are so high it is sometimes cheaper to buy an equivalent drug which does not require a prescription over the counter. Ask your chemist or GP about this. If, however, you qualify for a State pension or benefit then you are entitled to free prescriptions.

Dental services

There is a NHS dental service which covers the whole country and most dentists can treat both private and NHS patients. The scale of charges and part payments is complicated and needs to be discussed when you have treatment. Most dentists will undertake expensive or cosmetic treatment only on a private basis.

Although NHS dental treatment is not free, many people on low incomes may qualify for free treatment. This includes pensioners in receipt of supplementary pension. Otherwise you pay the full cost up to £17 and 40% of any cost over £17. There are, however, separate additional charges for dentures, bridges, crowns, inlays, pinlays and gold fillings. The most you can be asked to pay for each course of treatment, irrespective of the amount of work needed, is £115. Some items are free to everyone including check-ups, stopping bleeding, repairs to dentures, calling a dentist out to his surgery in an emergency and home visits (though the treatment itself may have to be paid for). A DHSS leaflet D11 (April 1987) called *NHS dental treatment, what it costs and how to get free treatment* is available from social security offices.

The rota of local dentists on emergency call is usually posted in the surgery. They are also often printed in the local paper and you can get them by calling the Community Health Physician's department at the Town Hall.

You do not have to register with a dentist as you do with a GP and you can change dentist whenever you want to, but not in the middle of a course of treatment. It is advantageous to stick with one dentist if you can and in practice one finds that many people are more loyal to their dentist than to their doctor and are prepared to travel to them.

Optical services

An ophthalmologist, as well as being concerned with vision and glasses, is an expert on eye diseases, both medical and surgical. An optician, however, primarily prescribes and sells glasses, although most have also had sufficient training to detect at least the common eye diseases and would, if necessary, refer you to an ophthalmologist. This is important as not all visual difficulties are due to simple lens changes.

Your optician or eye specialist will give you the details on the lenses that you require. The payment that you will be required to make will depend on the frames you choose and thus the size of lenses required for them. Although only a qualified optician or ophthalmologist can prescribe glasses, the sale and availability of glasses has recently been reorganised to make a wider choice available. Now almost anyone can make up prescriptions and special discount shops exist for this purpose, even some department stores have spectacle dispensing counters.

Hearing centres

Most hospitals have an Ear, Nose and Throat (ENT) department which diagnoses deafness and supplies NHS hearing aids. These are also available commercially and may be bought through hearing centres. Most of these are reputable and give fair, unbiased advice. However, do not buy a hearing aid until you are certain that it is of benefit and that you can operate all the controls. As hearing aids are becoming more and more sophisticated, some have small controls and are operated by tiny

batteries which are difficult to manipulate with arthritic fingers. You should insist on a week's trial. There are basically two sorts of hearing aid:
- those that fit inside the ear – to improve air conduction of sound as in normal hearing
- those that rest on the back of the ear for bone conduction.

The right type of aid depends on the cause of deafness. Certain types of deafness may also be helped by reconstructive surgery.

Fringe, alternative and holistic medicine

The medical profession, like many others, tends to be protective of its rights and often seems to want a monopoly. Their legal rights largely concern certification and prescription. This apart, there is nothing to stop anyone from consulting whom they like for alternative therapy. For a variety of reasons, there has been a growth in a wide range of alternative therapies. As these have become better organised and regulated some, such as osteopathy and chiropractic, are considered respectable, while others such as reflexology and aromatherapy, are less so. Homeopathy is practised by many doctors, as is osteopathic manipulation, and faith healing is no longer entirely frowned on by the **British Medical Association**.

Alternative therapies are much more holistic in the evaluation of symptoms, being concerned with the whole person and their reaction to life. This is desirable and often beneficial because the cause of an illness is not necessarily physical. There is much to be said for some of the alternative therapies. The range is vast but alternative treatment is not suitable if you are suffering from conditions such as a hernia and require surgery, e.g. the removal of a lump or prostatic enlargement. These are best treated by a conventional approach.

Access to alternative practitioners may be direct but your doctor can put you in contact with a healer or osteopath if you ask. You will also get help by calling the **College of Health**.

Further information

Information about the health and social services in your area, as well as sheltered housing, nursing homes and other specialised facilities, can be obtained from the local director of social services, the local **Department of Community Medicine** (at your local authority office), the **Citizens' Advice Bureau**, the Town Hall or the public library. You will find them all in the telephone directory. **The College of Health** advises on a range of health and medical topics including hospital waiting lists. They also run a *Health Line* telephone tape service on most health related problem areas. Membership is £10 a year.

OLDER RELATIVES – SUPPORT AND CARE

It is one of the ironies of retirement that just as we begin to enjoy our new freedom an elderly parent or close relative becomes so frail that they either need to move in with us or at least need more help to maintain their independence. Certainly for most of us our first experience of frailty in old age comes from elderly relatives and they can impose anguishing physical and mental pressures on a family or individual.

There are no simple answers to this problem but often, because of the very natural desire to look after an elderly mother, father or aunt, your own needs or those of the family tend to get neglected and your goodwill over-exploited. A similar conflict often occurs if there is a younger seriously disabled member of the family. It is important to be objective about balancing your needs against those of the dependent member and to realise that there are alternatives to you having to cope with the problems alone. After all, if you become ill or depressed you will be unable to effectively help your family.

Back-up care

Many elderly people live alone in spite of growing frailty and are reluctant to move from the house they are used to. In such cases the house often has a capital value which, if realised, would facilitate supportive care, and it is worth broaching this idea gently. However, if they are not persuaded, the only thing you can do is to try to ensure as much back-up care from local organisations as can be negotiated.

Although the local social services are often short of staff and money, and some of the facilities are means-tested, there is an obligation to provide a wide range of domiciliary support, in the form of home helps, district nursing, dependency aids and even alterations to the home. These may have to be fought for and your GP should be able to help, but you can also approach the local director of social services. Appropriate assistance such as a stair lift, wheelchair, walking frame, incontinence pads or elevated lavatory seat, can be a great help. Some of these come through the occupational therapist who is part of the social services. Organisations like **Age Concern** and the **Disabled Living Foundation** also give helpful advice.

'Granny' flats

If you have had the good fortune, and foresight, to be able to offer this kind of accommodation it can be a very good arrangement, giving proximity and yet a certain amount of independence. This should be designed on one floor, or have a lift. It may be wise, if starting from scratch, to design in facilities for a wheelchair, large toilets, special bath and other useful special features. Again the social services may be able to help.

Sheltered housing

If the granny flat solution is not possible or desirable, an alternative is the growing network of what is called 'sheltered housing'. There are two parallel networks for this, either the public (local authority) or the private and voluntary. Your local social services department or the Citizen's Advice Bureau will have lists of what is locally available. You will have to investigate options as the costs and what is offered varies widely.

For reasonably active and independent people, some form of warden-supervised sheltered housing unit, with a bungalow or flatlet, may be sensible. This offers independence, some shared facilities plus a degree of social support (see *Moving to Your Retirement Home* page 278). As frailty and dependence increase, the nursing home or what is called Part III-type accommodation may be available. This should continue into terminal care or hospital admission for acute disease and is part of the social service provision.

It is worth remembering that legally the social services have a responsibility to provide care for dependent residents. If necessary they will have to subsidise such care in a voluntary or nursing home or residential care units.

Surrogate homes

'Surrogate' homes such as those provided by **The Abbeyfield Society** are ordinary houses in ordinary streets, custom built or converted to provide a bed–sitting room, furnished by the resident. Similar arrangements are made by the **Anchor Housing Association**, **Age Concern** and **Help the Aged** among others. Main meals are provided and a housekeeper is employed to look after a small 'family' of elderly people. Six or so residents live in each house and are expected to relate to each other, but they can otherwise come and go as they please. They pay their own way, even if they are on supplementary benefit, and each unit is financially self-supporting. These can often provide the answer to loneliness in old age.

There are now 900 Abbeyfield houses countrywide which provide the next best thing to a family home. Your parent may well be happier living in these circumstances and you may be under less stress. However, old people are often reluctant to move so it may be worth suggesting a week's holiday visit before taking any decisions.

The Abbeyfield Society also has a growing chain of Extra Care houses which look after those who cannot cope on their own. Even if confused, incontinent or physically dependent, the majority of residents can spend the rest of their days here.

The hospice movement

The hospice movement was pioneered by Dame Cecily Saunders with her work at St Christopher's Hospice in South London. Almost entirely voluntary and locally based, a hospice provides simple terminal nursing care, sophisticated pain control, domiciliary support and bereavement counselling, largely for cancer patients. Part of this movement, and largely through the **Macmillan Homes**, has formed an expanding network of training courses in home nursing and terminal care, for relatives and other carers. This is of great help to a family wanting to care for a relative right to the end. It is now realised that carers, be they personal, volunteer or professional, carry considerable burdens and they need support and encouragement. Caring for the carers is a recognised area of need and support agencies are beginning to develop for this purpose. These include the **National Association of Carers** and the **National Council for Carers and their Elderly Dependants**.

COMMON PROBLEMS IN LATER LIFE

It is worth saying a few words about some of the illnesses and changes encountered by the elderly so that if you have elderly relatives to deal with you can be on the look out. For most of us our first experience of frailty in old age comes from elderly relatives. As well as the physical demands on time there is often emotional anguish which can strain other relationships. Some of the more common problems are described here together with some hints on how to relieve them.

Vision

Most of us need reading glasses in middle age because the eye lens which alters its focal length to accommodate near and distant vision loses some of its elasticity. Thus the natural focal point for reading tends to retreat further away from the eye and you become long sighted. Reading glasses will compensate for this and bring the print back into focus. For similar reasons, a previously short-sighted person may find that the focal distance has changed in such a way that they can do without glasses.

Diseases common in older people, such as diabetes and raised blood pressure, can reduce vision. Glaucoma, which is due to raised pressure within the eye and often runs in the family, and cataract, which causes lens opacity, are common causes of severe visual difficulty. Both can usually be cured and lens implants have considerably improved the results of cataract surgery. The possibility of these and other conditions reinforces the need for regular eye testing.

Regular eye tests every two years will ensure optimum vision. If you do close work, such as needlework or painting, and have to hold your materials at a distance different from that for comfortable reading, it may be worthwhile asking for a pair of special glasses of the appropriate focal distance. They will help to minimise fatigue. It is also important that the older eye receives more light to function efficiently. Don't be mean about lighting, especially in the kitchen, corridors and stairs, as this will also help to reduce the risk of accidents.

Reading is a major pleasure for many people, particularly if they are disabled. For those partially sighted and those who find it difficult to either hold a book or turn the pages, joining a talking book or tape library can help overcome any feeling of loss in this area. The **Calibre Library of Recorded Books** offers a free service in this area. Also contact the **Royal National Institute for the Blind**.

Hearing

Hearing also deteriorates with age but as it has a wider functional spectrum than the eye, deafness may be less critical affecting only certain sound frequencies. For instance, life-long exposure to loud noise, as in a factory or to gun-fire, will cause deafness at these frequencies in later life.

Hearing is tested by exposing each ear to specific sound frequencies and noting the level at which each one is first heard. Plotted as a graph, this produces an audiogram against which an appropriate hearing aid can be prescribed or subsequent change measured. If either you or an older relative is becoming deaf it is well worth having this test, if only to have a firm baseline against which any further change can be measured.

A range of aids other than hearing aids are now available which make life easier for you if you are deaf, e.g. lights instead of bells for the telephone; special devices to make it easier to hear when using the telephone and headphones for radio and television (which make life easier for the rest of the family). The **Royal National Institute for the Deaf** (RNID) can give advice about coping with hearing problems.

Other hearing defects

Buzzing in the ears (*tinnitus*) is a common and infuriating disease prevalent amongst older people. If you suffer from this see an ENT specialist who may be able to help you either control it or treat it. Often, however, little can be done to reduce the irritating noise. Further information on this condition may be obtained from the **British Tinnitus Association.**

Wax remains a common cause of disability in older people and should, if present, be regularly removed by syringing.

Improving other aspects of communication
Hearing is a complicated synthesis of signals and depends as much on the ability to pick up speech clues as on the physical ability to hear. It can be a great help to face a deaf person and speak slowly and clearly without shouting. Speech therapists can be of assistance both in helping the deaf to speak clearly and to understand others. The whole family can co-operate in minimising the strain on a deaf member. Think of how difficult it is for the driver of a car and the passengers in the back to hold a conversation? The visual clues are just not there then. Deaf people sometimes tend to become paranoid about what they cannot hear, so remember to be gentle with them.

Strokes and raised blood pressure

A 'stroke' is a common cause of death or disability in older people. A stroke occurs, often suddenly and unexpectedly, when part of the brain is damaged either because its blood supply has been blocked (cerebral thrombosis) or because of direct damage by bleeding from a burst blood vessel (cerebral haemorrhage). Both are manifestations of *arteriosclerosis* and raised blood pressure, *hypertension*. The cause of this is not fully understood but it is known that both affect the heart, which works harder to maintain the higher pressure, as well as the arteries, which thicken and narrow, blocking the flow of blood or swell and burst (the swelling is known as an *aneurism*).

After a stroke
The effects of a stroke depend entirely on its extent and site within the brain. They can be minor, with little more than tingling, numbness or local muscle weakness, or serious, with partial or complete paralysis of one side. There may be limited recovery within the brain but as lost brain tissue cannot be replaced any real anatomical recovery is limited. Fortunately the body has surplus resources and some muscle groups can operate independently of the damaged brain so quite a lot of the bodily functions may be recovered. This is aided by physiotherapy, re-education and great determination on the part of the patient, supported by encouraging relatives and friends. A serious stroke will, however, leave great impairment.

Who is prone to this disease?
Kidney disease can cause hypertension and diabetes predisposes to arteriosclerosis, both of which can also lead to reduced vision. Inevitably, after a certain age, wear and tear take their toll and something gives. However, strokes amongst younger people can be prevented or delayed by the early diagnosis of hypertension and its active treatment (see page 250).

Fluid intake

There is a tendency for many older people to cut down their fluid intake towards the end of the day, largely to avoid getting up at night. This is usually a false economy because the kidneys go on working at night and you will often have to get up anyway. However, it is important, particularly in hot weather, to keep fluid intake up because the kidneys' function slows down and cannot handle concentrated fluids so effectively. They like dilute fluids and they need plenty of liquid to work on. It does not matter what form this takes – tea, coffee, water, squash or beer – all work in the same way. Some drinks contain stimulants, such as caffeine, others sugar as in squash, or alcohol as in beer, but you can drink whatever you enjoy in moderation.

Bear in mind that high calorie drinks and sugar in tea and coffee should be limited as part of the daily calorie balance for weight control. If you need to have sweet things consider using artificial sweeteners, reduced sugar or sugar free jams and other such items. These are widely available, are all safe and may allow you to have a treat or two in the form of a pudding.

Coffee is currently under mild suspicion as a possible contributor to coronary heart disease, but a large quantity (five or more cups a day) has to be taken to be dangerous and powdered coffee seems a little safer than ground.

Warmth

Old people look so partly because of their greying hair and partly because the skin loses its resilience due to breakdown of the elastic tissue in the deeper layers. This elastic tissue also acts as an insulator in younger people, and this 'double-glazing' becomes less efficient and less flexible with age. For these reasons, older people need to have a higher room temperature and more warm clothing. It is sensible to wrap up well in the winter and not to be proud about thermal underwear and woolly hats. Anything goes where warmth is concerned – gloves, scarves and hats all help. Also think about how you can keep the home warm and draught-free (see *Improving your Home*, page 325).

Mobility

This is critical in later life and your feet play a major part in this. It is a great disability not to be able to cut one's own toenails, put on stockings and tie shoe laces. Similarly, if older people cannot get at their feet they tend to become neglected. Corns, bunions, distorted toes and other causes of pain require attention and their presence can seriously limit mobility. Older people are the major users of chiropody services but sadly chiropodists through the National Health Service are in very short supply, although they can be found readily in private practice.

It is essential to wear comfortable, sensible shoes. The foot was developed to lie flat on the ground and wearing fashionable shoes that raise the heel for long periods can cause much of the pain arising from corns and bunions. These are formed by friction caused by wearing the wrong shoes and in severe cases, specially-made surgical shoes may be necessary. These are available through the NHS.

As you age the blood supply to the skin becomes less efficient particularly in the lower leg causing pain. It is important, therefore, to treat all minor injuries with great respect and if they don't heal reasonably quickly, seek medical advice.

Memory and reflexes

If you are to get the best use from your brain it has to be regularly exercised, just like your muscles, so continued mental stimulation or 'brain challenge' is a pre-requisite for maintaining general liveliness. Although brain cells do degenerate with age, there is such a vast reserve that new learning is perfectly possible no matter what your age. Research exists that proves that older people can acquire new skills and knowledge. You must, however, make an effort, and the methods of teaching and learning you need are not necessarily those that have been suitable in your youth.

There are two changes that occur with ageing:
- unreliable short-term memory
- slower response or reflex time

How the memory works is unknown. One theory is that it is an indexed databank of past experience with a built-in recall mechanism. It is, in practice, a library of experience. However, with age the basic mechanism of recall gets 'rusty', works more slowly and perhaps more unreliably. Past experience is usually recalled better than recent activity. For instance, your *short-term memory*, trying to remember what you went to fetch or what you were doing when the door bell rang, may become difficult. This is a normal age change and in no way heralds the onset of senility.

To compensate for this you will have to work harder to imprint your experience on the brain so that it is firmer and more positive. By writing things down they are more likely to stick. Like me, you may find that your short-term memory is fatigue sensitive, so that it is worse at the end of a day or week. Everyone experiences this and learning to cope is a part of growing old gracefully. Activities such as writing lists and reading them will help to keep you organised.

The effect of age on your reflexes is more difficult to overcome. Activities such as driving or crossing roads become more difficult as the scenario about you will begin to change more quickly than your powers of adjustment. Reflex time increases and response consequently takes longer. It may then be wise for you to stop driving and become a prudent pedestrian. General physical and mental alertness help to minimise this change but be aware of the difficulties and seriously consider giving up driving both for your health and that of other road users.

Confusion

This is something we all fear and about a fifth of people over 85 may become confused. As senile dementia is age related and women live longer than men, more women than men become seriously confused. There are three types of confusion:
- Mild confusion and eccentric dottiness, due to failure of short-term memory
- Multiple infarct confusion (previously called senile dementia). This can be severe and is a form of mini-strokes destroying the brain tissue. It is a manifestation of arteriosclerosis and is not necessarily progressive.
- Alzheimer's Disease. This is the result of a distinct disease process. It occurs at an earlier age than senile dementia, is progressive and may run in the family.

The care required for the last two are more or less the same and for severe cases full-time nursing or even institutional care may be necessary.

Confused people fall into two main groups, those who are aggressive and disruptive, and those who are irritating and disoriented but relatively calm. It is in dealing with the former that the needs of carers should be paramount and hospital admission is probably the best answer. 'Psychogeriatrics' is the new speciality which copes with this problem area.

For others there are now day centres in many areas for isolated elderly people, special ones for the confused and day hospitals for assessment and rehabilitation. Transport is usually available and getting out of the house in this way provides stimulation for the person and a break for the carer.

In all complicated cases of elderly frailty, it is sensible to get an assessment by a geriatrician or psychogeriatrician. Their expert knowledge will help in assessing the best use of drugs. A short period of hospitalisation for assessment may work wonders, particularly if the patient is on too many drugs which can increase their confusion and frailty.

USEFUL ADDRESSES

Abbeyfield Society
186 Darkes Lane
Potters Bar
Herts EN6 1AB
☎ 0707 44845

Age Concern
Bernard Sunley House
60 Pitcairn Road
Mitcham
Surrey CR4 3LL
☎ 01-640 5431

Alcoholics Anonymous
PO Box 514
11 Redcliffe Gardens
London SW10 9BQ
☎ 01-352 9779

Alzheimer's Disease Society
1st Floor, Bank Lodges
Fulham Broadway
London SW6 1EP
☎ 01-381 3177

Anchor Housing Association
Estra House
Station Approach
Streatham
London SW16 6ES
☎ 01-677 8161

Arthritis and Rheumatism Council for Research
41 Eagle Street
London WC1R 4AR
☎ 01-405 8572

Arthritis Care
6 Grosvenor Crescent
London SW1X 7ER
☎ 01-235 0902

ASH (Action on Smoking and Health)
5–11 Mortimer Street
London W1N 7RH
☎ 01-637 9843

Association of Carers
First Floor, 21–23 New Road
Chatham
Kent ME4 4QS

Association of Sexual and Marital Therapists
PO Box 62
Sheffield S1O 3TS

Back Pain Association
31 Park Road
Teddington,
Middlesex TW11 0AB
☎ 01-977 5474

BACUP (British Association of Cancer United Patients)
121–123 Charterhouse Street
London EC1M 6AA
☎ 01-608 1661

British Chiropractic Association
5 First Avenue
Chelmsford CM1 1RX
☎ 0245 358487

HEALTH AND WELL-BEING

British Diabetic Association
10 Queen Anne Street
London W1M 0BD
☎ 01-323 1531

British Homeopathic Association
27a Devonshire Street
London W1N 1RJ
☎ 01-935 2163

British Hypnotherapy Association
67 Upper Berkeley Street
London W1H 7DH
☎ 01-723 4443

British Medical Association
Tavistock Square
London WC1H 9JP
☎ 01-387 4499

British Rheumatism and Arthritis Association
6 Grosvenor Crescent
London SW1X 7EH
☎ 01-235 0902

British Tinnitus Association
105 Gower Street
London WC1E 6AH
☎ 01-387 8033

BUPA (Head Office)
Battle Bridge House
300 Gray's Inn Road
London WC1X 8DU
☎ 01-837 6484

Calibre Library of Recorded Books
Aylesbury
Bucks HP20 1HU

Chest, Heart and Stroke Association
Tavistock House North
Tavistock Square
London WC1H 9JE
☎ 01-387 3012

College of Health
14 Buckingham Street
London WC2N 6DS
☎ 01-839 2413

Counsel and Care for the Elderly
131 Middlesex Street
London E1 7JF
☎ 01-621 1624
They offer advice on the whole field of caring, accommodation and financing.

CRUSE (National Association for the Widowed and their Children)
CRUSE House
126 Sheen Road
Richmond
Surrey TW9 1UR

Disabled Living Foundation
380–384 Harrow Road
London W9 2HU
☎ 01-289 6111

General Council of Osteopaths
1–4 Suffolk Street
London SW1Y 4HG
☎ 01-839 2060

GRACE
PO Box 71
Cobham
Surrey KT11 2HW
☎ 09326 2928
They advise on residential and nursing homes in the south.

Health Education Council
78 New Oxford Street
London WC1A 1AH
☎ 01-631 0930

Hospice Information Service
51–53 Lawrie Park Road
London SE26 6DZ
☎ 01-778 1240

Incorporated Society of Registered Naturopaths
328 Harrogate Road
Leeds LS17 6PE
☎ 0532 685992

Institute of Psychosexual Medicine
11 Chandos Street
London W1M 9DE

Macmillan Homes
c/o Cancer Relief Macmillan Fund
Anchor House
15–19 Britten Street
London SW3 3TY
☎ 01-351 7811

Mastectomy Association
26 Harrison Street
London WC1H 8JG
☎ 01-837 0908

Migraine Trust
45 Great Ormond Street
London WC1N 3HD
☎ 01-278 2676

Multiple Sclerosis Society
25 Effie Road
London SW6 1EE
☎ 01-381 4022

National Association of Carers
58 New Road
Chatham
Kent ME4 4QR
☎ 0634 513981

National Council for Carers and their Elderly Dependants
29 Chilworth Mews
London W2 3EG
☎ 01-724 7776

National Marriage Guidance Council
Little Church Street
Rugby CV21 3AP

Northern Ireland Council for the Handicapped
2 Annadale Avenue
Belfast BT7 3JR
☎ 0232 640011

Parkinson's Disease Society
36 Portland Place
London W1N 3DG
☎ 01-323 1174

Relaxation for Living
21 Burwood Park Road
Walton-on-Thames
Surrey KT12 5LH
☎ 09322 27826

Royal National Institute for the Blind
224 Great Portland Street
London W1N 6AA
☎ 01-388 1266

Royal National Institute for the Deaf
105 Gower Street
London WC1E 6AH
☎ 01-387 8033

Scottish Council on Disability
Princes House,
5 Shandwick Place
Edinburgh EH2 4RG
☎ 031-229 8632

Weightwatchers
11 Fairacres
Dedworth Road
Windsor
Berks SL4 4UY
☎ 0753 856751

Women's League of Health and Beauty
18 Charing Cross Road
London WC2H 0HR
☎ 01-240 8456

BIBLIOGRAPHY

Brinson, W. (1986) *Deafness in the Adult* Thorsons Publishing Group, Wellingborough.
BUPA Manual of Fitness and Well-being (1983) Macdonalds, London.
Consumers' and Patients' Associations (1983) *A Patient's Guide to the NHS* The Consumers' Association, London.
Confusion in the Elderly (1987) The Abbeyfield Society, Herts.
Consumers' Guide to Health Information (1986) College of Health, London.
Eyton, A. (1982) *The F-Plan Diet* Penguin, London.
Hanisson, Maurice (1984) *E for Additives* Thorsons Publishing Group, Wellingborough.
Easing Grief – for oneself and for other people (1980) Relaxation for Living, Surrey.
Glasspool, M. (1984) *Eyes* Martin Dunitz, Oxford.
Guide to Alternative Medicine (1985) College of Health, London.
Inglis, B. and West, R. (1983) *The Alternative Health Guide* Michael Joseph, London.
Sheltered Housing – How Best to Avoid the Pitfalls (1987) Age Concern, London.
Smith, T. (ed.) (1987) *The New Macmillan Guide to Family Health* The Macmillan Press Ltd, London.
Stoppard, Miriam (1983) *Prime of Your Life* Penguin, Harmondsworth
Thompson, Dr Keith (1987) *Caring for an Elderly Relative* Martin Dunitz in association with Help the Aged, London.
Wright, H. B. (1986) *Ease and Dis-ease* Longmans Professional, London.
Youngson, R. (1986) *How to Cope with Tinnitus* Sheldon Press, London.

The BUPA *Facts About* series of booklets are available from the Marketing Dept, BUPA Medical Centre, Battle Bridge House, 300 Grays' Inn Road, London WC1X 8DU. They are:
Breasts and the importance of breast examination
Cancer in perspective
Cholesterol
Coronary thrombosis: Avoid it or live with it
Drinking and how to control it
The menopause and how to live through it
Obesity and how to control your weight
Posture and exercise and how to keep moving
Pre-menstrual syndrome
Sleep and rest
Smoking and how to stop

References

Wells, Nicholas (1987) *Coronary Heart Disease – the need for action* Office of Health Economics, London.

You need never lose the comfort of your own home.

Knowing that you don't have to leave home when you need nursing care brings real peace of mind. BNA can provide just the help you need.

Trained *local* nurses are available 24 hours a day, 7 days a week. How long you have the services of your nurses depends entirely on you – but it could be for as little as an hour a day.

Private nursing isn't a luxury when it allows you to stay in the place where you most want to be.

For a copy of our brochure and list of local branches post off the coupon today. No stamp needed.

British Nursing Association

British Nursing Association,
FREEPOST, Hatfield,
Herts AL9 5BR

Name _____

Address _____
_____
_____
_____

Tel no. _____

MH/87

Laing's new 1 and 2 bedroom homes are specially designed to meet the needs of the over 55's. They are warm and comfortable and very economical to use.
If you are seeking companionship and a care-free retirement, telephone Laing Retirement Homes or fill in your name and address and tick which development you are interested in.

- ☐ **BROMLEY**
  1 & 2 bed flats. Tel: 01 207 6619
- ☐ **BUSHEY**
  1 & 2 bed flats. Tel: 01 207 6619
- ☐ **CHESHUNT**
  1 & 2 bed flats. Tel: 01 207 6619
- ☐ **EASTBOURNE**
  1 & 2 bed flats. Tel: 0323 642083
- ☐ **HORSHAM**
  1 & 2 bed flats. Tel: 01 207 6619
- ☐ **KENTON**
  1 bedroom flats. Tel: 01 207 6619
- ☐ **NEW MALDEN**
  1 & 2 bed flats. Tel: 01 207 6619
- ☐ **PINNER**
  1 & 2 bed flats. Tel: 01 207 6619
- ☐ **WELWYN GARDEN CITY**
  1 & 2 bed flats and 2 bed bungalows. Tel: 0707 325175
- ☐ **WOKINGHAM**
  1 & 2 bed flats and 2 bed bungalows. Tel: 01 207 6619
- ☐ **WORTHING**
  1 bedroom flats. Tel: 0903 208413

NAME _____
ADDRESS _____
_____

LAING RETIREMENT HOMES
MANOR WAY, BOREHAMWOOD, HERTS WD6 1LN

RG3

Bryant

Freedom...security...peace of mind... ...and a life of leisure!

That's what you'll find in a superb and luxurious craftsman-built one or two bedroom Bryant retirement apartment. And we're carefully planning developments in prime locations for completion during 1987 and 1988.

If you're looking forward to a life of leisure, DIAL 100 AND ASK FOR FREEFONE BRYANT and we'll send you a free brochure and audio cassette containing full details of these superb developments. A video cassette is available for club viewing, on request. Please ask for details.

**Bryant Homes Limited, 90/92 High Street, Crawley, West Sussex. RH10 1BA.
Tel: 0293 545021**

Bryant Homes — Raising the Standard

The
HOME FOR LIFE
PLAN

The HOME FOR LIFE PLAN is designed to provide a retired person or couple with a new home, within the protected environment of a good quality "sheltered" development, without the need to pay the builders price in full.

For further information please write to:
HOME FOR LIFE PLC, 10-12 Spencers Road, CRAWLEY, West Sussex RH11 7DA
or telephone: **(0293) 552751**

Moving to your retirement home

DO YOU WANT TO MOVE?	278
Myths and reality	280
THINKING IT OUT	282
GETTING THE FACTS	282
The weather	282
House prices	285
Cost of rates	287
Health Service provisions	290
Communications	290
THE COST OF MOVING HOME	290
Estate agents	291
Selling without an agent	292
When agents are useful	292
Conveyancing	293
Surveyors	294
Removals	294
WHAT SORT OF HOME?	294
Houses and flats	295
Sheltered homes	296
Mobile homes	298
Rented accommodation	300
New houses	301
USEFUL ADDRESSES	302
BIBLIOGRAPHY	314

Why do you live in your present home? Is it because:
- You found it convenient for the job?
- You had to move to this area as a condition of your job?
- The house goes with the job?
- You chose it because it was in the catchment area for the school you wanted your children to attend?
- You have lived in this town all your life and in this house since you married?
- Because it is your dream house? You always wanted one like this and when it came up for sale you just had to buy it.

No doubt you can add a few explanations of your own, but before you decide what to do, to move or stay, think back to your reasons for living where you are now. If either of the two final options apply to you, you will probably not want to move and may prefer to skip to *Home Improvements* (p. 325).

Most people, however, live in their present homes largely because of their jobs. Originally you may have had to uproot yourself from the place you grew up, in order to find employment. Since then you may have moved several times – for your marriage, as you changed jobs, for the sake of the children, or because you could afford a better house. And now that retirement is looming on the horizon you are free, for the first time in your life, to live exactly where you wish.

DO YOU WANT TO MOVE?

Perhaps you fancy returning to that part of the country you hailed from. Indeed you may still have relatives and friends there who will be pleased to see you back. Perhaps you have had your eye on some other part of the country which appeals to you because of the weather, the countryside, the people, the cheapness of the property or because you want to be beside the seaside. On the other hand, there could also be very good reasons for staying where you are. Likely motivations both for and against are given below.

Reasons for moving
- Your children have moved away and you would prefer to be closer to them.

MOVING TO YOUR RETIREMENT HOME

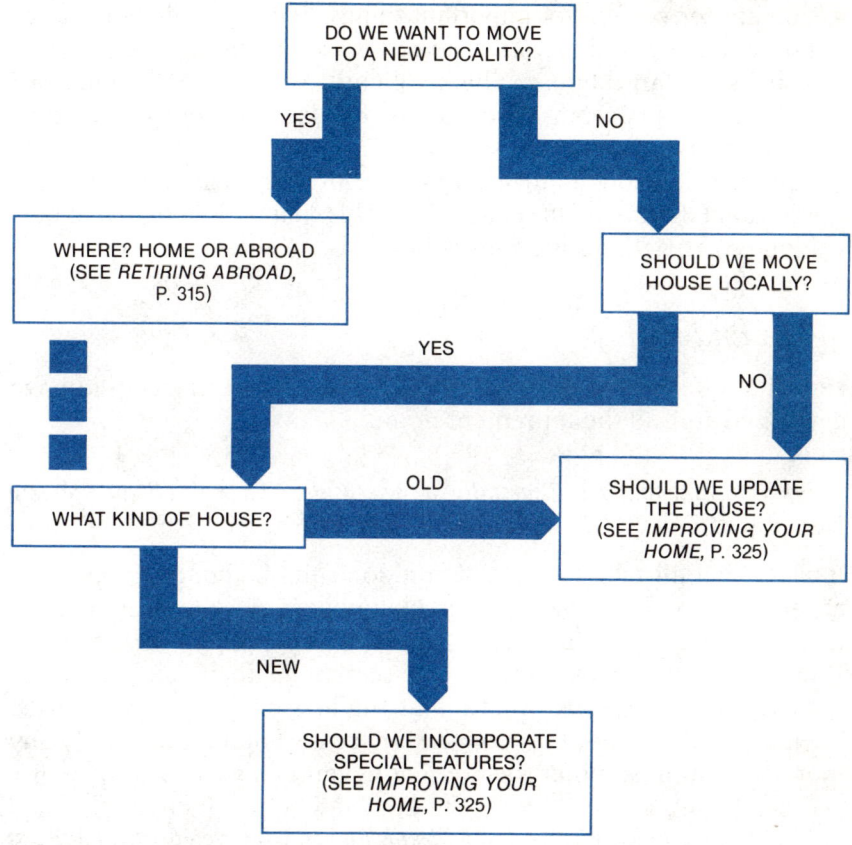

- Your present house was bought with raising a family in mind and is now really too big and too expensive for just the two of you.
- You are fed up with cities, with the traffic and noise, and with the anxiety about burglaries and muggings that go with them.
- The house is worth so much now and it's just sitting there doing nothing except costing you money.

Reasons for staying put
- This is where you now have your roots. You enjoy the company of friends and neighbours.
- One or more of your children lives nearby and you would not want to be inaccessible to them.
- You have a strong social life here. You are members of various clubs and societies. You feel wanted and needed here.
- You like it in the town. You have a good relationship with all the traders and services.

- You are convenient for important things, like a good doctor, a large hospital, a super library and the best cricket team.
- You like a large house. There's plenty of room to expand your hobbies and bedrooms to put up the children or friends when they come to visit.

Making the decision about where to live in retirement is much more complicated than it might seem at first. This chapter is designed to help you make the right decision for your needs.

Myths and reality

Let's first of all try to dispel a few of the myths which seem to have developed around the retirement home.

1. *It's a mistake to move. Especially to the seaside. You wait till you see how bleak it is in winter.*

It *might* be a mistake to move if you don't think about it properly in advance. If you did move to a seaside town simply because you once had a nice fortnight there, then you may very well be disappointed. However, many people move to the seaside for their retirement and have reported afterwards that it was the best move they ever made. Their complaint is not that they never see old friends and family any more but that in summer the house is never their own.

2. *Make sure you pick a house that will still suit you when you are frail and less able to cope*

Many of us embarking on retirement can expect to enjoy 20 years or more of active life. To cocoon yourself in a house at the age of 60 assuming that you will die in it is negative. In reality you may decide to move yet again. Perhaps twice. It is much more sensible to make sure you buy a house which suits your needs now and which is a sound investment so that if you do decide to sell it you will find ready buyers.

3. *You should move to a smaller house. You don't want to be rattling round this big old place like two peas in a drum*

What is wrong with a big house, assuming you can afford the upkeep? Or a big garden? In the early years of retirement you are in the best possible situation to enjoy them. Of all the mistakes people make about buying a home for retirement I suspect this is the most common. They go for a compact two-up two-down house because it is cheaper to run, easier to keep clean and quite adequate for their needs. This may be a mistake, however. Of course a big house will be more expensive to run but it may not be any more difficult to keep clean and tidy than a small one. Many people who have made such a move have told me it is quite the reverse. If you are accustomed to a sitting room 20 ft long and 14 ft wide, which contains a three-piece suite, a sideboard and an occasional table, there will still seem to be acres of space available. So if you drop a paper on the floor or leave garden catalogues on the side table, there is no apparent mess. When you move to a house with a sitting room 12 ft square, you are still likely to have a three-piece suite and an occasional table but when you drop your paper on the floor or leave your garden catalogues as before you may cause domestic disharmony.

Also, what happens if you take up new hobbies in retirement and need a table to work at them? If you have a spare bedroom there is no problem; you put a table in there and when it's time to eat you simply leave it. If the only available table is the dining room or kitchen table, this can be very awkward.

Moreover, as houses appreciate, big houses will appreciate faster in cash terms than small houses. Unless you desperately need to get your hands on the capital locked up in your house to help you make ends meet in retirement, why not let your home continue to increase in value so there is even more for you to capitalise on if the time should come? Unlike cash invested in a building society or a unit trust, you pay no tax whatever on the profits you make from selling your own home.

4. *Older people find it difficult to make friends in new areas*

Older people can make friends as easily as anyone else. There are far fewer areas of the country these days where you have to live for three generations before the locals recognise you. If you make an effort to get involved in local community activities you should have no problem making new friends. If you are particularly shy, however, it might be worth asking yourself if you are *sure* you will make the effort.

5. *People who emigrate to Spain and other sunspots invariably regret it and are desperate to come home*

No doubt it is true of some. But the same arguments apply in this case as to people who move to the seaside. Obviously you won't do it without spending some time in the area you plan to move to; you will take proper legal and financial advice; and you will make sure you know all the ins and outs so far as health care, taxation, travel restrictions and such like are concerned. (See page 315 for more on emigration.) In fact, many people who emigrate to Spain have an extremely comfortable life, enjoying the warm climate. As regards social life, they have the choice either of integrating into the Spanish way of life or living in the mainly-British communes.

THINKING IT OUT

Whether you decide to move or to stay put in retirement is a subject for serious thought. There are so many factors to consider that it is not a bad start for you to actually list your thoughts on a piece of paper. Couples should do their own lists individually and then compare notes. Do it in two stages:
1. Make two columns, one listing what you think would be the benefits of moving somewhere else in the country (or the world) and another listing the disadvantages of moving from your present area. (Never mind for the moment about what *sort* of home you want or happen to live in.)
2. You now have two possible options:
   (a) If you have decided to move to another location you should first decide *where* and then decide *what kind of house*.
   (b) If you have decided to stay in the same area you should still ask yourself the questions, 'Shall we stay in this house or move to another one nearby?' and 'Is there anything we should do to make our home more suitable?'

Generally, of those who are about to retire about 40% plan to move and 10% are undecided. Of those who have retired only 25% do actually move.

GETTING THE FACTS

Let's assume you decide you want to move to another part of the country. The decision may already be made in your own minds, of course, because you specially want to go to a seaside area or some county you find particularly attractive. If you are not quite sure, there are a few quesions you could ask yourself to help you pinpoint the right area.
What about
- the weather
- house prices
- cost of rates
- health service provision
- communications

The map and charts on pages 283–9 have been designed to help you check these points.

The weather

The weather information on pages 283–5 gives basic information about the local climate in 30 towns in the British Isles.

MOVING TO YOUR RETIREMENT HOME 283

The following weather information was compiled with the help of the Meteorological Office and the London Weather Centre. Basic information about local climate is given for 30 towns around the British Isles.

🌧️	TOTAL ANNUAL RAINFALL IN INCHES
🌧️	NUMBER OF DAYS ON WHICH AT LEAST ¼ MM OF RAIN (0.01 INCHES) WAS RECORDED
🌡️	AVERAGE MAXIMUM (DAY-TIME) TEMPERATURES FOR THE MONTHS OF JANUARY AND JULY RECORDED IN FAHRENHEIT
🌡️	AVERAGE MINIMUM (NIGHT-TIME) TEMPERATURES FOR THE MONTHS OF JANUARY AND JULY RECORDED IN FAHRENHEIT
☀️	AVERAGE NUMBER OF HOURS OF BRIGHT SUNSHINE RECORDED ANNUALLY
☁️	AVERAGE NUMBER OF DAYS WITH NO SUNSHINE RECORDED AT ALL
❄️	AVERAGE NUMBER OF DAYS WITH SNOW LYING

	ABERYSTWYTH	AMBLESIDE	BELFAST	BIRMINGHAM	BRAEMAR
🌧️	41.37	72.87	33.26	30.07	35.39
🌧️	220	208	213	178	208
🌡️	44.42 / 64.04	42.26 / 67.46	42.8 / 65.12	41.54 / 68.36	38.66 / 63.68
🌡️	35.78 / 53.6	33.8 / 51.44	34.7 / 51.8	34.88 / 54.14	27.5 / 47.78
☀️	1455	1188	1285	1299	1120
☁️	69	112	78	78	*
❄️	4	10	9	15	63

	BUXTON	CAMBRIDGE	CARDIFF	CLACTON	CRANWELL (LINCOLN)
🌧️	49.40	21.96	41.92	21.85	23.62
🌧️	191	147	180	153	165
🌡️	39.56 / 64.22	43.34 / 71.96	44.6 / 68.54	42.62 / 68.72	41.72 / 69.8
🌡️	31.1 / 51.08	33.08 / 53.24	34.7 / 54.32	34.52 / 41.9	32.9 / 52.88
☀️	1133	1490	1553	1674	1497
☁️	91	70	74	64	68
❄️	34	11	8	10	18

★ INFORMATION NOT AVAILABLE

	CROMER	DOUGLAS (IOM)	DOVER	DURHAM	EDINBURGH
🌧️ rainfall	24.33	44.84	29.56	25.9	26.61
🌧️ rain days	173	197	157	179	191
🌡️ max temp	43.34 / 68.9	44.24 / 63.32	44.24 / 68.18	42.08 / 67.64	41.9 / 65.12
🌡️ min temp	33.98 / 54.32	36.86 / 52.7	35.96 / 56.3	33.8 / 51.26	33.98 / 52.16
☀️ sunshine	1561	1584	1709	1332	1384
☁️ cloudy	66	71	65	79	71
❄️ snow	9	6	8	26	14

	EXETER	FALMOUTH	FELIXSTOWE	ILFRACOMBE	LONDON (KEW)
🌧️ rainfall	31.49	42.91	20.74	40.39	23.34
🌧️ rain days	163	193	157	180	153
🌡️ max temp	45.86 / 70.88	48.2 / 67.1	42.26 / 69.26	47.3 / 65.66	43.34 / 71.24
🌡️ min temp	36.32 / 53.78	39.74 / 55.4	35.6 / 56.66	39.74 / 57.02	35.96 / 56.3
☀️ sunshine	1636	1683	1667	1618	1514
☁️ cloudy	59	61	59	77	68
❄️ snow	4	1	7	3	7

	MORECAMBE	OXFORD	PLYMOUTH	RENFREW	ROSS-ON-WYE
🌧️ rainfall	37.91	25.98	37.40	43.66	28.14
🌧️ rain days	174	126	178	201	162
🌡️ max temp	42.98 / 66.2	43.7 / 71.06	46.76 / 66.2	41.72 / 66.2	43.52 / 69.62
🌡️ min temp	34.34 / 55.22	33.8 / 54.32	39.2 / 55.4	33.44 / 51.98	35.6 / 53.78
☀️ sunshine	1476	1501	1677	1243	1458
☁️ cloudy	74	62	62	79	57
❄️ snow	10	13	3	6	7

	SCARBOROUGH	SHREWSBURY	SKEGNESS	SOUTHAMPTON	YORK
☂	25.47	25.94	22.95	31.65	25.15
☔	179	185	158	166	177
🌡	43.7 67.28	43.88 69.62	42.44 67.82	45.32 70.88	42.62 69.8
🌡	35.06 54.5	32.9 53.24	33.44 54.5	35.06 54.86	33.44 53.78
☀	1397	1356	1530	1625	1342
☁	89	71	75	67	81
❄	14	17	10	6	15

House prices

House prices vary considerably depending on where you want to live. In 1986 houses of any kind in the London area were still the most expensive, with the cheapest housing to be found in Northern Ireland, closely followed by Wales, Yorkshire and Humberside. Anyone who decided to move out of a detached house in London could afford to buy two similar houses in Wales and still have change to buy a Rolls-Royce and a round-the-world cruise.

The tables on pages 285–7 show the typical cost of houses by the end of 1986 in the 12 principal regions of Great Britain, in order of expense. We have taken the average prices of new, modern and older properties for detached, semi-detached and terraced houses as well as for bungalows, flats and maisonettes which have been taken as a single category. The annual change in price during 1986 is also given.

		GREATER LONDON	OUTER METROPOLITAN AREA
🏠	DETACHED HOUSES	£112,230	£93,080
🏠	SEMI-DETACHED HOUSES	£74,980	£62,500
🏠	TERRACED HOUSES	£63,610	£50,580
🏠	BUNGALOWS/FLATS/MAISONETTES	£53,670	£53,350
		1986 CHANGE + 23%	1986 CHANGE + 19%

The above information on house prices has been compiled with help from the Nationwide Building Society.

	OUTER SOUTH EAST	SOUTH WEST	EAST ANGLIA	EAST MIDLANDS
🏠 (detached)	£70,790	£59,000	£52,860	£44,930
🏠 (semi)	£46,950	£40,730	£35,520	£29,720
🏠 (terrace)	£40,080	£32,600	£30,860	£22,330
🏠 (bungalow)	£46,300	£43,890	£39,510	£35,710
	1986 CHANGE +17%	1986 CHANGE +14%	1986 CHANGE +15%	1986 CHANGE +15%

	WEST MIDLANDS	NORTH WEST	NORTHERN ENGLAND	YORKSHIRE AND HUMBERSIDE
🏠 (detached)	£48,050	£47,810	£43,450	£42,190
🏠 (semi)	£29,360	£29,590	£28,660	£28,130
🏠 (terrace)	£21,870	£18,950	£20,400	£19,280
🏠 (bungalow)	£30,730	£34,530	£29,240	£31,640
	1986 CHANGE +7%	1986 CHANGE +7%	1986 CHANGE +3%	1986 CHANGE +5%

	NORTHERN IRELAND	SCOTLAND	WALES	UNITED KINGDOM AVERAGES
🏠 (detached)	£40,450	£47,020	£40,750	£61,800
🏠 (semi)	£25,340	£34,970	£30,490	£41,210
🏠 (terrace)	£17,010	£30,460	£22,710	£32,460
🏠 (bungalow)	£31,920	£30,280	£34,380	£39,900
	1986 CHANGE +2%	1986 CHANGE +3%	1986 CHANGE +7%	1986 CHANGE +14%

MOVING TO YOUR RETIREMENT HOME

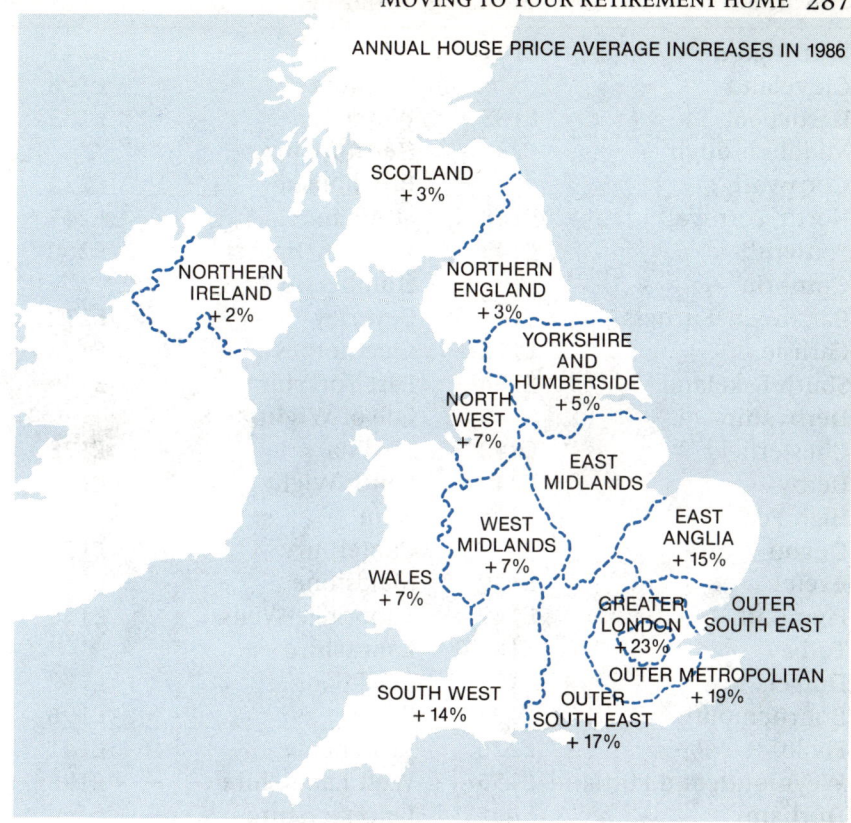

ANNUAL HOUSE PRICE AVERAGE INCREASES IN 1986

Cost of rates

The average rate bill per head of the ratepayer population in various towns in 1986/87 is given in the table below. They formed part of a Parliamentary written answer (to a question from MP Robin Corbett of Birmingham) by the Minister of State Department of the Environment in April 1987.

Avon
Bath   £197
Bristol   £219
Bedfordshire
Luton   £232
North Beds   £209
South Beds   £238
Berkshire
Newbury   £200
Reading   £178
Wokingham   £228

Buckinghamshire
Aylesbury Vale   £226
Chiltern   £351
Milton Keynes   £240
Cambridgeshire
Cambridge   £221
Huntingdon   £186
Peterborough   £198
Cheshire
Chester   £216
Macclesfield   £251

Warrington	£191	Hereford	£141
Cleveland		Redditch	£196
Hartlepool	£188	Worcester	£183
Middlesbrough	£230	**Hertfordshire**	
Cornwall		Broxbourne	£222
North Cornwall	£148	St Albans	£247
Penwrith	£143	Welwyn/Hatfield	£260
Cumbria		**Humberside**	
Barrow-in-Furness	£141	Beverley	£212
Carlisle	£172	Cleethorpes	£176
South Lakeland	£194	East Yorkshire	£159
Derbyshire		**Isle of Wight**	
Chesterfield	£212	Medina	£178
Derby	£249	South Wight	£191
High Peak	£202	**Kent**	
Devon		Canterbury	£153
Exeter	£139	Maidstone	£153
Plymouth	£147	Tunbridge Wells	£155
Torbay	£180	**Lancashire**	
Dorset		Blackpool	£172
Bournemouth	£198	Fylde	£196
Poole	£226	Rossendale	£141
Weymouth and Portland	£155	West Lancashire	£198
Durham		**Leicestershire**	
Darlington	£173	Harborough	£202
Derwentside	£141	Leicester	£155
Durham	£149	Melton	£171
Teesdale	£111	Rutland	£154
Essex		**Lincolnshire**	
Braintree	£195	Boston	£144
Chelmsford	£232	Lincoln	£139
Epping Forest	£260	South Kesteven	£138
Southend-on-sea	£244	**Inner London**	
Gloucestershire		Camden	£440
Cheltenham	£185	Islington	£305
Forest of Dean	£133	Wandsworth	£185
Gloucester	£143	Westminster	£501
Hampshire		**Outer London**	
East Hampshire	£205	Barnet	£265
Gosport	£177	Bromley	£192
New Forest	£187	Croydon	£207
Southampton	£154	Haringey	£468
Winchester	£200	Kingston-upon-Thames	£212
Hereford and Worcester		Redbridge	£183

Sutton	£208	South Staffordshire	£206
Waltham Forest	£230	Stoke-on-Trent	£145
Greater Manchester		**Suffolk**	
Bolton	£188	Ipswich	£192
Manchester	£225	Mid Suffolk	£173
Stockport	£222	Suffolk Coastal	£204
Merseyside		**Surrey**	
Liverpool	£251	Guildford	£225
St Helens	£208	Surrey Heath	£246
Wirral	£265	Tandridge	£199
West Midlands		Woking	£246
Birmingham	£206	**East Sussex**	
Solihull	£245	Brighton	£227
Wolverhampton	£204	Eastbourne	£233
Norfolk		Hastings	£183
Broadland	£174	Hove	£205
Great Yarmouth	£165	**West Sussex**	
Norwich	£170	Chichester	£192
Kings Lynn & W. Norfolk	£147	Horsham	£197
Northamptonshire		Worthing	£194
Corby	£185	**Tyne and Wear**	
Kettering	£173	Gateshead	£196
Northampton	£201	Newcastle-upon-Tyne	£307
Northumberland		**Warwickshire**	
Berwick-upon-Tweed	£157	Nuneaton and Bedworth	£202
Blyth Valley	£183	Stratford-on-Avon	£242
Tynedale	£164	Warwick	£232
Nottinghamshire		**Wiltshire**	
Ashfield	£146	Kennet	£162
Newark	£158	Salisbury	£173
Nottingham	£172	Thamesdown	£187
Oxfordshire		**North Yorkshire**	
Oxford	£183	Harrogate	£174
Vale of White Horse	£205	Scarborough	£143
Shropshire		Selby	£138
Bridgnorth	£159	York	£113
Oswestry	£134	**South Yorkshire**	
South Shropshire	£136	Barnsley	£161
Somerset		Sheffield	£230
Mendip	£167	**West Yorkshire**	
Taunton Deane	£170	Bradford	£161
Staffordshire		Calderdale	£169
Lichfield	£203	Leeds	£164

Health Service provisions

Some years ago, a number of doctors expressed a fear that certain seaside and spa towns which attracted large numbers of retired people were unable to cope with the demands they made on the health services. Their fears were overstated; both the **Patients' Association** and the **Department of Health and Social Security** confirm that services in such areas are well able to cope with demand. Nevertheless, it may pay to check with local people about the best doctors and other facilities. (See also *Using the Health Service* on page 257.)

Communications

There are two aspects to this
- ease of travel to other parts of the country you may want to visit regularly
- ease of travel to local shops, doctor and other services.

Retired people do not necessarily cut themselves off if they live in a rural area but it is true that 'It's fine so long as you can drive'. 'But what about when you are too old?' Well, that's likely to be some time off and there is nothing to stop you moving if that is the case. It is highly sensible for *both* husband and wife to be drivers. I have come across cases where non-driving partners, usually women, have become virtually isolated because their spouse died suddenly or became ill.

If you have no car and plan to live without one, then clearly the situation is different. If you are relying on public transport then you should try it out and make sure it is as convenient as you would like it to be. Villages, in my view, are no places for non-drivers. There is even a strong case for two cars.

THE COST OF MOVING HOME

Let's suppose you live in a detached house in the Home Counties close to London and decide to move to a new home in the South-West – you won't be alone because thousands of people have migrated to the warmer (though sometimes wetter) climate of Cornwall, Devon, Somerset, Dorset and Wiltshire. You have decided to go for a bungalow rather than a house.

The house price table on page 285 shows that you can expect to sell your detached home in the Home Counties for £93,080. Your new home will cost about £44,000. What other costs are involved? If you take the traditional course you will pay an estate agent to sell your house and a solicitor both to sell and buy. There is also stamp duty to pay on all properties over £30,000 as well as the cost of removal men.

The costs are typically those shown opposite.

THE COSTS IN BUYING AND SELLING A HOME

Selling a detached house for £93,000

Estate agent's fees (at 1.75%)	£1,627.50
Plus VAT (15%)	£244.12
Solicitor's fee (1% of selling price)	£930.00
Plus VAT (15%)	£139.50
Total	£2,941.12

Buying a bungalow at £44,000

Survey	£150.00
Plus VAT	£22.50
Solicitor's fee (at 1% of purchase price)	£440.00
Plus VAT	£66.00
Stamp duty (1%)*	£440.00
Land registry fees†	£70.00
Total	£1,188.50

Total

Selling price of house	£93,000.00
less purchase price of bungalow	£44,000.00
less costs of selling	£2,941.00
less costs of purchase	£1,188.50
less cost of removal	£350.00
Balance	£44,520.50

*There is no stamp duty on property purchases up to a value of £30,000. Over £30,000 the levy is a standard 1% of the whole amount. If you buy a house for £31,000, therefore, you pay stamp duty on the whole £31,000 not just £1000.

†Not all areas of the country are yet covered by compulsory land registration but 80% of the population lives in registered property. Fees are on a sliding scale according to the value of the property. These start at £20 for property worth up to £15,000. A house costing between £50,000 and £60,000 would cost £90, while a house costing between £90,000 and £100,000 would cost £175. Scotland has its own system of land registration but the scale of fees is much the same.

Estate agents

Estate agents' charges are one of the most resented yet significant costs involved in selling a house. These vary and are, to some extent, negotiable. If you have a particularly nice house in an attractive site which is obviously likely to be popular, then you can afford to be firm and insist on a reduced fee. These will probably vary between 1.75% and 2% of the sale price, but sometimes you can get them to 1.5% or lower. A lower rate may be offered anyway, provided you appoint them as sole agents. If you have time in which to sell your house you may like to agree to this for, say, a month and then offer it to other agents if no sale or prospect of one has materialised.

Charges are generally all-inclusive of expenses so do not agree to any additional charges such as advertising costs. You should also make sure your estate agent is a member of either the Incorporated Society of Valuers and Auctioneers, the Royal Institution of Chartered Surveyors or the National Association of Estate Agents.

Selling without an agent

It is possible, of course, to sell your house yourself, without using an agent, though relatively few people actually do it. There is nothing to stop you sticking up a 'For Sale' sign in the front garden or taking advertisements in the local press or one of the magazines specialising in property. Your rate of success is likely to be determined by where you live. In London, where property is still in short supply and rapidly increasing in price, you are more likely to be successful than in a depressed area, where houses are harder to sell anyway. Two difficulties you will encounter are:
- fixing the right selling price
- establishing the bona fides of your purchaser

In a year like 1986, when the normal increase in prices was between 10% and 23%, it is not easy to keep pace with the value of your property. You risk offering at too low or too high a price. The prices commanded by neighbouring houses of a similar situation and character can help you decide. Alternatively, you could employ a surveyor (who may also be an estate agent) to value your house for you for a fee.

When agents are useful

Estate agents maintain that they are better placed than the individual seller to establish whether or not the potential purchaser can actually raise the cash and mortgage necessary to go through with the deal. Many people who make bids for houses overreach themselves and have to withdraw, sometimes at a late stage. Agents may be able to help with mortgages or even with the sale of the purchaser's property, and so avoid the so-called 'chain' of buyers and sellers all waiting impatiently in a queue because one of them cannot sell his house or raise his mortgage. This can lead to the need for bridging loans, frayed nerves and lost tempers. This situation is well known in England and Wales, but the Scottish system precludes this. There a system of tendering exists which includes fixed dates for the payment of deposits and for completion. The **Prudential** is one national chain of estate agents that has been helping customers in some parts of the country by offering to buy their homes at the market price. This is in order to break the long chains that form.

Conveyancing

Solicitors

Solicitors have gone through turmoil in recent years, with their monopoly on handling conveyancing well and truly broken. The result is good news for the house buyer and seller because fees have certainly come down. Generally charges for conveyancing through a solicitor should not exceed about 1% of the selling or buying price, but there is no longer a fixed percentage and you should negotiate a fee *before* you agree to engage a solicitor to act for you. The higher the value of your house the lower the percentage charge should be, and you may get the work done for as little as $\frac{1}{2}$% if you press the case. Now that they are allowed to advertise, some solicitors have even been offering flat rate fees to handle any house.

Conveyancing firms

What has caused such an upset has been the arrival of a new breed of agent specialising in nothing but conveyance work. The movement was started in the early 1970s by a group of former solicitors' clerks (the people who do the work of conveyance) led by David Ashford who is now the chairman of the National Association of Conveyancers. The Association has 20 members nationwide, all with at least ten years' experience of conveyance work and charging between $\frac{1}{4}$% and $\frac{1}{2}$% of the buying or selling price.

One of the problems of going to a non-solicitor for conveyance work has been the fact that no licensing arrangements have been in force. This will be remedied by the end of 1987 when any conveyancer who is not licensed by the Lord Chancellor will not be allowed to offer his or her services.

Estate agents generally have an arrangement with local solicitors for payment whereby they send their commission bills direct to your solicitor who automatically deducts this, as well as his own fee, from the sale proceeds. You will receive the balance. However, if you are unhappy about this arrangement, you should instruct your solicitor accordingly.

Surveyors

Whether you use a surveyor or not is a personal decision. If it is a modern house covered by a National House Building Council 10-year guarantee then you probably have little to fear. But if it is an older house which has already had a number of structural alterations, then a survey might buy you peace of mind. Building societies and banks always employ a surveyor to check over a property before they will grant you a mortgage. This is charged to you and is a fairly superficial affair designed mainly to check the value of the property rather than provide a detailed structural report.

The Royal Institution of Chartered Surveyors does not lay down any particular scale of charges for survey work and it depends how detailed an examination you want. Usually when you buy a house you will have certain anxieties, whether a structural change was properly done, for example. Speak to the surveyor about this and ask him to look particularly into such aspects. Detail any other points you want a report on. Some surveyors charge on an hourly rate, some agree a fixed fee in advance. You should shop around.

Removals

There is nothing to stop you moving your own furniture in the back of a hire van, but it's hard work and most people prefer to put the removal into the hands of a professional. The experts are all members of the **British Association of Removers** from whom you can obtain a list of members in your area.

The cost of a removal varies depending on the volume of materials to be moved, the distance and any storage period to be taken into account. A simple local removal might be as little as £200 while a removal from a large house to another several hundred miles away could be over £1000. If you are going abroad it might be several thousand pounds. Clearly it is important to shop around and obtain a number of quotes. If you have friends who can recommend removal companies so much the better.

WHAT SORT OF HOME?

The choice open to you is probably wider in retirement than at any other stage in your life. You have few restrictions now, other than those of finance, and if you are moving from a high price to a lower price area even that may not be a problem. Here we shall look at the choices that are available, summarising the main advantages and disadvantages for each option.

Houses and flats

Detached or semi-detached houses
These are likely to be a popular choice, particularly among people who already live in such properties.

Advantages
- They afford a high degree of privacy
- They are widely available
- They are popular and therefore easy to sell
- They are spacious

Disadvantages
- They may be *too* spacious for the amount of maintenance, cleaning and decoration that you are prepared to do.
- They have stairs which may prove a problem in later years.

Terraced houses
These were very fashionable during the 19th century and early part of the 20th century. They rather went out of fashion between the wars but have recently been 're-discovered', especially in large cities. Modern ones are called 'town houses'.

Advantages
- They are often spacious and well built.
- Because of the neighbouring houses on both sides they tend to be warmer.

Disadvantages
- They are often on more than two floors (older ones may also have a cellar).
- Gardens tend to be long and narrow and are often overlooked by neighbours.

Bungalows
These have become extremely popular among retired people in recent years.

Advantages
- There are no stairs to climb.
- They are easy to manage, particularly if you are planning to do your own exterior maintenance and decoration – even with a short ladder you will be able to reach the gutters.
- Being popular and in short supply, they are easy to sell.

Disadvantages
- Some people do not like the idea of sleeping downstairs. This is not a great problem, however, and any strangeness you may experience is quickly overcome.
- For the space provided, bungalows can be a good deal more expensive than two-storey homes. This is because the cost of land represents a significant part of a house price and a bungalow takes up just as much of it, if not more, than a house.
- Since they are in short supply, bungalows tend to be quite hard to come by.

Flats and apartments

Moving to a flat is probably an option that you will consider if you are hoping to capitalise on the equity that is tied up in your present home.

Advantages
- They are usually less expensive than a house (London apart).
- They are easily maintained.
- Many do not have gardens (this of course may be a disadvantage for some people).
- Some have security entrances (with intercoms and remote control) or even resident caretakers.
- You may wish to live in close proximity to neighbours, which is more likely in a flat than a house.

Disadvantages
- If you are surrounded by other flats, above and below, you could be inconvenienced by noisy or inconsiderate neighbours.
- Flats are invariably sold leasehold, which means you may have to pay a ground rent.
- Complexes of flats usually have shared general maintenance charges for cleaning of stairs, hallway, grounds etc, which can be quite expensive. You should check this out in advance.

Sheltered homes

These have been one of the growth industries of recent years and have proved extremely popular with many older people looking to the future. The idea is that a complex of houses, bungalows or flats is purpose-built for older people and each complex has a warden or even a nurse on hand who can be called in case of emergency. At 65 you may well scorn such a thought, but later in life the comfort which comes with such an arrangement proves very appealing.

Advantages
- They provide extra safety and security, while enabling you to maintain a totally independent lifestyle.
- They have been built with easy running in mind.

Disadvantages
Largely financial and dependent on the particular arrangements:
- Many are offered on leases only, and some developers have sold merely a 'licence' to live in the property, which means that when you come to sell, the full market value may not come to you, but to the developer or site owner. All you get back is whatever you put in initially. There will probably be a weekly or monthly service charge, so you should not only find out how much this is but how often it can be increased and if there are any limits to the increase.
- There may even be a clause which would allow for your removal from the home if you should ever become in need of constant medical attendance. It is therefore imperative that you take careful legal advice and fully understand the implications of the move before you make it.

The success of these schemes would suggest that any disadvantages are greatly outweighed by the advantages, and there is no doubt we shall see many more sheltered developments in future. A list of sheltered home developers is given on pages 304–14.

'Home for Life' scheme
At least one financial company, **Home for Life**, has devised a scheme under which people who want to move into sheltered housing schemes can do so at a great deal less than the market price.

Who is this scheme intended for? The scheme is available only to those who are at least 60 and no medical examination is required. It will suit you if
- you prefer not to pay the builder's price in full
- paying that price for a long lease or freehold would leave you insufficient income to live on in reasonable comfort
- you have no children to whom you would wish to leave your home on your death
- your children feel they are already adequately provided for.

It is of less interest to anyone who
- can afford the full builder's price for a long lease or freehold and still have enough to live on in comfort
- want to leave the value of their sheltered home to their children or other dependants

unless they wish to release part of their own capital for other purposes or for the immediate benefit of their children.

How does the scheme work? Once you have found a suitable sheltered property, Home for Life helps you to buy it. How much they contribute depends on your age and sex, but a man in his mid-seventies or a woman in her late seventies could expect to pay about half the normal cost of a long lease or freehold interest. The older you are the more they would be prepared to advance.

During your lifetime you make no capital repayments and pay no interest, no occupational rent and no ground rent. However, on your death, or the death of the survivor in the case of a couple, ownership of the property passes to the company and is then sold on behalf of the pension fund investors who put up the contribution initially. They are thus able to recover their capital, loss of interest and other costs, benefiting from any increase in value in the property. Your estate has no interest in the outcome.

What if circumstances change? If you are single and desire to share your home with a friend, relative or new marriage partner after making the original agreement, the Management Company will normally allow a new agreement to be signed which adds the right of lifelong occupation for the new person, who must also be over the age of 60. As this additional right may extend the expected length of the occupancy a further single payment is required for the additional occupant and quotations are available on request.

Should you decide to surrender your life interest, on doing so you will become entitled to an annuity from a major insurance company. Where a medical examination shows you are in good health for your age you may choose to take a lump-sum instead. The amount of annuity or lump sum will depend on your age and sex, and on the value of the property at the time.

If you would like to move to another sheltered property within the scheme, the surrender procedure will be modified to allow you to do so. You will have to meet the normal costs of the deal, e.g. estate agency and legal fees. In addition, if the new property costs more than the old one, then you must pay a proportion of the difference. However, if the value of the new property is lower than the old one, then you will receive some compensation.

The company has a brochure outlining the scheme and stresses that you should take legal advice before proceeding with any plans for moving into sheltered housing.

Mobile homes

Although the words 'mobile home' may provoke thoughts of 'No thanks! You won't get me living in a caravan', there are many people who do spend happy retirements in mobile homes. If cashing in on your former bricks and mortar home is one of your main reasons for moving, then it will merit serious consideration.

What are mobile homes?
Contrary to its name, there is nothing mobile about a mobile home. Its mobility lasts the length of the journey from the factory where it was built to its site. They usually have no wheels and become permanent fixtures, so they are much more like pre-fabs in concept than caravans. Referred to as 'park homes' in the trade, they are invariably installed on sites with other mobile homes.

A typical mobile home may well consist of interconnecting sections with overall dimensions of about 20 ft by 40 ft. They usually come ready for occupation complete with fitted kitchen, bathroom, central heating, carpets on the floors, curtains at the windows, and even furniture and a bed installed. (You will get a price allowance if you decide to supply your own furniture.)

Price
They are not necessarily cheap. A new mobile home could cost you as much as £30,000. You will almost certainly not get a mortgage on a mobile home. Building societies can, but don't accept them, but you can get hire purchase loans and the interest can be offset against income tax just like a traditional mortgage. Unfortunately, hire purchase interest rates are more than double mortgage interest rates at around 28%, though tax relief reduces this to around 20%. The normal period of loan is about ten years.

Sites
If you decide to live in a mobile home, you must first find a suitable site. Some of the better ones do enjoy some lovely locations. The **British Holiday and Home Parks Association** publishes a *Caravan and Sites* Annual which will list sites in the areas that interest you. Members of the Federation abide by a voluntary code of standards.

There have been some unhappy stories of alleged harassment by unscrupulous owners so it is vital that you investigate the site properly. Make sure you speak to the owner and also some of the other residents. The **Park Home Residents' Guild** will also offer guidance on sites to avoid.

Some of the larger companies reserve sites specially for older people and I have visited communities where residents are warm in praise of their new lifestyle. They can be, to all intents and purposes, much like bungalows with plenty of space, nice gardens and congenial neighbours. But they can be a trap for the unwary as well and you *must* take professional advice before committing yourself to anything. The *Mobile Homes Act 1983* gives security of tenure to mobile home dwellers but you should still seek the guidance of a solicitor to examine your contract with the site operator. The Department of the Environment booklet *Mobile Homes* is also useful and may be obtained from your town hall or **Citizen's Advice Bureau**.

Extra costs involved
- Invariably the purchase of a mobile home is made through the site operator who gets a commission from the supplier.
- If you sell your mobile home to someone else the site operator is entitled to a commission not exceeding 10% of the sale price.
- Once on your site you will have to pay a 'pitch fee' to the site operator as well as being liable for rates and electricity bills.

Cautions
- Although mobile homes are similar in many ways to traditional buildings, they tend to depreciate in value over the years rather than increase.
- Site operators are entitled to stipulate standards of maintenance and decoration of your home and surrounds. Ultimately they have the power to evict you for failure to comply (provided they obtain a court order).

Rented accommodation

There are two viewpoints on this type of accommodation. If you already live in rented accommodation you might be wondering about moving to other rented accommodation elsewhere; if you are a house owner at present you might think this is the ideal way to cash in on the value of that home.

Renting in the private sector
The main disadvantage is that rented accommodation is expensive by comparison with paying a mortgage. It may also be difficult to find the accommodation you want, particularly if you want a house, as opposed to a flat.

Council tenants
If you are a council house tenant and do not wish to take advantage of the opportunities that exist to buy your house, you may be able to move from a larger house to a smaller one, or even a flat, in your locality. There are limited opportunities for transferring a tenancy to another part of the country as this usually relies on a reciprocal swap being

arranged with someone from your destination town. By contacting your local housing department, you can find out what the opportunities are for change.

Housing Associations
Housing Associations are an alternative renting opportunity and there are many associations of various kinds scattered around the country. They fall into two main groups, one specialising in the provision of subsidised rented homes and the other providing co-ownership schemes which enable people to pool resources, usually in a flat-building enterprise. This is known as 'equity sharing'. **The Housing Corporation** is the central agency for housing associations and publishes directories, region by region, for the associations registered with it. The **National Federation of Housing Associations** can help with information about individual associations. *Housing Association Rents* and *Shared Ownership* are useful booklets on this subject, and are available from the local council offices.

New houses

If you decide to buy a new house you have an ideal opportunity to make sure that things are done to your specifications. Extra money spent now may well make the house more comfortable, easier to run and more economical in retirement.

Some suggestions
- Make sure you have plenty of power points and position them at a convenient height. They don't have to be at skirting level.
- Make sure lighting is more than adequate and include outside lights over the front and back doors.
- Do all you can to make the house energy efficient. It is far cheaper to insulate lofts, fill cavity walls and install double glazing as the building is in progress rather than have them done at a later stage.
- In the kitchen you could have an oven and grill at waist and shoulder height to eliminate too much bending. Plenty of raised cupboards and shelves are a good idea too. (All these things are sensible at 25 years old, never mind 65.)
- If you have a choice of kitchen flooring, something non-slip is an advantage.
- In the bathroom, you could have hand grips on the sides of the bath. A shower can also be a useful addition.

A list of builders specialising in building homes for retired people is given on page 302. All housing that is offered is sheltered unless otherwise specified.

USEFUL ADDRESSES

British Association of Removers
277 Gray's Inn Road
London WC1X 8SY
☏ 01-837 3088/9

British Holiday and Home Parks
Association
Chichester House
31 Park Road
Gloucester GL1 1LH
☏ 0452 26911

Home for Life plc
Concept House
193 Three Bridges Road
Crawley
Sussex RH10 1LG
☏ 0293 552751

The Housing Corporation
Maple House
149 Tottenham Court Road
London W1P 0BN
☏ 01-387 9466

National Association of
Conveyancers
2–3 Chichester Rents
Chancery Lane
London WC2A 1EJ
☏ 01-549 3636

National Federation of Housing
Associations
175 Gray's Inn Road
London WC1X 8UP
☏ 01-278 6571

Park Home Residents' Guild
6 Morn Gate Park
Dorchester
Dorset DT2 9DS
☏ 030 588491

Patients' Association
Room 3, 18 Charing Cross Road
London WC2H 0HR
☏ 01-240 0671

Housebuilders offering housing for sale, especially for the retired. Each region has a number of operators which are given by the order in which they appear. All offer sheltered housing except those marked by * (not sheltered) and † (only some sheltered). (NOTE: ‡ Higher price range.)

England

Avon
32 65 75 83 109 111 113 144

Bedfordshire
53 81 92 111 130 152

Berkshire
13 26 48 80 91 101 114 147

Buckinghamshire
51 53 79 106 120

Cambridgeshire
1 6 16 69 74 85 92 133 152

Cheshire
77 90 92 98 99 108 129

Cleveland
144 151

Cornwall
32 101 103 127

Cumbria
70

Derbyshire
19 63 144

Devon
3 32 48 68 83 92 96 99 111 113 127 130 142

Dorset
48 60 83 92 144

Co. Durham
40 151

Essex
1 5 30 33 54 58 59 72 81 89 92 94 125 152

Gloucestershire
20 53 78 92 96 113 144

Hampshire
7 10 22 29 43 45 73 81 84 92 95 106 111 113 127 130 131 137 139 143 144 145

Hereford & Worcester
36 48 64 79 83 106 111 113 133 144 146

Hertfordshire
46 74 81 92 104 112 116 132 153

North Humberside
21 105 144

Isle of Wight
76

Kent
31 38 48 49 56 67 71 81 86 91 92 93 100 101 111 116 118 126 133 134 135 144

Lancashire
8 25 39 53 61 77 90 98 107 148

Leicestershire
52 144

Lincolnshire
19 121 125

London
1 14 38 49 56 81 91 92 101

Greater Manchester
8 77 90 92 98 102 120 129 144

Merseyside
25 77 92 99 144

Middlesex
81

Midlands, West
27 36 63 92 99 127

Norfolk
16 53 144 152

Northamptonshire
48 51 63 152 153

Northumberland
151

Nottinghamshire
19 127 141

Oxfordshire
34 47 80 111 149

Shropshire
44 50 96 127 136

Somerset
12 32 43 57 65 92 101 103 117

Staffordshire
19 27 35 36 43 87 90 115

Suffolk
1 16 48 54 85 124 140 144 152

Surrey
7 41 56 82 92 93 97 109 111 118

Sussex, East
7 42 43 48 54 91 92 100 106 111 112 118 128 130 144 153

Sussex, West
15 22 55 81 84 86 91 92 93 100 106 111 118 135 138 144 153

Tyne & Wear
40 92 151

Warwickshire
83 112 116

Wiltshire
24 32 37 48 62 65 75 92 99 119 127 133 150

Worcestershire
127

Yorkshire, North
2 11 17 21 28 63 92 105 123

Yorkshire, South
21 63 120

Yorkshire, West
17 21 28 84 120 151

Scotland
4 9 19 66 144

Wales
18 23 88 92 110 111 122 127

---

1 Anglia Secure Homes plc
145a Connaught Avenue
Frinton-on-Sea
Essex CO13 9AH
☎ 02556 79111

2 Arncliffe Holdings plc
Devonshire Hall
10 Devonshire Avenue
Street Lane
Leeds LS8 1AW
☎ 0532 668481

3 Barratt Bristol Ltd
7 Hill Street
Bristol BS1 5RU
☎ 0272 214701

4 Barratt Construction Ltd
Golf Road
Ellon
Aberdeenshire
☎ 0358 20765

5 Barratt East Anglia Ltd
Oak House
25 St Peter's Street
Colchester CO1 1XG
☎ 0206 68431

6 Barratt East Midlands Ltd
Broadgate House
Humber Road
Beeston
Nottingham NG9 2EF
☎ 0602 222421

7 Barratt Guildford Ltd
Chestnut Avenue
Guildford GU2 5HG
☎ 0483 505533

8 Barratt Manchester Ltd
Worrall House
683 Chester Road
Manchester M16 0QS
☎ 061 872 6004

MOVING TO YOUR RETIREMENT HOME

9   Barratt Falkirk Ltd
    Mayfield House
    7 Maggie Woods Loan
    Falkirk
    Stirlingshire
    ☏ 0324 20011

10 Barratt Southampton Ltd
    Mitchell House
    40–60 Southampton Road
    Eastleigh SO5 5PA
    ☏ 0703 619812

11 Barratt York Ltd
    Richmond House
    Millfield Lane
    Poppleton
    York YO2 6PH
    ☏ 0904 797961

12 Bartlett Housing Services Ltd
    The Abbey
    Preston Road
    Yeovil
    ☏ 0935 24251

13 Beechcroft Developments Ltd
    1 Church Lane
    Wallingford
    Oxon OX10 0DX
    ☏ 0491 34975

14 Bellway (North London) Ltd
    Raeburn House
    Northolt Road
    South Harrow HA2 0BA
    ☏ 01-864 9726

15 Bellway (South East) Ltd
    Long Lodge
    269 Kingston Road
    Merton Park
    London SW19 3NW
    ☏ 01-543 3011

16 Bennett Homes
  * Hallmark Building
    Lakenheath
    Suffolk IP27 9ER
    ☏ 0842 860765

17   Walter G Birch (Builders) Ltd
*†   Montpellier House
     Cold Bath Road
     Harrogate HG2 0NQ
     ☏ 0423 68261

18   Bishton Holdings Ltd
  * Market Hall
     Tywyn
     Gwynedd
     ☏ 0654 710500

19   Henry Boot Homes Ltd
  * Storforth Lane
     Chesterfield
     Derby S40 2TX
     ☏ 0246 209606

20   Brampton Park Homes Ltd
     Somerset House
     Knapp Road
     Cheltenham
     ☏ 0242 576519

21   Broseley Homes
  * Yorkshire Region
     Raines House
     Wakefield
     ☏ 0924 384141

22   Bryant Homes Southern Ltd
     90–92 High Street
     Crawley RH10 1BA
     ☏ 0293 545021

23   Builth Building Services
  * Castle Road
     Builth Wells
     Powys
     ☏ 0982 552746

24   R. Butcher & Son
  * 39 George Street
     Warminster
     Wilts BA12 8PU
     ☏ 0985 213047

25 S. Byron Ltd
*† Elm Lodge
    Elbow Lane
    Formby L37 4AF
    ☏ 07048 74437

26 Caversham Bridge Homes Ltd
    The Mitford
    Three Mile Cross
    Reading RG7 1AT
    ☏ 0734 884747

27 Clarke Homes Ltd
    Guardian House
    Lichfield
    Staffs WS13 6JG
    ☏ 0543 414131

28 Claxton & Garland (Homes) Ltd
    Millbank House
    18–20 Skeldergate
    N Yorks YO1 1DH
    ☏ 0904 20021

29 Colten Developments
*† Western Road
    Lymington
    Hampshire
    ☏ 0590 76033

30 Costain Homes (Eastern) Ltd
 * 20 Nails Lane
    Bishop's Stortford
    Herts
    ☏ 0279 58264

31 Costain Homes (South Eastern)
    19–21 Ashford Road
    Maidstone ME14 5DF
    ☏ 0622 59887

32 Costain Homes (SW) Ltd
 * 4/6 The Crescent
    Taunton TA1 4EA
    ☏ 0823 52061

33 Countryside Properties plc
    Countryside House
    81–87 High Street
    Billericay CM12 9BH
    ☏ 02774 22686

34 Country Village Retirement Homes
    c/o Smiths Gore
    Eastgate House
    Eastgate Street
    Winchester
    Hants SO23 8DZ
    ☏ 0962 51203

35 Mark Coupe Ltd
 * 68 Stone Road
    Hanford
    Stoke-on-Trent
    Staffs ST4 6SP
    ☏ 0782 659023

36 Cox Homes Ltd
*† 101 Birmingham Street
    Stourbridge
    W Midlands DY8 1JR
    ☏ 0384 373770

37 Crest Homes plc
 * 39 Thames Street
    Weybridge
    Surrey KT13 8JG
    ☏ 0932 47272

38 Crewbridge Estates Ltd
    1 Kelsey Park Road
    Beckenham
    Kent BR3 2LH
    ☏ 01-658 5926

39 James Crosby & Sons Ltd
    Buckwood House
    14 Old Market Place
    Altrincham, Ches
    ☏ 061-928 9516

40 CTC (Builders) Ltd
*† 50a Durham Road
Blackhill
Consett
Co. Durham DH8 8NR
☏ 0207 504157

41 L. T. Deeprose Ltd
Midleton Industrial Estate
Guildford GU2 5YA
☏ 0483 503131

42 Delves Retirement
Homes Ltd
23 London Road
Hailsham
East Sussex BN27 3BW
☏ 0273 813142

43 Dominion Homes Ltd
1a South Street
Horsham
West Sussex RH12 1EL
☏ 0403 51961

44 D. W. Dulson Ltd
Brook Buildings
Gobowen
Shropshire
☏ 0691 650507

45 E. G. Dunford & Sons Ltd
41 Gosport Street
Lymington, Hants
☏ 0590 74277

46 Durkan Brothers Ltd
Durkan House
St Wilfrid's Road
Barnet
Herts EN4 9SN
☏ 01-441 4400

47 Builders Ede Ltd
16 Lyne Road
Kidlington OX5 1SR
☏ 08675 77555

48 The English Courtyard
‡ Association
8 Holland Street
London W8 4LT
☏ 01-937 4511

49 Epsom Estates Ltd
312–314 High Street
Sutton, Surrey
☏ 01-643 0649

50 Equamill Ltd
* Druid Works
66 Spring Gardens
Ditherington
Shrewsbury
☏ 0743 69229

51 Erostin Homes Ltd
* 130 High Street
Newport Pagnell
Bucks MK16 8EH
☏ 0908 614446

52 N. R. Fitchett & Son Ltd
Woodlands
Bradgate Hill
Groby
Leicester LE6 8FA
☏ 0530 2029/3962

53 E. Fletcher Builders
(Midlands)
Victoria Road
Fenton
Stoke-on-Trent
Staffs ST4 2LY
☏ 0782 271010

54 French Kier Homes Ltd
* 50 Epping New Road
Buckhurst Hill
Essex IG9 5TH
☏ 01-504 4444

55 Gleeson Homes Ltd
Haredon House
London Road
North Cheam
Surrey
☏ 01-644 4321

56 **Global Homes Ltd**
Global House
R/O 38–40 High Street
West Wickham
Kent BR4 0NJ
☎ 01-776 1666

57 **Goodwood Buildings Ltd**
Tanyard Lane
North Wootton
Shepton Mallett
Somerset BA4 4AE
☎ 074989 274

58 **Grandor Ltd**
Fircroft
Links Drive
Chelmsford
Essex CM2 9AW
☎ 0245 266540

59 **Grenville Wilson**
 * **Developments**
1 Shenley Hill
Radlett
Herts WD17 7AS
☎ 0621 782085

60 **Guild Estates**
Guild House
75 Christchurch Road
Ringwood
Hants BH24 1DH
☎ 04254 5586

61 **John Halstead Ltd**
 * Baron Road
Blackpool FY1 6JU
☎ 0253 41678

62 **Hannick Homes**
101 Victoria Road
Swindon SN1 3BD
☎ 0793 45351

63 **Hassall Homes**
 † 500 Charlotte Road
Sheffield S2 4ER
☎ 0742 760191

64 **P. Hassell Ltd**
Priory Court
Glasshouse Hill
Oldswinford
Stourbridge
☎ 0384 397561

65 **A. P. Hemmings Ltd**
 * Greengate House
87 Pickwick Road
Corsham
Wilts SN13 9BY
☎ 0249 714296/714346

66 **Heritage Housing Ltd**
36 Albany Street
Edinburgh
☎ 031-557 4720

67 **Hesketh Homes plc**
Barham Court
Teston
Maidstone
Kent ME18 5BZ
☎ 0622 812219

68 **Hillgrove Home Ltd**
Glendower
7 Belvedere Close
Fleet
Hants GU13 8JP
☎ 02514 28355

69 **Hillson & Twigden Ltd**
The Shrubbery
Church Street
St Neots
Huntingdon
Cambs PE19 2BU
☎ 0480 72728

70 **Holbeck Homes Ltd**
 * Holbeck Park Avenue
Barrow-in-Furness
Cumbria
☎ 0229 22646

71 **Hurstway Homes Ltd**
 * Hartley Road
Cranbrook, Kent
☎ 0580 712266

72 **Ideal Homes Anglia**
40a The Street
Capel St Mary
Ipswich IP9 2ED
☏ 0473 310494

73 **Ideal Homes Solent**
Drayton House
6 Station Road
Petersfield, Hants
☏ 0730 65118

74 **Ideal Homes Thames Ltd**
Cementation House
Denham Way
Maple Cross
Rickmansworth
Herts WD3 2SW
☏ 0923 776666

75 **Ideal Homes Western**
1 Portland Square
Bristol BS2 8RR
☏ 0272 425001

76 **Island Builders Ltd**
Rink Road
Ryde
Isle of Wight PO33 1LP
☏ 0983 63668/9

77 **Jones Retirement Homes**
Emerson House
Heyes Lane
Alderley Edge, Ches
☏ 0625 584531

78 **Jotcham & Kendall Ltd**
* No 4 The Chipping
Wotton-under-Edge
Glos GL12 7AD
☏ 0453 842391

79 **Kendrick Homes Ltd**
Tasker Street
Walsall WS1 3QW
☏ 0922 22263

80 **Kylment Ltd**
23 Russell Street
Reading
Berks RG1 7XD
☏ 0734 591773

81 **Laing Retirement Homes**
Manor Way
Borehamwood
Herts WD6 1LN
☏ 01-207 6522

82 **Laing Homes Ltd**
* 105 High Street
Crawley RH10 1DD
☏ 0293 544844

83 **Lansdown Homes Ltd**
2 Midland Bridge Road
Bath
Avon BA2 3EY
☏ 0225 28401

84 **Alfred G. Lansley
(Soton) Ltd**
174 Manor Road
North Itchen
Southampton, Hants
☏ 0703 448220

85 **Laughton Homes**
51 High Street
Brandon, Suffolk
☏ 0842 811321

86 **John Lelliott Homes Ltd**
St George's House
19–25 Bridge Street
Walton-on-Thames
Surrey KT12 1AS
☏ 0932 231515

87 **C. Littleton & Sons**
4 Brampton Gardens
Newcastle, Staffs
☏ 0782 627845

88 **Lodgeminster Ltd**
15/21 Adam Street
Cardiff
☏ 0222 499260

89 **D. L. & P. Luck Ltd**
Astra House
30 Astra Close
Hornchurch
Essex RM12 5NJ
☏ 04024 54144

90 **Alfred McAlpine Homes**
* **(NW) Ltd**
Overton House
West Street
Congleton
Ches CW12 1JY
☏ 0260 271137

91 **Alfred McAlpine Retirement Homes**
Caxton House
St John's Hill
Sevenoaks
Kent TN13 3NP
☏ 0732 458655

92 **McCarthy & Stone**
Hinton Buildings
Hinton Road
Bournemouth
Dorset BH1 2EF
☏ 0202 293031

93 **McInerney Homes Ltd**
McInerney House
The Green
Croxley Green
Rickmansworth
Herts WD3 3HN
☏ 0923 776622

94 **McLaughlin & Harvey plc**
Jeffreys Road
Brimsdown
Enfield EN3 7UB
☏ 01-805 0101

95 **Melly & Knight**
Bramblings Sway Road
Brockenhurst
Hants SO4 7RX
☏ 0509 23232

96 **Mercian Homes**
† Longden House
105 Longden Road
Shrewsbury SY3 9DZ
☏ 0743 52415

97 **R. G. Mole & Co Ltd**
Limecroft Road
Knaphill, Woking
Surrey GU21 2TH
☏ 04867 81312

98 **Mulberry Homes (NW) Ltd**
* Firdale Park
Burrows Hill
Hartford
Northwich
Ches CW8 4BE
☏ 0606 79117

99 **Nationwide Housing Trust**
New Oxford House
High Holborn
London WC1Y 6PW
☏ 01-242 8822

100 **Oakland Ltd**
62 Aldwick Road
Bognor Regis
Sussex PO21 2PE
☏ 0243 829151

101 **The Osprey**
‡ **Management Co Ltd**
John Day House
Lower Square
Old Isleworth
Middx TW7 6BN
☏ 01-568 3691

102 **Partington Homes**
* Stock Lane
Chadderton
Oldham OL9 9EZ
☏ 061-652 8424

103 **C. H. Pearce Homes Ltd**
Parklands
Stoke Gifford
Bristol BS12 6QU
☏ 0272 693951

104 **A. P. Pearson Ltd**
Vienna House
Park Avenue South
Harpenden
Herts AL5 2DZ
☏ 05827 68111

105 **Pilcher Homes**
31 Flaxley Road
Selby
N. Yorks YO8 0BW
☏ 0757 702445

106 **Prowting Holdings Ltd**
† Bury Street
Ruislip
Middx HA4 7SY
☏ 08956 33344

107 **The Rawlings Group**
St Ives House
St Ives Road
Intack
Blackburn BB1 2BX
☏ 0254 51543/62233

108 **Redrow Developments**
Redrow House
Alltami
Mold
Clwyd CH7 6HD
☏ 0244 548111

109 **Reema Construction Ltd**
39 Botley Road
North Baddesley
Southampton, Hants
☏ 0703 732151

110 **Rendell Partnership Development Ltd**
Ferrara Quay
Swansea Marina
Swansea
☏ 0792 53220

111 **Retirement Care Ltd**
Tubs Hill House
London Road
Sevenoaks
Kent TN13 1DB
☏ 0732 460664

112 **Retirement Community Homes**
Old Portsmouth Road
Guildford
Surrey GU3 1LR
☏ 0483 69201

113 **Retirement Properties of Bath**
General Wolfe's House
5 Trim Street
Bath
Avon BA1 1HB
☏ 0225 338000

114 **Rockhold Ltd**
19 Reading Road
Pangbourne
Berkshire
☏ 07357 4646

115 **Geoffrey Royston Ltd**
* 20 Market Place
Uttoxeter
Staffordshire
☏ 08893 4328

116 **Ruskin Homes**
1 Lonsdale Gardens
Tunbridge Wells
Kent TN1 1NU
☏ 0892 46655

117 **Rydon Hill Ltd**
10 Wellington Road
Taunton TA1 4EG
☏ 0823 53782

118 **Rydon Homes Ltd**
Rydon House
Lower Road
Forest Row
West Sussex
☏ 0342 824411

119 **Saitch & Carter Ltd**
Orchard Court
Arches Lane
Malmesbury
Wiltshire
☎ 06662 4800

120 **Salveson Homes**
Whelmar House
Holden Road
Leigh
Lancashire WN7 1HH
☎ 0942 608831/672488

121 **G. L. Savage Ltd**
* 493 Hucknall Road
Nottingham
☎ 0602 621395

122 **Sharpe & Ayers Ltd**
69 Lime Street
Gorseinon
Swansea
☎ 0792 892451/894214

123 **Simons of York Ltd**
271 Huntington Road
York
☎ 0904 641661

124 **William Sindall plc**
Babraham Road
Sawston
Cambridge CB2 4LJ
☎ 0223 836611

125 **Southend Estates Group plc**
Start Hill
Dunmow Road
Bishop's Stortford
Herts CM22 7TB
☎ 0279 52201-5

126 **Sovereign Homes**
68 & 69 The Strand
Walmer
Deal
Kent CT14 7DP
☎ 0304 362918

127 **Spiral Housing Management Ltd**
Rigby Hall
Rigby Lane
Bromsgrove B60 2EW
☎ 0527 36202

128 **Steele Wakefield Ltd**
15 South Street
Lancing
West Sussex
☎ 0903 752233

129 **Stirling Homes Ltd**
24 Manchester Road
Wilmslow
Ches SK9 1BG
☎ 0625 531602

130 **Stratheden Homes Ltd**
26a Avenue Road
Bournemouth
Dorset
☎ 0202 297661

131 **Swattons (Andover) Ltd**
Balksbury Way
Salisbury Road
Andover
Hants
☎ 0264 3892/65250

132 **T. & B. (St Albans) Ltd**
38 Upper Marlborough Road
St Albans AL1 3UZ
☎ 0727 67275

133 **Village Green Ltd**
‡ 3 Meadow Court
High Street
Witney
Oxon OX8 6LP
☎ 0993 76367

134 **Wards Construction Ltd**
† 2 Ash Tree Lane
Chatham
Kent ME5 7BZ
☎ 0634 55111

135 **Wates Built Homes Ltd**
    1260 London Road
    Norbury
    London SW16
    ☎ 01-764 5000

136 **Watkin Starbuck & Jones**
    Salop Road
    Oswestry
    Shrops SY11 2RJ
    ☎ 0691 655201

137 **R. J. Watts (Builders) Ltd**
  * Roman Road
    Hythe
    Southampton SO4 5QJ
    ☎ 0703 842022/861522

138 **Westbrooke**
  *‡ **Developments Ltd**
    15 Buckingham Road
    Worthing BN11 1TH
    ☎ 0903 202133

139 **Wiggins Homes**
    Park View House
    100 Wickham Road
    Fareham
    Hants PO16 7HT
    ☎ 0329 282832

140 **Wilcon Homes Ltd**
    Thomas Wilson House
    Tenter Road
    Moulton Park
    Northampton NN3 1QJ
    ☎ 0604 46121

141 **William Davis Ltd**
    Forest Field
    Forest Road
    Loughborough
    Leics LE11 3NS
    ☎ 0509 231181

142 **Francis Williams Ltd**
    1a South Street
    Exmouth
    Devon
    ☎ 0395 272041

143 **Wilson Homes Ltd**
    1 South Lane
    Clanfield
    Portsmouth PO8 0RB
    ☎ 0705 597011

144 **Wimpey Homes Holdings Ltd**
    Hammersmith Grove
    London W6 7EN
    ☎ 01-846 2000

145 **Wimpey Homes Holdings Ltd**
    High Street
    West End
    Southampton SO3 3JJ
    ☎ 0703 476711

146 **Martin Wilesmith**
  * Somers Park Avenue
    Malvern
    Worcs WR14 1SE
    ☎ 06845 3316

147 **H. Wood (Harrow) Ltd**
    11 Bridge Avenue
    Maidenhead
    Berks SL6 1RR
    ☎ 0628 30948

148 **Eric Wright Developments Ltd**
    Unit 506
    Walton Summit Centre
    Bamber Bridge
    Preston PR5 8AY
    ☎ 0772 34961

149 **Basil Wyatt & Son Ltd**
    29 Harpis Road
    Oxford
    ☎ 0865 511733

150 **Yorkclose Ltd**
    Sands Farm
    Easterton Sands
    nr Devizes
    Wilts SN10 4PY
    ☎ 038084 649

151 **Cecil M. Yuill Ltd**
Cecil House
Loyalty Road
Hartlepool
Cleveland
☎ 0429 66620

152 **Retirement Appreciation Ltd**
Cavendish House
18 Princes Street
Norwich NR3 1AE
☎ 0603 667556

153 **Coastal Counties Retirement Homes Ltd**
Ridgeland House
15 Carfax
Horsham
W Sussex RH12 1EP
☎ 0403 69131

Based on information supplied by:
New Homes Marketing Board
82 New Cavendish Street,
London W1M 8AD
☎01-580 5588

BIBLIOGRAPHY

Buying and Selling Your Home Law Society, London.
Caravans and Sites (Annual) British Holiday and Home Parks Association, Gloucester.
Housing Association Rents (Booklet No 13) Department of the Environment, London.
Mobile Homes (Booklet No 16) Department of the Environment, London.
Open Up a Brand New Home (free booklet) New Homes Marketing Board, London.
Shared Ownership (Booklet No 15) Department of the Environment, London
Which Way to Buy, Sell and Move House Consumer Association London.

Retiring abroad

BUYING A PROPERTY	317
Some pitfalls	317
Further information	318
CURRENCY REGULATIONS	318
TAXATION	319
Foreign tax liability	319
Residence and UK liability	319
Inheritance tax and domicile	321
Further information	321
STATE PENSION	321
HEALTH CARE ABROAD	322
Reciprocal health schemes	322
Insurance	322
USEFUL ADDRESSES	323
BIBLIOGRAPHY	323

The long British winters prompt many to dream of retirement to some sunny shore or paradise maybe glimpsed during an annual holiday. Yet how many step from dream to reality? Quite a number; some 400,000 people are having their State pensions paid to them in some foreign clime.

However, the dream can end in severe disillusionment. As with all preparations for retirement, your investigation and planning must be meticulous. Even if you are quite happy about severing lifelong ties and adapting to new customs in an alien environment you must first make sure that the environment you are intending to move into is what you believe it to be. One holiday, even several holidays at the same time of year, is not enough.

What is the reality?

You probably don't mind that the sun may not shine so long or so warmly in the winter – it is not likely to be worse than in Britain – but what about those favourite waterside restaurants, bars, shops and even supermarkets? Are they open when all the tourists have trudged home? Does the local transport service carry on at the same level when the population has dwindled to its indigenous components? Where are the nearest doctor and dentist?

Perhaps more than in any other field, moving abroad on retirement requires long term planning. You have to find out all the details on cost, facilities and weather as for any move, but from a distance. Take a week's holiday in the winter, or at various times during successive years, to get to know your Mecca in all its seasons. It will be no hardship if you like the place well enough to want to make it your home.

With fewer distracting tourists around you should have more opportunity to talk with others who have blazed the overseas retirement trail ahead of you. Learn from their experience and ask questions. For example, how long does it take to get a plumber or electrician to call and what delay is there between applying for a telephone to be installed and its connection. How have they found the cost of living over a period of years and, most important, how do they get on with 'the natives'? Many things which we take for granted become important in a different country.

BUYING A PROPERTY

It is astonishing how many people who would not consider buying a house in Britain without consulting a lawyer and a surveyor cheerfully part with cash as a deposit and enter into commitments to buy property they have hardly seen – even property that is not there to be seen at all.

Unfortunately, there will always be con men in every sphere of activity where a dishonest penny may be made from the gullible. Even honest business people sometimes find themselves in difficulties and it is wiser not to be embroiled in the consequences of their financial failure.

Always take legal advice before entering into any contract to buy. Of course, it is the law of the land in which you intend to live that is important, so ideally you should engage a British firm with experience of these matters. They will instruct a local lawyer to watch your interests.

Some pitfalls

Liability for debts
If you are buying an existing property there are many traps for the unwary in different countries. For instance, you might buy a lovely villa in Spain not knowing that it is encumbered with debts for which you become liable. If the previous occupant has been a bit lax, then the first communication you get may be from the local energy suppliers demanding, as they have the right to do, that you pay for the electricity he consumed. The debt is viewed as a charge on the property. Other possible debts may arise from unpaid builders or a mortgage taken out by the previous owner.

Local land development
Always check carefully the siting of the property and the surrounding land. Then pursue vigorous inquiries as to whether there is any possibility of a hotel tower block, or similar development that could transform the scene from the bedroom window from a beautiful view of the sea or mountains to a building site or developed town.

Property in new developments
Buying a property yet to be constructed as part of a wider development requires just as much caution, despite the blandishments of the developer who may tell you that he will arrange all legal matters for you. While it is perfectly true that most developers provide a comprehensive and honest service, if things do go wrong you need someone to represent *your* interests.

With new construction, it is preferable to enter an agreement to make staged payments as building work progresses. This is an incentive for the developer and builder to get on with the job and exposes less of your capital to risk.

Also be careful about development projects that incorporate communal swimming pools, tennis courts and restaurants. What happens if they do not materialise? Is there any penalty on the developer or, more important, any recompense for you? This might seem harsh on the developer, but is meant to be taken as an encouragement to deal with those who are well established and who hold proven track records. Take a look at what they have already achieved and speak to those who have bought properties from them. After all, it is probably your life's savings or the property that you intend to sell at home that is at stake.

Building to your own specifications
It is best to avoid undertaking this type of project. Having your own retirement home purpose-built for you by a local builder is the most difficult method of all. Imagine the problems that can arise with a British builder and architect then multiply them threefold to account for language problems and the anxiety of trying to observe from a distance of 1000 miles the activity, or inactivity, of the indigenous workmen.

Further information

Advice on lawyers, agents and developers may be sought from:
The **Federation of Overseas Property Developers, Agents and Consultants (FOPDAC)** who can assist by providing names of agents in various countries together with legal notes relating to those countries. Agents in their membership will almost certainly be able to recommend lawyers in the countries in which they operate.

CURRENCY REGULATIONS

Make sure you understand and conform to any requirement regarding the money with which you pay for your property. It might well be that unless you use currency that is foreign to the country where you are making the purchase you will not be able to take the cash out again if you later change your mind and sell. That, in itself, is not a difficulty because you will probably be importing sterling, but it is vital to ensure that it is properly certified according to the law so that you can, if necessary, prove the purchase was made with imported foreign currency.

TAXATION

By retiring abroad, you will not, of course, escape income tax altogether, but you can avoid the iniquity of double taxation if the country of your choice has a bilateral agreement with the UK to cover this. In that case, where you pay tax depends on how much time you spend in the country of your choice and in that of your birth.

Foreign tax liability

To take an example, if you live in Spain for 182 days in one year your income and that of your spouse, whether or not he or she has spent the same amount of time there, becomes liable to Spanish tax.

In order to cope with the complexities of foreign tax returns you will need the assistance of a tax adviser in that country. In the case of Spain, this would be an Asesor Fiscal who, like any decent British accountant, will save you his fee and much more in completing the *Declaration Ordinaria* for you.

Residence and UK tax liability

If you spend six months or more, a total of 183 days, in Britain in any one tax year you will be liable for UK tax. (The tax year is the 12 months ending on April 5.) There is no exception to this rule and it makes no difference whether the 183 days were successive or the result of an accumulation of visits. However, days of arrival and departure are not normally counted.

It is perfectly possible to be regarded as resident in two countries at the same time and it is in these cases that double taxation agreements between the countries are important. Countries with such an arrangement are shown in the table on page 320. These agreements are not uniform, however, and copies of each one may be purchased from HM Stationery Office.

If you go abroad permanently but have accommodation here that you could use then you cannot return for even the briefest visit without being regarded as resident in this country and thus liable for tax. The fact that you may not own the house or apartment here is immaterial; the governing factor is its availability to you. A house owned, or rented, by your spouse will also be regarded as available to accommodate you. On the other hand, if you own a property which you let under an agreement that precludes you from staying in it, then it is no longer available to accommodate you and would not make you liable to be regarded as resident in this country, so long as your visits did not exceed the total of 183 days in one year.

Countries with double taxation agreements with the UK

Antigua	Guernsey	Philippines
Aruba	Hungary	Poland
Australia	India	Portugal
Austria	Indonesia	Romania
Bangladesh	Ireland	St Kitts
Barbados	Isle of Man	St Lucia
Belgium	Israel	St Vincent
Belize	Italy	Sierra Leone
Botswana	Jamaica	Singapore
Brunei	Japan	Solomon Islands
Burma	Jersey	South Africa
Canada	Kenya	Soviet Union
China	Kiribati	Spain
Cyprus	Korea	Sri Lanka
Denmark	Lesotho	Sudan
Dominica	Luxembourg	Swaziland
Egypt	Malawi	Sweden
Falkland Islands	Malaysia	Switzerland
Faroe Islands	Malta	Thailand
Fiji	Mauritius	Trinidad and Tobago
Finland	Montserrat	Tunisia
France	Namibia	Tuvalu
Gambia	Netherlands	Uganda
West Germany	Netherlands Antilles	USA
Ghana	New Zealand	Yugoslavia
Greece	Norway	Zambia
Grenada	Pakistan	Zimbabwe

Establishing non-resident status

The Inland Revenue will grant you temporary non-resident status provided you can supply them with evidence of your intention to return here for periods of not more than three months per tax year (on average). This evidence could be that you have sold your home here and established one overseas, for example. Usually, this provisional status becomes permanent after you have been abroad for a period which includes a full tax year and during which you have not made visits amounting to an average of three months per year.

If you cannot produce sufficient evidence to satisfy the tax inspector, confirmation of your non-resident status may take three years. Your liability will be adjusted, according to the decision, at the end of that period.

Having established that you are no longer resident you will not be liable to pay UK tax on any income arising outside this country (part time earnings, for example). But income arising in the UK is liable to be

taxed here unless there is a double taxation agreement with your country of residence, in which case the tax will be payable in that country. These could be:
- pension, both occupational and State
- purchased annuities
- dividends
- interest on bank and building society deposits
- profits from letting property in the UK

Non-residents are not liable to tax on capital gains made here *after* their residence has ceased.

Inheritance tax and domicile

Even though you may be resident abroad, inheritance tax will be payable in the UK at this country's rates on your estate. To avoid this you have to become *domiciled* abroad not simply *resident*.

Residence is readily understood by the layman, but *domicile* is a term with specific legal implications. For tax purposes, you may be resident in more than one place, but *you can have only one domicile*. This is where you make your permanent home and where you intend to remain. To satisfy the taxman that this is abroad, it would be necessary to cut all ties with this country, dispose of all property, for example, and settle in your domicile of choice with the clear intention of staying. A long period of residence is not, by itself, sufficient evidence to establish domicile nor is it a requirement.

Before setting out to achieve this status, make sure it is what you want. Rates of inheritance tax in some countries are higher than in the UK and by becoming domiciled in your country of choice you may lose some concessions that are available to those whose presence is regarded as of less permanent nature.

You need two lawyers or at least two tax experts, one in each country, to advise you of the advantages and consequences.

Further information

Useful leaflets on this subject are available, free from the **Inland Revenue** or local tax office.

STATE PENSION

There should be no difficulty in having your pension paid to you in whichever country you choose to settle in. The DHSS is currently happily sending them off all over the world, including some to pensioners who have chosen to live in Russia for their retirement. Whether you receive the inflation proofing increases depends on whether the UK has an agreement with the country you retire to (see page 48). however, this proofing is only against UK inflation, not the inflation rate of the country in which you have chosen to reside.

HEALTH CARE ABROAD

We take health care for granted in the UK where our National Health Service provides medical care, free of charge, when needed. What is the situation in your new home? Generally, it is not the standard of care that needs to be questioned so much as the cost of it, whether it be by direct payment or through insurance. This is a subject for careful examination as the situation varies from country to country.

Reciprocal health schemes

Although reciprocal health schemes exist in some countries, you should discover the extent to which this covers you and decide on whether you need to take out additional insurance. You will certainly not be covered by the reciprocal arrangements that apply to UK residents making short term visits overseas and you should consult the DHSS on the situation relating to the country where you intend to live.

Insurance

Generally speaking, it is best to take out medical insurance with a British company for the simple reason that you are more likely to understand the terms and provisions of the policy. For instance, abroad you might take out a policy that you thought gave you complete cover only to find, too late, that it is restricted to the area in which you are residing. If you are taken ill or have an accident on a trip to another part of the country you will not be covered. Some policies cover treatment by any hospital and any doctor, while others impose restrictions. By dealing with this in your first language you will at least be able to understand the small print before you pay the premium. It is vital that you understand the exclusion clauses fully. Some are unlikely to bother you; e.g. childbirth, hang gliding, mountaineeering and deep sea diving, but age is an important factor. Some companies have a maximum age above which they will not accept the risk, others charge more for the over 65s.

In general, the sooner you join a scheme the better. The **Exeter Hospital Aid Society** will issue policies to the over-65s but there is a joining fee, a once and for all payment, in addition to annual premiums. The joining fee varies on a sliding scale that increases the older you are.

Once in the scheme, you may remain in it for life, subject to you paying the annual premiums. Another firm specialising in overseas medical and nursing care cover is **Kent Insurance and Securities Services** which provides a variety of plans for different parts of the world. The maximum cover provided depends on the premium you are prepared to pay.

USEFUL ADDRESSES

Department of Health and Social Security
Overseas Branch
Newcastle-upon-Tyne NE98 1YX
Local DHSS offices are listed under Health and Social Security in the telephone directory.

Exeter Hospital Aid Society
5–7 Palace Gate
Exeter EX1 1VE
☎ 0392 75361

Federation of Overseas Property Developers, Agents and Consultants (FOPDAC)
International House
15–19 Kingsway
London WC2B 6UU
☎ 01-891 5444

HMSO
49 High Holborn
London WC1V 6HB
☎ 01-211 5656 (general enquiries)
☎ 01-622 3316 (orders)

Inland Revenue Headquarters
Somerset House
The Strand
London WC2R 1LB
☎ 01-438 6622

Kent Insurance and Securities Services
PO Box 30
Ashford
Kent TN24 9YY
☎ 0233 38374

BIBLIOGRAPHY

Capital gains tax (CTG8) Inland Revenue, London.
Double taxation relief (IR6) Inland Revenue, London.
Residents and non-residents liability to tax in the UK (IR 20) Inland Revenue, London.
Taxation of income from real property (IR27) Inland Revenue, London.
Hoppit, D. (1986) *Overseas Property Guide* Daily Telegraph Publications, London.

Improving your home

THE BENEFITS OF INSULATION	326
Loft insulation	327
Cavity filling of walls	328
Wall cladding	329
Double glazing	330
Draught proofing	331
CONTROLLING HEATING SYSTEMS	
FUEL	332
Economy seven	332
Alternative fuels	332
Coal and wood fires	333
COMFORT AND CONVENIENCE	333
Appliances and fittings	333
Aids for the disabled	333
HOME IMPROVEMENT GRANTS	333
Improvement grants	334
Intermediate grants	334
Repairs grants	334
Special grants	334
USEFUL ADDRESSES	335
BIBLIOGRAPHY	336
REFERENCES	336

Whether you stay put or move to another house, it is worth giving consideration to the suitability of the house for your retirement. There may be things you can do to improve both its comfort and convenience.

THE BENEFITS OF INSULATION

The extent of heat loss from a typical home with no insulation at all is illustrated below. This shows the relative heat loss from:
- windows
- doors
- roof
- walls
- floors

It makes sense, therefore, from the point of view of comfort and economy to insulate your home as far as possible. There are sometimes dramatic savings to be made.

SOURCE: DEPARTMENT OF THE ENVIRONMENT

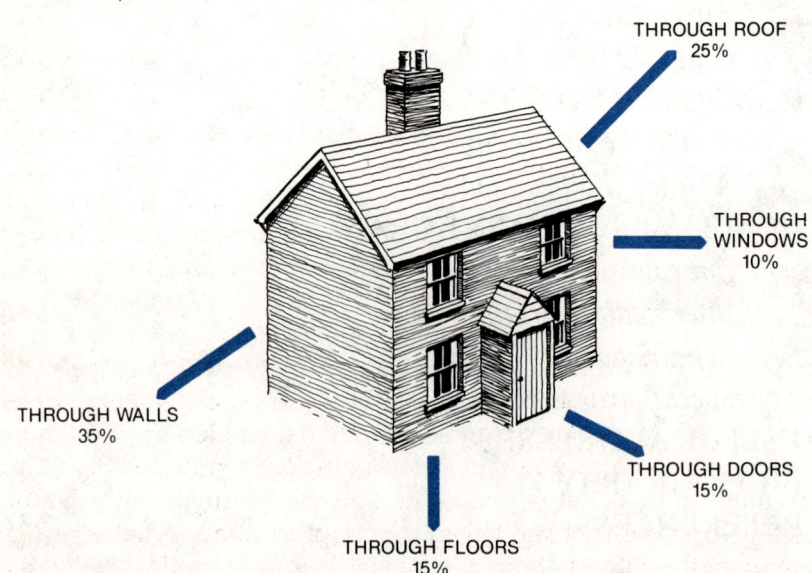

THROUGH ROOF 25%
THROUGH WINDOWS 10%
THROUGH DOORS 15%
THROUGH FLOORS 15%
THROUGH WALLS 35%

Loft insulation

This is one of the easiest, cheapest and most efficient ways of reducing heat loss from your home. Figure 2 (below) shows a common arrangement for loft insulation. The cost of loft insulation for a typical three-bed semi is likely to be between £90 and £180 with fuel savings of £60 to £190 a year, according to the Government's Energy Efficiency Office.

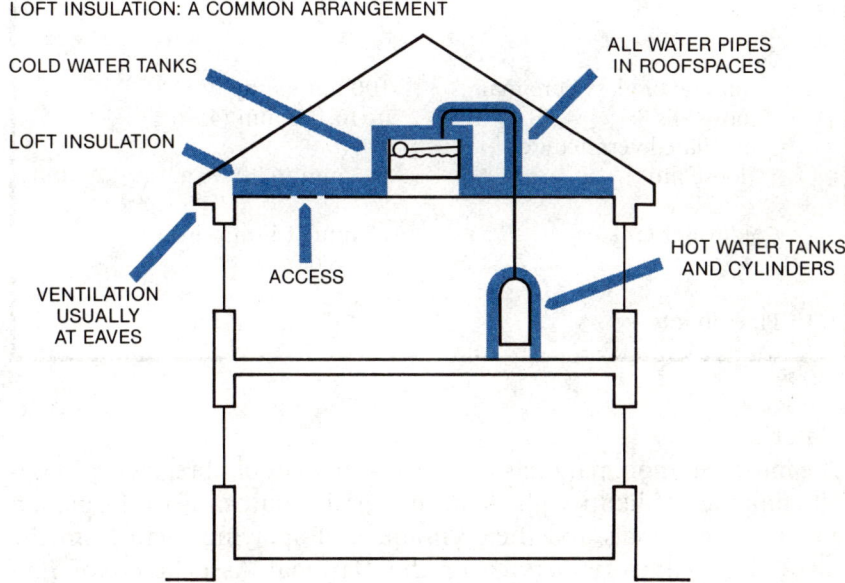

LOFT INSULATION: A COMMON ARRANGEMENT

REPRODUCED WITH THE PERMISSION OF THE CONTROLLER OF HER MAJESTY'S STATIONERY OFFICE

Getting a grant

If it has not been done previously and your house was built before 1976 then the chances are your local council will help you pay for it. Anyone is entitled to apply for a loft insulation grant which amounts to 66% of the total cost up to a maximum of £69. If you or your spouse is over retirement age the council will give you a grant of 90% of the cost up to a maximum of £95.

Conditions The grant applies whether you do it yourself or employ a contractor, but the job has to be done to meet certain minimum standards. The insulation has to be to a depth of not less than 100 mm (about 4 inches) and you will continue to get significant heat loss reductions up to a depth of 200 mm. You must insulate any pipes or water tanks in the roof and lag your hot water storage cylinder at the same time. It will cost about £10 to lag the cylinder adequately and produce savings of between £30 and £80 a year. This is the most efficient energy saver of all. The leaflet *All about Loft, Tank and Pipe Insulation*, available from your local council offices, gives some useful information on this topic.

Recommended insulation thicknesses

Hot water cylinder	80 mm (3 in) or jacket to BS 5615:1978
Loft:	
mineral or glass fibre mat	100 mm (4 in)
loose fills	up to 100 mm (4 in)
exfoliated vermiculite (loose fill)	155 mm (6 in)
Cold water tank	25 mm (1 in) for frost protection
Pipes in loft	up to 32 mm ($1\frac{1}{4}$ in)

Materials

The most common materials for the job are mats of fibreglass or loose-fill chippings of lightweight foam material. You can get information about the materials and the techniques of applying them from the **Insulation Advisory Service** or the **National Association of Loft Insulation Contractors**. Rolls of glass fibre matting can be bought that are cut to fit between the normal joists of a roof. This makes rolling out relatively straightforward. Remember *not* to lag underneath any cold water storage tanks. It is worth keeping an eye on special offers at your local building material supply company; insulation materials often seem to feature in such offers, especially in summer.

You can find out about jackets for hot water cylinders by writing to the **Insulating Jacket Manufacturers' Federation**.

Cavity filling of walls

About 35% of heat loss goes through the walls. By filling the cavities with insulation material fuel bills may be cut by up to 25% in a typical semi-detached house. The cost of the operation is likely to be between £260 and £355 with annual savings of between £75 and £225.

Cavity filling can be done during house construction using sheets of fibreglass matting or, in older properties, injected into the walls through a series of drill holes in the brickwork opposite. The material used is either a liquid foam that dries rapidly inside the wall or tiny dry glass fibres which are blown into the cavity through special nozzles. All suitable materials have to be approved by the **British Board of Agrément**, who also publish a list of approved contractors. They have a 'Hotline' you can use for checking on firms. Other contacts are listed at the end of this chapter.

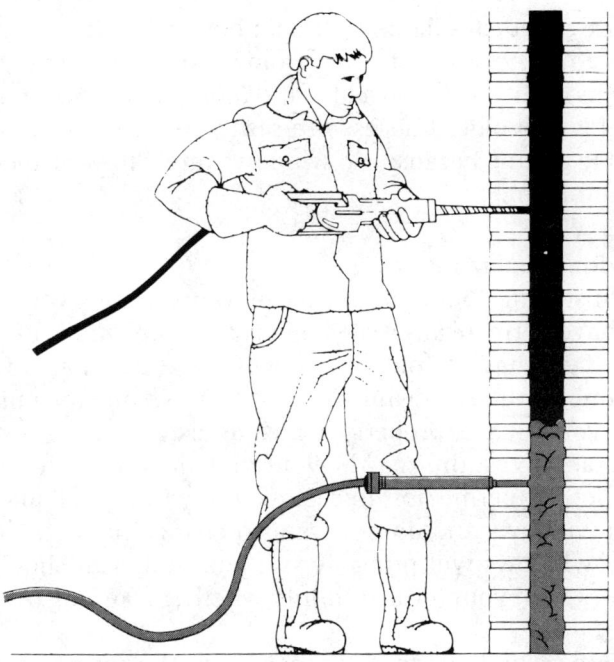

Wall cladding

If your house is of solid wall construction (as most pre-First World War houses are) then the only thing you can do is to clad your walls with insulating materials. This can be done either on the inside by fixing battens to the wall and constructing a false inner wall on them, or on the outside by bonding an insulating material to the outside wall which is then covered by a protective layer of rendering. Either way is extremely expensive. Internal cladding costs about £14 per m^2, and there would be the additional cost of redecorating, and external materials cost about £35–£45 per m^2, so the total cost would amount to about £4000 for a two-storey Victorian semi. (The heat savings are similar to cavity filling but you will wait a long time to get your money back in fuel savings on that sum.)

Double glazing

This requires careful thought because it is expensive. Approximately 10% of heat loss is through single glazed windows and double glazing can halve that. If you consider that putting in secondary double glazing units can cost £650–£1800 in an average house resulting in annual fuel savings of only £25–£70 it will, again, take a long time to recoup the outlay.

There are other considerations to double glazing, however, because it also cuts down noise interference from outside, and reduces draughts and condensation. It can also add to the resale value of your house. My own belief is that older houses with sash windows have most to gain from double glazing because old windows rarely fit well and draughts are a real problem.

Types of double glazing

If you are installing double glazing in a new house then you will almost certainly have hermetically sealed units which look much like ordinary windows. If you have an older house you have the choice of replacing the windows with sealed units or installing secondary units on the inside. If you own a property which is listed for its historical or architectural interest this may be your only option because you probably will not get permission to remove the windows. Equally, if you have sash windows and do not want to change their character then secondary windows will probably suit you best. You should, in any event, check with your local authority whether planning permission is required.

If you use secondary windows make sure the contractor is able to match the external frame and crossbars exactly. You should not be able to detect the internal frame by a casual glance from outside.

Problems with condensation

If you have double glazing, you are less likely to suffer from condensation on windows, as the inside pane of glass will be warmer, but be careful not to ignore the source of moisture which causes the problem. Usually it originates from the bathroom or kitchen, and if there is no cold glass to settle on it might well do so on the walls instead. Moisture should preferably be extracted by fans or leaving windows open rather than by opening internal doors.

Choosing your supplier

Because double glazing is costly, it will pay you to shop around and get at least two quotations. Don't be rushed into decisions by salesmen who try to pressure you into signing on the spot by offering special dis-

IMPROVING YOUR HOME 331

counts. If they want your business you will still get the discount a week later. You should, however, make sure they are members of the **Glass and Glazing Federation**, as they will abide by a code of practice. Two important aspects of this code are:

- Members will ensure that all windows comply with building regulations; that there will be sufficient ventilation and means of escape in the event of fire; and that the design and materials are suited to local conditions.
- You will almost certainly be asked to pay a deposit. If the firm goes bust in the six weeks or so it is likely to take from placing an order until installation, your deposit should be secure. Members are covered for deposits up to 25% of £6000.

Draught proofing

Draughts are uncomfortable and costly because whatever blows in must blow out taking your heat with it. There are various strips and attachments available for windows, doors and floorboards that can make life more comfortable for you (see Figure 4). Mastic around the joint between a window frame and wall can cut down many draughts, but you must be careful not to seal the entire house, especially if you are using open fires, gas or paraffin heaters.

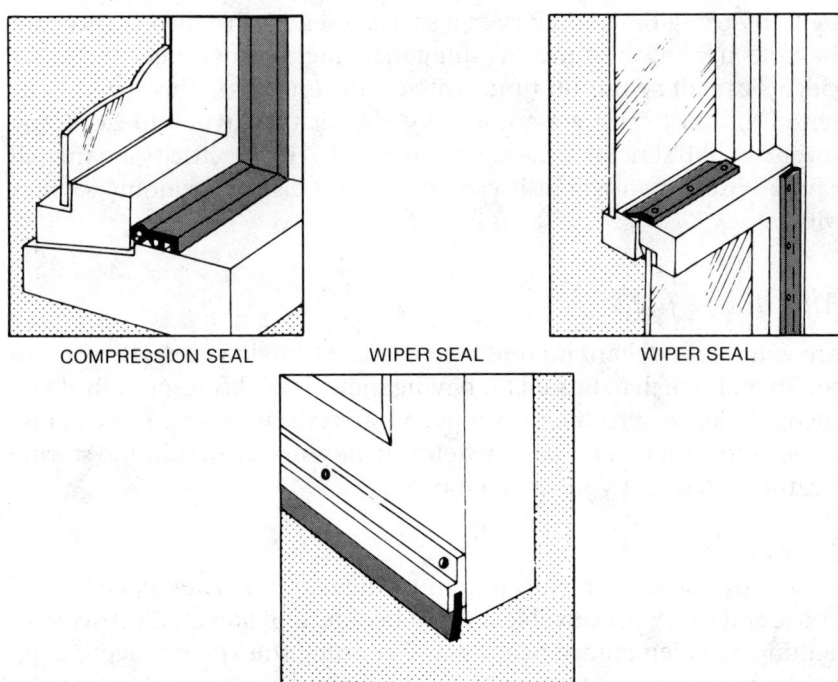

COMPRESSION SEAL   WIPER SEAL   WIPER SEAL

The cost of draught proofing a typical house is about £55 with annual savings of the order of £15–£45. Further information can be obtained from the **Draught-proofing Advisory Association**.

CONTROLLING HEATING SYSTEMS

You will not be making the most of insulating your home unless you also take the trouble to fit thermostats and time clocks on your heating appliances. There are a wide range of these, from room thermostats to mini-computers designed to get the most from a central heating boiler. Details can be obtained from the **Association of Control Manufacturers**, the **National Association of Plumbing, Heating and Mechanical Services Contractors** and the **Heating and Ventilating Contractors' Association**. The **Government's Energy Efficiency Office** publishes free leaflets which you can obtain on request.

FUEL

Economy Seven

Those using electricity as their main fuel can get cheaper rate supplies at night. By using Economy Seven a special meter is installed to measure the units used at this time. Washing machines, dishwashers and other gadgets can all be put on time switches to run during this seven hour period. If you heat a greenhouse by electricity a switch to Economy Seven would almost certainly be justified. The electricity boards all have advisers who will visit your home and discuss economy savings with you.

Alternative fuels

Are you totally reliant on one kind of fuel? If so do you really want to be? There is much to be said for having some flexibility, especially if you choose to live in a rural area supplied by overhead cables. You can lose power altogether and usually when you most need it in cold and stormy weather. No doubt you can go too far.

Example
I know of one couple who retired to the country. They have a large house and every conceivable form of heating and power. Electricity for lighting, supplementary heating and running the kitchen oven; a gas hob run from Calor tanks. Oil-fired central heating; and, because a

power cut would stop the boiler motors, they also have a stand-by generator. Just to be sure they don't get cold they also have three open fires which burn a mixture of coal and wood.

Coal and wood fires

Coal and wood fires are fine provided you don't have to rely on them. Central heating is much better for general warmth and comfort, leaving the open fires to provide a pleasant focal point and extra warmth when you want it. Wood-burning stoves have become very popular in recent years and you will usually find a local supplier who specialises in them. But whether they are special stoves or not, wood burns quickly and they need constant replenishment. Contact **The Wood and Solid Fuel Association of Retailers and Manufacturers** or the **Solid Fuel Advisory Service**.

COMFORT AND CONVENIENCE

Appliances and fittings

There are many other, often quite inexpensive ways of improving the comfort of your home. With later years in mind you may find it worthwhile to:
- relocate electric power points to a more convenient height
- install an eye level oven in the kitchen
- fit hand-grips to the bath
- improve security with locks, chains on the door, alarms, etc
- install a downstairs lavatory.

Aids for the disabled

Information on the various aids that are available for the disabled is given in the Health Section (page 225).

HOME IMPROVEMENT GRANTS

These are designed to benefit people owning or living in older property which lacks basic amenities or is in need of substantial repair work. You can apply for them whether you are a tenant, owner–occupier or landlord. They are paid by your local council with help from central government. Full details are to be found in *Home Improvement Grants – a guide for home-owners, landlords and tenants* available from town halls and Citizens' Advice Bureaux.

There are four kinds of grant:
- improvement grants
- intermediate grants
- repairs grants
- special grants

Improvement grants

These are for major improvements, and associated repairs and replacements. In priority cases – that is, houses that are in a particularly bad state of repair, lacking standard amenities, in housing action areas or need improvement for a disabled occupant – grants may be awarded for work up to £13,800 in Greater London and £10,200 elsewhere. For non-priority cases grants may be available for work up to £9000 in London and £6600 elsewhere.

Intermediate grants

These are for putting in missing standard amenities, such as an inside lavatory, bath, sink, wash basin, hot and cold water plus associated repairs and replacements. Intermediate grants are mandatory, so if you qualify for them your local council cannot refuse the grant. Grants are available for amounts up to £3005 in Greater London and £2275 elsewhere, with a repairs element of £4200 and £3000.

Repairs grants

These are for pre-1919 houses needing substantial and structural repairs up to £6600 in Greater London and £4800 elsewhere.

Special grants

These are for putting in standard amenities and means of escape from houses with multiple occupation. They are not available to tenants. Grant levels for standard amenities depend on the number of occupants, but grants are available for fire escapes up to a total value of £10,800 in Greater London and £8100 elsewhere.

These figures are merely the maximum sums for which grants can be considered. Your council can pay up to the following limits:
- priority cases   75%
- houses in general improvement areas   65%
- all other cases   50%

Higher grants may be available in cases of hardship.

USEFUL ADDRESSES

Energy Efficiency Office
Room 1312, Thames House South
Millbank
London SW1P 4QJ
☎ 01-211 6811 ext 6774

Cavity filling of walls

British Board of Agrément
PO Box 195
Bucknalls Lane
Garston, Watford
Herts WD2 7NG
☎ 0923 670844
☎ 0923 662900 ('hotline' for checking on firms)

Cavity Foam Bureau
PO Box 79
Oldbury
Warley
West Midlands B69 4PW
☎ 021-544 4949

Expanded Polystyrene Cavity Insulation Association
5 Belgrave Square
London SW1X 8PH
☎ 01-235 9483

National Cavity Insulation Association
PO Box 12
Haslemere
Surrey GU27 3AN
☎ 0428 54011

Controls

Association of Control Manufacturers
Leicester House
8 Leicester Street
London WC2H 2BN
☎ 01-437 0678

Heating and Ventilating Contractors' Association
34 Palace Court
Bayswater
London W2 4JG
☎ 01-229 2488

National Association of Plumbing, Heating and Mechanical Services Contractors
6 Gate Street
London WC2A 3HX
☎ 01-405 2678

Double glazing

Glass and Glazing Federation
44–48 Borough High Street
London SE1 1XB
☎ 01-403 7177

Draught proofing

Draught-proofing Advisory Association
PO Box 12
Haslemere
Surrey GU27 3AN
☎ 0428 54011

Loft insulation

Insulating Jacket Manufacturers' Federation
Little Burton West
Derby Street
Burton-on-Trent
Staffs DE14 1PP
☎ 0283 63815

Insulation Advisory Service
Pilkington Insulation Ltd
PO Box 10
St Helens
Merseyside WA10 3NS
☎ 0744 24022

National Association of Loft
Insulation Contractors
PO Box 12
Haslemere
Surrey GU27 3AN
☏ 0428 54011

Wood and Solid Fuel Association
of Retailers and Manufacturers
PO Box 35
Stoke-on-Trent ST4 7NU
☏ 0782 44311

Solid Fuel

Solid Fuel Advisory Service
Hobart House
Grosvenor Place
London SW1X 7AE
☏ 01-235 2020

BIBLIOGRAPHY

Cutting Home Energy Cost (1986) Department of the Environment, London.
Handy Hints to Help You at Home (1985) Department of the Environment, London.
Help with your Winter Heating (1986) Department of the Environment, London.
Home Improvement Grants – a guide for home-owners, landlords and tenants (Housing booklet No. 14) Department of the Environment, London.
How to Get Help with Insulation (1986) Department of the Environment, London.
Reader's Digest New D-I-Y Manual (1987) The Reader's Digest Association Limited, London.

References

All about Loft, Tank and Pipe Insulation (1984) Department of the Environment, London.
Make the most of your heating (1986) Energy Efficiency Office, London.

Cashing in on your home

TRADING DOWN	338
HOME INCOME PLANS	338
Advantages	339
What if I want to move?	339
Conditions	339
Mortgage loan	340
Annuity	340
Tax	340
Cautions	341
Capital protection	341
HOME REVERSION SCHEMES	341
LETTING	342
Flats	342
Letting whole houses	343
Tax	344
LODGERS	344
USEFUL ADDRESSES	344
BIBLIOGRAPHY	345

Many of us own our homes (or very nearly own them) by the time we reach retirement age and beyond. It is not unusual for people to have £25,000 to £100,000 worth of equity locked up in their bricks and mortar and yet still be hard up. As inflation eats into the value of an occupational pension, releasing that locked up cash could make an enormous difference to our lifestyles especially in the later years of retirement. There are several ways in which you may like to do this and the options available are:
- Trading down
- Taking out a home income plan
- Taking out a home reversion scheme
- Letting
- Taking in lodgers

TRADING DOWN

Some people may have the opportunity to sell a larger house and buy a smaller one, or move to an area where property prices are lower. If a move to a smaller home fits in with your retirement plan, the balance between what you get for your old house and what you pay for the new one will, after deduction of conveyancing, moving and all the other bills, be all yours (see page 291 for example). Remember that there will be no capital gains tax liability arising from the sale of your principal residence.

There may be the additional bonus that a smaller house, with fewer rooms to heat and quite possibly a lower rateable value, is going to be less expensive to run. But if you are content in your home, are firmly attached to the garden that has taken years to fashion to your liking, or need those beautifully decorated spare rooms for visiting children, grandchildren or friends, then there are other ways to improve your income later in life.

HOME INCOME PLANS

These schemes use the security of your bricks and mortar, to raise a cash lump sum as a mortgage. The lump sum is invested in an annuity and some of the monthly payments resulting from this are used to meet the interest charges on the mortgage. You do not need to pay off any of the capital you have borrowed, so what is left after paying the interest charges is yours to spend.

The capital has to be paid off at some time, of course, but only after your death and the death of your spouse in the case of married couples.

Advantages

The advantage these plans provide over other schemes is that the house remains yours. You and your spouse have the unfettered right to occupy the property for the whole of your lives. Moreover if you wish to leave it to your children, or any other beneficiary in your will, you may still do so. They then have the option to pay off the mortgage from their own resources or to sell the house to settle the debt and keep the balance.

What if I want to move?

If you want to move to another property this can normally be arranged subject to the new property being acceptable to the lender. The loan is then effectively transferred to the new home. If the move is to a property of lower value you might be required to repay part of the loan capital from the proceeds of the sale of the previous home, while if you decide to sell because you are going to live with relatives or move into a nursing home, for example, the mortage loan capital will need to be repaid out of the proceeds of the sale; you keep the balance. Your income will rise as a result because, having repaid the capital, there will be no further mortgage interest deductions to be made from the annuity payments.

These schemes are a long term fall-back which can be used in future years if capital has been spent and income eroded.

Conditions

Age qualification

The minimum is generally 69. If it were possible to enter a scheme at a lower age the benefits would be considerably reduced and not worthwhile. Where couples are concerned the combined ages must be at least 145 with the minimum age of 69 for the younger person. Marriage is not a condition. For example, a couple could be brothers, sisters or simply two people living together. When the occupants are both women, higher minimum age limits apply because women have a longer survival expectancy than men.

Property qualification

Money is raised only on a house, flat or maisonette that is freehold or that has at least 65 years of unexpired term if it is leasehold. It must be free of mortgage, in good repair and not let, or sublet. It must also have a sale value of at least £22,000.

Mortgage loan

This can be up to 80% of the property value but there is a ceiling of £30,000. This is because the tax advantage offered by MIRAS (Mortgage interest relief at source) does not apply to the excess above this limit.

Annuity

The level of annuity bought depends entirely on the capital raised by the mortgage and the age, or ages, of those entering the scheme. It is fixed for life, so over a long life you will almost surely see it devalued by inflation. Most schemes take into account the increasing value of your home in subsequent years, and allow you to take out a further mortgage at a later date with which to buy another annuity, subject to the present overall limit of £30,000.

Your income is the sum that is left after the deduction of the interest payments due on the mortgage. As the interest rate is also fixed at the outset, these payments will be unchanged. No deduction is made to repay any part of the capital element of the mortgage which remains constant until redeemed in full through the sale of the house or by other means.

Tax

Provided the mortgage is on your main residence, the interest qualifies for tax relief at source thus effectively reducing the level of interest repayment and increasing income. Loan interest is deducted net of basic rate tax relief and higher rate tax payers may claim additional relief from the Inland Revenue. Variations in tax rates do affect the final benefit but the effect is usually minimal. Annuities are regarded as partly a repayment of the capital used to buy them and partly as interest earned by the capital. No tax liability arises on the capital repayment element so only a portion of the annuity income is taxable and the tax due is deducted at source.

If there is a potential liability to inheritance tax (see page 188) it may be reduced or eliminated by the mortgage outstanding which represents a debt to be settled out of the estate before it is assessed for tax.

Cautions

Entering such schemes can affect the payment of supplementary pensions and housing benefits, such as rate rebates. There are so many factors to examine that expert advice, including that of a lawyer to look over the final agreement before you sign it, is essential. **Hinton & Wild (Home Plans) Ltd** have experience of all the schemes on offer and can advise on which is most suitable to your individual circumstances.

Capital protection

One obvious drawback for those who want to leave something to their heirs is the fact that if they die fairly soon after entering such a scheme they will have got comparatively little out of it and their property will be heavily mortgaged and consequently of less value to the beneficiaries. To offset this, some companies provide plans which protect the capital in the event of death within the first three years. Only 25% of the loan is repayable if death occurs in the first year, 50% in the second and 75% in the third. Thereafter the full loan is repayable.

Examples of benefits available from home income plans in 1987, on a house valued at £50,000 for persons aged 75 years

Company	Loan (£)	Net annual income (£) for (after basic rate income tax)		
		Single man	Single woman	Married couple (both aged 75)
Allied Dunbar Provident	30,000	2103* 2365†	1529* 1676†	1094†
Home Reversions Ltd	30,000	2147* 2414†	1592* 1737†	1197* 1215†
Abbey National	30,000	1891* 2420†	1283* 1607†	972†

*Limited capital protection provided
†Higher income without capital protection

HOME REVERSION SCHEMES

These differ from home income plans in one vital respect: you sell your house outright when you enter the scheme and although you have an absolute right to occupy it for the lifetime of yourself and your partner, you have no further interest in the equity and consequently nothing to leave from it in your will.

For higher priced properties it is generally possible to obtain a higher income from such schemes than would be achieved with a home income plan, and they may appeal to those who have no-one to leave their property to. In effect, you become the tenant at a nominal rent – a few pounds a year – with a lifelong tenancy. As there is no mortgage, there is no interest to repay and consequently an annuity bought with the cash will result in a higher net income. Under some schemes you do not have to use the money for an annuity – you can spend it or invest it, in fact, do anything you like with it.

Under such a scheme you would be obliged to keep the property in good repair and if you moved, into a nursing home for instance, it would revert immediately to the company that had bought it from you.

As the once and for all payment deprives you of all rights to benefit from the future appreciation of your house these schemes lack appeal for many.

LETTING

Careful thought to all the implications should be given before taking a decision to let part of your home. If you do not get on with your tenants you may find you are stuck with them for a considerable period, like it or not.

No doubt there are many successful ventures in this field, yielding both income and company to the landlord, but the risks are high. Even if you take a friend as a tenant can you be sure that by living in close proximity you will remain such good friends? However, if you have spare accommodation which can produce needed income and you are prepared to take a chance there are basically two ways in which this can be done.

Flats

You can convert some rooms to create a flat or bedsitters in which your tenants will lead a separate existence, providing their own meals. If you are living in the house yourself, the tenancy will be a *restricted contract* and there need be no written agreement. Whether or not the accommodation is furnished makes no difference.

Rent
The rent will be agreed between the landlord and tenant. Both, either individually or together, can apply to the rent tribunal for a reasonable rent to be registered. Once a reasonable rent has been fixed in this way

the landlord cannot charge more and must wait at least two years before having it reviewed unless there has been a change in circumstances which is likely to affect the rent such as improvement works. This applies even if the tenant leaves and is replaced by a new one. When the accommodation is unoccupied the landlord can, of course, have the registration cancelled, but the new tenant will have the same right to apply to the rent tribunal.

Rates The reasonable rent, when fixed, does not include the rates so the landlord may take a charge on account of that and may increase the charge if the rates rise.

Notice to quit Under a restricted contract a tenant does not have the security of tenure enjoyed by those occupying property in which the landlord himself does not live.
- If the letting was for a fixed period of time it automatically comes to an end at the expiry of the term and no notice to quit is required from the landlord.
- If no period was fixed and rent was paid weekly or monthly with no specified end then it is a *periodic tenancy* and the landlord must serve written notice to quit, allowing the tenant at least four weeks further occupancy.

Court orders If the tenant does not go, you cannot gain possession without a court order and the quickest you are likely to get before the county court is three weeks. The court has no option but to grant you an order but it can defer the date at which it comes into effect by up to three months. The court will make conditions on the tenant regarding payment of rent, and any arrears, during a period of postponement.

This may not sound a very long time, but if a relationship has turned sour the four weeks' notice plus three weeks to come to court and then a possible three months' postponement can add up to a very miserable and uncomfortable five months. That is why you should consider seriously all the implications. If you do have to give notice to quit, make sure it is in the form required by the law or that could lead to further delay (see the *Bibliography* on page 344).

Letting the whole house

If you are intending to go abroad for a period, or for some other reason and your home is going to be empty, you might be tempted to let the whole house rather than leave it to take care of itself. Again there are pitfalls. If you can let to a company, the risks are reduced but to give yourself the best chance of regaining possession at the end of the agreed period, do not embark on this course without a lawyer who will draw up a shorthold tenancy agreement for you. Alternatively, use a reputable agent who can keep an eye on your property during your absence.

Tax

Income received from any form of letting will be liable for income tax if you are a tax payer or if, indeed, the rents push you up to the tax liability level. Do not forget the rules that apply to the age allowance (see page 181) and the earnings rule relating to the State pension (page 47).

Capital gains tax comes into the reckoning if you convert part of your home into a self-contained flat and let it. You may not qualify for the exemption that applies when an owner sells his principal residence and could be liable for any gain made on the converted portion. So the advice of an accountant or lawyer should be sought at the outset.

LODGERS

Taking in a paying guest or guests means that your own accommodation is shared and you will be providing some service – at least one meal a day and perhaps cleaning. This is an informal arrangement and payment is entirely a matter for agreement between the parties. The owner/occupier is in a much stronger position for getting rid of an unwelcome guest or lodger fairly expeditiously, although it may still be necessary to go to the county court if a lodger refuses to quit.

USEFUL ADDRESSES

Consultants/agents specialising in home income plans

British Insurance Association
Aldermary House
Queen Street
London EC1N 1TT
☎ 01-248 4477

Bentley Wood Insurance Consultancy
The Old Cottage
Laughton
Lewes
E Sussex BN8 6BQ
☎ 032 183 616

Hinton and Wild (Home Plans) Ltd
374/378 Ewell Road
Surbiton
Surrey KT6 7BB
☎ 01-390 8166

Companies offering home income plans.
*Reversion schemes also offered.

Abbey National Building Society
Abbey House
Baker Street
London NW1 6XL
☎ 01-486 5555

Allied Dunbar Provident
9–15 Sackville Street
Piccadilly
London W1X 1DE
☎ 01-434 3211

Halifax Building Society
Trinity Road
Halifax HX1 2RG
☎ 0422 65777

*Home Reversions Ltd
30 Windsor Place
Cardiff CF1 3UR
☎ 0222 371726

Kent Reliance Building Society
Reliance House
Manor Road
Chatham
Kent ME4 6AF
☎ 0634 48944

National and Provincial Building Society
Provincial House
Bradford BD1 1NL
☎ 0274 733 444

Newcastle Building Society
Hood Street
Newcastle-upon-Tyne NE1 6JP
☎ 091-232 6676

BIBLIOGRAPHY

Letting Rooms in Your Home (Housing Booklet No. 4) Department of the Environment, London.
Letting your Home or Retirement Home (Housing Booklet No. 5) Department of the Environment, London.
Shorthold tenancies (Housing Booklet No. 8) Department of the Environment, London.
Notice to quit (Housing Booklet No. 11) Department of the Environment, London.

According to motoring connoisseurs it travels well.

In 1986, Autocar sampled the Orion and decided that it was "one of the best integrated 'hatchback-with-a-boot' designs of the current crop and one of Ford's best sellers".

In the same year, Motor savoured our car and concluded that it "...takes some beating in GL form. It offers competitive performance and economy, fine brakes, safe handling and an improved ride... the Orion is roomy with a comfortable driving position".

We're sure you'll find the Orion GL as much to your taste as these experts did. Especially if you enjoy touring around. There's lots of space inside so you and your passengers can travel in comfort. And the GL's standard sunroof slides open for cruising around those country roads or tilts so you can still use it when you're moving at speed down the motorway.

Tinted-glass will keep the dazzle from your eyes. So you can make the most of the beautiful scenery.

A four-speaker radio/stereo cassette will keep you entertained on the journey. And we've added lots of little touches like a digital clock to make life easier.

The GL comes with the clean power of the lean burn engine in a choice of 1.4 or 1.6 litre engine sizes. With t kind of performance you'll fairly eat up the miles.

If you would like a copy of the Ford Cars Brochure a details of your nearest Ford dealer, just fill in and send coupon below.

Achieved in government fuel economy tests: mpg (1/100 Orion 1.4 GL: constant 56 mph (90 kmh): 60.1 (4.7), constant 75 (120 kmh): 46.3 (6.1), simulated urban driving: 34.9 (8.1), Orion 1.6 constant 56 mph (90 kmh): 54.3 (5.2), constant 75 mph (120 kmh): (6.7), simulated urban driving: 34.0 (8.3).

The Orion GL. *Ford*

To: Ford Marketing Information, Dept. MHR, FREEPOST, PO Box 61, Greater London House, Hampstead Road, LONDON NW1 7QP

Please send me a Ford brochure and details of my nearest Ford dealer.

Name _____

Address _____

_____ Post Code _____

Current Car (Make/model/engine size) _____

Year of Purchase _____

Work and leisure

Retirement is an ideal time for you to become active and involved in your interests and hobbies. Some people leave their jobs for the last time and become as busy as when they were working. However, those who have been so wholly absorbed by work or other demands may not have had time to develop a suitable hobby or leisure interest to take up the extra 2000 to 2500 hours a year that retirement brings. The transition from work to full-time leisure will be a lot easier if you:
- start to develop interests long before you retire
- approach retirement as a challenge and an opportunity rather than as the 'end of the road'.

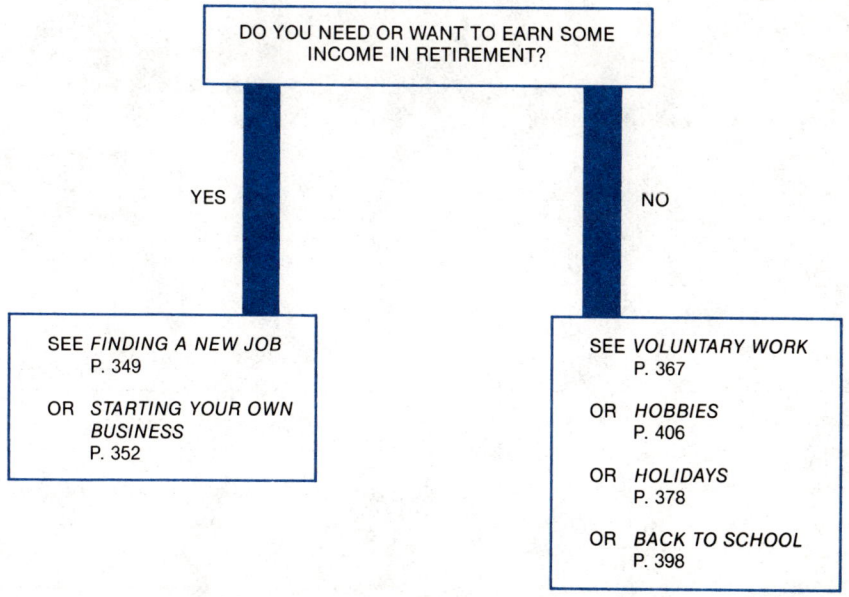

DO YOU NEED OR WANT TO EARN SOME INCOME IN RETIREMENT?

YES

SEE *FINDING A NEW JOB*
P. 349

OR *STARTING YOUR OWN BUSINESS*
P. 352

NO

SEE *VOLUNTARY WORK*
P. 367

OR *HOBBIES*
P. 406

OR *HOLIDAYS*
P. 378

OR *BACK TO SCHOOL*
P. 398

Fortunately there are so many worthwhile and stimulating ways of spending your time that retirement is a full-time job which is adaptable to different people's temperaments. There really *is* something to suit everyone.

For some it will be another full-time job, either in your own business or working for someone else. For others nothing will be more appealing than spending all day in front of the television. Whatever your choice, make sure it is planned so that you avoid doing something because you 'couldn't think of anything better'.

This section aims to help you explore some of the opportunities that are open to you, whether it is to earn money in retirement or not (or a mixture of both).

Work after retirement

FINDING A NEW JOB	350
Redundancy and early retirement	350
Professional and Executive Recruitment	350
Job-splitting scheme	351
Job-release scheme	351
Training for enterprise	352
Independent agencies	352
STARTING YOUR OWN BUSINESS	353
Weighing up the risks	353
Types of business	354
Courses, help and advice	357
Financial and legal matters	358
TURNING YOUR HOBBY INTO PROFIT	362
A few tips	363
Suggestions for businesses	363
VOLUNTARY WORK	368
Social welfare organisations	368
Animal charities	374
Sick and disabled	375
Third World	376
USEFUL ADDRESSES	377
BIBLIOGRAPHY	379

There are many reasons why people who 'retire' want to carry on working in some way. Money is often one compelling incentive, as well as the need to retain an identity. Some people may be able to stay on with their present employer, but many will be seeking a new challenge.

For those who have been made redundant in their fifties or who have taken early retirement there are a number of government schemes to help them find alternative work. Those who are beyond retirement age are likely to find it more difficult. The best approach is by self-advertisement amongst friends, relatives and acquaintances. An advertisement in the local newspaper and a visit to the Jobcentre can also be productive.

Realistically, the type of work you are likely to get will not be comparable with the one you have left. But the skills of accountancy, book-keeping, office administration and secretarial work are useful to many small employers.

Working beyond retirement will affect your pension and tax position. Further information on this can be found on pages 180–184.

FINDING A NEW JOB

Redundancy and early retirement

Sadly, many who have never thought of retirement or see it looming on the horizon only shortly before it happens, feel rushed into it prematurely. For those in their fifties, redundancy is often indistinguishable from retirement, but without the benefits of a planned and orderly withdrawal from full-time work. This chapter lists some government schemes as well as some independent agencies which can be of help to those seeking some form of work.

Professional and Executive Recruitment

A register of those seeking work in these fields is maintained by PER. Among the services is the publication of a list of vacancies and job opportunities in *Executive Post*. Detailed information is available at Jobcentres.

Job-splitting scheme

There are always two sides to every coin and, while so many are desperately seeking jobs, others are wishing that they could ease down on the amount of work they do. This, and the Job Release scheme, aim to capitalise on the latter sentiment. For some this may be the ideal way to approach retirement, not with a sudden full stop, but by a phasing down period during which you have a gradual introduction to more leisure time and the opportunity to plan how to fill it. This will minimise any shock that is normally associated with a change to a new phase of life.

The scheme does exactly what it says: it splits one full-time job into two part-time ones. (Part-time usually means between 16 and 29 hours per week, averaged over a 13-week period.) Employers are encouraged to achieve this in three ways:

- Split an existing full-time job or vacancy into two, one of which goes to an unemployed person
- Combine existing regular overtime hours into a new part-time job for an unemployed person
- Create two new part-time jobs

Employers who satisfy these conditions receive £840 towards administration and training.

Further information
Jobcentres can provide further information, but employers interested in the scheme should contact their nearest **Employment Measures Unit** (see page 377) who supply leaflets on this scheme available these centres.

Job-release scheme

For those who would like to give up work a little early, this scheme provides an allowance to help tide them over until the State pension is due. However, it applies only to those entering their last year of work because to be eligible women must be 59 and men 64. The minimum age for disabled men is 60, however.

The allowance varies between £51.95 and £74 a week depending on the employee's personal circumstances. You cannot take a unilateral decision to retire early under this scheme but must have the agreement of your employer who, in turn, must replace you with an unemployed person.

Further information
Your first approach should be to your employer, who should contact the nearest **Employment Measures Unit** (see page 377).

Training for enterprise

This scheme is aimed at those who are thinking of starting their own businesses, but the scheme also provides short courses in subjects such as finance and marketing for those already running small businesses and who wish to improve their skills.

Further information
The Manpower Services Commission offices (listed in the local telephone directories) can provide further information and leaflets on this scheme.

Independent agencies

There are a number of organisations that jobseekers in many categories of employment may find worth contacting. Some concentrate on executive and professional positions, but others are less specialised. All of those listed say they are sympathetic to the problems of the 50 plus age group.

British Legion Attendants Co Ltd
47 Glisson Road, Cambridge CB1 2HH
☎ 0223 61676
Commissionaires, car park attendants and security guards are the job specialities of this organisation. It no longer recruits exclusively from the ranks of ex-service men and women, although many of the applicants it places do have experience with the armed forces, police and fire services.

Country Cousins Employment Bureau
10a Market Square, Horsham, West Sussex RH12 1EU
☎ 0403 61960
A nationwide agency that specialises in temporary residential jobs, such as caretaking, cooking, caring for elderly people or looking after children when parents are away or ill. Jobs can last for up to one month. Applicants must be prepared to travel and have good references. Some jobs, particularly caretaking, are available for couples.

Executive Standby Ltd
Office 51, The London Wool and Fruit Exchange, Brushfield Street,
London E1 6EU
☎ 01-247 5693
Regional offices:
Northwich, Cheshire
☎ 0606 883849;
Bristol ☎ 0272 173118.
Skilled executives and professional workers are placed in jobs both in the UK and overseas. A large proportion of applicants for whom jobs are found are aged between 40 and 60.

Part-time Executive Appointment Service
Institute of Directors, 116 Pall Mall, London SW1Y 5ED
☏ 01-839 1233
This service is *not* exclusive to members of the Institute. It finds work for executives on its register who have been made redundant. Many of them will have already set up consultancy businesses from their homes and there are opportunities for them to act in a stand-in capacity. Work may be for two or three days a week, or for a month or more if a special project is involved.

Success after Sixty
40–41 Old Bond Street, London W1X 3AF
☏ 01-629 0672
Operates in London and Croydon, it finds jobs for the 50-plus age group. A wide range of employment is covered, both skilled and semi-skilled.

Temporary Executive Service
Manpower Department, Confederation of British Industry, Centre Point, New Oxford Street, London WC1A 1DU
☏ 01-379 7400
Provides companies with the right people for specialist jobs at a senior level that need doing on a temporary basis. The scheme provides companies with senior and middle management personnel to fill gaps created by sickness or to cope with sudden pressures, for example, the introduction of new technology with which the permanent executives are not familiar.

STARTING YOUR OWN BUSINESS

There has never been a time when so much encouragement and help has been given to people to go it alone. It is a logical solution to the contraction of employment opportunities, the problems of redundancy and early retirement. But before you start, ask yourself why, if you think you could now be your own boss, you didn't make the break and launch into a successful business career years ago. The answer probably comes down to risk and security.

Weighing up the risks

All business enterprise, large and small, has always involved risk for the employer or entrepreneur, the possibility of failure, or even bankruptcy. For the employee, employment most often meant security, the surety of a regular pay cheque at a constant and pre-determined level; a routine that enabled you to relax at home in the evenings and at weekends; two or three weeks' holiday every year and probably the prospect of a pension when you reached retirement age.

The risk is still there for the employer, but security for the employee, as we knew it, has gone. Only the fortunate can now say with absolute certainty how many years they will be allowed to continue working in the same employment, or look forward to a pension based on a full working life.

So, is self-employment or starting a more ambitious business a better solution for the redundant and those retired early, than seeking alternative employment? It depends entirely on your temperament. Are you and, equally important, is your wife or husband, prepared to sacrifice your social life, do without days off and holidays, and at the same time put your personal savings, perhaps even your home, at risk? Age has nothing to do with it; mental attitude, resilience, stamina and health do.

Before you commit yourself, there is ample opportunity to explore fully the implications of setting up on your own. In today's climate, advice on this subject is not in short supply but there are two main considerations:

- *The market* It is no good making things that no-one wants to buy at the price at which you could afford to sell them, nor to offer services for which there is little demand. Your first step is to discover whether there is a market for your ideas and whether it is already supplied by others against whom you would have to compete.
- *Finance* Even the smallest one-man enterprise will need money to get started and keep going while the business is being built up. If you cannot find enough from your own resources you are going to have to persuade some hard-headed bank manager to lend it to you and he will not be impressed by a proposal that is woolly, only partly thought through and sloppily presented.

Types of business

Sole trader

Being a sole trader means that you are in business on your own. You are self-employed for tax purposes and keep all your net profits, but your personal possessions are at risk if your business fails, leaving you in debt. You will not have to go through any legal formalities if you trade under your own name.

This is probably the best way in which a formerly employed person can put existing skills to use: a typing service, jobbing in the building trade, hairdressing, car repairs and a multitude of similar occupations. (See *Turning your hobby into profit*, page 360 for some suggestions.) Alternatively, you might get away from your past and open, or buy, a small shop, take up window cleaning or landscape gardening, if you have a talent for it.

The advantage of starting out as a sole trader is that normally the set-up costs are not too daunting, although you will be living on your savings, or borrowed money, until the business starts to make a reasonable profit. If you are buying an existing business, a shop for instance, you will need a lawyer and a financial expert, too, unless you are skilled in accountancy and can unravel the mysteries of the vendor's books to discover if he really is making the profit he claims.

Further information The Manpower Services Commission (MSC) runs self-employment courses under their *Training for enterprise* scheme. Ask at your local Jobcentre for the leaflet *Planning to Set Up Your Own Business* and contact the nearest MSC training division area office. All the High Street banks also produce excellent literature to put you on the right track initially and the bank manager is one of the first people to talk to. If you need a loan or an overdraft facility for your business; the sooner you take him into your confidence the better. The fact that you have got to marshall your thoughts and your plans to convince him it is a good idea, will itself be a useful exercise for you.

Partnerships

These can be between two or more people who share the work, the responsibility and the profits, often split in the same ratio as the amount of money that each has put into the business. However, there is an important legal point. If it all goes wrong, your liabilities are not apportioned in the ratio of the financial interest you have in the partnership. Irrespective of any agreement between you, the partners are 'jointly and severally' responsible for all the debts of the partnership. As with sole traders, your own assets outside the business are at risk. You will be treated as self-employed for tax purposes.

You need a solicitor to frame a partnership agreement. Informal agreements, even between good friends, are unsatisfactory because they rarely provide for all contingencies such as the introduction of new partners; the dissolution of the partnership; the restriction on individual partners in the matter of undertaking financial obligations on behalf of the partnership; and the authority to sign cheques which it may be sensible to limit both in size and frequency.

Further information The advice available to sole traders from the Manpower Services Commission and the banks is equally valuable to proposed partnerships.

Co-operatives

It takes only two people to start a co-operative. Members of co-operatives jointly own and work for the business. They share equally in decision-making and generally take the same amount in pay. Most co-operatives are limited companies (see page 354) which removes the risk to your personal assets in the event of failure. You would be treated as an employed person as far as National Insurance contributions and tax are concerned.

Further information Your local authority and Jobcentre will be able to tell you of co-ops in your area. Also available from your Jobcentre is *Co-operating for Work* which provides further information on this. Information and advice on setting up and running co-operatives are also available from the organisations found on page 376.

Franchising

This has been a fast growing area in recent years. In essence, you set up in business on your own but under licence from a company whose name you will use and, frequently, whose products you will sell. The franchise company has to be paid for the licence and will take an annual cut from the business. Banks look more favourably on franchise businesses when asked to lend money because the failure rate is much lower than that which afflicts other new business ventures.

More than 100 companies are now offering a wide range of franchises, including food stores, driving schools, drain clearing services, plumbing, photo processing, fast food restaurants, photocopying facilities and a host of others. However, considerable caution is required. The best franchisers, jealous of their good name, provide training, help in deciding the best location and premises for the business, as well as assistance with promotion and publicity. Others do not. Be wary of agreements that bind you to the exclusive sale of the franchiser's stock unless you are sure it is going to be supplied to you at a reasonable wholesale price. Enquire closely into the back-up services that are provided, and take legal advice before signing an agreement – an accountant would be well worth his fee for advice as well.

Further information The **British Franchise Association** can supply an information pack which will advise you on whether the franchiser you are proposing to deal with is on their approved or provisional register. Those on the full register have been going for some time and have satisfied the Association's code of conduct. The provisional register is for new companies which appear to satisfy requirements for full registration but have not yet undergone a sufficiently long testing period.

Limited company

In this case your personal finances are divorced from the business and your personal assets cannot be held forfeit, but a more complicated process is involved as regards the company accounts.

1. The business must be registered with the Registrar of Companies. Although you can file the memorandum and articles of association yourself it would be simpler and safer to ask your solicitor or accountant to do it for you.
2. Your books have to be audited annually by a qualified accountant and a set of figures, including the profit and loss account, have to go to the Registrar.

Cost of registration is £50 and £20 has to be paid each year when the accounts are returned. You can buy a previously registered company from a company registration agent (you can find them in the *Yellow Pages*). This is a quicker process and will cost between £110 and £180. You get a ready made package deal but if you want to change the name it could cost you a further £75 or so.

Courses, help and advice

Manpower Services Commission

In addition to the short courses provided for those starting in a small way as self-employed, the Commission runs longer courses for those whose horizons are somewhat wider. Small business courses last from 6 to 10 weeks while the new enterprise programme spans 16 weeks and is for those wishing to start a business with real growth potential. Details of the courses are obtainable from the Jobcentre or the nearest MSC Training Division area office.

The Commission also operates an enterprise allowance scheme under which you may qualify for £40 a week to supplement your income during the first year in which you are establishing your new business. You must have been unemployed for at least 13 weeks and be receiving unemployment or supplementary benefit to be eligible for this scheme.

A useful leaflet, *Guide to the Enterprise Allowance Scheme*, is available from the Jobcentre.

The Small Firms Service

This will give advice, free at the outset, on how to set up a small business. The service has offices in many centres and can be contacted by Freefone 2444.

Local authorities

Many have set up advice centres, called Local Enterprise Agencies, for the self-employed. It is worth asking if yours has one.

Council for Small Industries in Rural Areas (CoSIRA)

CoSIRA can help through all the stages from finding a workshop and working capital to production and selling, but its services are for rural areas. Advice and short training courses are provided for small retail businesses and village shopkeepers. Loans may also be made for equipment purchase or for the improvement of premises. Up to 30% of project costs with a ceiling of £75,000 may be made with repayment terms ranging from 2 to 20 years.

Further information Useful leaflets, *Action for jobs* and *Jobhunt 2. Be your own Boss* are available free from your local Jobcentre.

Financial and legal matters

Raising capital

If you need to raise money to start up your business and to see you through the early stages, you must approach the potential lenders in a business-like manner. They will need to be satisfied that you have gone into the project in depth and have taken a realistic view of its prospects. The first, and most important, person that you deceive by over optimism is yourself.

Resources First examine all of your resources. What assets can you convert into cash to reduce, as far as possible, the expensive business of borrowing money? Stocks and shares, insurance policies, premium bonds – it is worth considering them all. What are you going to put up as security for the loan you may need? Are you prepared to pledge your home, and if so what is it worth?

Cash flow forecasting How long is it before you are likely to be in a position to start reducing the loan? In order to get sensible answers to these questions you must make a cash flow forecast. Cash flow – too much of it in the wrong direction – has been the downfall of many a fledgling business. Forecasting cash flow is less difficult if you are buying an existing business, so long as there is a reasonable guarantee that you will retain existing customers. If you are starting from scratch then it needs *intelligent* guesswork. A simple example is given on page 358.

Pensions for the self-employed

The self-employed are allowed to convert 17.5% of their earnings to retirement annuities with a life assurance company. When over 50, the percentages may be higher. Tax relief can be claimed on the contributions at the highest rate of tax being paid and, if the full allowance is not taken up in any one tax year it can be claimed in the following six years (see page 79).

Insurance

If you are working from home, your insurances may need to be extended as loss or damage through burglary or fire could adversely affect your business as well as your domestic life. Also if your car is essential for your business, that too should be covered for the additional use. It might be worth it for you to consider insuring against the effects of accident or illness that compel you to be absent from your business and oblige you to take on someone to run things until you return.

Licences

Many forms of business (including food preparations and sale, sale of alcohol, and nursing homes) require a licence and you may be involved with a variety of authorities – local council, police, justices of the peace, fire service, environmental health authority. You should seek advice at your local council offices and should also try to make yourself familiar with all the regulations: they are many and varied, particularly where the sale of food and drink is concerned.

Tax and National Insurance

You must inform your local tax office if you are starting your own business. It may not be the same office that dealt with you under PAYE when you were an employee. Give the tax office the P45 form from your last employment so that the tax paid so far in the year can be taken into account.

From the outset you must keep accurate records of all business transactions plus receipts, bills and bank statements. The tax inspector, or your accountant if you employ one, will want a copy of the accounts at the end of each trading year. This is a period of 12 months which can start in any month you choose. It does not have to conform to either the calendar or tax years.

If you are conducting the business from home, a percentage of some expenses such as lighting, heating and the telephone may be set against the profits. Take professionl advice on this because if you claim this you may also lose part of the exemption from capital gains that is allowed on property that is used *only* for domestic purposes as the principal residence. An accountant will also be able to tell you which additional expenses you can claim against your tax bill.

You must also inform the local DHSS office to ensure that you are paying the correct National Insurance contributions. The addresses of both will be in your local telephone directory under Inland Revenue and Health and Social Security.

If you are taking on employees you also assume responsibility for their PAYE and National Insurance deductions and, of course, for the employer's contribution to National Insurance.

CASH FLOW FORECASTING

The table below gives an idea of how to go about assessing the likely position month by month. It enables you, and the bank manager, to judge what financial support you are going to need in the initial stages.

	1	2
Income Balance b/f	20,000*	4,090
Sales	—	1,500
Total	20,000	5,590
Expenditure		
Setting up costs, professional fees, etc.	2,200	500
Rent and rates	1,400	220
Equipment, etc.	2,500	100
Raw materials	5,000	1,000
Leasing payments	1,500	400
Own wages	600	600
Employees' wages, etc.	1,600	1,600
Advertising	1,000	1,000
Heating and lighting	—	750
Telephone	—	180
Loan interest	—	—
Post and sundries	110	110
Total	15,910	6,460
Balance c/f	4,090	(−870)

VAT

You must register for VAT with the Customs and Excise Office if your taxable turnover exceeds a certain level (£20,500 in 1986/87). You will be charged VAT by your suppliers and this is known as *input tax*. In turn, you should charge VAT to your customers, *output tax*. At the end of the year, input is deducted from output and you pay the difference to the Customs and Excise office. (The local Customs and Excise Office will be in the telephone directory.) Some items and transactions are zero rated, or exempt altogether, but most are liable to the tax at the rate of 15%.

Even though it is estimated that sales will double by the end of the first six months the business will still be operating at a loss. Projected further, there will come the break-even point after which the business may be expected to operate at a profit and begin to pay off its accumulated debts.

Cash flow (£) by months

3	4	5	6
(−870)	(−3,850)	(−6,030)	(−8,640)
1,500	2,000	2,500	3,000
630	(−1,850)	(−3,530)	(−5,640)
200	—	—	—
220	220	220	220
100	—	—	—
1,000	1,000	1,000	1,000
400	400	400	400
600	600	600	600
1,600	1,600	1,600	1,600
250	250	250	250
—	—	750	—
—	—	180	—
—	—	—	1,000
110	110	110	110
4,480	4,180	5,110	5,180
(−3,850)	(−6,030)	(−8,640)	(−10,820)

Even if your taxable turnover is insufficient to require registration, it may pay you to register on a voluntary basis. For anyone going it alone for the first time it is best to employ an accountant at the outset. You will have enough to do, concentrating on getting the business off the ground, without having to wade through the reams of regulations that now apply to you.

The sole trader may, in time, decide to deal with the tax affairs without help, but it is more likely that he, or she, will discover that if the business is successful an accountant is well worth the fee.

Health and Safety Regulations
You must also be aware of the health and safety regulations which apply not only to employers and employees, but also have a bearing on the use of your home as business premises and the effect it may have on neighbours. For further information contact **The Health and Safety Executive**. A free leaflet, *Don't Wait Until the Inspector Calls*, is available on request. The planning system and guidance on working from home is explained in a booklet *Planning Permission for Small Businesses*. You can also obtain this from your local authority.

TURNING YOUR HOBBY INTO PROFIT

Too many people overlook the possibility of turning their hobbies to modest profit. What better than to improve your financial situation with an activity that you already enjoy doing for nothing? Your object may not be to start up a business. Often, people who 'make a little money' from their hobby are not doing so at all. Their sales merely cover their expenses for raw material. In such cases, although the hobby may pay for itself, they are not making a profit. But sometimes what starts as a hobby can grow, alarmingly, into a business.

Once you start to make a real profit and are really turning your hobby into a business you should keep books and disclose the income to the Inland Revenue. You will also have to think about the *age allowance* and *earnings rule* (page 181). If you are in doubt, go to the local tax office who will advise you, not only of your liabilities but also of the items that you may offset. Of course, if the business grows, you may need the services of an accountant.

Example
One successful business began with a lady who, in one year, had a glut of garden produce. She made large quantities of chutney which she persuaded a local shop and a large store to buy from her. The chutney must have been very good because the orders flowed in. Soon the car was evicted from the garage which became a store room for the hundreds of empty jars she had to buy to meet the demand.

In next to no time the whole family was involved, including her husband who kept the books, dealt with the licensing requirements and general administration. The children made deliveries and helped with production, but all had their own careers and it got to the stage where staff would have to be employed which would have severely affected the overheads and profitability of the enterprise. It would also have meant taking up too much precious leisure time and the lady concluded that it had gone far beyond her intentions and the business was wound up.

A few tips

Costing
When costing your work, take into account the raw materials and overheads such as electricity, telephone and delivery. If you are merely selling to friends with the idea of covering your costs, stop there. Otherwise, add on your hourly rate for the job. If you intend selling on a market stall, at a car boot sale or to a shop, other costs must be added, e.g. rental for the stall or space, and a shop will want a commission.

Taking orders
Never take orders that you cannot fulfil or you will soon get a reputation for unreliability.

Working at home
Try to use a spare room as an office or workshop, because cluttering up the house with your little business can cause domestic dissension. If you convert a room, garden shed or garage into a workshop you may need permission from the local authority. Also check your house and car insurances which may not cover you for business use.

Advertising
You can advertise your products or services in shop windows, the local newspaper or even have leaflets printed to push through doors. If you are taking samples of work to shops or galleries it is courteous to make an appointment first.

Suggestions for businesses

Art
If you are a competent artist, there may be outlets for your work at art and craft shows, fêtes, market stalls and car boot sales. Try the local art shop or gallery, and ask local restaurants and pubs if they will allow you space on their walls. They will expect commission on any sales you make through them.

It is always better to try to sell pictures ready framed, but as framing is expensive you might consider taking a course in it yourself. In either case you should cover the cost in the sale price of the picture.

If you like to paint in a decorative manner, then you can paint stones and pebbles using a quick dry undercoat, acrylic paints and finishing with varnish to make interesting doorstops and paperweights. Junk furniture can be brightened up with hand-painted or stencilled decoration – fun for a nursery.

Antiques
If dealing with genuine antiques you must have a good knowledge of your subject, especially if you intend to carry out restoration and repair work. However, you might find junkroom or saleroom buys quite lucrative if you clean them up to re-sell on a market stall or local craft fair. Further information on this can be found in *The Complete Book of Furniture Restoration* by Tristan Salazar and *Secondhand Bargains made new* by David Fisher.

Bee-keeping
Selling surplus honey and beeswax could help to cover the cost of keeping hives and provide you with 'free' honey. If you make mead for sale, you will need a licence from Customs and Excise (see page 434).

Baby sitting
As clients would need to know you very well, offer your services to friends and neighbours. If they do not keep you busy word will soon spread. It is best to have your own transport, but most parents will be prepared to collect you and return you home.

Carpentry/plumbing
It is often difficult to find a carpenter or plumber, or indeed any such tradesman, willing to undertake small jobs. Those who possess such skills should find little difficulty in making profitable use of them once they have spread the word.

Chair caning/basket making
Caned furniture is becoming popular again. Not long ago you could pick up a small Victorian dining chair that needed caning for £3.50–£5. Soon they were in the £7.50–10 region, and once they are restored they are worth considerably more, of course. You can learn the craft of caning from *The Caner's Handbook* by Bruce Miller and Jim Widess or *Baskets and Basketry* by Dorothy Wright. It requires patience and a degree of dexterity. Instruction in caning and basket making is available (see page 423).

Cooking and catering
Buffets, dinner parties, wedding and other celebrations provide scope for small caterers who are able to prepare the food in their own homes and transport it to the customer. You need a modern, well-equipped kitchen with plenty of space. These small enterprises are often embarked on by friends who live close to one another. As well as cooking, they frequently supply a waitress or waiter service.

There are strict hygiene regulations covering the sale of food to the public. This is a complex subject and the best policy is to tell your local authority Environmental Health Officer what you intend to do so that he can advise you. Guidance notes and leaflets will also be sent. (You will find the number in the telephone directory under *Local Information*.) If you sell food from a Women's Institute stall (see page 448) the WI takes care of the legal side for you.

Crafts
From bobbin lace to quilting, there is demand for good quality craftsmanship and you will find appreciative customers at craft shows and local fêtes. You may find outlets in local shops which are willing to take a few items on a sale or return basis. A good photograph of your work displayed in a shop window can also bring in orders.

Decorating
Many building firms are interested only in the bigger jobs so there is scope for the individual who can competently tackle home decorating and minor repair work. You could advertise but generally your business builds up by personal recommendation.

Dressmaking
A brisk trade can be built up in this area, particularly in bridal wear or children's clothes. You could also offer an alteration and repair service.

Driving instruction
To qualify as a driving instructor you must pass both written and practical examinations set by the Ministry of Transport, Department of the Environment. Schools approved by the Ministry such as the Driving Instructors' Association, will provide tuition and a course which generally takes about six months for you to obtain your qualification. The cost will be in the region of £700; it costs a further sum (currently £100) to be placed on the Department of the Environment *Register of Approved Drivers*. It has to be renewed every four years. Further information may be obtained from the **Driving Instructors' Association** and the **British School of Motoring**.

Floristry
Local florists sometimes require freelance assistance when there are big orders to be satisfied. If you are adept at making bouquets and floral arrangements make your availability known to the local shops. You may also try growing and drying flowers to sell to the florist in bunches or in arrangements. *Complete Flower Arranging* by Sheila MacQueen is a useful book on this area.

Other ideas for flowers include pressing flowers to make cards and pictures; making flowers from fabric, shells and seeds, feathers, paper and bread dough. A number of ideas can be seen in *How to make beautiful flowers* by Valerie Jackson.

Gardening
There is always a demand for jobbing gardeners. An advertisement in the local newspaper or printed leaflets put through doors should bring an ample number of clients.

Knitting
The hourly rate for hand knitting is pretty low because of the length of time it takes to make most garments. Knitting machines are much quicker and can produce intricate designs which are often sought after by local shops. If this is of interest the book, *Machine Knitting to suit your mood* by Johanna Davis may give you some ideas. Contact your local boutiques to see if they are interested in your products.

Lace-making
This is a highly valued craft working with linen. It requires skill and patience but boutiques and craft shops may be interested in taking orders. *Modern Lace Designs* by Veronica Sorenson is a good source for ideas.

Languages
If you have a sound knowledge of foreign languages then you may teach students or business people. Advertise in the local newspaper for private students or approach your local education authority which might be looking for competent linguists to teach adult classes. You could also offer a translation service to local businesses.

Mail order
You will not earn a fortune as an agent with a mail order catalogue, generally you can expect about 10% commission on the goods you sell. You have to find your own customers and, if you have a salesperson's temperament, it is quite a sociable part-time occupation. Most of the women's magazines carry advertising from mail order companies looking for agents.

Needlework
Initials embroidered on plain sheets or dresses and the like, add a touch of style and you may be able to take orders to personalise household linen and garments. The more artistic forms of needlework, such as samplers, wall hangings and appliqué pictures take considerable skill

and much time, and command higher prices. Items such as christening gowns can become family heirlooms. So you could offer a service, not only making them, but in embroidering the names of the babies and their dates of birth around the hems.

Organic gardening
There is currently a demand for food grown organically, which means without use of chemicals. The produce may be sold at the house gate, on WI stalls or perhaps at your local health food shops.

Photography
You need a good camera and considerable expertise before daring to offer yourself at weddings, christenings and other such functions. A studio is not vital; you can even do portraits in people's homes if you have the correct lighting equipment, but you do need a dark room for developing (see page 410).

Picture framing
After a relatively small investment in mitre equipment and materials, and a lot of practice you could set up business by advertising locally. You can also offer your services to a local photographic or art shop, who may take work in for you and share the proceeds.

Quilting/patchwork
You need a good eye for colour and design and a deal of patience, but quilts fetch high prices. Cot blankets take less time and are quite popular (see page 425). Your local boutique or baby shop might provide an outlet for you.

Soft furnishing/upholstery
Curtains, lampshades and loose covers are just some of the things that sell. Many women positively detest sewing and are only too pleased to find, and pay, others who enjoy it. Again, it is a matter of getting the word round about your expertise. If you are really good, offer your services to local interior decorators.

Teaching
Your valuable skills as a tradesman or professional may well mean that you can work as a part-time teacher taking evening or day classes at the local Institute of Adult Education. Contact your local education authority about the opportunities available.

Writing
The market is enormous but the chances of success extremely limited. Always study the market to which you intend to offer your work and

submit it in a professional manner. Type your work with double spacing, whether it be aimed at the editor of the local free sheet or a major publishing house or agent. *The Writers Handbook* edited by Barry Turner, gives more specific advice about this.

VOLUNTARY WORK

Despite all the services provided by the Welfare State to protect those in need there is increasing pressure on voluntary services to take over where the State organisation finds difficulty in coping. If the idea of voluntary work appeals to you, you must first think long and hard about the *kind* of voluntary work for which you would be best suited. Many jobs such as those caring for the frail and elderly, or the mentally and physically handicapped require a great commitment to others and if you let them down, you will do more harm than good. If you do not have the temperament or patience to deal directly with the elderly, the handicapped or with children, maybe your skills could be put to better use in fund raising activities, or clerical and administrative work.

The animal charities always need help with fund raising, or perhaps you might like to become involved in a pet fostering scheme. Conservation groups also use volunteers on all sorts of countryside projects (see page 415).

Committee work with local clubs or societies can mean either occasional work or a much heavier commitment especially if you take office as chairman, treasurer or secretary.

If you are politically minded, local constituency parties will welcome your services, especially at election times.

Further information
Your local library, the church and Citizens' Advice Bureau will know of local needs and the voluntary associations which serve them. There are also hundreds of national, independent charities, many of them listed in *Voluntary Organisations* and *The Family Welfare Association Charities Digest* which contains over 1200 charities with details of their objectives and work. Here are a few which might appeal to you.

Social welfare organisations

General

Citizens Advice Bureaux
See the telephone directory for your local office. The CAB can provide information on voluntary organisations and local needs. It also uses voluntary workers to help with interviewing and counselling. Training is given for this.

The National Council for Voluntary Organisations
26 Bedford Square, London WC1B 3HV
☎ 01-636 4066
This is the main umbrella for the voluntary sector in England. It publishes leaflets and books and can give advice on a wide range of matters of concern to voluntary organisations.

Pre-Retirement Association
19 Undine Street, Tooting, London SW17 8PP
☎ 01-767 3225
This association encourages the provision of retirement planning courses up and down the country. It is always in need of helpers and speakers for its programmes.

REACH (Retired Executive Action Clearing House)
89 Southwark Street, London SE1 0HD
☎ 01-928 0452
The Retired Executive Action Clearing House recruits and places retired executives with business skills in voluntary organisations with charitable aims. The jobs are unpaid, but expenses are reimbursed. REACH is a charity and no fees are charged to individuals or organisations.

Children

Dr Barnardo's
Barkingside, Essex IG6 1QG
☎ 01-550 8822
Dr Barnardo's is a charity that always needs help with fund raising, charity shops and flag days.

The Church of England Children's Society
Edward Rudolf House, Margery Street, London WC1X 0JC
☎ 01-837 4299
This organisation cares for and supports children, young people and families in need, whether the problem is material, physical, mental, emotional or spiritual. The society needs volunteers to assist with fund raising. If you are interested in helping out contact the head office and you will be put in touch with the honorary secretary of a group, which is usually connected with your local church.

Girl Guides Association
17 Buckingham Palace Road, London SW1V 0PT
☎ 01-828 1488

Scout Association
Baden Powell House, Queensgate, London SW7 5JS
☎ 01-584 7030
Both associations welcome help in running local units/troops, organising local events and helping with badge testing work.

National Association for the Welfare of Children in Hospital
Argyle House, Euston Road, London NW1 2SO
☏ 01-833 2041

NAWCH is a national organisation that gives advice and practical help to parents with children in hospital. There are 70 branches. Voluntary work varies according to the region and could, for example, be visiting children in hospital or in their homes (so that mothers can have some free time), helping with transport or fund raising. The national office will put you in touch with a local branch.

National Children's Home
85 Highbury Park, London N5 1UD
☏ 01-226 2033

The NCH runs residential children's homes, day care centres and a telephone careline. They need volunteers for fundraising, social work projects, counselling and the careline service. Training is given if necessary. The Head Office will put you in touch with a regional branch.

National Society for the Prevention of Cruelty to Children
67 Saffron Hill, London EC1N 8RS
☏ 01-242 1626

Needs volunteers for fund-raising. Head office will put you in touch with a local group.

Community

New Horizons
c/o Choice Publications, 12 Bedford Row, London WC1R 4DU
☏ 01-404 4320

This is a recently established charity which aims to encourage the retired to join together and use their skills and expertise to benefit their local communities. The charity will provide grants of between £500 and £5000 to existing organisations, or newly formed groups of individuals, to help them start up and operate worthwhile projects. The groups have to devise the projects and convince the charity they will fill a need. Other qualifications for a grant are:
- there must be at least 10 people in the group, more than half of them aged 60 or over
- their project must involve as many retired people as possible and have a real prospect of becoming financially self-supporting.

Examples of successful projects are a home repair service for the elderly; hairdressing for the housebound; memorial site and park beautification.

Counselling

National Association for the Care and Resettlement of Offenders
169 Clapham Road, London SW9 0PU
☏ 01-582 6500

Voluntary help is needed for educational projects and in running leisure activities for young people. Training is given to volunteers. Schemes are centred around London, the Midlands, North Tyne and Knowsley.

National Association of Victims Support Schemes
17a Electric Lane, London SW9 8LA
☎ 01-737 2019
Volunteers help victims of crime with sympathy and advice. Training is given. Write to the association for details of the 300 training schemes which are run in various parts of the country.

National Marriage Guidance Council
Herbert Gray College, Little Church Street, Rugby CV21 3AP
☎ 0788 73241
The council will train volunteers as counsellors, but it takes three years to qualify and there is a rigorous selection process. Volunteers are also needed for teaching in schools and youth clubs. Again, training is given. There are 160 centres throughout the country and the head office will put you in touch with the one nearest to you. The main criterion for volunteers is that they are free from personal stress.

Catholic Marriage Advisory Council
Clitherow House, 15 Lansdowne Road, London W11 3AJ
☎ 01-727 0141
The Council provides a service for anyone, not necessarily catholics, who needs help and advice on preparing for marriage, personal relationships and family planning. They only train people to be counsellors if they are *under* 50 years, but use volunteers with office skills to help in regional centres.

The Samaritans
17 Uxbridge Road, Slough SL1 1SN
☎ 0753 32713
Telephones are manned every day and night of the year by volunteers who listen and talk, to anyone in distress. Volunteers are given training and blind volunteers are welcome. Write to the director of your local branch, which will be in the telephone directory.

The Society of Voluntary Associates
1–4 Brixton Hill Place, London SW2 1HJ
☎ 01-671 7833
Trained volunteers work with offenders, ex-offenders and their families in a supportive role. Volunteers work with professionals in association with the probation service. Some of the work may include prison visiting.

Education

Adult Literacy and Basic Skills Unit
Kingsbourne House, 229–231 High Holborn, London WC1V 7DA
☎ 01-405 4017
Could you teach someone to read and write? Help with basic maths and numeracy? A surprising number of adults have problems with reading and writing. Even those who can read a little have difficulty with official letters, timetables and the like. Many of the teachers working with ALBSU are volunteers who, after initial training, teach individuals or assist in a group.

The elderly

The Abbeyfield Society
186–192 Darkes Lane, Potters Bar, Herts EN6 1AB
☏ 0707 44845
This is a federation of voluntary local societies, each with charitable status, which have set up and managed family-sized houses in each of which seven to nine elderly people have their own bed-sitting rooms. A resident housekeeper prepares meals which are taken communally. There is need for volunteers to give practical help such as shopping, gardening, taking residents for car rides, decorating and setting up new schemes.

Age Concern
Bernard Sunley House, 60 Pitcairn Road, Mitcham, Surrey CR4 3LL
☏ 01-640 5431

Age Concern Northern Ireland
128 Victoria Street, Belfast BT2 7BG
☏ 0232 245729

Age Concern Scotland
33 Castle Street, Edinburgh EH2 3DN
☏ 031-225 5000

Age Concern Wales
1 Park Grove, Cardiff CF1 3BJ
☏ 0222 371566/371821
Age Concern needs an army of volunteers to help with their wide range of services to the elderly which include information, good neighbour schemes, organised holidays, home decorating, gardening, visiting the lonely and housebound, operating meals-on-wheels, transport to hospitals, social clubs and shopping trips. They are also starting a pets fostering scheme to help the elderly who have to go into hospital.

The Beth Johnson Foundation
Parkfield House, 64 Princes Road, Hartshill, Stoke-on-Trent ST4 7JL
☏ 0782 44036
Volunteers take part in, or initiate, projects that will benefit the over-60s in their communities. The foundation will help with initial finance but the aim is for the projects to become self-supporting. Volunteers are offered travelling expenses and a mileage rate is available to car owners who undertake transport work. Cooking, teaching, counselling, home visiting, helping with a telephone 'care line' and public speaking all come within the scope of the foundation which operates in the north Staffordshire area.

Contact
15 Henrietta Street, Covent Garden, London WC2E 8QH
☏ 01-240 0630
If you are willing to invite a group of elderly people to your home for tea on one Sunday a year, *Contact* would be pleased to hear from you. All you need is a

kind heart, a large teapot and a downstairs lavatory. Groups vary in size and can number up to 12 elderly people. Volunteer drivers collect them and bring them to your home between 3 and 4 p.m. leaving around 5.30 p.m. You will need seating for your guests. If there is no group in your area, *Contact* will be pleased to help you start one.

Help the Aged
St James's Walk, London EC1R 0BE
☎ 01-253 0253
Dedicated to improving the quality of life of the elderly, *Help the Aged* funds and supports mini-buses, day centres, day hospitals and hospices, domestic emergency alarms, research, development and education. There is a network of sheltered housing schemes and registered residential care homes. Older people who live alone, who are bereaved and have no nearby relatives suffer loneliness and depression. Home visits and day centres help them to feel part of the community again. At the day centres they can have their hair done, their feet looked after, take up keep fit classes or start a new hobby. Volunteers are needed to help in most of these areas.

Jewish Welfare Board
212 Golders Green Road, London NW11 9DW
☎ 01-458 3282
This body provides services such as meals-on-wheels and day centres for elderly Jews. Volunteers also help with office work, publicity and appeals. The office in Golders Green will put you in touch with other related autonomous organisations.

First Aid

Casualties Union
1 Grosvenor Crescent, London SW1X 7EE
☎ 01-235 5366
Volunteers take part as casualties in specially staged accidents organised by the local authorities, the emergency services, by hospitals for nurse training and other organisations concerned with first aid. You need a strong stomach because theatrical make-up is used to simulate wounds and it gives volunteers an opportunity to exercise their histrionic skills in the roles of shocked or pain afflicted victims.

St John Ambulance Brigade
1 Grosvenor Crescent, London SW1X 7EF
☎ 01-235 5231
A well-known first aid organisation, the brigade celebrates its centenary in 1987. Volunteers are given training in first aid and there is a yearly test to ensure standards are maintained. Help is given in hospitals and with home visiting; transport and escort is another aspect of the service; and advice and assistance are given to those who care for the elderly and handicapped. Work varies from county to county according to the needs. Untrained helpers are always welcome to assist with fund raising.

Medical research

British Heart Foundation
102 Gloucester Place, London W1H 4DH
☎ 01-935 0185
Volunteers needed for fund raising, the Head Office will put you in touch with a regional office. Activities vary according to the local group.

Cancer Research Campaign
2 Carlton House Terrace, London SW1Y 5AR
☎ 01-930 8972

Imperial Cancer Research Fund
PO Box 123, 44 Lincoln's Inn Field, London WC2A 3PX
☎ 01-242 0200
Both need volunteers for fund raising through coffee mornings, jumble sales, charity shops and so on. The Head Office will put you in touch with a regional office if you write to the Appeals Department. The chain of charity shops is increasing and more help is always needed. There are 'Groups of friends' which are autonomous bodies of volunteers who also help with various fund-raising activities.

Animal charities (see also *Hobbies*, page 406)

British Union for the Abolition of Vivisection
16a Crane Court, London N7 8LB
☎ 01-700 4888
The BUAV is a radical campaigning organisation committed to the total abolition of vivisection. Volunteers are needed by local groups and to help in the London office but they should be vegetarian or vegan. Membership is £4 a year which includes copies of their newspaper, *Liberator*, published 6 times a year.

Crusade against all Cruelty to Animals
Avenue Lodge, Bounds Green, London N22 4EU
☎ 01-889 1595
This is an educational organisation and one of the first to campaign against the slaughter of whales. It occasionally needs volunteers to help with office work. Membership is £2 a year which includes two magazines.

Royal Society for the Prevention of Cruelty to Animals
Causeway, Horsham, Sussex RH12 1HG
☎ 0403 64181

Zoo Check
Cherry Tree Cottage, Coldharbour, nr Dorking RH5 6HA
Actress Virginia McKenna and her husband, Bill Travers, set up Zoo Check, a trust that aims to seek out and prevent abuse to captive animals. They are opposed to zoos. Volunteers are welcome to help with the campaign.

Sick and disabled

British Red Cross
8 Grosvenor Crescent, London SW1X 7EJ
☏ 01-235 5454
An independent voluntary organisation, the Red Cross is part of a worldwide non-political movement based on the fundamental principles of humanitarianism, neutrality and impartiality. There are some 1200 centres in the UK operating more than 50 welfare services for the sick, handicapped, young, old, housebound and convalescent.

Training is given to volunteers. Some of the services undertaken include transport and escort (taking housebound people to hospital, on social trips and to visit clubs); helping at clubs and day centres; offering practical help to those returning home from illness or operation; helping stroke victims in their own homes; a foot care service, beauty care and cosmetic camouflage.

Trained *Red Cross* members can ease the strain on carers of handicapped and elderly people by sitting in to give the carer a break. A medical loan service provides walking sticks and wheel chairs, and holidays are organised for the handicapped and elderly. The organisation also performs services in hospitals.

Chest, Heart and Stroke Association
Tavistock House North, Tavistock Square, London WC1H 9JE
☏ 01-387 3012
The association has 500 or so clubs where volunteers help those who are recovering from a stroke, with activities to promote speech and movement. Activities include board games, outings and social events. Anyone who can provide transport is particularly welcome.

National Association of Leagues of Hospital Friends
38 Ebury Street, London SW1W 0LU
☏ 01-730 0103
There are more than 1000 leagues which operate on behalf of hospitals, hospices, children's homes and homes for the elderly. Each is autonomous and voluntary work varies according to the needs of the area. For example, fund raising, running hospital shops, helping in tea bars and visiting patients all form part of the work. The head office will put you in touch with a local group.

National Association for Mental Health (MIND)
22 Harley Street, London W1N 2ED
☏ 01-637 0741
MIND helps the mentally ill and their families. There is a wide network of clubs, day centres, social schemes and self-help projects where volunteer help is welcome.

The Royal National Institute for the Blind
224 Great Portland Street, London W1N 6AA
☏ 01-388 1266
Among its many activities, the RNIB provides schools for blind children, gives grants and special equipment, trains and finds employment for blind adults. Help is needed with fund raising.

The Shaftesbury Society
Shaftesbury House, 2a Amity Grove, London SW20 0LJ
☏ 01-946 6635
This society needs volunteers to talk to local clubs and organisations about the work of the society. It provides sheltered accommodation for the elderly and hostels for young people who are physically or mentally disabled. Training and the necessary information and literature, are provided.

The Spastics Society
12 Park Crescent, London W1N 4EQ
☏ 01-636 5020
Helpers are needed to run open days, provide transport, work in charity shops, and take part in fund raising and door-to-door collections.

Women's Royal Voluntary Service (WRVS)
17 Old Park Lane, London W1Y 4AJ
☏ 01-499 6040

WRVS Scotland
19 Grosvenor Crescent, Edinburgh EH12 5EL
☏ 031-337 2261

WRVS Wales
26 Cathedral Road, Cardiff CF1 9LJ
☏ 0222 28386
Among the many services provided by the WRVS are children's holidays; meals on wheels; and help for the disabled, elderly, young families, families of offenders and hospital patients. Members give what time they can to assist in their own communities; no special qualifications are required except that volunteers (including men) should be able to give regular service even if they can spare only a couple of hours. There are many jobs for those who can type, do accounts or clerical work, cook, knit, re-cycle clothes, organise clubs, drive a van or car, serve in a hospital shop, help with children and run toy libraries.

Third World

British Executive Service Overseas
10 Belgrave Square, London SW1X 8PH
☏ 01-235 0991
An independent organisation initiated by the Institute of Directors, it has the backing of the government and the CBI. It aims to improve managing skills in developing countries by sending executives with successful records in commercial and industrial fields. Projects last up to six months and can be many and varied from helping to set up new businesses and manufacturing processes to publishing and agriculture. On the spot training of the local workforce may also be required in some instances. Spouses may be taken, and travel expenses and insurances are paid by BESO. The organisation requesting your help pays your accommodation and subsistence allowances, but do not expect to receive rates comparable with the UK.

International Voluntary Service
Ceresole House, 53 Regent Road, Leicester LE1 6YL
☎ 0533 541862

Craftsmen and women, aged up to 65, are particularly needed to work in underdeveloped and deprived areas, mainly in southern Africa for a minimum of two years. Free living accommodation is provided, plus a modest living allowance. Air travel, insurances, and kit and equipment are paid for by IVS.

Oxfam
Oxfam House, 274 Banbury Road, Oxford OX2 7DZ
☎ 0865 56777

Oxfam works to relieve poverty, distress and suffering in any part of the world by supplying food, clothing, medicines, housing, training and education. It needs volunteers for fund raising, administration and to work in *Oxfam* charity shops.

Voluntary Service Overseas
9 Belgrave Square, London SW1X 8PW
☎ 01-235 5191

Every year, in response to requests from more than 40 countries, VSO send 600 or so volunteers to work in less developed communities. Volunteers are from all walks of life, including bricklayers, agriculturists, business advisers, doctors, mechanics, carpenters, electricians, midwives, social workers and teachers. Volunteers, aged between 20 and 65 are carefully selected to work abroad for two years or more. No provision is made for spouses. Experience, skill and strong motivation are the primary qualities needed.

VSO will pay for training, air fares, national and medical insurance, and equipment. Volunteers get free accommodation and are paid at local rates. Help with fund raising is also needed in this country in which there are 70 support groups. You can become a member for £5 a year and receive the quarterly magazine *Orbit*.

USEFUL ADDRESSES

British Franchise Association
Grove House
75a Bell Street
Henley-on-Thames
Oxon RG9 2BD
☎ 0491 578049

British School of Motoring
81 Hartfield Road
London SW19 3TJ
☎ 01-540 8262

Council for Small Industries in Rural Areas (CoSIRA)
141 Castle Street
Salisbury
Wilts SP1 3TP
☎ 0722 336255

Department of the Environment
Building 3
Victoria Road
South Ruislip
Middx HA4 0NZ

Driving Instructors' Association
Lion Green
Coulsdon
Surrey CR3 2NL
☎ 01-660 3333

Health and Safety Executive
Library and Information Services
  Department
Broad Lane
Sheffield S3 7HQ
☎ 0742 752539

Manpower Services Commission
  (Head Office)
Moorfoot
Sheffield S1 4PQ

Registrar of Companies for England and Wales
Companies House
Crown Way
Maindy
Cardiff C84 3UZ
☎ 0222 388588

Registrar of Companies for Scotland
Companies Registration Office
Exchequer Chambers
102 George Street
Edinburgh EH2 3DJ
☎ 031-225 5774

Co-operatives

The Co-operative Development Agency
Broadmead House
21 Panton Street
London SW1Y 4DR
☎ 01-554 3797

Industrial Common Ownership Movement (ICOM)
7–8 The Corn Exchange
Leeds LS1 7BP
☎ 0532 461737

London ICOM
7 Bradbury Street
London N16 8JN
☎ 01-249 2837

The Scottish Co-operatives Development Committee
Templeton Business Centre
Templeton Street
Bridgeton
Glasgow G40 1DA
☎ 041-554 3797

Wales Co-operative Development and Training Centre
Llandaff Court
Fairwater Road
Cardiff CF5 2XP
☎ 0222 554955

Employment measures units

Midlands
2 Duchess Place
Hagley Road
Birmingham B16 8NS
☎ 021-456 1144

North East
Condercum House
171 West Road
Newcastle-upon-Tyne NE15 6PL
☎ 091-272 2294

North West
Sunley Buildings
Piccadilly Plaza
Manchester M60 7JS
☎ 061-832 9111

South East
Unicorn House
28 Elmfield Road
Bromley
Kent BR1 1LR
☎ 01-464 6418

Scotland
Pentland House
47 Robb's Loan
Edinburgh EH14 1UE
☏ 031-443 8731

Wales and South West
1st Floor, Government Buildings
Block 4, St Agnes Road
Gabalfa
Cardiff CF4 3UF
☏ 0222 693131

BIBLIOGRAPHY

Davis, Johanna (1982) *Machine Knitting to Suit your Mood* Pelham, London.
Dudeney, Charles (1980) *A Guide to Executive Re-employment* Macdonald and Evans, Plymouth.
Earning Money at Home (1979) Consumer's Association, London.
The Family Welfare Association Charities Digest Family Welfare Association, London.
Farrell, Peter (1983) *Spare Time Income* Kogan Page, London.
Fisher, David (1983) *Secondhand Bargains Made New* Marshall Cavendish, London.
Humphries, Judith (1986) *Part-time Work* Kogan Page, London.
Jackson, Valerie (1984) *How to Make Beautiful Flowers* Search Press, Tunbridge Wells.
Johnson, Joanne (1980) *Working at Home for Profit* Basil Blackwell, Oxford.
MacQueen, Sheila (1983) *Complete Flower Arranging* Ward Lock, London.
Miller, Bruce W. and Widess, Jim (1984) *The Caner's Handbook* Collins, London.
Salazar, Tristan (1982) *The Complete Book of Furniture Restoration* Batsford, London.
Sorensen, Veronica (1984) *Modern Lace Designs* Batsford, London.
Swanson, Christine, Phillips, Patrick and Barrow, Beverley
Turner, B. (ed.) (1987) *The Writer's Handbook*. The Macmillan Press Ltd, London.
Voluntary Organisations National Council for Voluntary Organisations.
Worker's Co-operative Handbook Industrial Common Ownership Movement, Leeds.
Wright, Dorothy (1979) *Baskets and Basketry* David and Charles, Newton Abbot.
Free publications from the Customs and Excise
  Selling or Transferring a Business as a Going Concern.
  Should I be registered for VAT?
Free publications from the DHSS
  Employee's Guide to Statutory Sick Pay (NI 227)
  Employer's Guide to NI contributions (NP 15)
  More than one job? (NP 28)
  National Insurance Contribution Rates (NI 208)
  National Insurance for Company Directors (NI 35)
  National Insurance Guide for the Self-employed (NI 41)
Free publications from the Inland Revenue
  Capital allowances on machinery and plants (CA 1)
  Capital gains tax and the small businessman (CGT 11)
  Employer's Guide to PAYE (P7)
  Starting in Business (IR 28)

Thinking of taking someone on? (IR 53)
Thinking of working for yourself? (IR 57)

Free publications from Jobcentres

Action for Jobs (1987) Department of Employment, London.

Cooperating for work. Careers and Occupational Information Centre, MSC, Sheffield.

Employee's rights on insolvency of employer (PL 718)

Guide to the Enterprise Allowance Scheme (1987) Manpower Services Commission, Sheffield.

Jobhunt 2. Be your own Boss (1985) Manpower Services Commission, Sheffield.

Planning to Set Up your Own Business Manpower Services Commission, Sheffield.

Written Statement of main terms and conditions of employment (PL 700)

Free publications from the Health and Safety Executive

Don't Wait Until the Inspector Calls

Planning Permission for Small Businesses

Holidays

NEW HOLIDAY OPPORTUNITIES	382
Travelling out of season	382
Taking your time	383
Being more adventurous	383
SPECIAL PACKAGES	384
Cruises	384
Exotic tours	384
SAGA holidays	385
TIME-SHARING	385
What is a time-share?	386
Exchanging time-shares	386
Main advantages	386
Points to watch	387
Time-shares in Britain	387
CARAVANS AND MOTORHOMES	388
CAMPING	389
ACTIVITY HOLIDAYS	389
TRAVEL CONCESSIONS	389
Air travel	389
Bus travel	390
Rail travel	390
USEFUL ADDRESSES	394
BIBLIOGRAPHY	397

Holidays are different in retirement. They are just as enjoyable as ever they were, but we take them for different reasons. When we were at work or had young families, holidays were to help us all to relax, recharge our batteries, forget for a couple of weeks the pressures of life at home and office, and perhaps bask in a little unaccustomed sunshine.

In retirement they are not so much for relaxation and recuperation, as for stimulation and broadening of the horizons. Even the lure of sunshine might begin to wane and instead of searching for beaches to laze on we begin to look for new places to explore, new activities to try out and new people to meet.

NEW HOLIDAY OPPORTUNITIES

Retirement opens up very interesting possibilities for travel. Here are a few of the benefits that retirement can offer:

- *You can travel out of season* when almost any place you choose is less crowded than it would be in the height of the season.
- *You can stay longer.* A fortnight or three weeks was almost certainly the limit when you were at work. What (apart from finance) is going to stop you from spending a month (or even three) on holiday now? You could choose to spend the winter in sunny Spain, or perhaps this is the moment you will choose to visit children who emigrated to Australia or some other far-flung part of the world.
- *You can be more adventurous.* Many people start retirement with a 'dream' holiday. This may be a specially expensive or luxurious one they have dreamed about for years.

Travelling out of season

This is probably the great bonus of retirement holidaymaking. It is both cheaper and less crowded. For instance, Majorca is horribly crowded in the summer, but, out of season when the young holidaymakers from Britain, France and Germany have gone back to work, it remains one of the most beautiful islands in the Mediterranean with a fascinating history, beautiful walks, warm hearted hospitable residents and genuine tranquillity.

Taking your time

A tremendous market has grown up in recent years for cheap winter package tours. Retired people can go to the Costa del Sol in Spain for periods up to three months. Rather than close down in winter and lay off their staff, hotels are prepared to offer extremely low cost accommodation. Coupled with cheap flights, it can be almost as cheap to fly off to Spain for the winter as it is to stay at home and heat the house.

SAGA Holidays, which pioneered the growth of holidays specially for older people does an enormous trade in winter holidays, mostly to southern Spain. They reckon the basic cost is about £10 a day per person inclusive of flight, accommodation, two or three meals a day and an extensive entertainment programme. If you want to hire a small car at that time of year you can do so for about £15 a week.

Of course you have to make your selections with care according to your preferences. Torremolinos on the Costa del Sol is very popular with British retirees but has become a very commercial resort. This suits some people, but if bingo and dancing lack appeal for you, you will almost certainly be happier a little further down the coast at Marbella, which is quieter.

A list of holiday companies specialising in retired people appears at the end of this chapter. Write to them for details or simply walk in to your local travel agent and let them do the work for you.

Being more adventurous

This is where travel in retirement becomes really exciting. Many people are prepared to spend substantial sums on unusual holidays. For instance, I know a retired schoolmaster in Lincolnshire who is a seasoned traveller and seems to spend as much time abroad as in England. He has become so expert at travel in relatively primitive countries that he now leads parties of others who want to do so but are not quite sure how. Typically, he may go to Mexico for a couple of months with his entire luggage on his back in a hiker's rucksack so small that he can take it on to an aircraft as handbaggage. He washes his clothes as he travels and says the most important item of clothing is a large white napkin which ensures he doesn't spill soup on his trousers the first day out! He doesn't expect his companions to travel quite so lightly, though. He is particularly conscious of how tummy upsets and other minor illnesses can spoil a holiday both for the individual and the party they happen to be with, so he takes great care to advise his clients on the dos and don'ts of maintaining a clean bill of health while overseas. If you would like to know more about his accompanied tours write to the **Rev. Reg Woodword** (see page 396).

SPECIAL PACKAGES

Cruises

If relaxation, sunshine, luxury, good food and wine, perhaps even a hint of romance, are still as important to you as visiting new places, then the chances are that a cruise on one of the big liners has at least crossed your mind.

A very good top line range is offered by the Princess liners of P&O. A glimpse through their brochure quickly gives you a taste of the luxury and style they offer. In 1987 they are offering (among other things) a 73-night trip on the *Royal Princess* starting in Los Angeles and travelling to Honolulu, Christmas Island, Papeete, Auckland, Sydney, Bali, Singapore, Manila, Hong Kong, Peking, Nagasaki and Tokyo, to name just a few of the stopping points.

They do things in style on these ships. Everyone dresses for dinner (black ties for preference) and the meal is a seven-course affair. If you can still stand afterwards you will find plenty of entertainment and dancing through the night.

All rooms are first class, but they go from plain 'twin rooms, outside' to 'luxury deluxe suites, outside'. The main difference is the price: the former will cost £7,772 per person and the latter £18,894.

At the other end of the scale six nights on the *Pacific Princess* cruising in the Mediterranean starts at only £737 which includes your flight out and back so you don't waste a moment out of the sunshine.

A trip to your local travel agent will introduce you to plenty of other cruise lines offering a range of holidays. SAGA the specialist holiday company for the over-sixties also has a selection of cruises on offer.

Cruising is a special kind of holiday and one which appeals to large numbers. Certainly it has many attractions, but there are also some drawbacks. On board a ship there is no escape from the dinner-table bore, drinks may not be as cheap as you would hope even though duty free and, despite the idyllic pictures of romantic tranquillity, when a boat is in motion it can be very draughty on deck.

Exotic tours

If you prefer to be more firmly planted on *terra firma*, the whole world beckons. China has opened its doors in recent years; you could spend a lifetime getting to know a small part of India; and the game reserves of Africa beat any amount of animal filming on television. If your knowledge of Russia is confined to what you read in newspapers perhaps you should go there. It's funny how the little things stick. One retired man after a visit to Moscow said what struck him most was the immaculate cleanliness of the place (Londoners would think a Moscow street fit to eat off) and the fact that they didn't seem to use lawnmowers. All the parks had grass six inches long!

Specialist companies such as **Kuoni** and **Jules Verne** are good starting places for the intrepid traveller. In searching for the wonders of the world I felt spoilt for choice flipping through a **Kuoni** brochure. The Pyramids (Egyptian or Mexican), Ayers Rock in Central Australia, the palaces of India, the Terracotta Army, Mount Fuji, The Bridge over the River Kwai – they were all featured in one or another section of the **Kuoni** brochure. Thankfully, **Kuoni** are honest enough to warn would-be clients that some of their trips are arduous and cannot be described as 'holidays'. So before embarking on such a strenuous holiday make sure that you are fit enough (see page 391 for advice).

SAGA holidays

SAGA Holidays is without doubt the leader in the provision of holidays for the over 60s. About 250,000 people book with them each year to go on holidays ranging from short breaks at British universities out of term to round-the-world cruises. Their holidays are complete, with the rail fare from your home town to your destination in this country or to port or airports for overseas journeys included in the price.

In order to become a SAGA customer you must be 60 or, in the case of married partners, at least one of you must be 60.

The company was founded in the early 1950s when its founder Sydney De Haan a hotelier in Folkestone was pondering ways to keep his hotel open and its staff employed during the winter. He hit on the idea of advertising for retired people in the North of England, brought them down to Folkestone by coach and effectively discovered a new growth business. Since then **SAGA** has grown to be a giant in the holiday world and is now a public company quoted on the London Stock Exchange. Sydney De Haan has retired but the company is still based in Folkestone and his son Roger has taken over as chairman and managing director.

Other companies offering special packages to older people may be found at the end of this chapter (page 397).

TIME-SHARING

This is still a fairly new concept and, although we British have been fairly cautious about it, it is estimated that during the last ten years about 50,000 Britons have bought time-share apartments, joining the ranks of about a million time-sharers around the world. If that gives the impression of a big happy family, it is intentional. One of the merits of buying a time-share is the fact that you can swap it for another almost anywhere in the world. A large percentage of time-share owners do just that after spending the first few holidays in their own property. (Time-shares in boats are also possible.)

What is a time-share?

It is essentially a holiday apartment, which may be a single unit or one of many others in a block, that is 'sold' on a weekly basis. One apartment can be sold in this way 52 times in a year. When you buy a time-share apartment you buy the right to live in that property for a specific week (or more) each year. In a few instances time-sharers buy a share in the actual freehold of the property.

The price is determined not only by the quality of the apartment but also by the time of year which is bought: a high season week costs more than a low season week. It can cost anything from £1500 to £10,000 or more a week depending on the location and standards, which are usually very high.

Exchanging time-shares

Although some time-sharers begin the venture feeling that they love the place so much that they will be happy there for the rest of their lives many, in fact, end up joining the international exchange organisations who, for a relatively small fee, will let your apartment to a time-share owner from another country and find you an alternative time-share apartment in the country of your choice. They claim something like a 90% success rate. The two main exchange organisations are: **Interval International** and **Resort Condominiums International**. This ability to swap your time-share for another overturns one of the misconceptions about time-sharing which is thought to have put many people off – the idea that once you have bought a time-share you are stuck with it for ever. You are not. You can usually swap it, or you can sell it on. You might even make a profit, though that is not a wise reason to buy one.

Main advantages

- You buy a holiday week in a location of your choice in *your own place*.
- You are effectively buying inflation-proofed holidays. Although the initial expense may seem high, all you have to pay in future is your fares out and an annual charge for each week you own, typically between £75 and £150 a week.

- When you tire of your present time-share you can let it, sell it on, or swap with someone else in some other resort or country.
- If you die it can be willed to someone else.

Points to watch

- As with any other property purchase overseas you need to exercise great caution in the payment of deposits and ensuring legal title. You should use a local solicitor when buying into a scheme overseas (see *Retiring Abroad* page 315).
- Make sure you see the finished apartments before you buy, or at least one in the same development.
- It is worth ensuring that one of the international exchange organisations has accepted the development on to its exchange scheme.
- Check on the period of ownership. In some cases you can buy a time-share *in perpetuity*, but in others only on a long lease basis.
- Read the small print concerning the weekly service charges and check on any periodic reviews.
- Make sure that as *owners* you and other time-sharers in the same development have control over the managers, so that you can sack them if you are not satisfied.
- Don't be browbeaten by agents and their representatives on site. Some time-share developers have done the movement no good at all in recent years by operating high-pressure sales techniques. People are often stopped on the streets of overseas holiday resorts and offered all manner of inducements to go and see a time-share development. Once there they are subjected to quite powerful pressure to pay a deposit.

Time-shares in Britain

The fact that you are able to swap one time-share for another means there are good reasons for buying your time-share in this country. There are a growing number of high class developments around, including the conversion of some of our ancient and historic homes. They are much in demand as swaps by people from other parts of the world, so it would be perfectly feasible to buy a time-share in Britain and never use it.

The main advantage over buying abroad is that you have the opportunity to monitor a development in this country which you would not enjoy to the same extent overseas. Furthermore, you are protected by British laws. In this country you should go for developers who are members of the **British Property Time-Share Association (BPTA)** which imposes a code of ethics and good practice.

CARAVANS AND MOTORHOMES

Of course you don't have to go overseas to enjoy a holiday, nor do you have to go by aircraft. Many retired people choose a caravan or a motorhome instead. (A motorhome is a caravan with its own engine and four (or more) wheels, often conversions of a commercial vehicle chassis with custom-built living accommodation.) Either mode of travel comes as close to the nomadic gipsy life as any of us is likely to experience these days. You simply drive to your destination and stop. You are in all respects self-contained.

Which you choose depends on the amount of use you expect to get from your outfit and the depth of your pocket (see below). A second-hand two-berth caravan could, no doubt, be found for between £1000 and £2000, but a new one can cost anything from £3000 to £16,000. Of course, the more you pay the more home comforts you get. Modern vans include central heating, full cooking and refrigeration facilities, shower, lavatory and mains electricity hook-ups. Living in one is not exactly a hardship.

New motorhomes start at around £5000 but could cost anything up to £50,000 for vehicles which carry every comfort of home.

CARAVAN vs MOTORHOME

Caravan

Advantages
- They are less expensive
- Once at your destination you can unhook it from your car which is then free for local journeys

Disadvantages
- Handling a caravan requires more skill, especially in reversing
- There is a speed limit of 60 mph on motorways and dual carriageways and 50 mph on other roads.

Motorhome

Advantages
- They offer maximum freedom and manoeuvrability and enjoy the same speed restrictions as a motor car
- They can double-up as a second vehicle

Disadvantages
- They are more expensive than caravans
- If you want to make a local journey from a holiday base, everything has to be put into its proper place and secured

HOLIDAYS 389

Further information
The Caravan Club has more than 250,000 members and offers a wide range of services which are invaluable to the caravanner or motorhome owner. This includes the ownership and licensing of sites, insurance both for home and overseas travel, and home and international rescue services. They also publish a magazine, *En route*, eight times a year and a number of guides. Membership costs £15 a year.

The club also runs practical caravanning courses at weekends in various parts of the country which gives you an opportunity to practise basic towing and reversing skills, safety and maintenance. The courses cost £31.50 including VAT.

CAMPING

Life under canvas may not have such a great appeal to retired people, but if you still retain some of the youthful outlook of the Scouts and Guides, why not? Tents have become pretty sophisticated these days, though they still seem to get in a tangle when you put them up. Membership of the **Camping and Caravanning Club of Great Britain and Northern Ireland** can provide you with further information and advice. Membership costs £16 a year.

ACTIVITY HOLIDAYS

Activity holidays in which you follow some particular hobby or special interest pursuit are growing in popularity. You will find a number of these in *Back to School* (page 400) and *Hobbies* (page 408) see *Cycling* and *Rambling*) as well as a list of companies catering for such holidays at the end of this chapter (page 396).

TRAVEL CONCESSIONS

One of the good things about retirement is that many travel organisations are prepared to offer you reduced rate travel.

Air travel

Visiting friends and relatives abroad has become such big business for the travel industry that they use the shorthand VFR to describe it. It relies mostly on traffic between Britain and Australia, New Zealand, Canada, the United States of America and some African countries. Parents and grandparents often dream of visiting their faraway offspring in retirement, and those who achieve it represent big business for the airlines.

It is possible to make worthwhile savings on standard fares for these long haul flights through what are known as 'excursion' fares. Even so, they are not cheap. A return trip to Sydney to enjoy an Australian Christmas with your children and grandchildren can cost up to £1000, depending on which month you choose to travel. You no longer have to book these flights months ahead, but obviously the closer you get to your planned departure date the less likely you are to get a flight on the day of your choice. Other conditions are you must stay a minimum of 14 days and a maximum of 12 months.

Bus travel

Bus travel is either free or subsidised in many parts of the country, but the extent of the concession depends on the decision of the local authority or bus company concerned. In London, pensioners who live in Greater London are entitled to free travel on both buses and tube trains at off-peak hours. This represents a tremendous saving on travel costs for those who live in and around the capital. Few other authorities are so generous, however, and you should check with your local authority or Citizens' Advice Bureau to see what the situation is where you live.

Rail travel

British Rail

A *Senior Citizens Railcard* is available to anyone over the age of 60. There are two versions: one costing £7 and the other £12. The £7 card enables you to buy, at half the normal price, cheap day returns for second class journeys of up to 50 miles. While the £12 card entitles you to additional concessions of

- One third off *Saver* tickets. These tickets are available for second class return journeys over 50 miles. You must return within one month.
- Half price on standard first or second class day returns for journeys up to 30 miles away. There are no restrictions on travelling times.
- One third off standard first or second class single tickets.
- One third off standard first or second class for journeys over 30 miles. You must return within three months.

Disabled people, which includes the blind and deaf, are entitled to buy a *Disabled Person's Railcard* for £12. This entitles the disabled person and his or her travelling companion to various fare reductions including 50% off normal cheap day returns.

You can get a brochure outlining all the services available from your local railway station.

European rail travel

The *Rail Europ Senior Card* offers significant reductions in rail fares to British pensioners travelling in Europe. This costs £5 and is available to men aged 65 and women aged 60 who also hold a British Rail *Senior Citizen Railcard*.

The *Rail Europ* card entitles you to fare savings of
- Up to 50% on railway journeys in Belgium, France, Finland, Greece, Ireland, Luxembourg, The Netherlands, Norway, Portugal, Spain, Sweden, and Switzerland
- Up to 30% on railways in Austria, Denmark, West Germany, Hungary, Italy and Yugoslavia
- Up to 50% on British Rail when you buy a 'through' international rail/sea ticket
- Up to 30% on sea crossings to the Continent by *Sealink*, *Hoverspeed* hovercraft and *Townsend Thoresen* services between Dover and Ostend, or between Portsmouth and Le Havre when these are part of a through rail/sea journey
- At least 30% on sealink crossings to the Republic of Ireland.

You can get the application forms from your local station and the cards from **British Rail Travel Centres** or European Rail appointed travel agents.

Further information

A regularly updated list of the concessions you may find available in various European countries is published in a booklet called *Holidays* available from the **Greater London Association for Pre-Retirement (GLAP)**.

SAFE TRAVEL

Although age is no bar to active holidays under difficult conditions it is important to be adequately prepared. Not only for the actual journey but also for the conditions you may find at your destination if you are going abroad. While escaping the English winter can be a way of minimising the risk of flu and bronchitis, other diseases can become more likely. With prudence and planning there is every reason for you to enjoy an exciting holiday.

'Fit' to travel

If you are planning a fairly strenuous holiday (such as trekking in the Himalayas) or even one in which you are proposing more physical activity than you are used to, it is essential to get reasonably fit well before you go. Do a few 20-mile walks in the sort of country you are expecting and carry an appropriate load. Moderately high altitudes should present no serious problem to the reasonably fit, but those with poor chests or raised blood pressure may have difficulty and should consult their GP or a chest specialist.

If you are already on medication then make sure you tell your doctor where you are going and for how long so that he can make sure you have adequate supplies. If you are prone to tummy upsets of the 'Montezuma's revenge' variety he might also prescribe you a suitable general purpose antibiotic to help you overcome the infection. You may have to pay your doctor a small fee for this service as well as the full prescription fee at the chemist.

Take it easy at the beginning, take time to acclimatise and recover from jet lag. Remember that you are no longer 29 and don't take silly physical risks.

HEALTH HAZARDS ABROAD

A recent Consumers' Association survey looked at the health advice given in various travel brochures and was alarmed at its paucity. The occupied parts of developed countries are reasonably safe, but given the present state of much of the world, the health dangers are probably greater than they were a few years ago and you need protection. This requires expert advice which can be obtained from the **Medical Advisory Service for Travellers Abroad (MASTA)**. Operated through the **London School of Hygiene and Tropical Medicine**, they give up-to-date health briefings which include advice on inoculations and suitable medical kits to take with you. There is a modest fee for this but it is well worthwhile. One such brief is the *MASTA Healthy Holiday Brief* for people going on holiday in Europe for relatively short periods. Comprehensive briefings and a self-medication guide for people spending long periods overseas are available for about £25.

Inoculations

It is essential to check the need for inoculations, as the rules for these change constantly. Hepatitis, for instance, is both common and dangerous, even in Mediterranean countries, while malaria is an increasing hazard, and it is essential to take pills for a few days before and for six weeks after you get back from an infected country because the parasites lurk in the blood for this length of time. Thomas Cook and British Airways both offer excellent inoculation services and there are centres in most large towns. Your doctor can advise you on this.

If you should get any serious symptoms after returning from abroad, go at once to your doctor and *say where you have been*.

Medical kit

It is also wise to take a simple medical kit with remedies for tummy upsets, allergy, sunburn, bites and so on. Your doctor or the **London School of Hygiene** can advise you. Remember also that the Mediterranean becomes a cesspit by midsummer and many beaches are unsafe because of sewage pollution. Check on this with other visitors when you get there, the locals may tend to play it down for commercial reasons.

A TRAVEL MEDICAL CHEST

Here are some useful contents for a medical chest that you might like to take with you if you holiday anywhere in Europe.

aspirin, paracetamol, ibuprofen (*Nurofen*)
loperamide (*Imodium*) antidiarrhoeal agent
 (available as tablets or syrup)
antihistamine tablets
antiseptic solution and cream
calamine cream
eyewash solution
thermometer
cotton wool
cotton wool buds
Vaseline
tweezers
small scissors
teaspoon
insect repellent
sunscreen cream
sticking plasters

Medical insurance

It is imperative, especially on long trips, that you are well covered by insurance for medical treatment. EEC member countries have reciprocal agreements about this, but in order to benefit you must apply on form E111 for a certificate *before* you go.

The only way to ensure that you get free medical cover while overseas is to take out special medical insurance. Members of **BUPA** and similar health care organisations will usually organise this as an extension of normal cover. Travel agents can also arrange it for you, or you can go to your usual insurance broker. As you may well have to pay at the point of treatment and claim it back when you return home, you should keep your receipts.

Reciprocal agreements
Britain has reciprocal health care arrangements for *urgent* treatment with a number of countries including all member states of the EEC (see page 394). However, this does not necessarily mean you are entitled to

the same free treatment that you would get at home, only to the same medical care to which nationals of the country you are visiting are entitled.

In some countries you must pay the cost of treatment and then claim all or some of it back. In France, for example, you must normally pay for hospital, dental and other medical care and 70–80% of the charges are refunded by the French Sickness Insurance Office.

In order to qualify for treatment it is sensible to get hold of the DHSS leaflet *Medical Costs Abroad* from the local social security office well in advance and apply for a certificate called an E111. This has to be produced when you are seeking medical attention in an EEC country except in Gibraltar, Eire or Portugal where a UK Passport is sufficient.

Reciprocal health agreements

EEC countries

Belgium	Denmark	France
West Germany	Gibraltar	Greece
Eire	Italy	Luxembourg
Netherlands	Portugal	Spain

Non-EEC countries

Anguilla	Australia	Austria
British Virgin Islands	Bulgaria	Channel Islands
Czechoslovakia	Falkland Islands	Finland
East Germany	Hong Kong	Hungary
Iceland	Isle of Man	Malta
Montserrat	New Zealand	Norway
Poland	Romania	St Helena
Sweden	Turks & Caicos Islands	USSR
Yugoslavia		

USEFUL ADDRESSES

BUPA
Provident House
Essex Street
London WC2R 3AX
☎ 01-353 5212

Caravan Club
East Grinstead House
East Grinstead
W. Sussex RH19 1UA
☎ 0342 26944

Camping and Caravanning Club of Great Britain and Northern Ireland
11 Lower Grosvenor Place
London SW1W 0EY
☎ 01-828 1012

Greater London Association for Pre-Retirement
St Margaret Patten's Church
Eastcheap
London EC3M 1HS
☎ 01-623 6630

Medical Advisory Service for Travellers Abroad (MASTA)
London School of Hygiene and Tropical Medicine
Keppel Street
London WC1E 7HT
℡ 01-636 4403

Time-shares

British Property Time-Share Association (BPTA)
Westminster Bank Chambers
Market Hill
Sudbury
Suffolk CO10 6EN
℡ 0787 310749

Interval International
Standbrook House
2/5 Old Bond Street
London W1X 3TB
℡ 01-499 7383

Resort Condominiums International
Parnell House
19 Wilton Road
London SW1V 1LW
℡ 01-821 5588

Tour operators giving special packages to older people. A trip to your local travel agent will usually enable you to collect some brochures without going to the expense of phoning or writing for one. They will also make the necessary booking arrangements. Make sure they are members of the Association of British Travel Agents (ABTA).

Enterprise Holidays
British Airways Holidays
PO Box 100
Hodford House
17–22 High Street
Hounslow
Middlesex TW3 1TB
℡ 01-572 7373
There are special deals for people over 55 including long stay winter holidays. Ask for their *Winter Fun* brochure, available from travel agents or by calling 01-897 4545.

Global
26 Elmfield Road
Bromley
Kent BR1 1LR
℡ 01-464 7515
Global runs *Golden Circle* holidays for people over 50, including long winter breaks. You can get a copy of the *Golden Circle* brochure by writing or phoning the brochure department on 0274 726676.

Horizon
Broadway
Five Ways
Edgbaston
Birmingham B15 1BB
℡ 021-643 2727
Horizon offers special holidays, including long stay winter breaks, to people over 55.

Intasun
Intasun House
Cromwell Avenue
Bromley
Kent BR2 9AQ
℡ 01-290 0511
Intasun offers a range of holidays for the over 50s including long stay winter escapes. Ask for their *Golden Days* brochure.

SAGA Holidays
Bouverie House
Middleburg Square
Folkestone
Kent CT20 1AZ
☏ 0303 47000

Thomsons
Greater London House
Hampstead Road
London NW1 7SD
☏ 01-387 9321
Thomsons offer special holidays, including winter long stays, to people over 55. Their brochure goes under the name of *Young at Heart*.

Activity holidays

Butlins
Bognor Regis
Sussex PO21 1JJ
☏ 0243 820202
Both companies organise special interest holiday weeks and weekends including dancing. Although not necessarily for retired people modern sequence dancing is specially attractive to this age group.

Countrywide Holidays Association
Birch Heys
Cromwell Range
Manchester M14 6HU
☏ 061-225 1000
This company offers special interest holidays in a variety of centres including Scotland and Orkney.

The Holiday Fellowship
142 Great North Way
London NW4 1EG
☏ 01-203 3381
This is one of the oldest holiday organisations in the country. It runs a wide range of special interest holidays from bird watching to bridge, bowls to pony trekking.

Jules Verne Travel
10 Glentworth Street
London NW1 5PG
☏ 01-486 8080

Kuoni Travel Ltd
33 Maddox Street
London W1
☏ 01-499 8636

Pontins
Crest House
South Bar
Banbury
Oxon OX16 9XB
☏ 0295 4500

Rev. Reg. Woodward
104 Harrowby Road
Grantham
Lincs.

Holidays in the British Isles

For other holidays at home either at hotels, small boarding houses and farmhouses, it is worthwhile contacting the various tourist authorities who will be able to provide you with booklets of names and addresses.

English Tourist Board
24 Grosvenor Gardens
London SW1 0DU
☎ 01-730 3488
They publish a useful booklet of holiday addresses called *Let's Go*, which is available free from tourist information centres, from **Admail 14**, London SW1W 0YE or by telephoning 0272 277917.

Irish Tourist Board
Borde Failte
150 New Bond Street
London W1Y 0AQ
☎ 01-493 3201
They publish a free address and ideas book called *Ireland 87*.

National Holidays
George House
George Street
Wakefield WF1 1LY
☎ 0924 383838
or **Wallace Arnold**
Gelderd Road
Leeds LS12 6DH
☎ 0532 636456
Details of coaching holidays are available from their brochure *Coach Holidays in Britain and Ireland*.

Northern Ireland Tourist Board
River House
48 High Street
Belfast BT1 2DS
☎ 0232 246609

or 11 Berkeley Street
London W1X 6BU
☎ 01-493 0601
They publish *Northern Ireland – the main guide*, free of charge.

Scottish Tourist Board
23 Ravelston Terrace
Edinburgh EH4 3EU
☎ 031-332 2433
They publish *Scotland Getaway*, free of charge and have a booklet of small hotels and guest houses.

Welsh Tourist Board
Brunel House
2 Fitzalan Road
Cardiff CF2 1UY
☎ 0222 499909
They publish *Wales Holidays* and a bed and breakfast guide. Both are free and are available from PO Box 1, Cardiff CF1 2XN.

BIBLIOGRAPHY

Dawood, R. (1986) *Traveller's Health* Oxford University Press.
Ireland 87 Irish Tourist Board, Dublin.
English Tourist Board (1987) *Let's Go* British Tourist Authority, London.
Medical Cost Abroad DHSS, London.
Northern Ireland – the main guide (1982) Northern Ireland Tourist Board, Belfast.
Scotland Getaway Scottish Tourist Board, Edinburgh.
Wales Holidays Welsh Tourist Board, Cardiff.

PONTIN'S HOLIDAYS

PREPARE FOR YOUR RETIREMENT AND HAVE FUN

One week Retirement Planning Courses run by the Pre-Retirement Association. Covering everything you need to know on finance from pensions to tax; health, hobbies and a host of other subjects.

In addition there will be a full programme of entertainment available plus good food and accommodation all set in glorious Devon.

**FOR FULL DETAILS CONTACT:
PONTIN'S SPECIAL INTEREST HOLIDAYS
TELEPHONE: (0257) 452452**

NCDL
FOUNDED 1891

The National Canine Defence League is Britain's leading Charity caring for stray and unwanted dogs. Through our 14 Rescue Centres in the UK we rescue, rehabilitate where necessary, and rehome thousands of dogs each year. These dogs, through no fault of their own, have been discarded by their owners, usually because they have grown too large, are too expensive to feed, or have not been properly trained.

Any dog which cannot be rehomed, will stay in our care for life. NO HEALTHY DOG IS EVER DESTROYED. To help look after these dogs, the League has set up a Dog Sponsorship Fund whereby supporters who, for some reason, are unable to have a dog of their own, can sponsor one in our care, visit it and take it for walks, and treat it is as their own pet.

The League relies totally on voluntary donations and legacies. Membership of the League costs £7.50 per year (£3.45 for Senior Citizens) and entitles members to free 3rd party public liability insurance for damage caused by their dog up to £1,000,000; a free identity disc with veterinary guarantee, full voting rights in the League's affairs, an Annual Report and bi-annual Newsletter giving an up-date on our activities.

If you feel able to support our work, either by making a donation, rehoming a dog from us, or remembering us in your Will, please contact us at:
National Canine Defence League, 1 Pratt Mews, London NW1 0AD, Tel: 01-388 0137.

Registered Charity No. 227523

Leisure

BACK TO SCHOOL	400
Adult education classes	400
Universities and polytechnics	402
Open University	402
Short residential courses	404
Correspondence courses	406
Local network organisations	406
The library	407
HOBBIES	408
Index	408
Directory	410
USEFUL ADDRESSES	450
BIBLIOGRAPHY	453

BACK TO SCHOOL

Retirement often triggers off an urge to get 'back to school' in various forms. Night school language classes, pottery and painting classes, weekend and week-long residential courses, correspondence courses, even the pursuit of a degree through the Open University – all attract enormous interest from many age groups. For those of you who believe you are never too old to learn here are a few ways you might like to go about it.

Adult education classes

Most local authorities run Adult Education Institutes and Colleges of Further Education with day and evening classes. The Adult Education Institutes are designed primarily for older people who wish to improve their qualifications, take refresher courses or develop special interests. They offer mostly evening classes. The Colleges of Further Education are designed primarily for young people leaving school who wish to gain higher qualifications or trade skills, often on a day-release basis from their employers but, provided there are places free, there is no reason why a retired person should not enrol for the same classes.

The range of subjects covered under the heading of 'adult education' is enormous. The general rule seems to be that if sufficient people are interested in having a class, no matter how esoteric the subject, the adult education authorities will do their best to put it on.

What classes are available?
Either contact your local Adult Education Institute direct or keep an eye on the noticeboard of the local library where details are invariably listed and where you will probably be able to pick up a prospectus. In London the ILEA publishes a booklet called *Floodlight*, which is also available from the **Information Centre** of the ILEA. The 1986 version was a fat 332-page paperback in which the alphabetical list of subjects available ran to 232 pages. In Scotland you can get more information about adult education facilities by getting in touch with the **Scottish Institute of Adult Education** and asking for the *Handbook of Adult Education in Scotland*.

ADULT EDUCATION COURSES

The list of sample subjects given below was taken from the prospectus of the adult education facility of a small town college of further education in Suffolk. It listed over 80 evening class subjects alone and is likely to be a pattern replicated all over the country.

- Ladies keep fit
- Cooking for men
- Horse care
- Cake decorating
- Life painting
- German conversation
- Spinning & weaving
- Computers
- Lip reading
- Lacemaking
- Japanese
- Flower arranging
- Badminton
- Spanish
- Dance exercise
- Calligraphy
- Cosmetic make-up
- Word processing
- Historical documents
- First aid
- Wholefood cookery
- French
- Cooking for fun
- Round the world cookery
- Dressmaking
- Pottery
- Oil and watercolours
- Decorative pewterwork
- Field archaeology
- Starting painting
- Dutch
- Yoga
- Slimnastics
- China restoration
- Sociology
- Typing for beginners
- Dynamics of nuclear age
- Better driving
- Advanced yeast cookery
- Tracing your ancestors
- Ghosts
- Astronomy
- Craftwork
- Suffolk alehouses
- Canvaswork and embroidery
- Crochet
- Upholstery
- Growing vegetables
- Italian
- Self-defence for women
- Over-60s keep fit
- RYA competent skipper
- Car maintenance
- Craft brickwork

Enrolling

The majority of classes start in the September term so you have to keep your eyes open for enrolment dates during August. There is great flexibility about these classes and you will find a niche for yourself whatever your standard in a particular subject. If you want to learn French, for instance, there will usually be a beginners' class, an improvers' class, one for those who want to take examinations in the subject and others for those whose only interest is in developing their conversational skills.

Once you know when enrolment starts it pays to put down your name quickly as the more popular classes are often over-subscribed. If they are enormously over-subscribed then a second class may well be introduced but it often seems to be the way that the last half dozen or so have to be turned away.

Universities and polytechnics

If you have a university or polytechnic nearby it is also worthwhile checking to see if they run courses for members of the public in the evening or during the holiday periods. There are departments of adult education or extra-mural studies at many universities and polytechnics, and they produce a wide range of interesting and stimulating courses. In some cases this includes part-time study for degree courses spread over a number of years. The University of London, for example, has a particularly active department of extra-mural studies. Their prospectus for 1986–87 ran to 192 pages and is worth a read in its own right if only to marvel at the range of subjects available for study. You could have chosen a two-term course on:

- Recent archaeological work in London (Fee £39 for 24 evening meetings)
- Mathematics refresher course (Fee £15 for a three-day course on two Saturdays and a Sunday)
- Mahler's later symphonies and their influence (Fee £39, an advanced class for 24 evening meetings)
- Psychoanalysis and female identity (Fee £39, a first year tutorial course on Friday evenings for 24 meetings)

Courses vary in length from 1 day to 30 weeks and fees vary accordingly. You would also have to choose your course carefully if travel can be difficult, because they are scattered around London and held in a variety of adult education institutes and other venues. Many courses are organised in association with the **Workers' Educational Association**. (See also the section on short residential courses, p. 404.)

Further information is available from the **University of London, Department of Extra-Mural Studies**. Prospectus requests can be made during out-of-office hours by calling ☎ 01-636 9720.

Open University

Degree courses

If gaining an academic qualification is what you want then the Open University or 'University of the Air' is more likely to be the answer to your needs.

Since it was founded in 1971 thousands of retired people have enrolled on to its courses and every year about 150 retired people gain degrees for their work. At any one time there are about 65,000 men and women undertaking some form of Open University course.

Qualifications You do not need any academic qualifications, not even GCE 'O' levels or CSE grades. No matter what course you choose to take at the OU any present lack of qualifications will be ignored.

Course requirements Undergraduate courses run from February to October each year during which time you will be required to put in between 12 and 14 hours' work a week. This will include reading set texts, watching and listening to broadcasts, carrying out experiments and exercises, and submitting regular assignments to your personal tutor for marking and comment. At the end of each successfully completed year you will earn a 'credit'. You need six credits to gain the BA degree and eight for a BA Honours degree.

Enrolling You must apply for enrolment by the end of September of the preceding year *at the latest*. However, due to the increasing popularity of some courses there may be a waiting list of over one year.

Non-degree courses
Not everyone enrols with the OU for the sake of earning a degree. There are also updating courses for science and industry, management education courses and 'family, community and personal interest' courses which have proved attractive to older students. Examples of the personal interest subjects that are currently available and for which no previous qualifications or previous knowledge are required are given below:

- Looking into paintings
- Health choices
- W.B. Yeats
- Introduction to Hinduism
- Start your own business

- Introduction to economics
- Healthy eating
- James Joyce
- Rise of Christianity
- The changing countryside

- Planning retirement
- Governing schools
- Introduction to psychology
- Introduction to sociology
- Popular culture

Enrolling If you enrol for one of the personal interest subjects you will probably receive a pack of text material, audio cassettes or records, wall charts and similar material. Enrolment is twice yearly so the most you will have to wait is six months.

Cost The cost of an OU course obviously varies enormously and ranges from £10 for some of the short courses up to about £250 for a full credit course. This is made up of £150 for the course and another £100 for the week-long summer residential school. Payment can be by credit card if you wish. For longer courses fees can be paid in installments. The unemployed, or people on low income, may be eligible for grants or other financial assistance.

Example The *Planning Retirement* course costs £29.95. It covers the cost of a 256–page book supported by an audio cassette and various 'resource materials'. There are also regular, individual, computer-generated reports on your progress and achievements during the course.

Further information If you would like to know more about OU courses you can either write to their Enquiry Office direct, or contact one of their regional offices (listed at the end, on page 449), which will offer advice on courses.

Short residential courses

There is a host of small, sometimes privately owned academic establishments up and down the country which offer short residential courses on a wide range of subjects from financial management to painting, archery to wine appreciation. Here is a sample of some establishments and their courses.

The Earnley Concourse
Earnley Concourse offers two- and four-day courses in a wide range of arts and crafts, music, drama and dance, communication skills, literature, keep fit, languages, food and wine, and computer studies which are mostly designed for people with a little previous knowledge.

In 1987, the price of a two-day course is £63.95 plus VAT per person, and four-day courses cost £121.65 plus VAT. Both are inclusive of accommodation and meals.

Edward James Foundation, West Dean College
West Dean College offers weekend, five and seven-day courses in arts, crafts and music. The charges in 1987 are £74.50 per person for weekends, £174 for five days and £243.50 for seven days. All prices are inclusive of VAT and full board.

Denman College
Owned and operated by the Women's Institute, it is open to members only (although husbands are also welcome) and provides more than

200 courses to about 3000 students a year. Courses normally run from Monday to Friday, or over weekends. Subjects covered are wide-ranging, including public speaking, various forms of cookery, needlework, various art and craft subjects, self-defence, the countryside, health care, calligraphy and understanding the weather.

Charges for 1987 are £29 per day for a shared room (£4 supplement for single rooms) and £65 for husband and wife. Prices are inclusive of full board and VAT.

Field Studies Council

Many subjects are covered in the Council's programme of educational courses which are held at one of the ten field centres, each set in beautiful surroundings. The programme includes: general interest; natural history; ecology and conservation; flowers and other plants; birds and other animals; geology; landscape and climate; archaeology; history and architecture; painting and drawing; photography and crafts. Many of the courses are for beginners, for example:
- Painting for pleasure (1 week, £133) at the Drapers Field Centre, Betws-y-Coed
- Orchids in South-East England (5 days, £105) at Juniper Hall, Dorking
- A weekend fungus foray at the Leonard Wills Centre in Taunton (3 days, £55)
- A beginner's guide to marine biology for divers (1 week, £149) at Orielton, Dyfed.

Other subjects include heraldry, insects, waterways, calligraphy and ferns. Expeditions abroad are also organised, e.g. to France, Spain, Nepal and New Zealand.

Main courses, which are usually one week, and short courses of 2–3 days vary from £55 to £185. Those attending courses are expected to be members or to belong to an institute which is a corporate subscriber. Membership is £3, but it can be deducted from the fees of the Course. Further information is available from the membership office, while the **Flatford Mill Field Centre** deals with overseas programmes.

The University of Stirling

The University holds summer schools in the beautiful setting of Airthrey Castle which is situated on the campus. Courses are for one or two weeks and subjects include hand and machine knitting, hand spinning, tapestry weaving, tracing your ancestors, Scottish wildlife, Scottish gardening, bagpipes, accordion, handwriting, folk dancing, Scottish culinary tradition and the traditional fiddle.

Prices include tuition, meals and accommodation and are about £150 a week. Contact the Director of Continuing Education.

Further information
A comprehensive list of residential courses is available in *Residential Short Courses* published by the **National Institute of Adult Continuing Education**. This is published in January and August each year.

Correspondence courses

National Extension College
This is a non-profit making organisation which offers a comprehensive range of subjects for study by correspondence. Among nearly 100 topics are a wide range of studies for GCE 'O' and 'A' level examinations, preparatory courses for the Open University, computer courses, business and professional courses, and four leisure courses: birds and birdwatching; making a garden; the lawn; successful playwriting.

Courses include a mixture of written and taped material; you have a personal tutor. If you fail a GCE course examination you will get free additional tuition until you pass (or presumably until you give up in despair).

Costs of typical GCE courses are about £65 for 'O' level, and about £80 for an 'A' level, while the two gardening courses are £25 each. Further details and an enrolment form may be obtained by writing to the NEC (see p. 451).

There is a wide range of other (mostly profit-making) organisations offering correspondence courses. To make sure you get a course from a *bona fide* company write first to the **Council for the Accreditation of Correspondence Colleges** who will give you a list of member colleges that teach any subject which interests you.

Local network organisations

National Adult School Organisation
This was founded in 1798 in Nottingham by a Quaker and a Methodist who were moved by the plight of working people handicapped by illiteracy. They set up the first adult schools to teach reading and writing. Although there is a strong religious background to NASO, it is a non-sectarian non-political organisation with the motto 'Friendship through study'. The three keys which make up its symbol stand for Friendship, Knowledge and Understanding.

The Organisation has a national headquarters and county unions, but it is the small local groups which are its backbone. There are now about 120 of these. Members may meet in each other's homes if the groups are small or in community centres if larger. Discussions are based on an annual study book with background material on a range of topics. The 1987 study theme was 'Security' and discussions ranged from self defence to financial security, from international diplomatic relations to the Inca Civilisation.

Membership fees are variable depending on local needs (e.g. hire of a hall, etc.) but are not likely to exceed £6 a year. Meetings take place on a weekly or fortnightly basis throughout the year. It has a strong appeal to older people and many members are at or approaching retirement.

University of the Third Age

Commonly known as U3A, it is a development of the French idea, Université du Troisième Age. In Britain it has developed as a co-operative idea in which members who may be retired, redundant or unemployed, learn from each other, organising talks and study groups on a varied range of subjects. There were 130 groups around Great Britain at the start of 1986, and the idea is catching on fast. There is no national organising body as such; each group is started by the initiative of local people who want to work together.

Further information is available from the Executive Secretary of **U3A**. On sending a 6 × 10 inch s.a.e., you will receive a list of local organisations or advice on how to establish a group of your own. There is a practical pack designed to guide groups and individuals who want to set up a local U3A called *U3A DIY*.

Workers' Educational Association

This association organises talks and demonstrations on a wide range of subjects in most parts of the country. They are mostly evening classes but some full-time and part-time courses are also available. For details of the subjects available locally it is best to look up the WEA in the local phonebook under *Workers Educational Association*, or contact the national headquarters (see p. 451).

The library

In your pursuit of further education never forget the local library which has enormous resources to find text material for you at no cost. The majority of library staff go out of their way to find material for people embarked on special educational projects.

Quite apart from the range of books they stock on the premises they have access to works which may be held only by larger county or city libraries. These take a little longer to arrive, but arrive they will. All libraries have extensive reference sections and it is worthwhile spending an afternoon browsing through one to find out just what is available.

HOBBIES

The range of hobby activities is vast including sailing, golf, chess and stamp collecting. The cost will depend on your choice. To help you in this a number of interests have been listed giving likely cost and sources for further information.

Index

Academic interests 410
  Astronomy 410
  Geneaology 410
The Arts 411
  Fine arts 411
  Music 412
  Photography 412
  Poetry 412
  Theatre 413
Collecting 414
  Antiques 414
  Coins 414
  Militaria 414
  Model aircraft 415
  Stamps 415
Conservation 415
  Civic planning 415
  Heritage 416
  Rural conservation 417
  Fauna and flora 418
  General ecology 423
Cookery 423
Crafts 425
  General information 425
  Basketmaking 425
  Brass rubbing 425

Calligraphy 426
Flower arranging 426
Needlecraft 426
Weaving/spinning 428
Folk dancing 428
Gardening 428
Indoor games 430
  Bridge 430
  Chess 430
  Jigsaws 430
  Scrabble 430
Keep fit 431
  Movement and music 431
  Yoga 432
Pets 432
  Cats 432
  Dogs 433
Radio hams 434
Railways 434
Outdoor pursuits 435
  Archaeology 435
  Bee-keeping 436
  Rambling 437
  Treasure hunting 438
Sport 439
  General organisations 439

Angling 441
Archery 441
Athletics 442
Badminton 443
Bowling 443
Cycling 444
Golf 444

Shooting 446
Swimming 447
Table tennis 448
Tennis 448
Yachting/Sailing 448
Winemaking 449
Women's Organisations 450

Directory

Academic interests

ASTRONOMY

The complex working of the solar system and the movement of the stars and planets have long held a fascination for man. Many constellations can be seen with the naked eye, but if you do want a telescope at home a 3-inch reflector will cost from £150.

British Astronomical Association
Burlington House, Piccadilly, London W1V 0NL
☎ 01-734 4145
Many societies throughout the country are affiliated to the Association. They welcome new members and beginners. To join costs £21 a year for which you receive an annual handbook detailing the position of the planets throughout the year, six copies of the association's journal. Meetings are held in London every last Wednesday in the month and regularly in the regions.

Further reading *Stargazing: Astronomy without a telescope*, by Patrick Moore (Aurum Press, London).

GENEALOGY

Tracing your family tree can be a fascinating pursuit. You may be able to find out about more recent generations from within the family but when you start the real detective work at the **Registry of Births, Marriages and Deaths** and among ancient parish records you may need some help. The following organisations will give you advice.

The Centre for Heraldic and Genealogical Research
Northgate, Canterbury, Kent CT1 1BA
☎ 0227 462618
The Institute, an educational charitable trust, runs a series of residential courses at Allington Castle, near Maidstone and a correspondence course. It is supported financially by a company called **Achievements Limited** (same address). They provide a research service for anyone who wants a family history compiled professionally and also undertake the production of heraldic art-work. *Family History*, the Institute's journal, is published at least four times a year and is included in the membership fee which is £15 a year plus a £5 enrolment fee.

The Heraldry Society
45 Museum Street, London WC1A 1LH
☎ 01-430 2172
A friendly association mostly staffed by volunteers. Membership £14 a year.

Society of Genealogists
14 Charterhouse Buildings, London EC1M 7BA
☏ 01-251 8799
Members may use the library and receive the quarterly *Genealogists' Magazine* and newsletter from the society, which is also concerned with heraldry. Joining fee £7.50; annual membership £20; country members £14.

Further reading *Debrett's Guide to Tracing Your Ancestry* (Papermac, London).

The Arts

FINE ARTS

Even with a late start it is possible to become an accomplished painter, and if you never become a Grandma Moses, what does it matter? You paint for your own satisfaction. Do not give up if you think your first efforts are a failure. You will improve with practice.

You can buy paints and brushes, and start at home, but it is better to go to an adult education class for lessons, or even take a short course at a summer school. There are so many mediums you can work in that expert advice will help you choose the one most suitable for the style you want. Water colour is perhaps the most popular, but also the most difficult and tuition is advised. Acrylics are probably the easiest medium for beginners.

Courses
Galleon Art Holidays
Units 40 & 41, Temple Farm Industrial Estate, Southend on Sea, Essex SS2 5RZ
☏ 0702 617900
Offers a variety of courses: general painting, watercolour, oils and acrylics for beginners, improvers and experienced artists. Most holidays take place in colleges, although they do use a few hotels. Full board is provided in the colleges and half board in hotels. Prices for one week would be around £200, depending on location.

Sotheby's Works of Art Course
30 Oxford Street, London W1R 1RE
☏ 01-408 1100
A programme of study weeks offers a wide variety of courses. Most take place in London, although they have an exclusive series, the *Buccleuch Studies*, at Boughton House in Northamptonshire and Bowhill in Scotland. Fees are from £395 for 3 days. They also run a conservation week at Arundel Castle. A twelve week decorative arts course costs £1200 plus VAT.

Further reading *Painter's Progress* (*An Art School Year in Twelve Lessons*) edited by Ian Simpson (Allen Lane, London).

(See also 'Back to School', p. 400.)

412 THE MACMILLAN HANDBOOK FOR RETIREMENT

Appreciation

British Association of Friends of Museums
66 The Downs, Altrincham, Cheshire WA14 2QJ
☎ 061-928 4340
Hon. Secretary Mrs R. Marsh
Membership £17. Entitles you to free access to hundreds of museums and galleries, a directory of all those offering discounts to members, a free monthly museums bulletin, and discounts on admission to special exhibitions, publications, seminars and conferences.

The National Association of Decorative and Fine Arts Societies
38 Ebury Street, London SW1W 0LV
☎ 01-730 3041
NADFAS consists of member societies throughout the country whose aim it is to increase enjoyment, knowledge and care of the arts, and to stimulate interest in the preservation of our cultural heritage. The member societies plan a programme of monthly lectures, visits to museums, art galleries, country houses and other places of interest. The list of member societies is available from the secretary.

MUSIC

The Amateur Music Association
Medlock School, Wadeson Road, Manchester M13 9UR
☎ 061-273 3094
The Association covers the whole range of music from classical to rock. Their main membership comprises national organisations, local authorities and music groups, but individuals are welcome. Membership is £5 a year. The Association will give advice and information to non-members and put you in touch with a local music society.

PHOTOGRAPHY

Royal Photographic Society
The Octagon, Milsom Street, Bath BA1 1DN
☎ 0225 62841
Sponsors meetings, lectures, conferences and exhibitions. Membership is open to amateurs and professionals and costs £38 a year, plus an enrolment fee of

£10. Over 65 years, £23. Regional groups organise their own workshops, field days and other activities. Photography is not a cheap hobby. A good camera can cost well over £100. To set up your own dark room for basic black and white developing and enlarging will cost from £150.

POETRY

The Poetry Society
21 Earls Court Square, London SW5 9DE
☏ 01-373 7861
For those who enjoy either writing, reading or listening to poetry. London members £14; out of town members £11; retired £10. The society holds many events in London and members receive a quarterly magazine, *Poetry Review*, and newsletter as well as an events leaflet and discounts on admission to various literature festivals and half price admission to the society's own events.

THEATRE

There is enormous pleasure to be had from amateur dramatics at any age and you are almost certain to find a local group. Even if acting does not appeal to you, such groups are always on the look out for people to take an active backstage part be it in stage management, lighting, making and painting scenery, prompting or taking bookings. Many women find great satisfaction in making the costumes, particularly those requiring historical accuracy.

As well as a local drama group you will probably find a local operatic group and perhaps an old time music hall society so the range of opportunities is wide. Many of the music hall societies have smaller groups who spend much of the winter months taking short shows to entertain the elderly in hospitals and homes, and you may derive much satisfaction from joining them. Your local library will probably be able to put you in touch with local secretaries.

British Theatre Association
Regent's College, Inner Circle, Regent's Park, London NW1 4NW
☏ 01-935 2571
This gives advice on setting up an amateur theatre group and there are training courses for professionals and amateurs. There is a loan scheme for play sets and members have access to the association's library. Visits to plays in and around London are organised and discounts are available on the purchases of records, tapes and theatrical supplies. Membership £25 a year, £12.50 (retired).

Society of West End Theatres
Bedford Chambers, Covent Garden, London WC2E 8HQ
☏ 01-836 0971
The society runs a scheme for admission to West End theatre matinée performances at reduced prices for the retired. Write for an application form enclosing a stamped, addressed envelope.

Collecting

ANTIQUES

The Antique Collectors Club
5 Church Street, Woodbridge, Suffolk IP12 1DS
☎ 03943 5501
Weekend seminars and an annual ceramic conference are among the events organised by the club which has more than 70 autonomous regional clubs. Members bring items to be authenticated. Annual subscription is £14.95 and members receive monthly, except in August, the full colour magazine *Antique Collecting*. Most issues contain articles on antiques priced under £10. Dealers pay to advertise, but private owners of antiques may advertise them free of charge.

COINS

British Association of Numismatic Societies
Department of Numismatics, Manchester Museum, The University,
Oxford Road, Manchester M13 9PL
☎ 061-273 3333 ext 3125
Co-ordinates the activities of local societies and specialises in coins relating to the British Isles. For your nearest branch write enclosing an s.a.e.

Royal Numismatic Society
c/o British Museum, Great Russell Street, London WC1B 3DG
☎ 01-636 1555
A society with about 1000 members throughout the world. Meetings are held in London on all aspects of coins and medals. It publishes the *Numismatic Chronicle*. Annual membership £18.

Seaby Ltd
8 Cavendish Square, London W1M 0AJ
☎ 01-631 3707
Specialist booksellers who specialise in publications on coins and medals.

MILITARIA

British Model Soldier Society
22 Priory Gardens, Hampton, Middlesex TW12 2PZ
☎ 01-979 7137
Covers all aspects of military modelling and is of interest to anyone who collects lead toy soldiers and other figures. The Society runs auctions, and buys

and sell pieces. There is a monthly meeting in London and 28 groups exist throughout the country. Annual subscription, £7. Curator, John Ruddle.

The Miniature Armoured Fighting Vehicle Association
15 Berwick Avenue, Heaton Mersey, Stockport, Cheshire SK4 3AA
☎ 061-432 7574
Although military model collectors form the major sector of the association, many ex-army pals keep in contact and often trace one another through it. They hold branch meetings, but it is mainly a correspondence society. There is a bi-monthly magazine, *Tankette*, which contains articles on tanks, self-propelled guns, armoured cars, trucks, artillery, uniforms and so on.

Occasional meetings are organised in France and Germany and there is an annual get-together. Yearly membership, £4.50. Contact G.E.C. Williams. Please enclose a stamped, addressed envelope.

MODEL AIRCRAFT

Society of Model Aeronautical Engineers
20 Links Road, West Wickham, Kent BR4 0QW
☎ 01-777 5533
This will put you in touch with local groups and organises competitions for model aircraft enthusiasts.

STAMPS

The British Philatelic Bureau
Freepost, Department 87 LAA, 20 Brandon Street, Edinburgh EH3 0HM
☎ 031-556 8661
Set up to help all collectors from beginners to experts. As well as information on British issues, they sell a range of albums, presentation and collectors' packs, and publish *The Bulletin*, a monthly magazine that costs £4 per year.

Conservation

CIVIC PLANNING

Civic Trust
17 Carlton House Terrace, London SW1Y 5AW
☎ 01-930 0914
The Civic Trust works to protect and improve our environment, to help to make sure our children grow up with a heritage of which they can be proud. It has pioneered new techniques for the reclamation of derelict land and planting of semi-mature trees so that urban and rural scars can heal more quickly. There is an excellent library which can usually supply information about matters of urban and planning design.

This is an independent charity supported by voluntary contributions. If there is no local group the Trust will let you have a 'Starting kit' with advice on how to start one. The Trust journal, *Heritage Outlook* is published six times a year and costs £7.

Town and Country Planning Association
17 Carlton House Terrace, London SW1Y 5AS
☎ 01-930 8903
A voluntary body concerned with planning and the environment. It provides an independent voice on issues by means of policy statements, through attendance at public inquiries, periodicals and conferences.

HERITAGE

The Georgian Group
37 Spital Square, London E1 6DY
☎ 01-377 1722
1987 is the fiftieth anniversary of the founding of the group which aims to save Georgian buildings, monuments, parks and gardens.

Membership, £10 a year; life subscription £250. This entitles you to take part in various activities and receive copies of the newsletter and the illustrated annual report.

Historic Houses Association
38 Ebury Street, London SW1W 0LU
☎ 01-730 9419
Members have free entry to some 260 historic houses and gardens, and receive the quarterly magazine *Historic House*. Lectures, concerts and other events are arranged. Membership, £12.50; joint membership, £20. For membership details write, enclosing an s.a.e. to
Spiralla House, Bridge Road, Letchworth, Hertfordshire
☎ 04626 79356

The National Trust
36 Queen Anne's Gate, London SW1H 9AS
☎ 01-222 9251
Founded in 1893, the Trust is a landowning charity. Its properties include 250 historic buildings which are open to the public, but the Trust is not just concerned with preserving historic houses and their contents, it also conserves and preserves gardens and landscaped parks. It owns half a million acres of countryside and miles of unspoilt coastline which is protected for us all to enjoy. Many properties have interesting and beautiful nature walks. They are listed in a free leaflet, *Nature Walks*, which you can get by writing, enclosing a stamped addressed envelope. All the Trust's properties are listed in a book, *Properties of the National Trust*, which is issued free to new members, or costs £1 from the National Trust shops. *Gardens of England and Wales open to the public* is also £1 from the shops or £1.40 by post.

The Trust offers a variety of holiday accommodation ranging from basic lodgings for hikers to a luxuriously furnished 10-bedroom house in Cornwall. A leaflet, *Holiday Cottages*, may be obtained free if you enclose an s.a.e.

The Trust does not receive regular, official funding and relies heavily on private donations. It is also grateful for volunteers to help with conservation work.

Yearly membership, £14.50; for each additional member of the family at the same address, £8.50; life membership, £300; over-60 life membership, £200;

joint life membership, £375; over-60 joint, £275. On joining, you receive a card which provides free admission to the Trust's properties, a guide, a regular colour magazine and a members' handbook. For membership details write to:
The National Trust
Freepost, Beckenham, Kent BR3 4UN

Society for the Protection of Ancient Buildings (SPAB)
37 Spital Square, London E1 6DY
☎ 01-377 1644
Founded by William Morris in 1877 to oppose harmful conjectural restoration of old buildings. The SPAB is a leading authority on the 'how' of repairing and maintaining old buildings, and performs an advisory, campaigning and educational role. Activities include a regular programme of repair courses, lectures and visits aiming to involve members in both the theory and practical problems of repairing and saving old buildings. Life membership, £150; annual membership, £12; associate membership, £5.

Further reading *Buildings of Delight*, Alec Clifton-Taylor edited by Denis Moriarty (Gollancz, London).

RURAL CONSERVATION

Association for the Protection of Rural Scotland
14a Napier Road, Edinburgh EH10 5AY
☎ 031-229 1898

Council for the Protection of Rural Wales
Ty Gwyn, 31 High Street, Welshpool SY21 7JP
☎ 0938 2525

Council for the Protection of Rural England
4 Hobart Place, London SW1 0HY
☎ 01-235 9481

These independent registered charities are the watchdogs for the countryside. They actively promote conservation, from tree planting to 'best kept village' competitions.

Rural Voice
26 Bedford Square, London WC1 3HU
☎ 01-636 4066
A national alliance of nine voluntary organisations, including the **Council for the Protection of Rural England**, concerned with the improvement of the social and economic life of country people.

Common Ground
45 Shelton Street, London WC2H 9HJ
☎ 01-379 3109
Promotes the importance of common animals and plants. Runs various projects with volunteer help.

Council for National Parks
45 Shelton Street, London WC2H 9HJ
☎ 01-240 3603
This national voluntary organisation aims to promote national parks. It has over 30 member organisations who represent voluntary wildlife, recreation and conservation interest in the parks and is supported by the **Friends of National Parks** to which individuals can subscribe.

The Countryside Commission
John Dower House, Crescent Place, Cheltenham GL50 2RA
☎ 0242-521 381
Regional Offices: Birmingham; Bristol; Cambridge; Leeds; London; Manchester; Newcastle-upon-Tyne; Newtown; Powys.

The Countryside Commission for Scotland
Battleby, Redgorton, Perth PH1 3EW
☎ 0738 27921
Both Government agencies are concerned with conservation of the natural beauty of the landscape and with providing facilities for access and recreation in the countryside. They produce a range of publications and leaflets some of which list the designated areas of outstanding beauty and the facilities available. A free catalogue may be obtained by writing, enclosing a stamped, addressed envelope, to:
The Countryside Commission
Publications Department, 19–23 Albert Road, Manchester M19 2EQ

Open Spaces Society
25a Bell Street, Henley-on-Thames RG9 2BA
☎ 0491 573535
Britain's oldest national conservation body, founded in 1865. In its early years it rescued Hampstead Heath, Wimbledon Common and Epping Forest from enclosure. It is concerned with the preservation of common land, village greens, public open spaces, rights of way and footpaths. Publications include booklets on the rights of the public in the countryside. Annual membership, £7 (over sixties, £3.50); life membership, £175 (over sixties, £100).

FAUNA AND FLORA

General
Fauna and Flora Preservation Society
c/o The Zoological Society of London, Regent's Park, London NW1 4RY
☎ 01-586 0872

Founded in 1903, it is the longest established international wildlife conservation society in the world. Members receive a quarterly magazine, *Oryx*. They can attend meetings to hear talks given by well known conservationists and can see excellent wildlife films. Members of the society enjoy access to the Linnean library in London and may take advantage of exclusive sales offers. Leaflets available to the public include: *I Love Bats*; *Don't Squash Me* (hedgehogs), and *Be Kind to Snakes*. Annual membership £15 (pensioner £7). Write for further information enclosing a stamped, addressed envelope.

The Royal Society for Nature Conservation
The Green, Nettleham, Lincoln LN2 2NR
☎ 0522 752326
The RSNC is the national association linking 46 nature conservation trusts. Founded in 1912, it is the major voluntary national body concerned with all aspects of conservation in the UK. The trusts are also active in urban areas, creating wild corners in cities and encouraging the decision makers to plan for wildlife. Members can visit reserves, learn more about wildlife and assist as wardens or in the management of reserves. There is a regular newsletter with information about field meetings, lectures and film shows. A colour magazine is published three times a year. Annual membership £4–£12 depending on your part of the country. Write, enclosing an s.a.e. for further details.
Further reading *RSNC Guide to British Wild Flowers*; *RSNC Ecology Wall Charts*; *New RSNC Guide to Butterflies of the British Isles*; *The Macmillan Guide to Britain's Nature Reserves*.

Fauna
The following organisations will give you information and put you in touch with local groups for your particular area of interest if you write enclosing an s.a.e.

The Mammal Society
141 Newmarket Road, Cambridge CB5 8HA
☎ 0223 351870

Institute of Biology
20 Queensbury Place, London SW7 2DZ
☎ 01-581 8333

Zoological Society of London
Zoological Gardens, Regents Park, London NW1 4RY
☎ 01-722 3333

Nature Conservancy Council
Northminster House, Peterborough PE1 1VA
☎ 0733 40345

Birds Bird watching is a hobby that can be enjoyed all the year round. It can take you to far away places or no further than the kitchen window. You do not need any equipment until you take it seriously; then a pair of binoculars will prove a good investment. A good book with illustrations of birds and descriptions of their habitats is also invaluable and you should carry a notebook to make field sketches and records. Amateurs can, and do, make a contribution to the knowledge of bird behaviour and distribution. The scope for study is wide.

British Trust for Ornithology
Beech Grove, Tring, Hertfordshire HP23 5NR
☎ 04482 3461
The BTO leads the field in research into Britain's bird population, mapping distribution, tracing migration patterns, studying breeding and identifying habitats. It has over 8000 bird watcher members, both amateur and professional, and correlates their reported observations to create an overall picture of Britain's bird life. Annual membership, £10.

The Royal Society for the Protection of Birds
The Lodge, Sandy, Bedfordshire SG19 2DL
☎ 0767 80551
This is Europe's largest voluntary nature conservation organisation. Its activities range from help and information for beginners to highly technical scientific courses and reserve management. The RSPB has also put a lot of resources into protecting nest sites of rare birds and its efforts over the years have saved the great skua, red kite, marsh harrier and bittern from extinction as British breeding birds. It has reserves throughout Britain and Northern Ireland. Many are open to visitors. Membership, £12 a year (pensioner £6); fellow, £20. Members receive a quarterly colour magazine, *Birds*; have free admission to most reserves and are eligible to join a network of members groups.

The Wildfowl Trust
Slimbridge, Gloucestershire GL2 7BT
☎ 045389 333
Sir Peter Scott founded the trust in 1946 and it now has the largest collection of wildfowl in the world. It has had some notable achievements in saving species threatened with extinction. Full membership, £12; retired, £9. Members receive the trust magazine twice a year and may visit the seven centres free of charge, accompanied by a guest.
Further reading *The RSPB Book of British Birds* Macmillan (London) Ltd.

Butterflies Butterflies can be encouraged into your garden by planting to attract them and, if possible, creating a small area of wild garden, including some nettles.

The British Butterfly Conservation Society
Tudor House, Quorn, nr Loughborough, Leicestershire LE12 8AD
☏ 0509 412870

Institute of Terrestrial Ecology
Monkswood Experimental Station, Abbots Ripton, Huntingdon PE17 2LS
☏ 04873 381
This will answer questions about butterflies. Contact Mr E. Pollard.

Wildlife
World Wildlife Fund
Panda House, 11–13 Ockford Road, Godalming, Surrey GU7 1QU
☏ 04868 20551
With every passing year our wildlife and natural resources diminish. Whole species are threatened with extinction: the environment on which they depend for survival is polluted and destroyed. The WWF is fighting to prevent this horrifying loss by raising money to develop and implement practical conservation policies worldwide. Membership £11; retired £5; benefactor £100.

Flora
Botanical Society of the British Isles
c/o The British Museum (Natural History), Cromwell Road, London SW7 5BD
The society maintains a panel of experts willing to answer questions from anyone interested in British flora.

Conservation Association of Botanical Societies
323 Norwood Road, London SE24 9AQ
CABS is the liaison organisation for those national voluntary organisations concerned with the conservation of the flora of the British Isles.

Wild Flowers
The Wild Flower Society
68 Outwoods Road, Loughborough, Leicestershire LE11 3LY
The primary aim is to encourage and develop a love of wild flowers and to promote the study of wild plants in their natural habitat.
 Amateurs and professionals are welcomed. Members have spoken of the pleasure of a developing expertise and of the friendships and shared enthusiasms which can grow from belonging to the society. A magazine is published three times a year.
 Membership £5. For further details, write enclosing stamped, addressed envelope.

South London Botanical Institute
323 Norwood Road, London SE24 9AQ
☎ 01-674 5787
Of value to those interested in wild flowers of Britain and Europe, and to gardeners and horticulturists. Membership £5 annually.

Woodlands
Woodland Trust
Autumn Park, Dysart Road, Grantham, Lincolnshire NG31 6LL
☎ 0476 74297
The **Woodland Trust** is a national charity which safeguards Britain's native woodland by raising money to buy and look after woods that might otherwise be destroyed. It also has an extensive tree planting programme.

Our trees are disappearing faster than they are being replaced. In the last 30 years almost half our ancient woods have vanished and more than 140,000 miles of hedgerows have been grubbed up. Farmers have been encouraged to produce more food and to do this efficiently they use larger machinery which needs more room in which to manoeuvre. So hedgerows make way for bigger fields. Other areas are threatened by the need for buildings and roads.

Joining the trust is a positive step to preserving our landscape for future generations. Members receive a *Woodland Directory* with details of nearly 200 woods across 42 counties, a regular newsletter and a car emblem. Annual membership £5; life membership £100. Write enclosing an s.a.e.

Forestry Commission
231 Corstorphine Road, Edinburgh EH12 7AT
☎ 031-334 0303
The main object of the commission is the efficient production of wood for industry, but it also safeguards woodlands as wildlife habitats and, where practical, improves them. Commission woodlands are open to the public and many offer forest walks, trails, picnic areas, visitor centres and camping grounds. There are also opportunities for fishing, orienteering, pony trekking, hill walking and nature study.

The commission publishes numerous books, leaflets and other forms of specialist advice. Their catalogue is available from:
Publications Section
Alice Holt Lodge, Wrecclesham, Farnham, Surrey GU10 4LH

The following organisations can also provide information. Please enclose a stamped addressed envelope when writing.

The Royal Forestry Society of England, Wales and Northern Ireland
102 High Street, Tring, Herts HP23 4AH

Royal Scottish Forestry Society
1 Rothesay Terrace, Edinburgh EH3 7UP

Northern Ireland Forest Service
PR and Education branch, Department of Agriculture, Dundonald House, Newtonwards Road, Belfast BT4 3NR

Tree Council
35 Belgrave Square, London SW1X 8QN

GENERAL ECOLOGY

The Conservation Society
12a Guildford Street, Chertsey KT16 9BQ
☎ 09328 60975
The **Conservation Society** is a voluntary group founded in 1966 to publicise and combat two global threats: the population explosion and the headlong industrialisation of the earth. Their members include people from all walks of life, from political parties as well as many with no political affiliation. No qualifications are needed for membership, only a concern for the quality of life now and for those who come after us. For more information write, enclosing an s.a.e., to Dr John Davoll. Membership £7.50; over 60 £3; fellow £10 (subscriptions are cheaper when paid by banker's order). Life membership £100.

Friends of the Earth
377 City Road, London EC1 1NA
☎ 01-837 0731
One of Britain's major environmental groups, campaigning on issues such as pollution, wildlife, the countryside, transport and energy. It has 250 local groups and 250,000 members. Family membership £12.50; individual £7.50; un-waged £5.

Greenpeace
36 Graham Street, London N1 8LL
☎ 01-251 3022
A direct-action environmental group which campaigns against nuclear and other pollution in favour of wildlife preservation. They need volunteers for fund-raising in local groups across the country.

Royal Zoological Society
London Zoo, Regent's Park, London NW1 4RY
☎ 01-722 3333
You can become a 'friend' of the zoo for £12 a year. Friends receive regular newsletters and are able to attend talks and receptions as well as having free admission to London Zoo and Whipsnade.

Cookery

Retirement is a time when you can expand culinary skills and experiment, with new recipes and techniques. There are countless books on every cuisine you could think of. Why not try to produce a special meal once a week? Have some wine and try to create an atmosphere. It all adds to the enjoyment.

Eating well does not mean spending a lot. As there will be more time for shopping around, you can select cheaper cuts of meat, and if you are near a 'pick your own' farm, going during the week usually means you get the best of the crop and avoid the weekend hordes. This flexibility gives you the chance to buy fresh fruit and vegetables at reasonable prices in season for freezing, and jam and chutney-making. Elderberries, blackberries, crab apples and sloes take a day to turn into wine. They are free for the taking and can give you a pleasant day out gathering them.

Most adult education institutes run a wide range of cookery courses (see p. 450). Costs vary but on average work out to around 90p an hour, but frequently those receiving State benefits, including pensions, are charged about 20p an hour. Commercially run courses cost a great deal more and vary from afternoon or evening lessons to a 12-week diploma course. Some combine tuition with a holiday. Fees vary considerably, but here are some examples:

The Cordon Bleu Cookery School
114 Marylebone Lane, London W1M 6HH
☏ 01-935 3503
Non-residential. Six afternoon lessons 'Entertaining Cookery', £75–£80
One week intensive, or beginners' course, £210–£220
Four week introductory course, £800–£840

Leith's School of Food and Wine
21 St Alban's Grove, London W8 5BP
☏ 01-229 0177
Non-residential. Beginners' five lesson course (Tuesday evenings), £100–£105
One week 'Entertaining' course, £165–£175
Four week intensive course, £650–£730

Cookery at the Grange
The Grange, Beckington, Bath BA3 6TD
☏ 0373 830607
Residential. Four week course, Basic to Bernaise, £885.50
Five days (Mon–Fri), Food with Flair, for those with some experience, £224.25
Five days (Mon–Fri), Self Preservation, for beginners, £207

Savoy Continental School of Cookery
Crossways, Whalley Road, Padiham, nr Burnley BB12 8JR
☏ 0282 72423
Residential. Weekend gourmet class in kitchens of traditional French restaurant, including lectures, picnic at local beauty spot, champagne reception and meals, £170.

Page & Moy Ltd
136–138 London Road, Leicester LE2 1EN
☏ 0533 552521
Five day gourmet cookery coach holiday in Brittany with classes hosted by a master chef, £139–£159.

Crafts

GENERAL INFORMATION

The Association of British Craftsmen
57 Coombe Bridge Avenue, Stoke Bishop, Bristol BS9 2LT
☎ 0272 686417
The Association publishes a free booklet, *Craft Vacation Weeks*, for those who would like to stay in the home of a craftsman teacher while learning.

The Crafts Council
12 Waterloo Place, London SW1Y 4AU
☎ 01-930 4811
Promotes the work of contemporary artists and craftsmen. The public is welcome to use the enquiry service which offers information on a wide range of subjects, for example, where to buy supplies. There is an extensive library of slides, magazines, video tapes and other reference material on craft subjects. The council maintains an index of craftsmen working in England.

You can find out about full-time and part-time courses on crafts ranging from musical instrument making to textiles, ceramics and jewellery. A magazine called *Crafts*, costs £15 a year on subscription for six issues, and the council also publishes books on craft subjects.
Further reading *Craft Workshops in the English Countryside* (AA in conjunction with CoSIRA)

BASKETMAKING

The Basketmakers' Association
17 Heathcote Grove, Chingford, London E4 6RZ
Hon. Secretary I. Pritchard
As well as basketmaking, the association encompasses caning and rush seating. It runs classes and workshops, holds occasional exhibitions and publishes a quarterly magazine. Membership, open to amateurs and professionals, costs £7 a year, joint membership £10.

BRASS RUBBING

Monumental brass plates, deeply engraved with figures were popular in churches in the Middle Ages and provide a visual record of people, their costume and armour in bygone days. Brass rubbing, to produce attractive wall hangings on waxed paper, was so popular that through sheer enthusiasm many brasses were damaged. Now, most rubbing is done on replicas because many churches, quite sensibly, will no longer allow the originals to be used.

There are a number of brass rubbing centres around the country where you may rub replicas without going to the churches. The biggest is the London centre at Piccadilly which has a variety of replicas. The cost of a rubbing starts at 50p and depends on the size of the figure. The price includes the special waxed paper.

Clark Patterson Ltd
Unit 1–2, Wye Estate, London Road, High Wycombe,
Buckinghamshire HP11 1LH
☎ 0494 444967
This company manufactures the special paper needed for rubbing. It is also the administrator of some brass rubbing centres.

CALLIGRAPHY

A pastime which does not involve a great outlay, all you need is paper, pens and a ruler. With a little patience, good lettering can be learned through observation and practice. Your local library should be able to give you information about local classes.

The Society of Scribes and Illuminators
54 Boileau Road, London SW13 9BL
☎ 01-748 9951
Funded by its members and run by volunteers. Membership, £12 a year. They organise meetings and lectures and publish a journal three times a year. There are self-help groups throughout the country.
Further reading *Learn Lettering – Calligraphy Step by Step*, by Gail and Christopher Lawther (Macdonald & Co, London).

FLOWER ARRANGING

National Association of Flower Arranging Societies of Great Britain
21a Denbigh Street, London SW1V 2HF
☎ 01-828 5145
Can put you in touch with local groups or recommend classes. Many local horticultural associations have flower arranging sections.

NEEDLECRAFT

In all its various forms, needlecraft is a hobby with a gigantic following. Knitting has long been popular and wool sales continue to increase. Embroidery, dress making, soft furnishings, toys, tapestry, macramé, patchwork, quilting and appliqué are all done mostly for pleasure, but make excellent gifts and often become family heirlooms. It is mostly inexpensive although some projects can be costly, for example, you can buy a simple tapestry kit for £3 or £4 but once the bug gets you, larger printed tapestry canvases and wool can cost £100 or more.

The Embroiderer's Guild
Apartment 41, Hampton Court Palace, East Molesey, Surrey KT8 9AU
☎ 01-943 1229
An educational charity founded in 1906 to promote the craft of embroidery. It does this through workshops and lectures held at Hampton Court Palace.
   Membership is open to men and women, beginners and experts, and costs £12.50 per annum (over 60 years, £7.50); life membership £150 (over 60

years, £75). Members receive the guild's quarterly magazine, *Embroidery*, which is supplemented by newsletters.

Affiliated branches have their own subscription rates and the name and address of branch secretaries may be obtained from the guild.

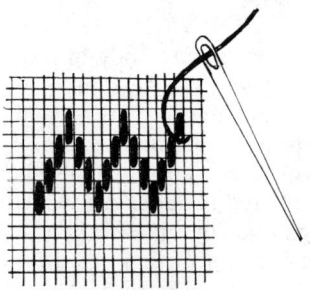

The Edinburgh Knitting and Crochet Guild
9 Lennie Cottages, Craigs Road, Edinburgh EH12 0BB
☏ 031-339 5350
Hon. Secretary Julie Matthews
The Guild organises practical workshops on subjects related to hand knitting, machine knitting and crochet, and exhibitions where members are invited to show their work. It publishes a magazine, *Hook & Needle*. Write, enclosing a stamped, addressed envelope for membership details.

The Lace Guild
The Hollies, 53 Audnam, Stourbridge, West Midlands DY8 4AE
☏ 0384 390739
The Guild, although founded in 1976, sprang from a group of enthusiasts who met at a 'Lace-in' in the small village of Elstow, Bedfordshire in 1975. 'Lace-ins' abound where lacemakers meet to discuss problems and to listen to lectures. Suppliers find it worthwhile to attend and sell. Teachers' conferences and weekend and midweek courses are held in many areas. Write for further information, enclosing a stamped addressed envelope.

Quilters' Guild
56 Wilcot Road, Pewsey, Wiltshire SN9 5EL
☏ 067-26 3230
The Quilters' Guild has an international membership and is open to those interested in patchwork, appliqué, quilting or quilts. They have a network of regional groups and members receive a quarterly magazine, opportunities to attend workshops, visit museums and to use the library. They may also submit work for selection for the Guild's national exhibition. For further details write, enclosing a stamped, addressed envelope to the Guild's secretary, Margaret Petit.

Further reading
Complete Guide to Needlework (Readers' Digest) £14.95 – covers 10 subjects. *Have you any wool?* by Jan Messent (Search Press). *In Stitches* by Una Stubbs (Ward Lock, London). *A Treasury of Embroidery Designs* by Gill Speirs and Sigrid Quemby (Bell & Hyman, London). *Made to Treasure* edited by Kit Pyman (Search Press).

WEAVING/SPINNING

The Association of Guilds of Weavers, Spinners and Dyers
3 Gillsland Road, Edinburgh EH10 5BW
☏ 031-337 3984
Hon. Secretary Isabella Ricketts
The Association is the co-ordinating body of more than 90 affiliated guilds throughout the country. There are also guilds overseas. Their object is to preserve and improve craftsmenship in weaving, spinning and dyeing. Amateurs and professionals are welcome to join.

The guild publishes a quarterly journal. It also holds summer schools every other year and courses offered include: rug weaving; tapestry; Ikat weaving with silks; fashion design and cut; creative hand-knitting and machine knitting. Write enclosing an s.a.e. for further details.

Folk dancing
Dancing is a pleasant way to keep fit and, of course, is a sociable activity. Afternoon tea dances seem to be regaining popularity and many local institutes run dance classes where people of all ages meet and mix happily. Your library will know about any local dance clubs.

English Folk Dance and Song Society
Cecil Sharp House, 2 Regent's Park Road, London NW1 7AY
☏ 01-485 2206
The society holds dances and festivals in London and throughout the country. Membership £12 a year, retired £6. Members have free use of the library, a yearly journal and a magazine *English Song and Dance* (six issues a year).

Royal Scottish Country Dance Society
12 Coates Crescent, Edinburgh EH3 7AF
☏ 031-225 3854
Branches and groups all over the world are affiliated and members pay £3 a year for which they receive the annual bulletin and a book of dances.

Gardening
If there is such a thing as the perfect hobby, gardening must surely be the main contender for the title. It is such an adaptable hobby. No matter how grand or modest a scale of gardening you want to tackle there will be interest (and work) aplenty. No matter how limited or deep your pocket there is a branch of gardening which will suit you. Even if you have no garden at all there is such a range of plants available for indoor cultivation that you need not miss out. Whether we like it or not, most of us have to be gardeners of a sort during our working lives even if it is limited to running the mower over a handkerchief-sized lawn once a week at weekends – weather permitting.

We may very well start our gardening lives with little real interest. Early on the garden may be seen as nothing more inspiring than a play area for the children and the animals. Later as the children grow up we begin to take more pride in its appearance, introducing flowers and vegetables, until by the time retirement is on the horizon we may already be well on the way to becoming enthusiasts.

It's a short step from there to becoming really involved in your garden which opens up all manner of possibilities – clubs and societies to join both at national and local level; new plants to grow; new techniques to try out.

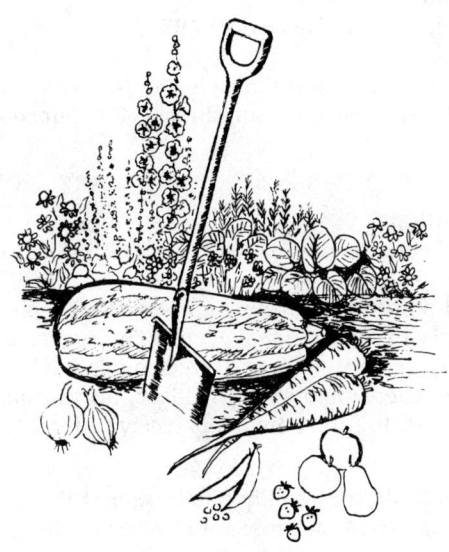

Join your local horicultural society and the
Royal Horticultural Society
80 Vincent Square, London SW1P 2PE
☏ 01–834 4333
Membership for one person costs £14 a year which entitles you to a monthly copy of the RHS journal, *The Garden*; entry for one to Chelsea Flower Show on any day including the private view day. It also entitles you to one further ticket for one of the public days, entry for three to the RHS gardens at Wisley. Free entry for one of the many RHS shows in London usually at the Royal Horticultural Halls in Vincent Square. If you wish, you can buy a double membership ticket for £24 which enables two people to go to Chelsea on private view day, provides two tickets for public days and enables you to take a party of six people to Wisley.

Further reading *The Garden Book* by John Brookes; *Decorative Trees for Country, Town and Garden* by Alan Mitchell and John Jobling; *Conifers for Your Garden* by Adrian Bloom; *In Your Greenhouse* by Percy Thrower; *The Vegetable Expert* Dr D. G. Hessayon. (There are several other *Expert* books including those on flowers, trees and shrubs, houseplants, roses, lawns and others. They are invaluable.) The **Royal Horticultural Society** also publish many useful pamphlets.

Indoor games

Card and board games need no more physical energy than the throwing of a dice, the laying of a card or the moving of a counter. There is usually an element of luck but most board and card games leave scope for skilful play.

BRIDGE

English Bridge Union
15b High Street, Thame, Oxfordshire OX9 2BZ
☏ 08442 2221
For an annual fee of £7, members are eligible to enter for all the English national championships. Write, enclosing an s.a.e. for your county association.

CHESS

British Chess Federation
9a Grand Parade, St Leonards-on-Sea, East Sussex TN38 0DD
☏ 042444 2500
The BCF is the focal point for managing and developing chess activities and represents this country in international events. They welcome new members and there are two ways to join, either as a direct member which can cost £20 or by joining a local club where membership fees vary but normally include £2.20 registration fee to the BCF. Direct members receive a free Year Book and are listed in it.

Further reading *Newsflash*, the weekly publication of the BCF costs £12 per annum; *British Chess Magazine*, monthly at £15.60 a year from 9 Market Street, St Leonards-on-Sea, East Sussex TN38 0DQ.

JIGSAWS

British Jigsaw Puzzle Library
Old Homend, Streeton Grandison, Ledbury, Hereford HR8 2TW
☏ 0531 83462
This is a postal lending library. Subscriptions are £21 for three months, £32 for six months and £48 a year. Postal charges are extra. The puzzles, which do not come with guide pictures, are wooden and vary in difficulty.

SCRABBLE

Scrabble Club Co-ordinator
42 Elthiron Road, London SW6 4BW
☏ 01-731 2631
There are clubs all over the country, some have their own premises, some meet in halls and others in members' homes. Some clubs are run by semi-retired and retired people who, the co-ordinator Leonard Hodges says, make excellent organisers.

'Evergreen' scrabble clubs are for the over 60s and members often visit disabled or housebound people for a game. Write, enclosing an s.a.e. for the address of your nearest club.

Keep fit

MOVEMENT AND MUSIC

Mixing keep fit with music is a pleasant way to exercise and in most towns and villages you will find movement and music classes. This kind of activity has been well tested and proven. It reduces tensions, gives enjoyment and keeps you fit, trim and healthy.

Women's League of Health and Beauty
18 Charing Cross Road, London WC2H 0HR
☏ 01-240 8456

Mrs Bagot Stack, a pioneer of physical education for women, founded the league in 1930. It has now grown with centres throughout Britain and overseas. Non-profit making, it receives a small annual grant towards administration costs from the Sports Council.

Classes are held in centres around Britain and teachers are all intensively trained. The rhythmic health exercises devised by Mrs Stack have since been expanded and developed for modern needs, and this long before aerobics and Jane Fonda were heard of! Women of all ages are welcome. You can start at 70 plus if you wish. Classes are usually held in the evenings but some are available during the day.

New membership costs £3; annual renewals £2.50. Classes cost from £1 a session according to the time of day and size of class. Exercises are graded to suit capabilities.

Retirement and disabled classes

Retirement and disabled classes, as well as general classes, are also organised by some local education authorities using the league's instructors. Information about these and private classes, will be supplied if you write to the league enclosing a stamped, addressed envelope.

The league, in association with **Extend** (see below), have produced a booklet with information and line drawings on how to follow the Bagot Stack system of exercises, adapted specifically for older people. It costs 50p plus a large, stamped envelope, from either organisation.

Extend
3 The Boulevard, Sheringham, Norfolk NR26 8LJ
☏ 0263 822479

Extend is a registered charity associated with the **Women's League of Health and Beauty**. It was founded by Penny Copple, a state registered nurse and a League teacher because she was concerned about the large number of elderly, frail people who sat inert all day, deteriorating through a lack of interest and exercise. She has set up a network of classes throughout the country, the aim being to improve the quality of life through graded recreational movement to music. As well as in clubs, classes take place in hospitals, day centres, and residential homes.

The set exercise routines can help everyone and booklets (75p each) or musical cassette tapes (£3.75) are available from Extend.

They are constantly looking for potential teachers, both men and women. If you would like more information about any of their activities write, enclosing a stamped addressed envelope to Mrs Copple.

YOGA

Yoga for Health Foundation
Icknell Bury, Northill, nr Biggleswade, Bedfordshire SG18 9EF
☏ 0767 27271

Yoga helps relaxation and improves fitness and may be taken up in later life. Many begin at 50-plus. The foundation has more than 70 clubs and runs residential courses at its centre. Some programmes are directed towards alleviating specific problems such as stress and backache. Weekend courses cost £48.50 including board and lodging; a week costs £168. Membership, £6 a year, for a quarterly magazine *Yoga for Fitness* and a monthly newsletter.

Pets

Probably there is no better time of life than retirement for keeping a pet because, relieved of the pressures and demands of work, we are able to discharge the responsibilities and fulfil the obligations that animal ownership entails. The loyal companionship they provide is comforting, particularly to those of us who live alone.

Choose your pet carefully, always having regard to your ability to care for it properly. Dogs and cats are the most popular pets, but not everyone lives in a home suitable for keeping them – flat dwellers, who have no garden and are covered by tenancy restrictions, for example. However, there is rarely a difficulty in keeping a budgerigar, feathered extroverts who love human company. I doubt that hamsters, gerbils, rats and mice would cause problems in a flat – unless you allowed them to escape! But always check your tenancy agreement first.

Always find out as much as you can about the pet you think you would like in advance. Libraries are well stocked with books on almost every type of animal and breed. The **PDSA** (see p. 373) has a series of useful leaflets free if you send a large s.a.e.

CATS

Cats may have a reputation for independence, but they still need, and give, affection. They also need grooming and if you start when they are kittens they will grow to enjoy it. Obviously they are not so demanding as dogs. You do not have to walk them and you can go away, leaving them at home where they will probably be much happier, provided you have arranged for someone to feed and keep an eye on them.

However, they can, in some respects, be more troublesome than dogs by scratching furniture and upholstery, leaping on to tables and other surfaces – often in pursuit of attractive smelling food. So do not leave food about, or if you have to, make sure it is adequately covered.

It is best to have cats neutered unless, of course, you wish to breed from them. Females can be a nuisance when 'calling' and an even greater nuisance when they produce a litter of kittens for which you have to find homes. Un-neutered males will continue to spray and make unpleasant odours to mark their territory and they are also more aggressive – which may disturb relations with your neighbours.

Cats Protection League
17 Kings Road, Horsham, West Sussex RH13 5PP
☏ 0403 65566
The League will find you a kitten if you can provide a good home for it. They will want to visit to ensure this. There is no charge, but the League is grateful for a donation, no matter how small. There are eight animal shelters and 150 local groups. Members pay £5 a year and for this receive six issues of the magazine, *The Cat*.

The Governing Council of the Cat Fancy
4–6 Penel Orlieu, Bridgwater TA6 3PG
☏ 0278 427575
An organisation for the show enthusiast and breeder.
Further Reading *Cat World*, a monthly magazine which carries an updated breeders directory in every issue.

DOGS

Apart from being the most companionable of animals, a dog's need for exercise encourages its owner to keep fit by taking a twice daily walk. The friendliest dog adds to the security of a home, even if its bark at strangers is one of welcome.

Cautions
There is no point in buying a large breed of dog unless you are able to give it adequate exercise and can afford to feed it properly. You must also face the fact that a dog may live an active life of 12 or 14 years or more. If you buy it as a puppy when in your sixties, it will still need exercise when you are well into your seventies. Another consideration is, if you are active and spend a lot of time away from home on holidays, weekend breaks and so on, the dog will have to go into kennels, which can be costly, unless you have friends willing to care for it.

All dogs, but especially the long-haired types, need regular grooming with brush and comb, and the occasional bath. Some require regular nail clipping, but if you intend to do this yourself, get an expert to show you how, and buy the correct clippers.

Always remember that, as an owner, you also owe a responsibility to other people for the behaviour of your dog, otherwise you could become quite unpopular. Kerb training and obedience on the lead, so that walking does not develop into a tug-of-war rather than pleasant exercise, should be a priority from the outset. However obedient your dog, it is never wise to walk it in the streets when not on a lead. Instinct can be more compelling than training when it spots a cat on the other side of the road and you could not only lose your dog but also be responsible for a nasty accident.

The Kennel Club
1 Clarges Street, London W1Y 8AB
☎ 01-493 6651
They publish, *Kennel Gazette* monthly at 65p.

Radio hams

Radio Society of Great Britain
Alma House, Cranborne Road, Potters Bar, Hertfordshire EN6 3JE
☎ 0707 59015
Offers advice on how to join amateur radio operators' organisations throughout the world. Membership fees vary. Write, enclosing a stamped, addressed envelope, for details.

Railways

In the days of steam most young lads' ambition was to drive a train. Although the great steam engines no longer thunder along British Rail's tracks, a large band of *aficionados* keep these magnificent engines alive and running.

Association of Railway Preservation Societies
3 Orchard Close, Watford, Herts WD1 3DU
Contact Douglas Whittle
The Association supplies a free leaflet listing steam railway preservation sites and centres throughout Britain. Please send an s.a.e.

The Locomotive Club of Great Britain
8 Lovatt Close, Edgware, Middx HA8 9XG
Members are supplied with 10 issues of the Club's magazine bulletin. It contains reports of tours and special visits here and overseas. From time to time the club arranges special train trips, visits to interesting lines and industrial railways. There is an annual photographic competition and many members are accomplished photographers.

The club organises visits to Austria, Belgium, France, Finland, West Germany, Holland, Italy, New Zealand, Switzerland and the USA. Local clubs hold regular meetings and a selection of publications, books and postcards are available through the club's sales department. Membership £7 a year. For further details write enclosing an s.a.e.

The Railway Correspondence and Travel Society
T. J. Edgington, Membership Secretary, 20 Baker Street, York YO3 7AX
The society is a non-profit making self-supporting organisation. It offers railway enthusiasts the opportunity to study various aspects of railway history, operation and development. There are about 30 centres and regular meetings are arranged, mainly between September and June. Membership costs £8.50 a year and there is a monthly magazine, *The Railway Observer*. Life membership is available to members over 50. Write enclosing an s.a.e. for more details.

Museums
The **National Museum of Steam** is at York and houses several famous locomotives, but one of the best 'working' steam museums is at Bressingham Gardens, near Diss in Suffolk (☎ 0379 88464). It opens on Sundays and Thursdays through most of the summer months and also Bank Holidays. Gardeners who are also steam enthusiasts will be in their element.

Further reading *Railway Magazine*, monthly (Prospect magazines, Cheam).

Outdoor pursuits

ARCHAEOLOGY

To play a part in the work of the experts who put together bits and pieces of the past in an intricate jigsaw that creates a picture of our heritage is an absorbing pastime. However, a dig can be exhausting. You could be on your knees in a trench, trowel in hand, for hours on end, so you need stamina and patience. You will probably end up with backache, sore knees and knuckles, but the joy of finding a tangible fragment of history can be so exciting that the discomforts are forgotten.

The Council for British Archaeology
112 Kennington Road, London SE11 6RE
☎ 01-582 0494
This can put you in touch with local societies and does its best to answer any of your queries. Please enclose a stamped addressed envelope. The Council provides liaison at national and regional level between archaeological organisations and the government bodies concerned with the preservation and presentation of ancient monuments and sites.

They publish a series of specialist books, handbooks and material for teachers. A list is available but the beginner would probably find their newspaper of most use and interest. *British Archaeology News* contains information about current events in archaeology, notices of excavations needing voluntary workers, educational courses and so on. The subscription is £7.50 for nine issues a year.

BEE-KEEPING

This is an absorbing hobby and can even be modestly profitable through the sale of surplus honey. But, as with any activity you are taking up for the first time it is wise to find out as much as you can before becoming involved. Your local library will have plenty of books on bee-keeping, but you should also try to talk to an apiarist and, if possible, watch him or her at work. They are generally friendly folk who respond to an interest in their hobby. Get in touch with the local bee-keeping association which may be able to arrange a meeting for you. They will also give you information about any courses that may be run locally.

If you live in town and have a large garden, you may be able to keep bees but have a word with your neighbours first. Most gardeners welcome bees because they are, of course, efficient pollinators.

The following organisations will put you in touch with local groups and supply information about bee-keeping. Please enclose an s.a.e.

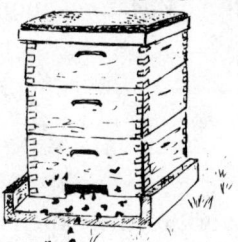

British Bee-keepers' Association
National Agricultural College, Stoneleigh, Kenilworth, Warwickshire CV8 2LZ
☎ 0203 552404

The International Bee Research Association
18 North Road, Cardiff CF1 3DY
☎ 0222 372409
This international association exists to promote the scientific study of bees. Members receive three journals, *Bee World*, *Apicultural Abstracts* and *Journal of Apicultural Research* and may have access to a large library. Annual membership £21.

Ministry of Agriculture, Fisheries and Food
MAFF Publications, Lion House, Willowburn Estate, Alnwick, Northumberland NE66 2PF
This department of the Ministry has a list of useful publications on bees and bee-keeping which they will supply on written request.

RAMBLING

There are over 120,000 miles of public footpaths, bridleways and byways in England and Wales. Most have been preserved or restored by volunteers working with organisations that strive to conserve our countryside (see pp 415–21). There are ten National Parks from 225 to 880 square miles in size which provide opportunities for relaxation and outdoor activities. There are also many designated 'Areas of Outstanding Natural Beauty' which are protected by legislation. Scotland, of course, abounds in beautiful mountain and moorland scenery. However, not all routes for walkers are signposted and there are occasional restrictions during certain seasons.

The best way to see the countryside is on foot and many paths have been joined together to form continuous, long distance trails from 30 to 515 miles in length. There is Offa's Dyke, a 168 mile walk along the great earthwork constructed around AD 800 to mark the frontier between England and Wales; Hadrian's Wall a 70 mile walk; and 85 miles of the Ridgeway Path which passes by many fascinating archaeological remains.

Equipment

Normal clothing and comfortable shoes are satisfactory for short walks but if you take up hiking and rambling seriously, practical clothing is essential. You will often be walking on tracks which are pitted and muddy, in rocky mountainous areas and through tangled woodland. Strong walking boots with good ankle support will cost you around £35 and it is wise to buy them half a size, or one size too large because you may need to wear two pairs of socks, one thin next to the skin for comfort, the other heavy for extra warmth. You should have a weatherproof jacket (£20–£80) with plenty of roomy pockets for your Ordnance Survey map and compass, perhaps a reference book and a notebook and pen. You may also need a rucksack, costing between £6 and £15, for your equipment, food and first aid kit.

Ramblers' Association
1/5 Wandsworth Road, London SW8 2XX
☎ 01-582 6878
Part of its work is the maintenance of footpaths and 250 local groups supply working parties to keep them clear, build stiles and put up signposts and waymarks. Membership £8.50 (joint £10.60); retired persons £4.25 (joint £5.30); life membership £298. Most groups run social events and walks and membership secures a free copy of *The Rambler's Yearbook* which contains 2300 bed and breakfast addresses where walkers are welcome. Also available is use of the Association's Ordnance Survey map library and information about clothes and equipment and discounts obtainable in more than 100 shops.

Further reading *Walking the Dales*, by Mike Harding (Michael Joseph); *Walkers' Britain 2* (Pan Books/Ordnance Survey); *Classic Walks*, by Ken Wilson and Richard Gilbert (Diadem).
Free guides *Walking in Britain* (British Tourist Authority) *See Your Forests, Scotland* (Forestry Commission) – see p. 422 for addresses.

[See also Cycling, p. 442].

TREASURE HUNTING

For around £50 you can equip yourself with an electronic detector and join the small army of hopefuls who sweep across the country at weekends like a battalion of sappers searching for war time land mines. The joy is perhaps more in the anticipation than the realisation although some important finds have been made.

More often than not, electronic 'discoveries' turn out to be bottle tops or buttons, but if you are among the fortunate the excitement of finding out about the age and historical significance of your find equals the thrill of making it.

Treasure hunting is basically a solitary hobby and many detectors prefer to be loners. However, others like to discuss their finds in the company of like-minded folk. Occasionally, detectors can help the police and farmers who lose equipment. They have even helped to trace electric cables under the floor of a church, saving the expense of digging them up. There is a code of conduct which you should always follow.

- Do not trespass and always ask permission when venturing on to private land
- Respect the Country Code
- Do not leave an unsightly mess. Take your rubbish home
- If you discover live ammunition or any lethal object, do not touch it. Mark the site carefully and report it to the police
- Report all unusual historical finds to the local museum
- If you discover a site of archaeological interest, get expert help.

Legal aspects
Make sure you know the law relating to archaeological sites. It is illegal for anyone to use a metal detector on a scheduled ancient monument unless permission has been granted by the **Historic Building and Ancient Monument Commission** in England or the Secretaries of State for Scotland and Wales. You will also need to know the laws of treasure trove. In essence, anything that has been deliberately hidden, however long ago, is treasure trove and will become the property of the Crown should it wish to keep it. However, the finder will be rewarded at market value. Items that have obviously been lost are not usually treasure trove, but it is always wise to check.

Federation of Independent Detectorists
3 Morton Close, Barton Court, Abingdon OX14 3XL
☎ 0235 23640
For those not wishing to join a club, the federation provides legal advice and insurance cover.

National Council for Metal Detecting
105 Bradwell Road, Sandbach, Cheshire CW11 9AN
☎ 0270 761301
There are two levels: the local clubs belong to a county federation and the federations are affiliated to the national council. Each club operates independently and sets its own annual fee. The average is £3–£5 a year. The national council offer public liability insurance cover and help with legal problems. For details about membership and affiliated clubs write to the general secretary, Gerald Costello, enclosing a stamped, addressed envelope.
Further reading *Treasure Hunting* monthly magazine from Sovereign Publications; cost £1.30.

Sport
The approach of retirement may mean you are looking forward to devoting more time to a sport that you already enjoy, thinking of taking one up again, or even trying one for the first time. Libraries and leisure centres are the ideal places to find out about new sporting opportunities. Most sports have governing bodies which will put you in touch with a local club. **The Sports Council**, a government supported body, will also provide information on local facilities.

If yours has been a sedentary life, it is wise to prepare your body with some introductory exercise. It will help to strengthen muscles and make you more supple and mobile. You can either work out a routine or, better still, go to a local club or adult institute class. (See *Health* p. 225 for advice.) If, on the other hand, you have expertise in a sport, you may like to use that in a more official capacity. Your services might be welcome by local clubs in helping with training, serving on the committee, and so on.

GENERAL ORGANISATIONS

The Sports Council
16 Upper Woburn Place, London WC1H 0QP
☎ 01-388 1277
The Sports Council will put you in touch with the governing body of the sport you are interested in, or suggest other ways in which you can become involved. They have regional offices throughout the country.

East Midlands
Covers Derbyshire, Nottinghamshire, Lincolnshire and Leicestershire
☎ 0602 821887

Eastern Region
Bedfordshire, Hertfordshire, Cambridgeshire, Suffolk, Norfolk and Essex
☏ 0234 45222

Greater London and South East
Greater London, Surrey, Kent, East and West Sussex
☏ 01-778 8600

North West
Northumberland, Cumbria, Durham, Cleveland, and Tyne and Wear
☏ 0385 49595

South West
Avon, Cornwall, Devon, Dorset, Somerset, Wiltshire and Gloucestershire
☏ 0460 73491

Southern Region
Hampshire, The Isle of Wight, Berkshire, Buckinghamshire and Oxfordshire
☏ 0734 595616

West Midlands
West Midlands, Hereford, Worcestershire, Shropshire, Staffordshire and Warwickshire
☏ 021-454 3808

Yorkshire and Humberside
West, South and North Yorkshire and Humberside
☏ 0532 436443

Scottish Sports Council
☏ 031 225 8411

Sports Council for Northern Ireland
☏ 0232 661222

Sports Council for Wales
☏ 0222 397571

Central Council of Physical Recreation
Francis House, Francis Street, London SW1P 1DE
☏ 01-828 3163
This embraces some 240 governing bodies of sport and physical recreative activities organised in divisions of games/sport; major spectator sports; outdoor pursuits; water recreation; movement and dance. The CCPR will put you in touch with a local organisation of interest.

Disabled
British Sports Association for the Disabled
Hayward House, Barnard Crescent, Aylesbury, Buckinghamshire HP21 8PP
☏ 0296 27889
This national organisation has ten regional offices.

UK Sports Association for Mentally Handicapped People
Blanche Neville Site, Phillips Lane, London N15 4JB
☎ 01-885 1177
The association will provide information of facilities throughout the country.

ANGLING

Angling is one of Britain's most popular sports with over $3\frac{1}{2}$ million anglers. Water has an hypnotic and soothing effect and angling can be a very relaxing sport (although sea angling can be quite strenuous). There are three disciplines:
- *Coarse* freshwater fishing for non-edible species on rivers, lakes and ponds.
- *Game* catching salmon, trout and sea trout from the bank, from a boat or in the river.
- *Sea* from beaches, the pier or jetties where, if you are lucky the fishing is free, or from boats which go out to sea.

You can write to one of the national organisations for the address of your nearest club, but it is probably easier to call in at your local tackle shop. The Water Authority too, will give you a list of local reservoirs where fishing is allowed and can issue the necessary licence.

The following national bodies can give you advice and information and will put you in touch with local affiliated clubs.

National Anglers Council
11 Cowgate, Peterborough PE1 1LZ
☎ 0733 54084

National Federation of Anglers
Halliday House, 2 Wilson Street, Derby DE1 1PG
☎ 0332 36200
This is the national body governing the three disciplines. They organise national senior championships for coarse angling.

The National Federation of Sea Anglers
26 Downside Crescent, Uckfield, Sussex TN22 10B
☎ 0825 3589

Further reading *Where to Fish*, edited by D. A. Orton (Thomas Harmsworth).

ARCHERY

Bows and arrows have been used since the Stone Age and archaeologists are still digging up ancient flint arrow heads. Modern bows are based on the long bow but styles vary according to the preference of the archer. There are three disciplines:
- Target archery which is shot over a fixed distance with the aim of hitting the gold centre of the concentric rings of the target.

- Field archery does not have fixed-range targets and you aim at pictures of animals or at small special targets set out in woodland areas.
- The crossbow which is used for fixed-target shooting. It is of long standing in Europe and is now gaining in popularity in Great Britain.

Archery can be taken up by both men and women at almost any age, and it is a sport in which the disabled can compete on almost equal terms. If you want to try your hand, clubs offer six introductory lessons and the cost of these is usually taken off your membership fee (about £20 a year) should you decide to continue. They will lend you the initial equipment, which you should never buy without professional advice. Basic equipment will cost around £100. Wear well-fitting but comfortable clothes, not loose garments which could catch in the bow, and sturdy shoes.

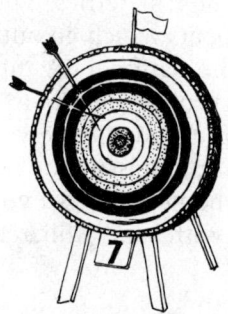

Crossbow Archery Development Association
Dock Meadow Drive, Lanesfield, Wolverhampton WV4 6UD
☎ 0902 47686
The Association produces an informative magazine, *Crossbow Shooting* which costs £7.50 for 6 issues.

Grand National Archery Society
Seventh Street, The National Agricultural Centre, Stoneleigh, Kenilworth, Warwickshire LV8 2LG
☎ 0203 23907

Further reading *The Challenge of Archery* by Don Stamp (A & C Black).

ATHLETICS

The most natural sport – walking, running, jumping and throwing. Though competitive athletics are for the young, older people can and do compete in marathons, provided they are fit, dedicated and not newcomers to long distance running. The **British Athletic Federation** also organises events for the 40-plus age groups and hold area, British, European and world veterans championships.

Amateur Athletics Association
Francis House, Francis Street, London SW1P 1DL
☏ 01-828 9326

British Athletic Federation
159 Marsh Lane, Erdington, Birmingham B12 0LF
☏ 021-382 1195

BADMINTON

Badminton is an indoor game played over a net with two or four players. A lightweight racquet is used costing from £12. Shuttlecocks are around £7 for a box of 12 and feather shuttlecocks about £12 for 12. Many sports and leisure centres have badminton courts, and some adult education institutes run classes for beginners. There are a few private clubs.

Badminton Association
National Badminton Centre, Laughton Lodge, Milton Keynes MK8 9OA
☏ 0908 568822

BOWLING

Indoor and outdoor bowling continue to increase in popularity and, with their weatherproof advantage, there is often a waiting list for membership of indoor clubs. There are well over half a million players of the various codes of bowls and, once a comparatively minority recreation, the game now ranks as a fast developing premier sport.

Some local leisure centres have an indoor bowls facility where the beginner can get a feel for the game. Usually you can hire woods and overshoes. The membership fee for a private indoor club can be anything up to £50. Green fees generally work out at 75p to £1 but vary from club to club. It is often easier to get a game on an outdoor green. The hourly fee is around £1.50 and most clubs will allow you to hire woods and overshoes, and to play a game before you decide whether to become a member. Then you pay a club fee of £2–£3 plus a capitation fee for the five months season that could cost in the region of £40. Unless you are playing in the league or a competition there is no additional green fee.

The woods used for indoor and outdoor games are the same and you would expect to pay anything from £50 to £100 for a set, although you might find some secondhand woods are available if you ask around at the club. Shoes must have flat, smooth soles and above all, be comfortable. They will cost around £20–£30.

The following associations are keen to help beginners and will put you in touch with your nearest club. If you write please enclose a stamped, addressed envelope.

English Bowls Council
15 Datchworth Court, Village Road, Enfield EN1 2DS
☎ 01-367 1269
The council acts as forum for the national associations which control the sport.

British Crown Green Bowling Association
14 Leighton Avenue, Maghull, Liverpool L31 0AH
☎ 051-526 8367

English Bowling Association (Men only)
2a Iddesleigh Road, Bournemouth, Dorset BH3 7JR
☎ 0202 22233

English Bowling Federation
62 Frampton Place, Boston, Lincolnshire PE21 8EL
☎ 0205 66201

English Women's Bowling Federation
18 Thorold Street, Boston, Lincs PE21 6PH
☎ 0205 68729

Indoor Bowling Association
290a Barking Road, London E6 3BA
☎ 01-470 1237

Women's Bowling Association
2 Inghalls Cottages, Ditteridge, Box, Wiltshire SN14 9PP
☎ 0225 742852

CYCLING

This is a cheap method of transport and a way to get good, regular exercise, but many people do not care to compete on the road with four-wheeled vehicles. So it is as a leisure activity that cycling has grown most in popularity, with many organisations creating opportunities for riding over paths and tracks in unspoiled stretches of countryside.

The **Forestry Commission** has created cycle routes away from main highways. Some sections of canal towpaths and disused railway lines are also available to cyclists. **British Rail** will allow you to take your cycle free of charge on many trains, but there are restrictions and charges on some because of limited space, so it is best to plan your route and check in advance. Ask for free leaflet, *The British Rail Guide to Better Biking*, at your local station.

A new bicycle can cost from £150 upwards. Clothing should be comfortable and include a waterproof jacket which can be bought for around £30. Proper cycling shoes cost from £20.

Cyclists Touring Club
69 Meadowrow, Godalming, Surrey GU7 23HS
☎ 04868 7217
Well worth joining for its free legal aid to members, free third party insurance, a competitive cycle insurance scheme, a bi-monthly magazine, technical advice, free touring itineraries (on scenic routes avoiding main roads), shop and mail order facilities, a biennial handbook and the companionship of some 250 local groups. The association also protects cyclists' rights in both town and country. Membership £14 a year.

The following organisations will also give information about cycling facilities. Please enclose a stamped, addressed envelope.

British Waterways Board
Melbury House
Melbury Terrace
London NW1 6JX
☎ 01-262 6711
Contact David Allison,
Leisure Department

Countryside Commission
John Dower House
Crescent Place
Cheltenham GL50 3RA
☎ 0242 521381
Contact Jeremy Worth,
Access Branch

Cycle Campaign Network
Tress House
3 Stamford Street
London SE1 9NT
☎ 01-928 7220
Contact Ian Maxwell

English Tourist Board
4 Grosvenor Gardens
London SW1W 0DU
☎ 01-730 3400

Forestry Commission
231 Corstorphine Road
Edinburgh EH12 7AT
☎ 031-334 0303
Contact Duncan Campbell, Design and Recreation Branch

Railway Path Projects
35 King Street
Bristol BS1 4DZ
☎ 0272 28893
Contact John Grimshaw

Sports Council
16 Upper Woburn Place
London WC1H 0QP
☎ 01-388 1277
Contact John Roberts, Sports Development Unit

GOLF

With most clubs there is no easy route to membership and in the South East it is quite common to have a two-year waiting list. You will probably have to get two members to sponsor your application and may even be vetted by the committee. If you don't know any members you will have to use your ingenuity to get to know some.

Many clubs will offer you weekday membership at first. This means you can play on Monday to Friday only. If you are retired this will probably not be a problem and it is cheaper than full membership. As full members drop out you will be invited to become a full member. Membership fees vary between £50 and £300.

You do not *have* to be a member to play on most courses. You can usually get a game by paying a 'green fee' which, depending on the quality of the course, is likely to be anything from £8 to £15. However, on certain competition days and weekends they may not be taking green fees so it is always wise to phone in advance.

There are also municipally-owned courses where you can usually play without restriction, although they are often very crowded. There are also lots of 'pitch and putt' courses on which you can practise a lot of your short-game work.

Further reading Library shelves are full of books by various golfing stars offering their own tips on how to improve your game. Essential reads when you begin to take your golf seriously are *The Inner Game of Golf* by W. Timothy Gallwey and (for women in particular but men will learn just as much) *The Golfing Mind* by Vivien Saunders.

SHOOTING

Target shooting is fundamentally a mechanical and mental exercise. If you think of taking it up in your fifties, go ahead. Age is no barrier, though you do need reasonable eyesight. Marksmen shoot primarily for pleasure but often go on to enjoy competitive shooting, even if they have no ambition to qualify for county teams. It is not a dangerous sport because it is highly organised and no risks are taken.

Small bore and pistol shooting usually take place indoors at firing ranges over distances of not more than 25 metres. At smallbore and pistol shooting clubs, as well as the club fee you can expect to pay about 50p nightly fee and 50p range fee. Ammunition costs from 30p for 10 rounds. Full bore shooting takes place over ranges of 100–1200 yards outdoors. The target fee is from £2 upwards and ammunition costs from 15p a round.

Instruction is necessary for beginners and most clubs provide this. Those affiliated to the **National Rifle Association** have qualified instructors. Initially you may hire, or borrow, a rifle. They can cost from £50 to £1500 to buy and you must first have a licence which is issued by the police. Gun rack and ammunition cabinets cost from £100.

Membership fees for both full and small bore clubs vary considerably, according to amenities. For example, some have social facilities, others do not. The following associations will give the address of your local clubs, but please enclose a stamped addressed envelope.

Clay Pigeon Shooting Association
107 Epping New Road, Buckhurst Hill, Essex IG9 5TQ
☎ 01-505 6221

The Joint Shooting Committee of Great Britain
Sandroyd Lodge, Green Lane, Cobham, Surrey KT11 2NM
☎ 09326 3120

National Rifle Association
Bisley Camp, Brookwood, Woking GU24 0NP
☎ 04867 2213
There are no facilities for novices at Bisley. Membership is £17.50 a year and members who shoot on the Bisley range pay around £15 a day. They also receive a quarterly magazine.

National Small Bore Rifle Association
Lord Roberts House, Bisley Camp, Brookwood, Woking GU24 0NP
☎ 04867 6969
Annual membership of the Association costs £14 and includes the bi-monthly magazine *Rifleman*.

SWIMMING

Swimming is one of the most highly recommended sports for older people. It is the complete exercise which gently uses all the muscles and stimulates the heart and circulation. You can learn at any age. Your library or town hall will tell you where your nearest public pool is. Many run adult beginners' classes and some give instruction at special times when the pool is closed to the general public. Others run swimming clubs. Once you are able to swim, you can enjoy other sports like sailing, canoeing or angling.

Facilities vary, so obviously you must ask at your own pools. It costs about £1 a session to swim, but again entrance rates vary: some have cheaper rates at certain times or special rates for the retired.

The Amateur Swimming Association
Harold Fern House, Derby Square, Loughborough, Leicestershire LE11 0AL
☎ 0509 230431
The governing body of the sport, it is concerned with national, international and regional competition and will help with individual queries if it can.

TABLE TENNIS

Veterans English Table Tennis Society
53 Solway, Hempstead Park, Hailsham, East Sussex BN27 3HB
☏ 0323 845583
Contact M. D. Watts

VETTS organise five regional single and doubles tournaments each season. Each has events for players in the over 40, over 50, over 60 and over 70 years age groups. Annual membership is £10, or £5 for senior citizens. You will automatically be sent entry forms for the tournaments and receive the society newsletters. Membership is open to men and women players over the age of forty. Obviously a lively lot, the optional entertainment on the evening of the Brighton tournament is a disco!

TENNIS

You will need to be fit and have reasonable eyesight if taking this game up for the first time. Public courts are not expensive (about £1 an hour) though private clubs cost a lot more and often have waiting lists. However, there is obviously a social atmosphere which you will not find on a public court. A racquet of reasonable quality costs around £20; tennis shoes about £16.

Your library, or council recreational department, will tell you where to find your nearest public courts; alternatively the *Yellow Pages* list private, public and indoor courts.

The Lawn Tennis Association
Palliser Road, Barons Court, London W14 9EG
☏ 01-385 2366
The association has an information department which you can use if you have difficulty in finding a court or coach.

YACHTING/SAILING

Royal Yachting Association
Victoria Way, Woking, Surrey GU21 1EQ
☏ 04862 5022
The Association is the national authority for the sport of sailing and can give you information about all aspects of sailing, including boardsailing and about training schemes. Courses are run in centres all over Britain, at independent sailing schools, sailing clubs or educational establishments. By attending a RYA

recognised course you will be taught by experienced instructors in suitable boats with adequate safety backup.

Membership of the RYA costs £8.50 a year. Members receive a quarterly magazine, free booklets and information sheets. Free access to the RYA lounge at the Boat Show, free allocation of sail numbers and special discounts. Write to them for more information.

Winemaking

Grapes have been grown in England since Roman times but almost disappeared in the Middle Ages. However, in recent years commercial vineyards have been planted successfully in England and the wines from them are popular. Some have even been exported to France! Because many new varieties have been bred for our climate it is quite easy to grow your own grapes. They need fairly poor ground, but good drainage. Vines do not like their roots to be disturbed and they need as much sun as possible. Once established, a vine will produce good crops and you never have to feed or water it.

Making wine from your own grapes is a fascinating pastime but requires patience as you wait for it to ferment and mature. If you want quicker results there is much fun to be had from making wine and beer from kits. They produce acceptable results – facsimiles of sauterne, chablis, graves, burgundy, claret and the like. You can even buy port and sherry in concentrated kit forms.

There are a wide range of kits and equipment designed for the home winemaker (and don't forget that you have access to lots of suitable materials for making wines absolutely free of charge in the garden and countryside). Armed with a few demijohns and some basic equipment it is amazing the variety of wines you can make at home, from elderflower to rose, from raspberry to parsnip. You will find a good selection of recipe books at Boots and other shops and you can be guaranteed lots of pleasure both in the making and in the drinking.

Further reading *Home Winemaking*, by Paul and Ann Turner. *The Hamlyn Basic Guide to Winemaking*, edited by Mary Lambert.

Women's organisations

National Association of Women's Clubs
5 Vernon Rise, Kings Cross Road, London WC1X 9EP
☎ 01-837 1434

There are approximately 620 clubs. They are non-political, non-sectarian and open to all women, whatever their ages or interests. Each club is self-governing and activities include various crafts, choral singing, drama, keep fit, lectures and outings to theatres, exhibitions and local industries. Hospital visiting and other community work is encouraged among the members.

National Federation of Women's Institutes
39 Eccleston Street, London SW1W 9NT
☎ 01-730 7212

The WI is the largest women's voluntary organisation in Britain with almost 352,000 members; 9216 institutes grouped into 70 county federations help to co-ordinate the activities of the local groups, suggest speakers, initiate competitions and organise other events. All the groups and county federations are affiliated to the national federation with headquarters in London.

The WI is not a religious organisation nor is it a political society. It holds courses, conferences, social events and many other activities including crafts, music, arts, drama, rural issues, cookery, current affairs, home-making and gardening. Anyone, member or not, can sell home-made produce on WI stalls, if they buy a share in the co-operative at 5p a share. It is a good way of making a profit from your hobby, be it craftmaking, garden produce, jams or chutneys.

The WI has its own adult education college, Denman. Over 200 short courses are run every year and cover a wide range of subjects. See page 404. They also take an active interest in public affairs and have their own magazine. Membership £5.60 a year.

Townswomen's Guilds
75 Harbourne Road, Birmingham B15 3DA
☎ 021-455 6216

There are 2250 guilds in all parts of the UK grouped into 114 federations. The aims of the guild are to enable women of all ages to make the best use of their talents. Meetings help members develop new interests and programmes include drama, music, health and beauty. Membership £5 a year. The magazine *Townswoman* is published 11 times a year and costs 30p an issue, plus 24p post and packing.

USEFUL ADDRESSES

Council for the Accreditation of Correspondence Colleges
27 Marylebone Road
London NW1 5JS
☎ 01-935 5391

Denman College
Marcham
Abingdon
Oxon OX13 6NW
☎ 0865 391219

The Earnley Concourse
Earnley
Chichester
Sussex PO20 7JL
☏ 0243 670392/670326

Edward James Foundation
West Dean College
West Dean
Chichester
West Sussex PO18 0QZ

Field Studies Council
Preston Montford
Montford Bridge
Shrewsbury SY4 1HW
☏ 0743 850674
Membership Office
62 Wilson Street
London EC2A 2BU
☏ 01-247 4651

Flatford Mill Field Centre
East Bergholt
nr Colchester
Essex CO7 6UL
☏ 0206 298283

ILEA Information Centre
County Hall
London SE1 7PB
☏ 01-633 1066

National Adult School Organisation
Norfolk House
Smallbrook Queensway
Birmingham B5 4LJ
☏ 021-643 8297

National Extension College
18 Brooklands Avenue
Cambridge CB2 2HN
☏ 0223 316644

National Institute of Adult Continuing Education
19b De Montford Street
Leicester LE1 7GE
☏ 0533 551451

Scottish Institute of Adult Education
30 Rutland Square
Edinburgh EH1 2BW
☏ 031-633 5000

U3A
6 Parkside Gardens
London SW19 5EY

University of London
Department of Extra-Mural Studies
  Information Office
26 Russell Square
London WC1B 5DQ
☏ 01-636 8000 ext 3833/3850
☏ 01-636 9720 (during out-of-office hours)

University of Stirling
Pathfoot Building
The University
Stirling FK9 4LA

Workers' Educational Association
Temple House
9 Upper Berkeley Street
London W1H 8BY
☏ 01-402 5608

Open University and regional centres

The Open University
PO Box 71
Milton Keynes MK7 6AG
☏ 0908 74066

London
Parsifal College
527 Finchley Road
London NW3 7BG
☏ 01-794 0575

South
Foxcombe Hall
Boars Hill
Oxford OX1 5HR
☏ 0865 730731

South West
41 Broad Street
Bristol BS1 2EP
☎ 0272 299641

South East
Wyvern House
230/232 London Road
East Grinstead
West Sussex RH19 1LA
☎ 0342 27821

West Midlands
66 High Street
Harborne
Birmingham B17 9NB
☎ 021-426 1661

East Midlands
The Octagon
143 Derby Road
Nottingham NG7 1PH
☎ 0602 473072

East Anglia
Cintra House
12 Hills Road
Cambridge CB2 1PF
☎ 0223 64721

Yorkshire
Fairfax House
Merrion Street
Leeds LS2 8JU
☎ 0532 444431

North West
Chorlton House
70 Manchester Road
Chorlton-cum-Hardy
Manchester M21 1PQ
☎ 061-861 9823

North
Eldon House
Regent Centre
Gosforth
Newcastle-upon-Tyne NE3 3PW
☎ 091-284 1611

Northern Ireland
40 University Road
Belfast BT7 1SU
☎ 0232 245025

Scotland
60 Melville Street
Edinburgh EH3 7HF
☎ 031-226 3951   or

2 Park Gardens
Glasgow G3 7YE
☎ 041-332 4364

Wales
24 Cathedral Road
Cardiff CF1 9SA
☎ 0222 397917

BIBLIOGRAPHY

Floodlight Inner London Education Authority
Handbook of Adult Education in Scotland Scottish Institute of Continuing Education, Edinburgh
Residential Short Courses National Institute of Adult Continuing Education, Leicester
U3A DIY U3A, London

INDEX

Abbeyfield Society, The, 265–6, 272
Age Concern, 265, 272
Anchor Housing Association, 265, 272
Annuities, 74–5, 76, 142, 214–15, 338
Association of British Insurers, 197, 198, 202, 206–7
Association of Control Manufacturers, 332, 335
Association of Futures Brokers and Dealers, (AFBD), 113, 119
Association of Investment Trust Companies, 168
Association of Sexual and Marital Therapists, 255, 272

Banks, 123–7
  accounts, 123–7
  investment advisory service, 147
  offshore accounts, 127, 129
Bequests *see* Gifts
Bereavement, 256–7
British Board of Agrément, 329, 335
British Franchise Association, The, 356, 376
British Holiday and Homes Parks Association, 299, 302
British Insurance Association, 119
British Medical Association, 263, 273
British Property Time-Share Association (BPTA), 385, 395
British Tinnitus Association, 268, 273
Budgeting for retirement, 96–9, 230
Building societies,
  accounts, 128–9
  deposits, 76, 127–9
Building Society Shop, The, 127, 142
Business, starting your own, 353–68
  information and advice, 353–4, 356–62
  pensions for self-employed, 79–82, 357
  types of business, 354–6

Calibre Library of Recorded Books, 267, 273
Camping and Caravanning Club of Great Britain and Northern Ireland, 389
Cancer, 233, 240, 242, 243, 244, 245
Caravan Club, The, 389
Chartered Institute of Public Finance and Accountancy, (CIPFA), 139, 142
Citizens' Advice Bureau, 12, 259, 265, 300, 390
Community housing, 253

Company Pensions Information Centre, 83
Compounded Annual Rates (CARs), 140
Coronary Heart Disease, 231, 233, 234–7
Council of Small Industries in Rural Areas (CoSIRA), 357–8
Covenants, 190–91
Credit cards, 126
CRUSE (National Association for the Widowed and their Children), 257, 273

Denman College, 404–5, 450
Department of Community Medicine, 263
Department of Health and Social Security (DHSS), 57
Department of the Environment, 377
Department of Trade and Industry, 119
Deposits, 102, 104–8, 126–42
  see also Banks; Insurance companies
Diet, 231, 233–41
  and heart disease, 231, 233, 234, 236–7
  and lung cancer, 233
Disabled Living Foundation, 266, 273
Draught-proofing Advisory Association, 332, 335
Driving Instructors' Association, 364, 377

Earnley Concourse, The, 404, 451
Education, adult, 399–407, 450–52
  correspondence courses, 406
  universities and polytechnics, 402–4
Edward James Foundation, 404, 451
Energy Efficiency Office, 332, 335
Equities, Personal Equity Plans, 169–71
  buying and selling, 169–70
  choosing a plan, 171
  tax benefits, 170, 192
  types of scheme, 169
Exercise and fitness, 230–33

Family Practice Committee, 258, 259
Federation of Overseas Property Developers, Agents and Consultants (FOPDAC), 318, 323
Field Studies Council, 405, 451
Financial advisers, 114–19
Financial Intermediaries, Managers and Brokers Regulatory Association (FIMBRA), 112, 114
Financial Services Act 1986, 116, 117
Flatford Mill Field Centre, 405, 451
Franchising, 356

Gifts, 111, 188, 189, 190
Gilts, 154–8
  buying and selling, 155–8
  index-linked stocks, 155
  monitoring performance, 157, 158
  tax advantages, 157
Glass and Glazing Federation, 331, 335

Health, 225–75
  checks, 241–4
  confusion, 271–2
  fluid intake, 269
  hearing, 267–8
  memory and reflexes, 270–71
  mobility, 270
  problems for men, 245–6
  problems for women, 244–5
  strokes and raised blood pressure, 268–9
  vision, 266–7
  warmth, 269
  see also Cancer; Coronary Heart Disease; Diet; Exercise and fitness; Smoking; Weight
Health Line telephone tape service, 263
Heating and Ventilating Contractors' Association, 332, 335
Help the Aged, 265
Hobbies, 12, 13, 408–52
  index, 408
  into profit, 362–8
Holidays, 381–97
  activity holidays, 389
  camping, 389
  caravans and motorhomes, 388–9, *see also* 298–300
  exotic holidays, 384–5
  health safeguards abroad, 391–4
  time-sharing, 385–7
  travel concessions (air, bus rail), 389–91
Home, cashing in on your, 337–45
  capital protection, 341
  home income, 338–42
  letting, 342–4
  trading down, 338
Home for Life plc, 297–302
Home, improving your, 325–36
  fuel, 332–3
  home-improvement grants, 333–4
  insulation, 326–32

Inland Revenue *see* Taxation
Inner London Education Authority (ILEA), 400, 451
Institute of Adult Education, 36
Institute for Psychosexual Medicine, 274

Insulation Advisory Service, 328, 335
Insurance, 193–216
  companies, 76, 119, 142, 213, 215–16
  Contents, 199–208
  Life, 209, 212–15
  Motoring, 208–9, 210–11
  Property, 195–9
  see also Annuities; Medical care, private
Interval International, 386, 395
Investment Advisers *see* Financial advisers
Investment Management Regulatory Organisation (IMRO), 113, 119
Investments, 23, 47, 56, 76, 100–19, 143–77, 184
  advisory service, 147
  high risk, 171–2
  see also Equities; Gilts; Investment trusts; Stocks and shares; Unit trusts
Investment Trusts, 166–9
  buying and selling shares, 167–8
  monitoring performance, 168
  split capital trusts, 166–7
  tax, 168
Investor protection, 112–3

Jules Verne Travel, 385, 396

Kuoni Travel Ltd, 385, 396

Life Assurance and Unit Trust Regulatory Organisation (LAUTRO), 112, 120
Life Expectancy, 3, 109, 110
Life Insurance and Unit Trusts Intermediary Regulatory Organisation, 114
Living alone, 253
London University, Department of Extra-Mural Studies, 400, 449
London School of Hygiene and Tropical Medicine, 392

Macmillan Homes, 266, 274
Manpower Services Commission, 352, 355, 357
Medical Advisory Service for Travellers Abroad, (MASTA), 392
Medical care, the health services, 257–63
  chemists, 261
  dental services, 261–2
  fringe, alternative and holistic medicine, 263
  general practitioners, 257–60
  hearing centres, 262–3
  hospitals, 259
  optical services, 262
Medical care, private, 260
  BUPA, 241, 246, 260, 273, 393

insurance for holidays abroad, 393–4
other medical insurance, 260
Mortgages, 100–102
   Mortgage Interest Relief at Source, (MIRAS), 100, 340
   see also Home, cashing in on your
Moving to your retirement home, 277–314
   buying and selling, 290–94
   conveyancing, 293
   council tenants, 300–301
   estate agents, 292–3
   housing associations, 301
   mobile homes, 298, 300
   new houses, 301
   rented accommodation, 300
   surveyors, 294
   see also Retiring abroad

National Adult School Organisation, 404–5, 449
National Association of Carers, 266, 274
National Association of Conveyancers, 293, 302
National Association of Estate Agents, 292
National Association of Loft Insulation Contractors, 328, 336
National Association of Plumbing, Heating, and Mechanical Service Contractors, 332, 335
National Association of Security Dealers and Investment Managers (NASDIM), 114
National Association for Carers and their Elderly Dependants, 266, 274
National Extension College, 404, 449
National Federation of Women's Institutes, 365, 404, 450
National Health Service (NHS), 258–62, 270
National House Building Council, 294
National Marriage Guidance Council, 255, 274
National Savings, 108, 130–39
   accounts, 103, 130, 132–3, 135
   bonds, 133–4
   certificates, 134–5, 136, 137
   premium bonds, 138–9
   taxation, 130–39
   yearly plan, 137
National Supervisory Council of Intruder Alarms, 207
Neighbourhood Watch Schemes, 204, 208

Older relatives – support and care, 264–6

   accommodation with assistance, 253, 264–5
   back-up care, 264, 266
   hospices, 266
Open University, 402, 404, 451
Over-the-counter (OTC) market, 172

Park Home Residents' Guild, 299, 302
Patients' Association, 290, 302
Pensions, occupational, 37, 39, 43, 45, 47, 52, 61–93
   Additional Voluntary Contributions (AVCs), 77–8
   calculating your pension, 62–4
   commutation/lump sum benefits, 65, 69, 72–9, 100, 102
   death-in-service provision, 70
   early retirement, 70–71
   Guaranteed Minimum Pension, 64
   inflation and pensions, 66–8, 76
   late retirement, 78–9
   payment of pension, 72
   pensions from previous jobs, 83a
   women and pensions, 65, 68–70, 74, 76
   see also Business, starting your own
Pensions, state, and other social security benefits, 25–60
   age addition, 27, 34, 41, 98
   attendance allowances, 30, 31
   basic state retirement pension, 27–60
   cashing a pension book order, 49
   Certificate of Age Exception, 31, 35
   child benefit, 31, 40
   choosing how your pension should be paid, 36
   Christmas bonus, 27, 34, 41
   deferred pension, 35, 44, 46, 47, 56
   dependants' allowances, 27, 37, 40
   divorce and pensions, 52–3
   early retirement, 45–6
   earnings rule, 39, 47–8
   graduated pension, 27, 34, 35, 37, 41, 44, 50, 52, 53, 55
   inflation protection, 34, 35
   invalidity allowances, 27, 29, 37, 40, 43–5, 182
   married couples pension, 29, 30, 34, 35, 38, 39, 43, 46, 48, 51
   maternity allowance, 30
   National Insurance contributions, 27–33, 50–51
   non-taxable benefits, 183
   reciprocal pension agreements with overseas countries, 48–9
   SERPS, 41

456 INDEX

Pensions Cont.
   sickness benefit, 27–9, 46, 51
   supplementary pension, 44
   unemployability supplement, 30
   unemployment benfit, 27, 29, 45–6, 51
   widow's bereavement allowance, 55, 182–3
   widow's pension, 45, 53, 54, 55, 56
   wives, non-working, 29, 30, 31, 34, 38, 43, 44, 46, 48
   wives, working, 29, 30, 38, 39, 48, 51
   see also Pensions, occupational, Guaranteed Minimum Pension
Personal Equity Plans *see* Equities
Planning for Retirement, 8–14
Policy Holders' Protection Act 1975, 119
Pontins Holiday Centre, 12–13, 396
Pre-Retirement Association, 11–13, 14–17
Pre-Retirement courses, 11–14, 20–21
Public Affairs Department, The, 148, 173
Public Trustee, 221–2

Relationships, 251–2
   see also Sexual relationships
Relaxation, 247–51
Resort Condominiums International, 384
Retirement
   age, 65
   courses on *see* Pre-Retirement courses
   early, 45–6, 70–71
   late, 78–9
Retirement Preparation Service *see* Pre-Retirement Association
Retiring abroad, 315–23
   currency regulations, 318
   health care abroad, 322–3
   state pension paid abroad, 321–2
   taxation, 319–21
Royal Institute of Chartered Accountants, 113
Royal Institution of Chartered Surveyors, 292, 294
Royal National Institute for the Blind, 267, 274
Royal National Institute for the Deaf (RNID), 267, 274

SAGA Holidays, 13, 14, 383, 384, 385
St Christopher's Hospice, London, 266
Savings, 23, 37, 56, 100–19
Securities and Investments board (SIB), 112, 117, 119
Securities Association (SA), 113, 119
Self-employment *see* Business, starting your own; Hobbies, into profit

Sexual relationships, 254–5
Sheltered homes, 296–8
Small Firms Service, The, 357
Smoking, 231, 233, 234, 237
Stockbrokers, 148–51, 155
Stock Exchange, 119, 145, 146, 147, 152, 156, 168, 172
Stocks and shares, 145–54
   buying and selling, 151
   dividends, 152
   increases in capital value, 152
   monitoring performance, 152, 153
   selecting, 154
Stress, 246–51

Taxation, 24, 37, 179–92
   allowances, 37, 181–4
   capital gains tax, 106, 108, 151, 168, 185–7, 189, 190, 321
   Capital Transfer Tax (CTT) *see* inheritance tax (below)
   Composite Rate Tax (CRT), 140–41
   income tax, 180–84
   inheritance tax, 102, 187, 188–9, 190
   non-taxable income, 183
   PAYE, 30, 180
   taxable income, 37, 69, 182
   tax-free lump sum benefits, 72, 78–9
   tax rates, 180–84
   VAT for the self-employed, 361
Third market, 172

Unit trusts, 100, 106, 159–66
   buying and selling, 160–61, 163–4
   monitoring performance, 162–3
   selecting, 165–6
   taxation, 163
   types of trust, 159–60
University of the Third Age, 407, 451
Unlisted Securities Market, 146, 172

Voluntary work, 368–77

Weight, 234, 237, 239
Wills, 217–24
   intestancy, 219
   invalid wills, 222
Work
   after retirement, 229, 348–79
   independent employment agencies, 352–3
   perspective on, 3–7
   see also Business, starting your own; Hobbies, into profit
Workers' Educational Association, 12, 402, 407, 451